JANE AUSTEN:
A FAMILY RECORD

This book is the outcome of years of research in Austen archives, and stems from the original family biography by W. and R. A. Austen-Leigh, *Jane Austen: her Life and Letters. Jane Austen: A Family Record* was first published in 1989, and this new edition incorporates information that has come to light since then, and provides new illustrations and updated family trees. Le Faye gives a detailed account of Jane's life and literary career. She has collected together documented facts as well as the traditions concerning the novelist, and places her within the context of a widespread, affectionate and talented family group. Readers will learn how Jane transformed the stuff of her peaceful life in the Hampshire countryside into six novels that are amongst the most popular in the English language. This fascinating record of Austen and her family will be of great interest to general readers and scholars alike.

Deirdre Le Faye has been actively researching the life and times of Jane Austen and her family for the last thirty years. In 1995 she prepared a completely new edition of *Jane Austen's Letters*. She has also written several other books: a short illustrated biography, *Jane Austen* (1998), *Jane Austen's 'Outlandish Cousin', the Life and Letters of Eliza de Feuillide* (2002) and *Jane Austen: The World of Her Novels* (2002) as well as numerous articles in literary journals.

JANE AUSTEN:
A FAMILY RECORD

SECOND EDITION

DEIRDRE LE FAYE

CAMBRIDGE
UNIVERSITY PRESS

CAMBRIDGE
UNIVERSITY PRESS

University Printing House, Cambridge CB2 8BS, United Kingdom

Published in the United States of America by Cambridge University Press, New York

Cambridge University Press is part of the University of Cambridge.

It furthers the University's mission by disseminating knowledge in the pursuit of
education, learning and research at the highest international levels of excellence.

www.cambridge.org
Information on this title: www.cambridge.org/9780521534178

First published by The British Library 1989
Second edition published by Cambridge University Press, 2004

A catalogue record for this publication is available from the British Library

Library of Congress Cataloguing in Publication data
Le Faye, Deirdre.
Jane Austen: a family record / by Deirdre Le Faye.
p.   cm.
Rev. ed. of: Jane Austen: a family record / by William Austen-Leigh and Richard Arthur
Austen-Leigh; revised and enlarged by Deirdre Le Faye, 1989.
Includes bibliographical references (p.) and index.
ISBN 0 521 82691 8 – ISBN 0 521 53417 8 (pbk.)
1. Austen, Jane, 1775–1817.   2. Austen, Jane, 1775–1817 – Family.   3. Novelists, English – 19th
century – Family relationships.   I. Austen-Leigh, William. Jane Austen, a family record.   II. Title.
PR4036.L433   2004
823'.7–dc21   2003053232

ISBN 978-0-521-82691-4 Hardback
ISBN 978-0-521-53417-8 Paperback

Contents

Plates

Foreword

Richard Austen-Leigh and his uncle Willie Austen-Leigh combined in 1913 to publish the first *Life and Letters of Jane Austen*. They were descended from Jane's nephew James Edward (respectively his grandson and his youngest son), and except for his *Memoir* little was known about her at that time.

Richie was educated at Eton and Trinity College, Cambridge, and worked most of his life at Spottiswode, the family publishing business, with his elder brother Eddie. Their sister Kathleen married Edward Impey, who became a well-loved housemaster at Eton and had three sons. It was her son Lawrence Austen Impey (my husband) who inherited from Uncle Richie books and papers about Jane and her family. Among Uncle Richie's books was his much-worn copy of the *Life and Letters*. It was stuffed to almost double its size with papers and correspondence he had about Jane, and filled with notes. Our friend Deirdre Le Faye considered he was clearly planning a revised edition. She is a scholar devoted to Jane Austen, working at the British Museum, and has written many papers on Jane and her family. She has studied the letters, diaries, etc., left by Uncle Richie and so I asked her if she would take on the task of revision, adding the new material and bringing it up to date for publication. We feel this book, being the first main source of knowledge about Jane Austen, will be welcomed by scholars all over the world.

JOAN IMPEY
1989

Preface

It will be seen from the Foreword (written when the first edition of this book was published) that the Impey family, heirs of R. A. Austen-Leigh, were kind enough to entrust to me the task of revising and updating the definitive biography of their collateral ancestress, *Jane Austen, her Life and Letters, a Family Record*, a task which I was both honoured and delighted to undertake.

Nearly forty years have now passed since I first became a member of the Jane Austen Society, and for the first ten of these I was content to pay occasional visits to Chawton Cottage, to attend the Annual General Meeting every July, and to read works of Austenian biography and literary criticism as well as, naturally, rereading the novels themselves. My own serious biographical studies did not commence until the late 1970s when, in the course of some local history work in the London Borough of Camden, I found out quite unexpectedly that Jane's aunt Mrs Hancock was buried in the parish churchyard of St John-at-Hampstead, London NW3, together with her daughter Eliza de Feuillide and her grandson Hastings de Feuillide. Attempts to discover why the trio should have been buried there made me realise that all current Austenian biography was in some way or other inadequate – lacking in detail, uncertain in its chronology, imprecise or contradictory in its statements and (with one or two honourable exceptions) showing little signs of any original research having been carried out since Dr R. W. Chapman published the first proper collection of *Jane Austen's Letters* in 1932.

Since the 1980s, therefore, I have concentrated on finding out anything and everything which has any kind of bearing upon the life of Jane Austen and her family, and this research has enabled me to publish various short articles on specific topics as I have come across them, as well as, in 1989, the first edition of this book. I have followed in Jane's footsteps round the south of England; searched for gravestones; corresponded with and visited County Record Offices and private persons, including several members of the Austen family; and read unpublished letters, memoirs, diaries, journals, parish registers, account-books, naval log-books, Wills, inventories and other miscellaneous documents held in public and private archives in this country and in America. The information found in this way, combined with what was accurately available in print, grew into a card-index of some 10,000 entries relating to the Austens and their connections and covering the period from approximately 1700 to 1900. The compilation of this index enabled me to identify errors in previous publications, fill in many of the gaps in the chronology of Jane's life as previously known, and locate correctly some of the anecdotes about her preserved in family tradition.

In the course of this work, I had the pleasure of meeting the Impey family, who gave me the unique privilege of months of study of their complete family archive, including R. A. Austen-Leigh's annotated copy of the original *Life* that he and his uncle William had first written in 1913. It seemed to me that R. A. Austen-Leigh had been intending to produce an updated edition; and so, with this aim in mind, in 1989 I revised and enlarged his original text in order to incorporate information which had been published since 1913 and also that stemming from my own original researches in recent years.

This revision led to a shift in the balance of the original text which was reflected in a change in the subtitling, making 'A Family Record' the second rather than the third element. In their book the Austen-Leighs relied largely upon quoting rather arbitrary extracts from such letters of Jane's as they could then find, which not only meant that there were breaks in the chronological continuity at times when no letters appeared to exist, but also that Jane's place in her family circle, and the family circle as a whole, were both left rather nebulous; the effect was something like being shown a picture of a solitary rose in a specimen vase, with no information as to the bush from which it was plucked or the garden in which the bush grew. For my enlarged version, therefore, I devoted more space to filling in the hitherto blank periods between her surviving letters, and to illuminating the background against which the progress of her life must be seen.

Perhaps more than any other writer, Jane was so much a product and a part of her family that neither her life, her letters nor her works can be properly understood without reference to the lives of the rest of the Austens. As a single woman, with no private income, she had no option but to live with her parents and abide by their decisions and, had she survived longer, she would always have remained beholden to her brothers for financial upkeep and social contacts. Luckily, the family group was close-knit and affectionate, and the letters exchanged between its members show how much Jane was valued as a daughter, sister, aunt and friend, and how sympathetic they were towards her literary work. In this respect, it is as well for posterity that she did remain single, since marriage and maternity would probably have left her no time for creative composition.

In 1995 I was able to publish a completely new edition of Jane's letters, including those which had come to light since Dr Chapman's second edition of 1952, so that Jane's own words have now become fully and freely accessible in this separate publication. Furthermore, since 1989 much original research has been carried out into the lives of Jane and her family, especially by members of the Jane Austen Society, and the new information from these various sources needs in its turn to be incorporated into the 1989 text, thus finally superseding the original *Life and Letters*.

As Jane herself was so modest and unassuming, it is very lucky from the biographical point of view that the Austens were a highly intelligent and literate group, quick to commit their thoughts to paper in letters, journals and memoirs; without these family records it would be otherwise very difficult to trace the course of her brief life. Some of this collective information was paraphrased by James Edward Austen-Leigh in his *Memoir of Jane Austen* in 1869 and also referred to again in the 1913 *Life*, but on this present occasion preference has been given to straightforward quotation from these original sources, so that the Austens can speak to us now with their own individual voices as they did to each other at the time.

DEIRDRE LE FAYE
2003

Acknowledgments

Apart from the Impey family, my grateful thanks are due to the following private individuals, librarians, archivists, curators and the staffs of their respective institutions, in both the United Kingdom and the United States, who have in their several and various ways extended most welcome hospitality, provided constant encouragement, corresponded with me, permitted me to read and quote from their archives and also supplied photocopies therefrom, in some cases for periods ranging over a number of years: Mr Matthew Alexander, the great-grandsons of Admiral Sir Francis Austen, Joan Austen-Leigh, Mr Jack Ayres, Miss S. J. Barnes, Mr and Mrs Peter Bell, Mrs E. S. Binnall, Miss Jean K. Bowden, Mrs Joyce Bown, Lord Brabourne, The British Library Board, Mr Herbert Cahoon, Dr Clive Caplan, Mr Tom Carpenter and the Trustees of the Jane Austen Memorial Trust, Dr June Chatfield, Mr G. C. R. Clay, Mr and Mrs John Coates, Dr Edward Copeland, Mr T. A. B. Corley, Mr John Cresswell, Mr T. Cross, Mr C. R. Davey, Prof. Peter Davison, Lord Deedes, Abbé Michel Devert, Miss R. C. Dunhill, Miss Elizabeth Einberg, Mr Oliver Everett, Mr J. M. Farrar, Mr Mark R. Farrell, Mr John Finch, Mrs Penelope Fletcher, Dr Levi Fox, Dr Michael Freeman, Miss M. A. V. Gill, Mr H. Gillet, Mr David Gilson, Mr Victor Gray, Mr J. A. S. Green, Mr Peter Hacker, Revd Dr A. Tindal Hart, Miss Carol Hartley, Revd Canon Philip Hobbs, Mr G. P. Hoole, Mr and Mrs Hopkinson, the Houghton Library of Harvard University, Mrs V. G. Hunt, Mrs Sarah Hynd, Mr Hugh Jaques, Revd W. A. W. Jarvis, Miss Elizabeth Jenkins, Mr Henry Jenkyns, Mr Colin Johnston, Mrs M. Joyce, Dr Bryan Keith-Lucas, Mrs Diana Kleyn, Dr G. A. Knight, Ms Edith Lank, Miss M. M. Lascelles, Miss Helen Lefroy, Lexbourne Ltd, Mrs Susan McCartan, Mr and Mrs McEvoy, Mr K. G. McKenna, Mrs C. R. Maggs, Dr Meg Mathies, Mr Duncan Mirylees, Mrs Jo Modert, Mrs V. Moger, Mrs T. M. Morrish, the Trustees of the National Maritime Museum, Mrs J. E. Neale, Lt-Col. R. W. Nye, Miss A. M. Oakley, Dr M. J. Orbell, Oxford University Press, Miss Daphne Phillips, Mr Patrick Piggott, Revd

Colin Pilgrim, Rear-Admiral and Mrs Philip Powlett, Dr Judith Priestman, Miss S. D. F. Radcliffe, Ms Jennie Rathbun, Mr W. Birch Reynardson, Mr and Mrs H. J. B. Rice, Mr K. H. Rogers, Mrs Elizabeth Rose, Mrs M. M. Rowe, Mr D. A. Ruddom, Mr George Sawtell, Mr David Selwyn, Mrs Margaret Shaida, Mrs Diana Shervington, Mr D. M. M. Shorrocks, Mr M. K. Skinner, Mr D. J. H. Smith, Miss J. Smith, Prof. Sir David Waldron Smithers, Dr Kathryn Sutherland, Miss S. D. Thomson, Prof. K. Tillotson, Mr Steven Tomlinson, Miss K. M. Topping, Mr George Holbert Tucker, Revd G. R. and Mrs Turner, Dr D. G. Vaisey, Mrs Gervaise Vaz, Mr Robin Vick, Mr Chris Viveash, Ms Emily C. Walhout, Dr Richard Walker, Miss Janet Wallace, Miss J. C. Ward, Mr C. J. Ware, Mr John Webb, Prof. Michael Wheeler, Mr A. M. Wherry, Miss A. M. Williams, Mrs Margaret Wilson, Dr C. M. Woolgar, Miss Bridget Wright, and Mr W. N. Yates.

Notes and abbreviations

Dates of birth, marriage and death are taken from R. A. Austen-Leigh's *Pedigree of Austen* unless otherwise stated. See Bibliography.

General information on the careers of Frank and Charles Austen can be found in William R. O'Byrne, *A Naval Biographical Dictionary*, and in J. H. and E. C. Hubback, *Jane Austen's Sailor Brothers*. See Bibliography.

To avoid confusion between similarly named members of the family, the following conventions have been adopted: Anne Mathew, Mary Lloyd, Martha Lloyd, Mary Gibson, Fanny Palmer and Harriet Palmer are referred to by their maiden names even after marriage. Eliza de Feuillide is best known by the letters she wrote while married to her first husband, and therefore continues to be referred to by this name after her marriage to Henry Austen.

Jane's brother Edward, and his eldest daughter Fanny, are referred to as 'Knight', although their change of name did not occur until 1812. Information on the Knight family between 1803 and 1817 is taken from Fanny's diaries and letters unless otherwise stated.

Similarly, Jane's nephew and biographer James Edward Austen-Leigh is referred to as such, although he did not add '-Leigh' to his name until 1837.

Where quotations from manuscripts are given, spelling and punctuation have been left as in the original.

In the references family names are abbreviated as follows:

JA	Jane Austen
CEA	Cassandra Elizabeth Austen
EAK	Edward Austen/Knight
HTA	Henry Thomas Austen
FWA	Francis William Austen
CJA	Charles John Austen
JEAL	James Edward Austen-Leigh
CMCA	Caroline Mary Craven Austen
JAMT	Jane Austen Memorial Trust.

Titles of reference works (for full details see Bibliography) are abbreviated as follows:

S&S	*Sense and Sensibility*
P&P	*Pride and Prejudice*
MP	*Mansfield Park*
E	*Emma*
NA	*Northanger Abbey*
P	*Persuasion*
MW	*Minor Works*
Alum Cantab	*Alumni Cantabrigienses*, J. A. Venn
Alum Oxon	*Alumni Oxonienses*, J. Foster
AP	*Austen Papers, 1704–1856*, ed. R. A. Austen-Leigh
Aspects	*Personal Aspects of Jane Austen*, M. A. Austen-Leigh
BC	*The Book Collector*
CMCA Rems	*Reminiscences*, Caroline Austen, ed. Deirdre Le Faye
CP James	*The Complete Poems of James Austen*, ed. David Selwyn
CPVA	*Jane Austen: Collected Poems and Verse of the Austen Family*, ed. David Selwyn
FCL Family History	Unpublished manuscript, Fanny-Caroline Lefroy
FP	*Jane Austen – Facts and Problems*, R. W. Chapman
Gents Mag	*Gentleman's Magazine*
JALM	*Jane Austen's Literary Manuscripts*, B. C. Southam
JAOC	*Jane Austen's 'Outlandish Cousin': the Life and Letters of Eliza de Feuillide*, Deirdre Le Faye
JEAL	*James Edward Austen-Leigh*, M. A. Austen-Leigh
Letters	*Jane Austen's Letters*, ed. Deirdre Le Faye
Life	*Jane Austen, her Life and Letters*, W. and R. A. Austen-Leigh
MAJA	*My Aunt Jane Austen*, Caroline Austen
Memoir	*A Memoir of Jane Austen*, J. E. Austen-Leigh, ed. Kathryn Sutherland
N&Q	*Notes and Queries*
Pedigree	*Pedigree of Austen*, R. A. Austen-Leigh
PULC	*Princeton University Library Chronicle*
Reports	*Collected Reports of the Jane Austen Society*
RES	*The Review of English Studies*
SB	*Jane Austen's Sailor Brothers*, J. H. and E. C. Hubback
TLS	*Times Literary Supplement*

Chronology of Jane Austen's life

1764

26 April   Marriage of Revd George Austen and Cassandra Leigh (in due course, Jane Austen's parents).

9 Oct.   Marriage of James Leigh-Perrot (Mrs Austen's brother) and Jane Cholmeley.

1765

13 Feb.   James Austen born at Deane.

Summer   Mr and Mrs Hancock (Mr Austen's sister) and their daughter Eliza ('Betsy') return from India.

1766

26 Aug.   George Austen the younger born at Deane.

1767

7 Oct.   Edward Austen born at Deane.

1768

July/Aug.   Austen family move to Steventon.

?Autumn   Mr Hancock returns alone to India.

29 Dec.   Marriage of Jane Leigh (Mrs Austen's sister) and Revd Dr Edward Cooper.

1770

1 July   Edward Cooper the younger born in London.

1771

8 June   Henry Thomas Austen born at Steventon.

27 June   Jane Cooper born at Southcote, near Reading.

?Autumn   Cooper family move to Bath, No. 12 Royal Crescent.

1773

9 Jan.   Cassandra Elizabeth Austen born at Steventon.

| 23 March | Mr Austen becomes Rector of Deane as well as Steventon. Pupils live at Steventon from now until 1796. |

1774
| 23 April | Francis William Austen born at Steventon. |

1775
| 5 Nov. | Mr Hancock dies in Calcutta. |
| 16 Dec. | Jane Austen born at Steventon. |

1776
| June | Mr and Mrs Austen in London, probably en route to or from Kent. |

1777
| Winter | Mrs Hancock and Eliza go to Continent. |

1779
23 June	Charles John Austen born at Steventon.
3 July	James Austen matriculates at St John's College, Oxford.
Summer	Mr and Mrs Thomas Knight II (cousins of Mr Austen) visit Steventon.

1780
| | Coopers move to No. 14 Bennett Street, Bath. |
| | Mr and Mrs Austen take HTA on a visit to Kent. |

1781
| ?Autumn | Marriage of Eliza Hancock to Jean-François Capot de Feuillide, in France. |

1782
| Summer | First mention of JA in family tradition. |
| Dec. | First amateur theatrical production at Steventon – *Matilda*. |

1783
	Edward Austen adopted by Mr and Mrs Thomas Knight II.
Easter	JA, CEA and Jane Cooper go to Mrs Cawley in Oxford; Mr and Mrs Austen, with HTA and FWA, visit relations in Kent.
3 May	Revd I.P.G. Lefroy instituted to Ashe.
Summer	Mrs Cawley moves to Southampton and the girls fall ill.
25 Oct.	Mrs Cooper dies in Bath.

1784

July   *The Rivals* performed at Steventon.
                Revd Dr Cooper moves to Sonning.

1785

Spring   JA and CEA go to the Abbey House School, Reading.

1786

                EAK abroad on Grand Tour from 1786 to 1790.
15 April   FWA enters Royal Naval Academy, Portsmouth.
25 June   Eliza de Feuillide's son Hastings born at Calais, while she
                is en route to London.
Nov.   James Austen goes to the Continent.
End Dec.   JA and CEA have now left school.

1787

                JA starts writing her *Juvenilia*.
Autumn   James Austen returns from Continent.
Dec.   *The Wonder* performed at Steventon.

1788

Jan.   *The Chances* performed at Steventon.
March   *Tom Thumb* performed at Steventon. A 'private theatrical
                exhibition' also performed at Steventon some time later
                this year.
1 July   HTA matriculates at St John's College, Oxford.
Summer   Mr and Mrs Austen take JA and CEA to Kent and
                London.
Sept.   Mrs Hancock and Eliza de Feuillide return to France.
23 Dec.   FWA sails to East Indies.
Winter   *The Sultan* and *High Life Below Stairs* performed at
                Steventon.

1789

31 Jan.   First issue of 'The Loiterer' appears – published weekly by
                James Austen in Oxford until March 1790.
Spring   Lloyd family rent Deane parsonage.

1790

April   James Austen takes up residence as curate of Overton.
Autumn   EAK returns to England from Grand Tour.

1791

21 June   Death of Mr Francis Austen of Sevenoaks.

20 July	CJA enters Royal Naval Academy, Portsmouth.
15 Sept.	James Austen becomes vicar of Sherborne St John.
27 Dec.	Marriage of EAK and Elizabeth Bridges, in Kent; they live at Rowling, near Goodnestone.

1792

Jan.	The Lloyds leave Deane for Ibthorpe.
26 Feb.	Death of Mrs Hancock, in London.
27 March	Marriage of James Austen and Anne Mathew, at Laverstoke; they presently take up residence at Deane parsonage.
27 Aug.	Death of Revd Dr Cooper, at Sonning.
Oct.	JA and CEA visit the Lloyds at Ibthorpe.
11 Dec.	Marriage of Jane Cooper and Capt. Thomas Williams, RN, at Steventon.
?Winter	CEA engaged to Revd Tom Fowle.

1793

21 Jan.	Louis XVI of France guillotined.
23 Jan.	EAK's first child, Fanny, born at Rowling.
1 Feb.	Republican France declares war on Great Britain and Holland.
Spring	HTA becomes Lieutenant in Oxfordshire Militia.
14 March	Marriage of Revd Edward Cooper and Caroline Lybbe-Powys; they live at Harpsden till 1799.
15 April	James Austen's first child, Anna, born at Deane.
3 June	JA writes last item of *Juvenilia*.
Winter	FWA returns home from Far East.
Dec.	JA and CEA visit Butler-Harrison cousins in Southampton.

1794

22 Feb.	M. de Feuillide guillotined in Paris.
Midsummer	JA and CEA visit the Leighs at Adlestrop.
? Aug.	JA and CEA visit EAK and Elizabeth at Rowling.
Sept.	CJA leaves Royal Naval Academy and goes to sea.
23 Oct.	Death of Mr Thomas Knight II.
?Autumn	JA probably writes *Lady Susan* this year.

1795

| | JA probably writes *Elinor and Marianne* this year. |
| 3 May | Death of Anne Mathew at Deane; Anna sent to live at Steventon. |

| Autumn | Revd Tom Fowle joins Lord Craven as his private chaplain for the West Indian campaign. |
| Dec. | Tom Lefroy visits Ashe Rectory. |

1796

Jan.	Tom Lefroy leaves Ashe for London.
	Tom Fowle sails for West Indies.
April	JA and CEA visit Coopers at Harpsden.
?Summer	Both HTA and James Austen courting Eliza de Feuillide.
June	Capt. Thomas Williams knighted.
Aug.	EAK and FWA take JA to Rowling via London; she returns to Steventon late September/early October.
Oct.	JA starts writing *First Impressions*.
End Nov.	James Austen engaged to Mary Lloyd.

1797

17 Jan.	Marriage of James Austen and Mary Lloyd at Hurstbourne Tarrant; Anna returns to live at Deane.
Feb.	Tom Fowle dies of fever at San Domingo and is buried at sea.
Aug.	JA finishes *First Impressions*.
1 Nov.	Mr Austen offers *First Impressions* to publisher Cadell; rejected sight unseen.
Nov.	JA starts converting *Elinor and Marianne* into *Sense and Sensibility*.
	Mrs Austen, JA and CEA visit the Leigh-Perrots in Bath, at Paragon Buildings.
	EAK and family move from Rowling to Godmersham.
Winter	Revd Samuel Blackall visits Ashe.
31 Dec.	Marriage of HTA and Eliza de Feuillide, in London.

1798

6 April	Death of Mr William Hampson Walter (Mr Austen's elder half-brother), in Kent.
Aug.	Mr and Mrs Austen, with JA and CEA, visit Godmersham.
	JA probably starts writing *Susan (Northanger Abbey)*.
9 Aug.	Lady Williams (Jane Cooper) killed in road accident.
24 Oct.	JA and her parents leave Godmersham for Steventon.
	Mrs Austen ill until end November.
17 Nov.	James Austen's son James Edward born at Deane.

1799

Feb.	JA possibly visits Lloyds at Ibthorpe.
March	CEA returns to Steventon from Godmersham.
17 May	Mrs Austen and JA arrive in Bath, with EAK and Elizabeth, and stay at No. 13 Queen Square.
End June	They return home.
	JA probably finishes *Susan (Northanger Abbey)* about now.
Late summer	The Austens pay round of visits to Leighs at Adlestrop, Coopers at Harpsden, and Cookes at Great Bookham.
14 Aug.	Mrs Leigh-Perrot charged with theft and committed to Ilchester Gaol.
Oct.	The Coopers move to Hamstall Ridware, Staffs.

1800

29 March	Mrs Leigh-Perrot tried at Taunton and acquitted. Probably stays at Steventon thereafter.
Oct.	EAK visits Steventon and takes CEA back to Godmersham with him via Chawton and London.
End Nov.	JA visits Lloyds at Ibthorpe; returns home mid-December.
Dec.	Mr Austen decides to retire and move to Bath.

1801

Jan.	HTA resigns commission in Oxfordshire Militia and sets up as banker and Army agent in London, living at 24 Upper Berkeley Street and with office at Cleveland Court, St James's.
End Jan.	JA visits Bigg-Wither family at Manydown.
Feb.	CEA returns to Steventon from Godmersham via London.
May	The Austen family leave Steventon; Mrs Austen and JA travel to Bath via Ibthorpe, and stay with the Leigh-Perrots.
	James Austen and his family move to Steventon.
End May	The Austens lease No. 4 Sydney Place and then go on West Country holiday; probably visiting Sidmouth and Colyton.
	JA's traditional West Country romance presumably occurs between now and the autumn of 1804.
Sept.	The Austens visit Steventon and Ashe.
5 Oct.	They return to Bath.
9 Oct.	Hastings de Feuillide dies, in London.

1802

Spring	Mrs Lybbe-Powys visits Austens in Bath.
25 March	Peace of Amiens commences.
April	James and Mary, with Anna, visit the Austens in Bath.
Summer	CJA joins Austens for holidays; they visit Dawlish and probably Teignmouth, also probably Tenby and Barmouth. HTA and Eliza go to France.
Autumn	FWA joins Austens in Bath.
1 Sept.	JA and CEA arrive at Steventon.
3 Sept.	CJA takes JA and CEA to Godmersham.
28 Oct.	CJA brings his sisters back to Steventon.
25 Nov.	JA and CEA visit Manydown.
2 Dec.	Harris Bigg-Wither proposes to JA.
3 Dec.	JA and CEA return to Steventon and set off at once for Bath.
Winter	JA revises *Susan (Northanger Abbey)*.

1803

Feb.	Mrs Lybbe-Powys visits Austens in Bath.
Spring	JA sells *Susan (Northanger Abbey)* to Crosby & Son of London.
	HTA returns from France; his office now in Cannon Row, Westminster.
18 May	Napoleon breaks Peace of Amiens; Eliza de Feuillide returns from France.
Summer	JA possibly visits Charmouth, Up Lyme and Pinny.
July	FWA stationed in Ramsgate.
Sept. to Oct.	Mr and Mrs Austen, probably accompanied by JA and CEA, stay at Godmersham.
Oct.	JA and CEA visit Ashe.
24 Oct.	They return to Bath.
Nov.	The Austens visit Lyme Regis.

1804

	JA probably writes *The Watsons* this year
Jan.	Mrs Lybbe-Powys visits the Austens in Bath.
Spring	Mrs Austen seriously ill.
	HTA moves house to 16 Michael's Place, Brompton, and moves office to Albany, Piccadilly.
Summer	The Austens, with HTA and Eliza, visit Lyme Regis.

25 Oct.	The Austens return to Bath and move to No. 3 Green Park Buildings East.
16 Dec.	Madam Lefroy of Ashe killed in a riding accident.

1805

21 Jan.	Death of Mr Austen in Bath.
25 March	Mrs Austen and her daughters move to No. 25 Gay Street, Bath.
16 April	Mrs Lloyd dies at Ibthorpe, and thereafter Martha Lloyd joins forces with Mrs Austen, JA and CEA.
June	Mrs Austen, JA and CEA, travel to Godmersham via Steventon, taking Anna with them.
18 June	James Austen's younger daughter Caroline born at Steventon.
17 Sept.	JA and CEA go to Worthing, and stay there with Mrs Austen and Martha until at least early November.
21 Oct.	Battle of Trafalgar – FWA unable to participate.

1806

Jan.	Mrs Austen and her daughters visit Steventon.
29 Jan.	Mrs Austen returns to Bath and takes lodgings in Trim Street.
Feb.	JA and CEA visit Manydown, returning to Bath via Steventon mid-March.
2 July	Mrs Austen and her daughters finally leave Bath, and go via Clifton to Adlestrop.
24 July	Marriage of FWA to Mary Gibson, at Ramsgate.
5 Aug.	Adlestrop family party go to Stoneleigh Abbey.
14 Aug.	Mrs Austen and her daughters go from Stoneleigh to visit the Coopers at Hamstall Ridware and stay about five weeks.
Oct.	The Austens call at Steventon, and with FWA and Mary Gibson take lodgings at Southampton.
Winter	CEA visits Godmersham.

1807

	HTA moves office from Albany to 10 Henrietta Street, Covent Garden.
March	Austens move into house in Castle Square, Southampton.
April	HTA brings CEA back to Southampton from Godmersham via London.

19 May	Marriage of CJA to Fanny Palmer, in Bermuda.
Aug.	The Coopers visit Southampton.
Sept.	EAK arranges family gathering at Chawton Great House, followed by further family gathering in Southampton.

1808

Jan. to March	JA and CEA staying at Steventon, Manydown, and with the Fowles at Kintbury.
15 May	HTA and JA at Steventon en route for London; JA stays with HTA.
14 June	JA goes from London to Godmersham with James and Mary Lloyd.
8 July	JA returns to Southampton.
28 Sept.	CEA goes to Godmersham.
10 Oct.	Death of Elizabeth Austen (Knight).

1809

Feb.	CEA returns to Southampton.
5 April	JA attempts to secure publication of *Susan (Northanger Abbey)*.
May	Mrs Austen and her daughters arrive at Godmersham.
June	HTA and Eliza move house to No. 64 Sloane Street, London.
7 July	Mrs Austen and her daughters move into Chawton Cottage.
Oct.	EAK and Fanny visit Chawton.

1810

July to Aug.	JA and CEA visit Manydown and Steventon.
Nov.	EAK and Fanny visit Chawton.
Winter	*Sense and Sensibility* accepted for publication by Thomas Egerton.
	The Leigh-Perrots buy No. 49 Great Pulteney Street, Bath.

1811

Feb.	JA planning *Mansfield Park*.
March	JA staying with HTA in London and correcting proofs of *Sense and Sensibility*; CEA at Godmersham.
May	JA returns to Chawton via Streatham.
Aug.	CJA and family return to England.
30 Oct.	*Sense and Sensibility* published.

| Nov. | JA visits Steventon. |
| ? Winter | JA starts revising *First Impressions* into *Pride and Prejudice*. |

1812

April	EAK and Fanny visit Chawton.
9–25 June	Mrs Austen and JA visit Steventon – the last time Mrs Austen does so; CEA goes to Godmersham.
17 June	America declares war on Great Britain.
14 Oct.	Death of Mrs Thomas Knight II; Edward Austen now officially takes surname of Knight.
Autumn	JA probably visits London and sells copyright of *Pride and Prejudice* to Thomas Egerton.

1813

28 Jan.	*Pride and Prejudice* published. JA halfway through *Mansfield Park*.
21 April	EAK and family come to Chawton Great House and stay for four months.
22 April	JA goes to London to attend Eliza de Feuillide.
25 April	Eliza de Feuillide dies.
1 May	JA returns to Chawton.
19 May	HTA takes JA to London again, for a fortnight.
June	HTA moves to live over office at No. 10 Henrietta Street.
?July	JA finishes *Mansfield Park*.
17 Aug.	Anna Austen engaged to Ben Lefroy.
Sept.	EAK and JA travel via London to Godmersham; her last visit there.
13 Nov.	EAK takes JA back to Chawton via London; *MP* probably accepted for publication at this time.
?Winter	HTA moves from No. 64 to No. 63 Sloane Street.

1814

21 Jan.	JA commences *Emma*.
1 March	HTA takes JA to London.
April	JA returns to Chawton via Streatham.
	EAK and family stay at Chawton Great House for two months.
5 April	Napoleon abdicates and is exiled to Elba.
9 May	*Mansfield Park* published, by Thomas Egerton.
Midsummer	JA visits the Cookes at Great Bookham.
	HTA moves house to No. 23 Hans Place, London.

Aug.	JA visits HTA in London.
	FWA and family move into Chawton Great House and stay there for about two years.
3 Sept.	HTA takes JA home to Chawton.
6 Sept.	CJA's wife Fanny Palmer dies after childbirth.
Autumn	Hinton/Baverstock lawsuit against EAK commences.
8 Nov.	Marriage of Anna Austen and Ben Lefroy at Steventon; they go to live in Hendon, near London.
25 Nov.	JA visits HTA in London.
5 Dec.	HTA takes JA back to Chawton.
24 Dec.	Treaty of Ghent officially ends war with America.
26 Dec.	JA and CEA stay with Mrs Heathcote and Miss Bigg in Winchester.

1815

2–16 Jan.	JA and CEA stay at Steventon, also visiting Ashe and Laverstoke.
March	Napoleon escapes and resumes power in France; hostilities recommence.
29 March	*Emma* finished.
?March or April	JA and CEA probably visit HTA in London.
18 June	Battle of Waterloo finally ends war with France.
July	Mary Lloyd and Caroline stay at Chawton.
8 Aug.	JA starts *Persuasion*.
Aug.	Anna and Ben Lefroy move to Wyards, near Chawton.
	JA possibly goes to London to negotiate publication of *Emma*, returning early in September.
4 Oct.	HTA takes JA to London; he falls ill, and she stays longer than anticipated.
13 Nov.	JA visits Carlton House.
16 Dec.	JA returns to Chawton.
End Dec.	*Emma* published, by John Murray.

1816

Spring	JA begins to feel unwell.
	HTA buys back MS of *Susan (Northanger Abbey)*, which JA revises and intends to offer again for publication.
15 March	HTA's bank fails; he leaves London.
May	EAK and Fanny stay at Chawton for three weeks.

22 May	JA and CEA go to Cheltenham via Steventon.
15 June	They return to Chawton via Kintbury.
Midsummer	FWA and family move from Chawton Great House to Alton.
18 July	First draft of *Persuasion* finished.
6 Aug.	*Persuasion* finally completed.
Sept.	CEA and Mary Lloyd go to Cheltenham.
Dec.	HTA ordained, becomes curate of Chawton.

1817

	FWA and family living in Alton this year.
27 Jan.	JA starts *Sanditon*.
18 March	Ceases work on this MS.
28 March	Death of Mr Leigh-Perrot at Scarlets.
27 April	JA makes her Will.
24 May	CEA takes JA to Winchester, where they lodge at No. 8 College Street.
18 July	JA dies in early morning.
24 July	Buried in Winchester Cathedral.
?Autumn	HTA arranges publication of *Northanger Abbey* and *Persuasion*.
End Dec.	*NA* and *P* published together, by John Murray, with 'Biographical Notice' added by HTA.

CHAPTER I

Austens and Leighs, 1600–1764

Jane Austen's paternal ancestry can be traced back with reasonable certainty to a William Astyn who lived in Yalding, a village in the Weald of Kent, and who died in 1522. His descendants moved to the neighbouring parish of Horsmonden, and by the end of the sixteenth century John Austen I (1560–1620) had become a man of considerable means, owning property in Kent and Sussex and elsewhere, and with the right to bear a coat of arms.[1] It seems likely that he lived in the manor-house of Broadford, close to Horsmonden, and his wealth was probably derived from the trade of clothier – the middleman who provided the capital and raw wool for the manufacture of cloth, and then sold on the finished product to merchants for retailing. Hasted, the eighteenth-century Kentish historian, instanced the Austens, together with the Bathursts, Courthopes and others, as being some of the

antient families of these parts, now of large estate, and genteel rank in life, and some of them ennobled by titles, [who] are sprung from and owe their fortunes to ancestors who have used this great staple manufacture, now almost unknown here . . . They were usually called, from their dress, The Grey Coats of Kent, and were a body so numerous and united, that at county elections, whoever had their votes and interest was almost certain of being elected.[2]

At his death in 1620 John Austen I left a family of eight sons, and the fifth of these, Francis I (1600–88), who described himself in his Will as a clothier, acquired another nearby manor-house, that of Grovehurst, and eventually inherited Broadford as well. Francis's son John Austen III (c. 1629–1705) lived on at Grovehurst, also following the trade of clothier, and one of this John's daughters, Jane, married Stephen Stringer, of a neighbouring family at Goudhurst; she numbered among her descendants the Knights of Godmersham, a circumstance which exercised an important influence over the subsequent fortunes of the Austen family in Jane's generation. John III's son John IV (c. 1670–1704) took over Broadford upon his marriage to

Elizabeth Weller of Tonbridge. This younger John seems to have been a careless, easy-going man, who thought frugality unnecessary, as he would succeed to the estate on his father's death; but he died of tuberculosis in 1704, predeceasing his father by more than a year, and leaving seven young children as well as debts unsuspected by his wife.[3]

Elizabeth Weller, a woman happily cast in a different mould from her husband, was an ancestress of Jane Austen who deserves commemoration. Though receiving only grudging assistance from her miserly father-in-law before he too died suddenly in 1705, of an illness that 'seiz'd his brains', she proved herself to be thrifty, energetic, a careful mother and a prudent housewife, and managed both to pay off her husband's debts and to give her younger sons a decent education. Her eldest son, John Austen V (1696–1728), was sent to Pembroke College, Cambridge, by his grandfather's executors in accordance with the old man's wish, but only minimal provision had been made for his brothers and sister. Elizabeth Weller therefore let Broadford for the highest rent she could obtain and moved to Sevenoaks, where she took the post of housekeeper at the town's Grammar School, boarding the Master and some of the boys in return for free schooling for her own sons. By the time she died in 1721 her daughter Betty was safely married to a Tonbridge lawyer, George Hooper, and the boys were already making their way in the world – Francis II (1698–1791) had been apprenticed to an attorney, Thomas (1699–1772) to a haberdasher (though he later became an apothecary), William (1701–37) to a surgeon, and Stephen (1704–51) to a stationer; the remaining son Robert (1702–28) died of smallpox.[4]

John Austen V and his son John Austen VI (?1716–1807) lived at Broadford during the eighteenth century, but the breach in the family caused by the inequality of John III's Will was never mended, and the senior Broadford line made no attempt to help or keep in touch with the younger Austen branches. It was left to Francis II, the legally trained brother, to retrieve the family fortunes and become the benefactor of his generation. After finishing his apprenticeship, he set up in Sevenoaks 'with £800 & a bundle of pens, as Attorney, & contrived to amass a very large fortune, living most hospitably, and yet buying up all the valuable land round the Town'. He remained single until he was nearly fifty, but then married two wealthy wives – first, in 1747, Anne Motley, who died in childbirth the same year, leaving a son, Francis Motley Austen – and second, in 1758, Jane Chadwick, the widow of Samuel Lennard of West Wickham, who had left her his estate. 'The widow was legally attacked by the nearest male relations of the defunct – she flung her cause into the hands of my Great Uncle, old Frank Austen; he won the cause & the wealthy widow's heart and hand.' Francis was also careful to ask the rich Lady Falkland to be godmother to his eldest son, and in due course Francis Motley received from her a legacy of lands worth about £100,000. He then 'completed his Father's various purchases of land about Sevenoaks by buying Kippington House & demesne a short mile from the Town – and so forming an extensive Park'.[5]

In the meantime, Francis's younger brother Thomas, now an apothecary at Tonbridge, had had a son, Henry (1726–1807), who graduated at Cambridge and took Holy Orders. As the advowson of West Wickham was part of the Lennard estate, Francis was able to present his nephew Henry to this living, where he remained as rector from 1761 until 1780.[6]

The next brother, William the surgeon, also resident in Tonbridge, was Jane Austen's grandfather. In 1727 he married Rebecca, daughter of Sir George Hampson, Bt, a physician of Gloucester, and widow of another physician, William Walter.[7] By her first husband Rebecca had a son, William Hampson Walter (1721–98), and by William Austen she had four children – Hampson (a daughter) (1728–30), Philadelphia (1730–92), George (1731–1805) and Leonora (1732–83). Rebecca died soon after the birth of Leonora. In 1735 William Austen made his Will, by which he left his property in trust to his brothers Francis and Stephen for them to use as they saw fit upon the education of his three children.[8] The following year he married again, his second wife being Susanna Kelk of Tonbridge, thirteen years his senior;[9] but unfortunately – perhaps with a touch of his father's carelessness – he did not bother to alter his Will to take account of this second marriage. When he died eighteen months later, Susanna Kelk was therefore under no legal obligation to care for her stepchildren and apparently felt no moral obligation either. She lived on for another thirty-one years, occupying William's house in Tonbridge,[10] but played no part at all in rearing her husband's children; nor, in turn, did she mention them in her Will.[11]

At the time of William's death in 1737 Francis was still a bachelor, but the next brother, Stephen, was married with one little boy and in business as a bookseller and publisher at the sign of the 'Angel and Bible' in St Paul's Churchyard, London. It must therefore have seemed most appropriate that he should be the one to give a home to the three little orphans. However, Stephen resented the charge, and treated the children 'with neglect, if not with positive unkindness'[12] – his 'idea of education developed itself strongly in a determination to thwart the natural tastes of the young people as much as possible'.[13] George was sent to live with his Austen aunt Betty Hooper and her family[14] while he attended Tonbridge School from 1741 to 1747.[15] Philadelphia may also have been sent back to Kent, though at some stage she did receive help and kindness from the Freeman family, cousins on the Hampson side, who lived in Hertfordshire;[16] and in 1745, on her fifteenth birthday, was apprenticed to a London milliner.[17] Leonora was the only one of the three children whom Stephen Austen was prepared to take into his household; she may perhaps have grown up handicapped in some way, for she never married and in later years lodged with various booksellers' families in London, supported financially by her brother and sister.[18]

Luckily, George was 'blessed with a bright & hopeful disposition which characterised him during the whole course of his life',[19] and 'proved by his mildness and gentleness of temper, and his steadiness of principle'[20] that he had not suffered from his Uncle Stephen's harshness. 'The knowledge too of his almost destitute circumstances joined to energy of character, and very superior abilities, might naturally lead to success both at School and College.'[21] In 1747, at the age of sixteen, he entered St John's College, Oxford,[22] and received there the Fellowship which had been reserved by the Founder of the College for a scholar from Tonbridge School. In 1751 he obtained his Bachelor of Arts degree, and two years later was awarded a Smythe Exhibition – again thanks to his Tonbridge School background[23] – which enabled him to remain at Oxford for a further seven years to study divinity with a view to eventual ordination. In 1754 he became Master of Arts, and in March of that year was ordained deacon in Christ Church Cathedral, Oxford. Soon after this he moved back to Kent, was priested at Rochester in May 1755, and for the next three years combined the duties of perpetual curate of Shipbourne, near Tonbridge, with those of Usher (Second Master) at his old school.[24] His appointment to the living of Shipbourne was probably due to his uncle Francis's influence in the locality.[25] When he went back to St John's in 1758 he became assistant chaplain of the College, and was also Junior Proctor for the academic year 1759–60. During this term of office he was nicknamed 'The Handsome Proctor' on account of his commanding height and outstanding good looks. 'His eyes, [were] not large, but of a peculiarly bright hazel . . . The complexion was clear, the countenance animated, & the whole appearance striking.'[26] In 1760 he gained his Bachelor of Divinity degree, and his future now seemed reasonably assured. If he wished to marry he would need to find a clerical living rich enough to enable him to support a wife and family, but if he were prepared to remain celibate he could stay a Fellow of St John's for the rest of his life.

However, while George was still single and relatively poor he could not offer a home to his sister Philadelphia, and when she finished her apprenticeship in 1750 her only alternative to becoming a drudging seamstress or penniless dependant like the unfortunate Leonora was to get married at the earliest opportunity. But by the standards of the time her lack of any dowry to bring to a marriage settlement would considerably reduce, if not entirely destroy, her chances of finding an eligible husband. As she had now come into possession of her share of what little was left of her father's estate, she petitioned the Court of East India Directors in November 1751 for leave to sail out by the *Bombay Castle* to friends at Fort St David, her sureties being James Adams of London and John Lardner of Southwark. The 'friends' may have been merely a form of words, for there can be little doubt that being without means or prospects she was going to India with the object of finding a husband amongst the European community there.

The *Bombay Castle* sailed from England on 18 January 1752, and reached Madras on 4 August of that year. Six months later, on 22 February 1753, Philadelphia married Tysoe Saul Hancock (1723–75), the surgeon at the East India Company's post at Fort St David.[27] Not much is known about Hancock's background – his family came from Sittingbourne in Kent, and he had a brother, Colbron, in business at Charing Cross, London, and a sister, Olivia, living in Margate.[28] He had been in India since at least 1748, when his name appears in the list of surgeon's mates serving out there with the East India Company.[29] As Francis Austen had for some years acted as his English agent or attorney it would seem quite possible that the match had been suggested to Philadelphia by her uncle, if not indeed pre-arranged by him direct with Hancock. The Hancocks stayed at Fort St David till 1759, and then moved to Fort William, Calcutta, where their only child, Elizabeth (known as Betsy in her childhood and as Eliza thereafter), was born in 1761.[30] It is thanks to Eliza's correspondence with her half-cousin Philadelphia, daughter of William Hampson Walter, that we get glimpses of the Austen family's life in the 1780s and 1790s.

The fourth member of William Austen's family, his stepson William Hampson Walter, is a shadowy but still quite significant figure in Austenian biography. There is no mention of him in his stepfather's Will, presumably because he was already adequately provided for out of his own father's estate.[31] He may have been employed as a steward or agent for some local landowner;[32] but in any event he passed all his life in the Tonbridge area and reared a family in reasonable comfort. He was on affectionate terms with George and Philadelphia and their families, as none of them made any distinction of the fact that they were related only by half-blood. A number of letters survive from the Austens to the Walters, written in the 1770s and 1780s, one of which gives news of the birth of Jane in 1775. William Hampson Walter, being some ten years older than his Austen brother and sisters, was the first to settle in life, marrying Susanna Weaver in the mid-1740s and having six children by her. Their youngest son, James (c. 1760–1845), who was George Austen's godson,[33] entered the church, married a cousin from London, Frances Maria Walter, and in turn settled down to rear a large family in Lincolnshire, where he was for many years rector of Market Rasen and Headmaster of Brigg Grammar School.[34] His sister Philadelphia (1763–1834), known usually as 'Phylly' or 'Phillida', lived alone with her parents in Kent until she eventually married very late in life.[35] She kept up a regular correspondence with James, and one of her letters provides an early mention of Jane Austen as a child.[36] Of James's numerous family, one son, Henry, remained in touch with his distant Austen cousins, and is mentioned in Jane's letters many years later.[37]

The other four children of William Hampson Walter have no direct bearing on Austenian biography, except in so far as their names are occasionally mentioned in family correspondence or memoirs; they were Sarah, who died in 1770 when on the verge of marriage;[38] Weaver, who also entered the church and eventually became the incumbent of Brisley in Norfolk, where he died in 1814;[39] and William and George, who both went to the West Indies, where the Hampson family had business interests, and died out there in 1787 and 1779 respectively.[40]

It was now George Austen's wish to marry, and as a necessary first step he turned to his richer relations to help him find a suitable clerical living. George's second cousin Jane Monk (granddaughter of Jane (née Austen) Stringer of Goudhurst) had married Thomas Knight of Godmersham in Kent. Thomas Knight had actually been born Thomas Brodnax, but had changed his name to May upon inheriting one family estate and changed it again to Knight by the Will of another distant cousin, Mrs Elizabeth Knight, in order to inherit her estates at Chawton and Steventon in Hampshire.[41] In the eighteenth century to change one's name required a private Act of Parliament, and Mr Knight's rapid alterations provoked one MP to remark: 'This gentleman gives us so much trouble, that the best way would be to pass an Act for him to use whatever name he pleases.'[42] Mr Knight was perfectly ready to help his wife's Austen cousins, and had already presented one of them, the Revd Thomas Bathurst, to the curacy of Steventon in 1754. He presented Henry Austen to the rectory of Steventon in 1759, and when Henry resigned Steventon in favour of Francis Austen's gift of West Wickham in 1761, Mr Knight passed on the Hampshire living to Henry's cousin George Austen.[43] It was a time of laxity in the church, and George, although he afterwards became an excellent parish priest, does not seem to have resided or done duty at Steventon before 1764, evidently content to leave the care of the parish in the hands of his cousin, Thomas Bathurst. George also turned to his kind uncle Francis Austen for assistance, and he purchased the two livings adjacent to Steventon, Ashe and Deane, so that George could have in the future whichever fell vacant first.[44]

Some time in the early 1760s George Austen met and became engaged to Cassandra, younger daughter of the Revd Thomas Leigh, the rector of Harpsden (then usually called 'Harden'), a small village near Henley-on-Thames in Oxfordshire. The Leighs were part of the large clan of the Leighs of Adlestrop in Gloucestershire, of which family the Leighs of Stoneleigh Abbey in Warwickshire were a younger branch. Both the branches descended from Sir Thomas Leigh, Lord Mayor of London, behind whom Queen Elizabeth I rode to be proclaimed at Paul's Cross in 1558. He was rich enough and great enough to endow more than one son with estates; but while the elder line at Adlestrop remained plain country squires, the younger at Stoneleigh rose to a peerage at the time of the Civil War. 'When Charles I was on his march to Nottingham there to set up the Royal Standard, he found on reaching Coventry that the gates of that city were closed against him by order of the Mayor. On this he rode off to Stoneleigh Abbey where he and his escort were hospitably received by the reigning Sir Thomas Leigh'[45] and for which act of loyalty Sir Thomas was created Baron Leigh of Stoneleigh in July 1643.

In the eighteenth century the Stoneleigh branch was approaching extinction, but the Adlestrop family flourished and was connected with many other wealthy families in Gloucestershire and Oxfordshire. A Leigh family history has much to say of one of the Adlestrop squires, Theophilus (*c.* 1643–1725), Jane Austen's great-grandfather.[46] He married Mary Brydges, sister of the first Duke of Chandos, and in honour of the Duke's wife, the 'excellent Cassandra',[47] gave this unusual Christian name to one of his daughters. For generations afterwards the name of Cassandra appeared in the Leigh family, and through them passed on to the Austens and their descendants. Theophilus was a strong character, the father of twelve children, and one who lived up to fixed, if rather narrow, ideas of duty. The family manuscript tells of his old-fashioned dress and very formal behaviour, of his affability to his neighbours and his strict but just government of his sons. His brother-in-law, the Duke of Chandos (Handel's patron), sent for Theophilus's daughters one by one to be educated in the splendour of the ducal estate at Canons, near Edgware, Middlesex, after which he arranged their marriages and provided them with dowries of £3,000 apiece.

Theophilus's third son, another Theophilus (1693–1785) – small, thin, clever and in his youth suffering from a pimply face[48] – was elected Master of Balliol College, Oxford, in 1727 and occupied this position until his death. He was renowned beyond the bounds of Oxford University for his witty and agreeable conversation and for the sense of humour which he retained up to his dying day.[49] The Master's younger brother was the Revd Thomas Leigh (1696–1764), elected Fellow of All Souls at so early an age that he was ever after called 'Chick' Leigh. He became rector of the All Souls college living of Harpsden in 1731[50] and remained rector till his death in 1764, living entirely on his benefice and greatly beloved in his neighbourhood as an exemplary parish priest. 'He was one of the most contented, quiet, sweet-tempered, generous, cheerful men I ever knew and his wife was his counterpart.'[51] Thomas Leigh married Jane Walker from Oxford, who was descended on her mother's side from the Perrot family, long settled in Oxfordshire but also known in Pembrokeshire at least as early as the fourteenth century. At Harpsden they had six children, of whom two died young, leaving James (1735–1817), Jane (1736–83), Cassandra (1739–1827), who became Jane Austen's mother, and Thomas (1747–1821). Thomas unfortunately was 'imbecile from birth', and according to the custom of the time was boarded out from the family but remained under their supervision until his death.[52]

The three young Leighs grew up in the rural but elegant rectory at Harpsden, a spacious red brick house of late seventeenth-century date.[53] They knew all the gentry families in the Henley area – for example the Vanderstegens at Cane End; the London goldsmith and banker Gislingham Cooper with his children Edward and Ann at their country home of Phyllis Court;[54] the Newells of Henley Park and their witty daughter Mary; the Lybbe-Powys family at Hardwick Hall with their tall, handsome sons Phil, Tom and Richard; and the widowed Mrs Girle, retired from London to Caversham with her short, plump, jolly daughter Caroline.[55] Mary Newell and Caroline Girle were the particular friends of Cassandra Leigh, friendships that endured to their lives' ends, and there is also a hint that Tom Lybbe-Powys was one of Cassandra's admirers.

Mrs Leigh's aunt, old Miss Anne Perrot, was one of the family circle at Harpsden Rectory, and taught her great-nieces to read and to do fine needlework, which latter skill Cassandra in turn passed on to her own daughters.[56] Miss Anne Perrot was also most unselfishly responsible for increasing the Leigh family fortunes; when her childless brother Thomas Perrot announced his intention of bequeathing to her his estate at Northleigh in Oxfordshire, she begged him to leave the bulk of his property to their great-nephew James Leigh, and to leave her instead only an annuity of £100. Her brother complied with this request, on condition that he took the surname and arms of Perrot. Accordingly, on the death of Mr Thomas Perrot in 1751, James, then in his teens, became Leigh-Perrot, and had the comfortable knowledge that in a few years' time he would enter into possession of the Northleigh house and lands. His sisters Jane and Cassandra also profited by the kindness of their great-aunt, who left £200 to each of them.[57]

Another legacy which filtered from the Perrots through the Walkers and so on to the Austens was the advantage of being 'kin' to Sir Thomas White, the Founder of St John's College, Oxford, an advantage of which several members of the Austen family later availed themselves.[58]

James Leigh-Perrot moved to Northleigh when he came of age, and while living there in 1762 had the pleasure of being one of the parties to the marriage settlement between his childhood friends Caroline Girle and Philip Lybbe-Powys.[59] However, Northleigh did not suit him, and a couple of years later he sold the estate to the Duke of Marlborough, buying instead for himself the small Berkshire property of Scarlets at Hare Hatch in the parish of Wargrave, situated on the Bath Road midway between Maidenhead and Reading. Scarlets had at one time been in the possession of James's mother, Mrs Leigh, and its ownership could be traced back through the Perrots and their maternal ancestors to the middle of the thirteenth century.[60] In October 1764 James married Jane Cholmeley (1744–1836), from an old Lincolnshire family and heiress to her late father's estate in Barbados.[61] Miniatures of James and Jane, painted presumably at the time of their engagement, show him as a gentle, quietly handsome man, while she is an enchantingly pretty but determined-looking young girl.[62] In early 1765 James completed the purchase of Scarlets, enlarged and improved the house,[63] and there he and Jane lived prosperously for the rest of their lives, amassing fine furniture and ceramics,[64] dining with thirty families in the neighbourhood[65] and, though childless, remaining a deeply devoted pair. It is this couple who are always referred to by Jane Austen in her letters as 'my Uncle' and 'my Aunt'.

Jane, the elder of the two Leigh daughters, did not marry until December 1768, when she was thirty-two.[66] She then became the wife of the Revd Dr Edward Cooper, the son of their Henley neighbour Mr Gislingham Cooper of Phyllis Court, and now a Fellow of All Souls: 'a rosy, round-faced divine, with a most amiable expression'.[67] Dr Cooper's father had just died, so his widowed mother sold Phyllis Court and moved to Southcote, a hamlet near Reading, where she rented a house – probably the old Southcote Manor

House[68] – from the Blagrave family.[69] Dr Cooper was of course obliged to resign his Fellowship upon marriage, so he and his wife joined his mother at Southcote for a few years till she died in 1771, when they moved to Bath. There are references to one or two visits made by the Austens to the Coopers during this Southcote period.

As for Cassandra Leigh, even at the age of six she had already achieved recognition for her cleverness. In 1745, when her witty uncle the Master of Balliol was visiting her parents, he wrote home praising his niece Cassandra for having delighted him by playing the lead in an extemporary nursery charade. At the same time Dr Leigh added that Cassandra was already 'the Poet of the Family' and had entertained him with several 'Smart pieces promising a great Genius'.[70] In later years Cassandra's granddaughter Anna Lefroy wrote:

The education of my Grandmother had not been, for a person in her station of life, much attended to; but whatever she had the opportunity of learning, there was quickness of apprehension, & a retentive memory to make the most of; and whilst her natural talent may well be supposed to have compensated in early life for many school room deficiencies, it certainly qualified her to be the companion of a Husband, who had little toleration for want of capacity in man or woman; and even, in an unpretending way, to assist in his labours of tuition. In regard to personal appearance, it was rather difficult to believe [her] own assertion that she never had been handsome; and I always attributed the low estimate she had of her own good looks to the circumstance of her Sister being a regular and acknowledged Beauty – The eyes, gray, & of rather a peculiar tint, were handsome, as also was the nose; the general contours of the face what might fairly be described as aristocratic; yet the face itself was too thin, especially about the mouth, and there could have been, habitually, no brilliancy of complexion. The hair was dark, & to a very late period of life retained its colour – The figure, rather falling below than exceeding the middle height, spare and thin.[71]

She was amusingly particular about people's noses, having a very aristocratic one herself, which she had the pleasure of transmitting to a great many of her children. She was a quickwitted woman with plenty of sparkle and spirit in her talk who could write an excellent letter either in prose or verse, the latter making no pretence to poetry, but being simply playful common sense in rhyme.[72]

Towards the end of his life the Revd Thomas Leigh moved to Bath for his health's sake, died there in January 1764 and was buried in St Swithin's church in Walcot parish.[73] The earliest surviving letter from his daughter Cassandra was sent from Princes Street, Bath, on 12 June 1762, to her old friend Tom Lybbe-Powys of Hardwick Hall, who had taken Holy Orders and had just heard that he was to be presented to the living of Fawley. 'We feel the care with which it was composed . . . Had there been any love passages between them, unsuccessful on his side? If so, it would account for the young lady writing and not her mother, on whom the duty would have more naturally devolved.'[74]

Permit me, dear Mr Tom Powys, to appear in the list of your congratulating friends, for not one of them, I am certain, can feel more real joy on the occasion than myself; in any instance of your good fortune I shd. have rejoiced, but I am infinitely happy to know you Rector of Fawley, as I well remember to have heard you wish for that appellation at a time when there was little probability of our living to see the day. May every wish of your heart meet with the same success – may every blessing attend you, for no one more deserves to be blessed; &, (as the greatest felicity on earth) may you soon be happy in the possession of some Fair one, who must be one of the very best of her sex, or she will not merit the good fortune that awaits her. If her heart is as full of love & tenderness towards you, as mine is of esteem & friendship, you will have no cause to complain, but will find yr.self completely happy in that respect, as you are sincerely wished in every respect, by your very affectionate & infinitely obliged

Cassandra Leigh

My Father, Mother & Sister join me in congratulatory compts. to all at Hardwick.[75]

It is not known when and how George Austen met Cassandra Leigh, but it would seem probable that it was at Oxford, through the good offices of either the Master of Balliol or Dr Cooper. In 1763 George had his miniature painted – his bright eyes looking very dark in contrast to his powdered wig with its four neat sausage curls over each ear – and Cassandra had herself painted wearing a blue gown; as in the case of the Leigh-Perrots, the young couple probably exchanged these miniatures upon their engagement.[76] Arrangements now had to be made for his move to Steventon in order to provide a home for his bride, which led to a problem – Steventon rectory was only a small, dilapidated seventeenth-century house,[77] 'of the most miserable description',[78] so the new young rector was obliged to look elsewhere for a residence. Luckily, the neighbouring rector of Deane, the Revd William Hillman, was a person of some private fortune and preferred to live in the large house of Ashe Park outside his own parish, so that Deane rectory was vacant.[79] This then was the Austens' first married home, though it too was far from ideal – 'a low damp place with small inconvenient rooms, and scarcely two on the same level'[80] – and for which George had to pay about £20 a year in rent to Mr Hillman.[81] It stood in Deane Lane, with a thatched mud wall round its garden, close to Deane House and All Saints church.[82] Damp it must certainly have been, for a note at the back of the Deane parish register records that:

From the 12th Day of July 1763 to the Fifth of Febry. 1764 There were seldom Two dry Days together in the seven Months and some times Twenty Days Rain together. The Waters rose at Dean Janry. 7th and there was no passing for Foot People until after Lady Day [25 March]; many Graves in the Church fell in and there was no getting to the Church but thro' Mr Harwoods Yard or Garden; a Large Stream ran from Shepherd's Pond by Hall Gate thro' the Common Field, the Parsonage Meadow and Garden; and the Wells in the Parish rose to their Tops, and Fish were taken between the Parsonage Yard & the Road leading from Overton, to Basingstoke.[83]

George went to Hampshire in the spring of 1764 to prepare Deane parsonage for occupation, and in his last bachelor evenings there prepared also for his duties at Steventon by copying out in his firm, clear handwriting the chaotic old Steventon parish register into a new book, from 1738 onwards to the entry for 11 March 1764.[84] On 15 March the marriage settlement between the young couple was signed – Cassandra had some leasehold houses in Oxford and the prospective sum of £1,000 to which she would become entitled by her father's Will on the death of her mother, and George brought to the settlement some freehold lands in Tonbridge and a third share of other properties there, all expectant on the death of his stepmother, Susanna Kelk.[85] On 26 April 1764 they were married by special licence in Bath, at St Swithin's, Walcot, the service being taken by Cassandra's friend Tom Lybbe-Powys, with her brother and sister as witnesses.[86] The sensible Cassandra, beginning as she meant to continue, did not waste money on elaborate wedding finery but was married in her travelling dress – hardwearing red woollen fabric cut trimly in the style of a riding habit.[87] The newly married couple set off straight away for Hampshire, their only honeymoon being the night spent at Andover en route.

CHAPTER 2

Deane and Steventon, 1764–75

Mr Austen's living of Steventon was then and is still a small village tucked away among the Hampshire Downs, in the north of the county, about seven miles south-west of Basingstoke. It can nowadays be glimpsed from trains on the Waterloo to Winchester line, on the south side of the high viaduct known as 'Steventon Arch', but there is no railway station nearby. In the eighteenth century it was almost equidistant from two main roads – one running from London through Basingstoke to Overton, Andover and the west, with the coach stop at the Deane Gate inn (the local roads are now numbered B3400/A303/A342) – and the other from London to Basingstoke, Winchester and the south-west, the coach stop for this route being at the Wheatsheaf inn on the corner of Popham Lane (A30/A33).

The surrounding country presents no grand or extensive views, but the features are small rather than plain. In the Austens' time sheep grazed on the chalky hills, and the streams in the winding valleys below watered fields which produced excellent cereal crops, turnips, sainfoin, peas and beans, with hay and clover in the meadows.[1] Peat and furze supplied fuel for the cottagers, and oak, beech, ash and elm grew in the woodlands and hedgerows – which in this part of the county were not thin formal lines of quickset, but irregular borders of copse-wood and timber, often wide enough to contain within them winding footpaths or rough cart tracks.[2] There were about thirty families in the parish, the men working on the land and their wives spinning flax or wool at home in the thatched whitewashed cottages that were scattered round the green, each set in its own vegetable garden with flowering creepers almost hiding the little casement windows.[3] On Sunday afternoons this green was the village playground, when the cottagers met to relax and gossip beneath the old maple tree there.[4]

The rectory stood at the end of the village, on the corner of the lane leading uphill for half a mile to the little stone-built thirteenth-century church of St Nicholas. Opposite the church, and on the site of an even earlier building,[5] stood the Tudor manor-house of flint and stone, with

Plate 1 'New Map of Hampshire', by Charles Smith, *c.* 1801.

18 Little Landon
Bramley
Bramley green
Buckley
Hartfordbridge Green
Heckfield
Bramshill Park
Yately
London Blackwater
Darby Green
Hawley Br.

Camber End
Sherborne Green
The Vine
Mildford Gr.
Sherfield Grs.
Hartley Wespall
Mattingley
Hazley Heath
Huntley Row
Harwood Bridge
Yately Heath
12

Sherborne St Johns
Sherfield
Rotherwick
West Gran
Hartley Wintney
Elvetham
10
Farnb

Monk Sherborne
Chinham
Basing Turnpk
Tilney Hall
Raven Inn
Shapley Heath
Cowllarden
Crookham Common
Basingstoke
Flet Pond

Pastrow
8
Newnham
Watermead Bridges
Old Basing
Yateley Skewers
Mapledurwell Marsh
Odiham Lodge
Odiham Hill
Snelsmell
Aldershot Common
Sapins Ewshot House
Aldershot Bottom

Hallway House
BASINGSTOKE 45
Natly
North Warnboro
Broad Oak
ODIHAM 41½
Great Rye
Ewshot
Aldershot Bottom

Cliddesden
Mapledurwell
Tunworth Dew
James End
Grewell
Horsdon Common
Mitchel
Bowling Alley

Winslade
Upton Grey
Weddington
Long Sutton
Swinthorpe
Cleor Ileax
Crondal
Dives Grean

Farleigh
12
Tunworth
Weston Corbett
South Warnborough
Well
12

Ellisfield
Herriard
Weston Common
Weston Patrick
Bowmer
Sutton Common
Sheep House Coppice
Slade Heath
FARNHAM 38

Nutley
Southrop
New Inn
Golden Pots
Lower Froyle
Coldrey
Bentley b

Old Arbor
9
Lasham
Froyle
Inn
Way
Moreland
Grove Land
Great Lodge

Bradley
Lower Weld
Benhams
Issington
Alice Holt
Forest

Shalden
Binsted
Goose Green Lodge
Docksfield
Bavins

Bentworth
Ansty
Holybourne
Forest

Meadstead
Weld
ALTON
Allen Burs
Monks Hill
Whitleigh
Old Close Lodge
Goose Green Lodge
Docksfield

Oldwston Park
Chawton
14
East Worldham
Kingsley
Badge Br.
Binglingwood Lodge
Headley 20

North Street
Chawton
Wm Worldham
Hartley
Headley Park
Bern

Brighton Woods
Silton Woods
Farringdon
Norton
Oakhanger
Woolmer
Bowling Green

ALRESFORD
6
Gilbert
Pelham Place
Newton Valence
Temple Farms
Echlake
Holt Pound
Lidshot

Ropley
Ropley Dean
Rother Park
Eastisted
Selbourn
Commons Pond
Great Pott Moor
Woolmer Pond
Upper Lodge
Langton Bridge
Bram

Zoward Pickles
Wm Tisted Place
Colemore
Theddridge
Forest
Lipheol

West Tisted
Colemore Common
Empshot
Greatham
Liphook

Basing Park
17
Priors Dean
Lower farm
Lyss
9
Bilmer Hill
Hawley

Plate 2   Front view of Steventon rectory; wood-engraving as used in the *Memoir* of 1870.

Plate 3   Rear view of Steventon rectory; drawing, probably by Anna Lefroy, 1814.

mullioned windows and vast living-rooms forty feet long.[6] It was so hidden amongst elms and sycamores that the dawn and evening sunlight could pick out only its gables and tall chimney-stacks.[7] This house was occupied by the Digweed family, who rented it from Mr Knight of Godmersham together with the 900-acre Manor Farm. As the Steventon glebe land was only a little over three acres,[8] Mr Knight had agreed that Mr Austen could use the 200-acre Cheesedown Farm in the north of the parish [9] for his secondary source of income, as the church living itself was estimated to be worth only £100 p.a.[10]

Of this somewhat tame country, Steventon, from the fall of the ground, and the abundance of its timber, is certainly one of the prettiest spots; yet one cannot be surprised that when [Cassandra Leigh], a little before her marriage, was shown the scenery of her future home, she should have thought it unattractive, compared with the broad river, the rich valley, and the noble hills which she had been accustomed to behold at her native home near Henley-on-Thames.[11]

However, from their marriage in the spring of 1764 until the summer of 1768 the young Austens lived in Deane parsonage, about two miles to the north of Steventon, whence Mr Austen could easily ride down the lane to do duty in his own church. Their way of life in these early days was so modest and unworldly that for two years after her marriage Mrs Austen had no new gown, relying just on her red wool wedding dress for her regular morning wear.[12] Their neighbours immediately across the road here were the Harwood family, who owned most of the land in the parish, in their fine red brick seventeenth-century Deane House next door to the church. 'The property at Deane was worth about £1,200 a year, and it had descended through a squirearchy of John Harwoods, fathers and sons, for five or six generations.'[13] The current Squire Harwood (1719–87) was a bucolic character who is reputed to have been the original of Squire Western in Fielding's *Tom Jones*.[14] The Squire had a great respect for his new neighbour's learning, and

referred the following difficulty to Mr Austen's decision: 'You know all about these sort of things. Do tell us. Is Paris in France, or France in Paris? for my wife has been disputing with me about it.' The same gentleman, narrating some conversation which he had heard between the rector and his wife, represented the latter as beginning her reply to her husband with a round oath; and when his daughter called him to task, reminding him that Mrs Austen never swore, he replied, 'Now, Betty, why do you pull me up for nothing? that's neither here nor there; you know very well that's only *my way of telling the story*.'[15]

Another squire in Deane parish was young Mr Wither Bramston of Oakley Hall, with his 'very excentric' sister Augusta,[16] and further afield were the Chute family in their Tudor mansion of The Vyne at Sherborne St John, whose daughter Mary married Mr Bramston in 1783, thus bringing the Chutes into the Austens' circle of acquaintances; and a few miles away to the south-east of Deane lay the village of Dummer, where the Terry family had been long established at Dummer Grange.

Soon after her daughter's marriage, Mrs Austen's widowed mother Mrs Jane Leigh came from Bath to join the young couple at Deane, probably bringing with her Mr Austen's first pupil, seven-year-old George Hastings. This little boy was the only surviving child of Warren Hastings, the future Governor-General of Bengal (1773–85); he had been born in India in 1757 and, as was then the custom, sent back by his father in 1761 to be educated in England.[17] Hastings had known the family of the Leighs of Adlestrop since his birth and childhood in the neighbouring parish of Churchill, where his impoverished grandfather, the rector of Daylesford, was obliged to live and act as curate, having sold the family advowson of Daylesford.[18] It is therefore logical to assume that little George was consigned to the care of this large and wealthy family, as his far-distant father could then be sure that upon arrival in England one or other branch of his old friends would be able to foster his son safely and happily in a home environment. It seems that the charge fell upon the Harpsden Leighs; and as Cassandra Leigh was by now probably engaged to George Austen, Hastings's friend Francis Sykes, who had brought the child to England, made a few payments to Mr Austen during 1763–4 on the child's account.[19] Poor little George Hastings did not live long, even in the Austens' good care, for he is said to have died in the autumn of 1764 of 'putrid sore throat' (diphtheria), and 'Mrs Austen had become so much attached to him that she always declared that his death had been as great a grief to her as if he had been a child of her own.'[20]

However, Mrs Austen did not have long to grieve over the empty place in the nursery, for her own babies soon appeared in the world. The first Austen to be born in Hampshire was James, on 13 February 1765, privately baptised by his father the same day. On 17 March he was taken across the road to Deane church for his public christening,[21] and afterwards Mr Austen noted in his family Bible that the godparents had been the baby's maternal grandmother Mrs Jane Leigh; Francis Austen, his father's uncle; and James Langford Nibbs, Esq.[22] This Mr Nibbs was a rich young man, heir to a West Indian plantation on the island of Antigua, who had matriculated at St John's College in 1758 but left without taking a degree.[23] In 1760, when

James Nibbs married his cousin Barbara Langford, he had asked his tutor Mr Austen to be one of the Trustees in their marriage settlement,[24] and Mr Austen now repaid the compliment by choosing Mr Nibbs as godfather for his firstborn son. In turn, maintaining the friendship in later years, Mr Nibbs sent his son George to be one of Mr Austen's pupils at Steventon rectory.[25]

Mrs Austen nursed her babies herself for their first few months of life, and then

followed a custom, not unusual in those days, though it seems strange to us, of putting [them] out to be nursed in a cottage in the village. The infant was daily visited by one or both of its parents, and frequently brought to them at the parsonage, but the cottage was its home, and must have remained so till it was old enough to run about and talk; for I know that one of them, in after life, used to speak of his foster mother as 'Movie', the name by which he had called her in his infancy.[26]

The foster parents for the Austen babies were John and Elizabeth Little-worth, who probably lived at Cheesedown Farm, and their young daughter Bet or Betsy was the little Austens' nursemaid and playfellow. The extended Littleworth family remained devoted friends and servants of the Austens for nearly a century, and several of them are mentioned in Jane's letters.[27]

In the summer of 1765 Mr and Mrs Hancock and their one little daughter arrived in England from India aboard the *Medway*, a voyage that cost them £1,500.[28] They were probably accompanied by Warren Hastings, and it is said that the first news he received upon landing in England was that of the death of his son George at Deane rectory the previous autumn, news which left a shadow on his face for years.[29] But in those days it was an accepted fact that children were very likely to die in infancy, and Hastings did not sever his friendship with the Hancocks and Austens on this account. He rented a house in Essex Street, off the Strand, in London, and the Hancocks took one close by in Norfolk Street.[30] First of all Mrs Hancock introduced her husband to the Freeman cousins who had helped her in her unhappy girlhood,[31] and then later in the summer Mr Austen went to London to renew acquaintance with the sister whom he had not seen for thirteen years and to meet his hitherto unknown brother-in-law.[32] It is probable that the Hancocks came in turn to stay at Deane, for when the Austens' second son, George, was born the following year on 26 August 1766, privately baptised the same day and christened on 29 September, Mr Hancock was one of his godfathers. The other godparents were the Revd Dr James Musgrave, rector of Chinnor, Oxfordshire, one of Mrs Austen's many cousins in that county, and a Mrs Cockell, about whom Mr Austen made no identifying comment when entering the event in his family Bible.[33]

The third Austen son, Edward, was born and baptised on 7 October 1767 and publicly christened at Deane on 22 November. He was named for his godfather the Revd Dr Edward Cooper (soon to become his uncle by marriage), and the other sponsors were Mr Leigh-Perrot and Mrs Cassandra Wight, one of Mrs Austen's aunts on the Leigh side. After these three births in successive years, there was a gap of nearly four years before the fourth son, Henry Thomas, was born at Steventon in 1771.

In the meantime the next family event was the death of Mr Austen's step-mother, Susanna Kelk, in January 1768, so that at long last the Tonbridge property which she had been occupying could be sold – later in the year Mr Austen received about £1,200 as his share from this source.[34] Old Mrs Leigh, now in her sixties, evidently also began to feel unwell, as she made her Will in July 1768.[35] Soon after this the Austens finally took up residence in their own rectory at Steventon, which presumably by now Mr Austen had been able to repair and enlarge sufficiently to make hab-itable for his young family. The summer had been very wet, and the lane between Deane and Steventon was so churned up 'as to be impassable for a light carriage. Mrs Austen, who was not then in strong health, per-formed the short journey on a feather-bed, placed upon some soft ar-ticles of furniture in the waggon which held their household goods.'[36] Mr Austen had insured this waggon-load of all his worldly possessions for £300.[37]

The rectory she approached, and which was to be her home for thirty-three years, 'stood in a shallow valley, surrounded by sloping meadows well sprinkled with elm trees . . . North of the house, the road from Deane to Popham Lane ran at a sufficient distance from the front to allow a carriage drive, through turf and trees.'[38] The parsonage had a red tiled roof, and beneath this the walls were a patchwork – some were plain brick, some were timber-framed with infill panels of brick, and part of the south side was plastered and weather-tiled – the whole building being valued at £300.[39] Inside it

consisted of three rooms in front on the ground floor – the best parlour, the common parlour and the kitchen; behind these were Mr Austen's study, the back kitchen, and the stairs; above were seven bedrooms, and three attics. The rooms were low-pitched, but not otherwise bad, and compared with the usual stile of such buildings, it might be considered a very good house.[40]

It was sufficiently commodious to hold pupils in addition to a growing family, and was in those times considered to be above the average of parsonages; but the rooms were finished with less elegance than would now be found in the most ordinary dwellings. No cornice marked the junction of wall and ceiling; while the beams which supported the upper floors projected into the rooms below in all their naked simplicity, covered only by a coat of paint or whitewash.[41]

Behind, on the sunny side of the house, was an enclosed garden, bounded by a straight row of spruce firs, and terrace walk of turf. At one end this terrace communicated by a small gate with what was termed 'the Wood Walk', which, winding through clumps of underwood, and overhung by tall elm trees, skirted the upper side of the Home Meadow. At the other end of the terrace a door in the garden wall opened to a lane that climbed the hill, and led through field or hedgerow to the Church . . . near the Wood Walk gate, and garden bench adjoining, was placed a tall white pole surmounted by a weathercock. How pleasant to childish ears was the scrooping sound of that weathercock, moved by the summer breeze! how tall its stem! and yet how much more stupendous was the height of the solitary silver fir that grew at the opposite end of the terrace, and near the church road door! How exquisitely sweet too the honeysuckle, which climbed a little way up its lofty stem![42]

There was

a well between the house and the Wood Walk . . . in the square walled-in cucumber garden. The walls of this inner garden were covered with cherry and other fruit trees. On the west side was a garden tool house. On the south a door communicated with the back yard – not far from the granary – another door opened into the larger garden, in the east wall, I think. I remember this sunny cucumber garden well – its frames, and also its abundance of pot-herbs, marigolds, etc. – Oh! me! we never saw the like again.[43]

The lower bow window, looking so cheerfully into the sunny garden, up the middle grass walk bordered with strawberry beds, to the sundial, belonged to my Grand Father's study; his own exclusive property, & safe from the bustle of all household cares. The Dining or common sitting room looked to the front, & was lighted by two casement windows; on the same side, the principal door of the house opened into a parlour of smaller size. Visitors, it may be presumed, were few and rare; but not a whit the less welcome would they have been to my Grand Mother on account of their finding her seated in this very entrance parlour, busily engaged with her needle, in making or repairing.[44]

The Austens' entry into their new home was unfortunately marked by sorrow, for Mrs Leigh died only a few weeks later, and was buried in the chancel of Steventon church on 1 September 1768.[45] The bulk of her property was divided between her daughters, and the earliest extant letter from Mr Austen is one he wrote to the Leighs of Adlestrop concerning Mrs Leigh's estate, of which he and his wife were joint executors.[46] Mrs Austen's eventual share amounted to £1,000 which, with other family monies, was invested for her in £3,350 of Old South Sea Annuities. This holding was set aside to provide her widow's portion, and with 3 percent dividends yielded annually £100.10s.0d.[47]

Later in 1768 the family circle was broken again, when Philadelphia's husband, Tysoe Hancock, was reluctantly obliged to return to India to try to make more money by business ventures out there, as the funds which he had brought back in 1765 now proved insufficient for their way of life in London. The unlucky Hancock never did succeed in amassing a fortune sufficient to enable him to rejoin his family in England, and he died in Calcutta in November 1775 at the age of fifty-two.[48] In his absence his wife and daughter Betsy or Bessy (as she was then nicknamed) lived in various smart rented houses in the newly developing West End of London, alternating with visits to the Walters in Kent and the Austens in Hampshire, and sometimes attempting country life on their own in a cottage in Surrey.[49]

From 1770 to 1775 a group of ten letters from the Austens to their Walter relatives provide vignettes of the busy rural life at Steventon rectory in the years immediately preceding Jane's birth. Although Hancock was no longer in England his place in the family was filled by the acquisition of the Revd Dr Edward Cooper as another brother-in-law; he and Mrs Austen's elder sister Jane were married in December 1768,[50] and Mrs Austen looked forward with pleasure to the idea of a large family of Cooper nephews and nieces. Of their own three sons, it had now become sadly clear to the Austens that little George was mentally abnormal and subject to fits. It may be that he was also deaf and dumb, for many years later there is a reference in Jane's letters to her knowledge of the deaf and dumb alphabet, an accomplishment which would not normally be acquired unless there were some good reason for so doing.[51] Mrs Austen tried to keep him at home, but the demands of her other children together with increasing family duties meant she could not give him sufficient attention. Like his 'imbecile' uncle Thomas Leigh, George had to be boarded out locally with a respectable village family, under the supervision first of his parents and later of his brothers.[52]

In the spring of 1770 Mr Austen went to London to visit Mrs Hancock in Bolton Street, and from there wrote to Mrs Walter inviting her to bring her little girl Phylly to join him upon his return to Hampshire and to stay at Steventon while Mr Walter was away on business.[53] This invitation was accepted, and following Mrs Walter's return to Kent at midsummer Mr Austen sent all the latest family news:

The Day I received your kind Letter, for which accept my thanks, your sister set out for London to enter on her office of Nurse in Ordinary, & the same Post likewise brought me intelligence that she was too late for the Ceremony She intended being present at, for Mrs Cooper was happily brought to bed last Sunday morning of a Boy, & both well [Edward, 1770–1835]; She came, it seems, rather before her time, & of course the Babe is a small one, but however very like to live; You may possibly have heard of this from Sister Hancock, but lest you should not I could not help mentioning it, as I am sure the News will give you great pleasure. – I don't much like this lonely kind of Life, you know I have not been much used to it, & yet I must bear with it about three weeks longer, at which time I expect my Housekeeper's return, & to make it the more welcome she will bring my Sister Hancock & Bessy along with her. – You may depend on it that if it is tolerably convenient we will return your Visit another Summer, & I say we, for I certainly shall not let my Wife come alone, & I dare say she will not leave her children behind her. I am much obliged to you for your kind wish of George's improvement – God knows only how far it will come to pass, but from the best judgment I can form at present, we must not be too sanguine on this Head; be it as it may, we have this comfort, he cannot be a bad or a wicked child . . . The only News I have to send you, & the chief subject of conversation in our Neighbourhood is the quarrels of Mr Hillman & Squire Harwood, they have commenced actions against each other & seem to promise good Sport for the Lawyers . . . My James . . . & his Brothers are both well, & what will surprise you, bear their Mother's absence with great Philosophy; as I doubt not they would mine, & turn all their little affections towards those who were about them & good to them; this may not be a pleasing reflection to a fond Parent, but is certainly wisely designed by Providence for the Happiness of the Child.[54]

Mrs Austen returned with relief from London to Steventon and her domestic employments, as she told Mrs Walter in her letter of 26 August:

I receiv'd your kind Letter in Town and should have thank'd you for it before now, but was so hurried while I was in Town that I deferr'd it till I got home . . . I was not so happy as to see my Nephew Weaver, suppose he was hurried in time as I think every one is in Town, tis a sad place, I would not live in it on any account: one has not time to do one's duty either to God or Man. I had the pleasure of leaving my Sister tolerably well & the Child quite so, they are now moved into the Country, I hope change of air will enable her to pick up her Strength – We talk of going there and to Scarlets in about three Weeks time, and shall be absent a full month, shall take both my Boys with me . . . What Luck we shall have with those sort of Cows I can't say. My little Alderney one turns out tolerably well, and makes more Butter than we use, and I have just bought another of the same sort, but as her Calf is but just gone, can not say what she will be good for yet . . . Neddy is not so ungrateful to forget so good an Aunt but talks of you very often.'[55]

The visit to the Coopers was in fact postponed till later in the year, perhaps because Edward ('Neddy') fell ill, as in her letter of 9 December 1770 Mrs Austen writes:

my little Neddy's Cough seems entirely to have left him – he was so well that I ventured to leave him with his Maid for a few Days, while we went to Southcote, where we found my Sister, Dr Cooper and the little Boy quite well, I had not seen her before since I left them in Town last July – We went on Monday & returned last night and found Neddy quite well. The Day after Christmas Day we are to go to my Bror. Perrot's for about Ten Days, but there I shall take Neddy as well as Jemmy, there being no little ones there to catch anything bad of us. I wish my Dear Brother & Sister Walter were not more than thirty instead of Eighty miles from us, for believe me tis the distance, not the place you live in, which prevents my visiting you so often as I could wish . . . Mr Hillman & Mr Harwood are still at Variance, but the former goes away at Lady Day; the House is lett to two very young single Gentlemen. My poor little George is come to see me to-Day, he seems pretty well, tho' he had a fit lately, it was near a Twelvemonth since he had one before, so was in hopes they had left him, but must not flatter myself so now.[56]

After a surprising gap following the birth of Edward in 1767 – perhaps the reference to Mrs Austen being 'not then in strong health' when the family moved to their new home meant either she had just miscarried, or that she was pregnant, in which case the upheaval of moving must have caused her to lose the child – the first baby to arrive at Steventon was Henry Thomas, born and baptised on 8 June 1771 and christened on 12 July.[57] His godparents were Mrs Austen's cousin, Revd Thomas Leigh, the rector of Adlestrop; her old friend and perhaps unsuccessful suitor, Revd Tom Lybbe-Powys, the rector of Fawley; and her sister-in-law, Mrs Hancock. Mrs Austen wrote happily to Mrs Walter on 21 July:

Thank God I am got quite stout [strong] again, had an extraordinary good time and Lying in, and am Bless'd with as fine a Boy as perhaps you ever saw, he is much the largest I ever had, and thrives very fast. Mr Austen and my other Boys are all well. I should rejoyce to see you my Dear Sister, but it is not in my power to take any Journeys at present, my little family grows so numerous, there is no taking them abroad, nor can I leave them with an easy mind. My Sister Cooper has got a little Girl [Jane, 1771–98], not quite three weeks younger than my little Henry. She had a very good time and is pure well, and so is the Child, only remarkably small, as I hear, the Boy wanted four days of being a year old when the Girl was born, so she seems to be making up for her lost time . . . Nothing has happen'd in these parts worth relating. Our very few Neighbours are just as they were, only instead of the Hillmans we have got two agreable [*sic*] young Men at Ash Park. Mr and Mrs Harwood are quite reconciled to their Son and Son's Wife, and I hear the young Woman behaves very well and the young Squire continues monstrously fond [of] her.[58]

The new tenant of Ashe Park was Mr James Holder, who lived there for many years and is mentioned in Jane's letters;[59] he never married, and towards the end of his life his West Indian fortune failed, so that 'he died, as I have been told, poor & imbecile and ill-treated by his former Butler under whose care he was placed'.[60] Mrs Austen unfortunately gives no explanation as to why the old Harwoods had disapproved of their son's marriage.

Although the Austens were obviously unfeignedly pleased to have more children, it was also equally obvious that their finances could not keep pace with the expenses of an increasing family. Despite the sale of the crops from Cheesedown Farm, and the produce of the rectory garden and domestic dairy for everyday consumption, it was still necessary for Mr Austen to have money in the bank to pay tradesmen and other creditors, and from 1770 onwards his funds were gradually dwindling away. His own holding of £800 of Old South Sea Annuities was sold off in stages, thus losing capital as well as income, and was finally exhausted in April 1772.[61] And his wife was soon pregnant again, as she told Mrs Walter:

As to my travelling into Kent it is not to be thought of, with such a young family as I have around me. My little boy [Henry] is come home from Nurse, and a fine stout little fellow he is, and can run anywhere, so now I have all four at home, and some time in January I expect a fifth . . . I begin to be very heavy & bundling as usual, I believe my Sister Hancock will be so good as to come and nurse me again . . .[62]

This fifth baby was their first daughter, Cassandra Elizabeth, born and baptised on 9 January 1773 and christened on the 25th, when her godparents were her great-uncle, the Master of Balliol, her aunt, Mrs Cooper and her mother's cousin, Miss Elizabeth Leigh of Adlestrop.

It must now have been of desperate urgency for Mr Austen to have further funds, for in February his bank account shows a payment to him of £300 from Mr Leigh-Perrot, without which he would have been hopelessly insolvent.[63] March 1773 brought longer-term relief, for now at last the living of Deane, which had been purchased for him by his uncle Francis Austen of Sevenoaks, fell vacant by the death of the Revd Mr Hillman and, following a dispensation from the Archbishop of Canterbury,[64] Mr Austen was able to become rector of this small parish as well – its inhabitants numbered about two dozen families of farm labourers, and it was estimated to be worth £110 p.a.[65]

However, the extra income from Deane would of course only trickle in gradually over the year, and money was needed more quickly than that, so Mr Austen now embarked upon the usual recourse of scholarly but impecunious clerics, that of taking in boys to prepare them for university entrance by teaching them the necessary classical studies. No such pupil had been brought into the Austens' household since the death of poor little George Hastings in 1764, but their first boarder now came to them in the summer of 1773. In June Mrs Austen wrote to invite the Walters to visit them soon:

Mr Austen wants to shew his Bror. his Lands & his Cattle & many other matters; and I want to shew you my Henry & my Cassy, who are both reckoned fine Children. I suckled my little Girl thro' the first quarter; she has been wean'd and settled at a good Woman's at Dean just Eight weeks; she is very healthy and lively, and puts on her short Petticoats to-day. – Jemmy & Neddy are very happy in a new Play-fellow, Lord Lymington, whom Mr Austen has lately taken the charge of – he is between five & Six years old, very backward of his Age, but good temper'd and orderly; he is the Eldest Son of Lord Portsmouth who lives about ten miles from hence . . . I have got a nice Dairy fitted up, and am now worth a Bull & Six Cows, and you would laugh to see them; for they are not much bigger than Jack-asses – and here I have got Turkies & Ducks & Chicken for Phylly's amusement. In short you must come, and, like Hezekiah, I will shew you all my Riches.[66]

Another boarder came later in the year, and in December Mrs Austen wrote:

I thank God we are all quite well, and my little Girl is almost ready to run away. Our new Pupil, Master Vanderstegen, has been with us about a month, he is near fourteen years old; is very good temper'd and well disposed. Ld. Lymington has left us, his mamma began to be alarm'd at the Hesitation in his Speech, which certainly grew worse, and is going to take him to London in hopes a Mr Angier (who undertakes to cure that Disorder) may be of Service to him.[67]

The stammering little Lord Lymington might well have benefited from being left longer with the kind and eminently rational Austens, for he grew ever more unpleasantly eccentric until finally being declared a lunatic in 1823.[68] Nevertheless he always remembered the Steventon family, and while he was still reasonably sane and able to take his place in society as the 3rd Earl of Portsmouth he never omitted to invite them to his annual ball at Hurstbourne Park, given on the anniversary of his marriage to his first wife.[69]

Once again Mrs Austen was pregnant, and her fifth son Francis William was born on 23 April 1774, baptised two days later and christened on 27 May.

His godparents were William Vanderstegen of Cane End, Oxfordshire, one of Mrs Austen's girlhood friends and the father of their latest pupil; William Hampson Walter, the baby's half-uncle, and Mrs Leigh-Perrot, his aunt. There is no letter surviving from Mrs Austen to Mrs Walter telling of Francis's birth, which suggests that perhaps the Walters were in fact staying at Steventon upon this occasion. The next news from the rectory is in Mrs Austen's letter of 20 August 1775:

We are all, I thank God, in good health, and I am more nimble and active than I was last time, expect to be confined some time in November. My last Boy [Francis] is very stout, and has run alone these two Months, and he is not yet Sixteen Months old. My little Girl [Cassandra] talks all day long, and in my opinion is a very entertaining Companion. Henry has been in Breeches some months, and thinks himself near as good a man as his Bror. Neddy, indeed no one would Judge by their looks that there was above three years and a half difference in their ages, one is so little and the other so great. Master Van is got very well again, & has been with us again these three months, he is gone home this morning for a few Holidays.[70]

However, November came and went, and it was not till 17 December 1775 that Mr Austen could pass on good news to Mrs Walter both of family and farming:

You have doubtless been for some time in expectation of hearing from Hampshire, and perhaps wondered a little we were in our old age grown such bad reckoners but so it was, for Cassy certainly expected to have been brought to bed a month ago: however last night the time came, and without a great deal of warning, everything was soon happily over. We have now another girl, a present plaything for her sister Cassy and a future companion. She is to be Jenny, and seems to me as if she would be as like Henry, as Cassy is to Neddy. Your sister thank God is pure well after it, and sends her love to you and my brother, not forgetting James and Philly . . . Let my brother know his friend Mr Evelyn is going to treat us with a plowing match in this neighbourhood on next Tuesday, if the present frost does not continue and prevent it, Kent against Hants for a rump of beef; he sends for his own ploughman from St Clair. Does my brother know a Mr Collis, he says he is very well acquainted with him, he visited me to buy some oats for Evelyn's hunters.[71]

The cold weather did continue, and the winter of 1775–6 was one of the bitterest for many years,[72] so it is not surprising that, after her private baptism on 17 December, the new baby was not taken out to the freezing little Steventon church for her public christening till 5 April 1776. She received just the single name of Jane, and her godparents were her great-aunt Jane, wife of Francis Austen of Sevenoaks; Mrs Jane Musgrave, wife of Mrs Austen's cousin, the rector of Chinnor; and the Revd Samuel

Cooke, the vicar of Great Bookham in Surrey and husband of another of Mrs Austen's Leigh cousins – her namesake Cassandra, daughter of the Master of Balliol.

Mr Austen's predictions for his younger daughter were fully justified. Never were sisters more to each other than Cassandra and Jane; while in a particularly affectionate family there seems to have been a special link between Cassandra and Edward on the one hand, and between Henry and Jane on the other.

CHAPTER 3

India and France, 1752–85

The title of this chapter may seem far removed from the life of Jane Austen, but her aunt and cousin, Mrs Hancock and her daughter Eliza, were the bright comets flashing into the otherwise placid solar system of clerical life in rural Hampshire, and the news of their foreign travels and fashionable London life, together with their sudden descents upon the Steventon household in between times, all helped to widen Jane's youthful horizons and influence her later life and works.

As mentioned in chapter 1, Mr Austen's sister Philadelphia had gone to India in 1752 to find a husband and married Tysoe Saul Hancock out there in 1753. For a few years afterwards they lived at Fort St David, Madras, until early in 1759 Hancock was appointed surgeon at Fort William, Calcutta, at the request of Robert Clive, then Governor of Bengal.[1] Here the Hancocks became very friendly with Warren Hastings, then also an employee of the East India Company; it seems probable that Philadelphia had known his first wife Mary Buchanan (née Elliott) before the two girls had travelled to India, since the James Adams of London and John Lardner of Southwark who acted as Philadelphia's sureties for the trip to the Far East had performed the same function for Mary Elliott.[2] In any case, Hancock and Hastings soon entered into a business partnership, trading in salt, timber, carpets, opium and rice.[3] The widowed Mrs Buchanan brought two little girls to her marriage with Warren Hastings, and by him had another two children – a son, George, born in 1757, who was sent home to be educated in England and died while in the Austens' care, and a daughter, Elizabeth, who lived for only three weeks in October 1758.[4] Arriving at Fort William in 1759, Philadelphia Hancock had only a few months in which to renew her friendship with Mary Hastings before the latter died in July of that year at Cossimbazar.[5]

Warren Hastings was a kind-hearted man, very conscious of the responsibilities of kinship and friendship and devoted to children,[6] and when the Hancocks' only daughter was born on 22 December 1761 he stood godfather to her, and gave her the name of Elizabeth in memory of his own lost little girl. While he was absent from Calcutta, doing his duty as Resident in Murshidabad, his friends knew that they could please him in no better way than by giving him news of the continued health and development of the children in the close-knit little English community. In April 1762 the Revd Samuel Staveley (nicknamed 'Old Rattle' as he himself cheerfully acknowledged) wrote almost every other day to Hastings, always including such information as: 'George and Bob [Vansittart] are both very well & Miss Betsy Hancock . . . Little Betsy is very fond of Miss Ironside & her Guitar, she is a sweet little Girl . . . I know nothing worth writing to You, but that George & Bob & Miss Hancock (I beg her Ladyships Pardon she should have been first mentiond) are well.' At this period Mr Hancock had to leave his own home in order to give full-time attendance to a dangerously ill patient, James Philip Lyon, and Mr Staveley told Hastings: 'I leave You to guess what he must have suffered by being so long absent from his Wife & Child. He has been Night and Day with Lyon. Mrs & Miss Hancock are both well.'[7]

The close friendship between Hastings and the Hancocks, coupled with the fact that the latter had been childless for so long before Betsy's birth, gave scope for spiteful gossip to suggest that she was not Hancock's daughter. This rumour was spread by the malicious Mrs Strachey, whose husband was secretary to Lord Clive, and her slander was successful in so far as Clive wrote to his wife in the late summer of 1765: 'In no circumstances whatever keep company with Mrs Hancock for it is beyond a doubt that she abandoned herself to Mr Hastings, indeed, I would rather you had no acquaintance with the ladies who have been in India, they stand in such little esteem in England that their company cannot be of credit to Lady Clive.'[8] There is no evidence as to whether Hancock was aware of this gossip, but he knew that Mrs Strachey had an unpleasant nature, and some years after wrote to Philadelphia:

You ought not I think have hesitated to tell Mrs Strachey that her Behavior to you while in India, which plainly proved her contempt of you, gave her no Right to expect any favor from you. I am much mistaken if Lady Clive's most extraordinary Coolness be not owing to the Pride of that Woman. Surely I did enough for her when I saved her Life; her return for which was the basest Ingratitude to you.[9]

He certainly had no doubt in his own mind that Betsy was indeed his child, and his fondest hope was that he would be able to spend his latter days in watching her grow up and supervising her education.

By the time Lady Clive received this warning letter from her husband the Hancocks had already returned from India and were renting a house in London, in the happy expectation that the capital they had amassed abroad would provide a sufficient investment income for them to live comfortably in England for the rest of their lives. Hastings too had resigned his position with the East India Company and returned to England, and the old friends were living close by each other in London. In July 1765 Mr Austen went to see his relatives and probably met Hastings at the same time. In his boyhood Hastings had been a brilliant classical scholar at Westminster, and his headmaster there had been greatly disappointed when the boy's guardian refused to allow him to go on to university but instead sent him out to India to start earning his own living with the East India Company. Hastings retained all through life a taste for Latin poetry, and for composing English verse in the classical style.[10] The scholarly Mr Austen was evidently equally impressed by Hastings's intellectual abilities, and years afterwards was still urging his own sons and pupils to emulate Hastings's achievements in the way of classical learning.[11]

In London lived also Hastings's sister Anne, married to a lawyer, John Woodman, with their son, Tommy, who was much of an age with little Betsy Hancock. The Woodmans had a house in Cleveland Row, St James's, and they and the Hancocks became very close friends, so much so that Hastings said he considered them to be one family and wrote joint letters to them. Philadelphia and her husband lived leisurely in London for some three years, but gradually realised to their dismay that they were spending at the rate of £1,500 a year, nearly double their actual income. There was nothing for it but for Hancock to return to India in the hope of amassing a second fortune that would increase their capital to £44,000 which, when invested in Government stocks, would yield 3 percent or $3\frac{1}{2}$ percent interest a year and so provide the income required for the lifestyle to which they had grown accustomed in the Far East.[12] He therefore set off again in the autumn of 1768, leaving his family behind but taking with him a miniature of Philadelphia painted by John Smart. This miniature shows that she was then a slender, elegant woman with large dark eyes and smoothly upswept dark hair, wearing a turquoise blue dress and a pearl choker.[13] The Hancocks had already used up so much of their funds that Warren Hastings had to make a loan to Philadelphia to tide her over until such time as Mr Hancock could reach India and start to remit money to her from there.[14]

Hancock's plan had been that he would stay in India only three years, reckoning that such a period would be long enough for him to acquire the funds he needed. But he was soon to find that this time-limit for a return to solvency was quite unrealistic; the cost of living in Calcutta had risen sharply during his absence, trading opportunities had diminished and there were constant difficulties in remitting money to England. He wrote regularly to Philadelphia, and at first hopefully, with details of his prospective business ventures, and carefully copied the text of his letters into a ledger for ease of reference. However, the uncertainty of sending letters by sailing ships, with all the hazards of wrecks and delays during the long voyage round the Cape of Good Hope, meant that no proper communication could be maintained between husband and wife. The minimum time for the sea-voyage was four months, and the average time nearer eight months; some letters were even longer delayed, others never arrived at all, and when a letter did reach its destination its news was already stale and overtaken by events. The copies in Hancock's letter-book show how his hopes of prosperity and a return to England in triumph were gradually destroyed, leaving him only the weary determination to struggle on as long as his continual ill-health would allow, in order to provide for the wife and daughter on whom he doted.

Upon arrival in Calcutta he managed to obtain the position of Surgeon-Extraordinary to the garrison, which he hoped would be a sinecure but which in fact involved him in considerable work. 'You know how much I hate the Practice of Physick, yet I am obliged to take it up again: nothing could have induced me to do so, but the Hopes of thereby providing for my family.'[15] This position as Surgeon enabled him to obtain a *dustuck* or licence from the East India Company to trade on his own account, and he now managed to send home either bills of exchange or diamonds and silver bullion that could be sold in England by Philadelphia's uncle, Francis Austen of Sevenoaks, who acted as Hancock's attorney or trustee for his English financial affairs. The funds raised by these means were enough to provide a livelihood for Philadelphia and Betsy, but the business transactions involved were so expensive that overall they represented a net loss to Hancock.

Everything he touched seemed to fail – in March 1771 he wrote: 'Lately all the Gentlemen of Council have entered into a Joint Trade on a very large Stock; they [made] me the offer of Managing the whole for them, with the Compliment of my being the most Capable Person in India',[16] – but only a few months later: 'my Hopes are totally frustrated by the Gentlemen having entirely given up the Scheme. All my Expectations are vanished like a Dream & have left me Astonished how I could, against all Experience, imagine that Fortune would be long kind to me.'[17] He tried to live as frugally as he could, as he told his wife:

When I first arrived I resolved by the utmost Parsimony to save as much as possible and to avoid every expense which was not absolutely necessary to my existence. I carried the Resolution into Execution, lived without company, seldom went abroad, & never invited a single Person to my Table, on which was never placed more than a Fowl or a Bit of Mutton, & that only at Noon . . . At last I was given to understand that I was looked upon as one whose Misfortunes had sour'd his Temper and made him unsociable; accordingly I was shunned by almost every Body. This had a bad effect on my Affairs.[18]

He therefore moved to share a house with another single man, Benjamin Lacam, and was persuaded by the latter to enter into a contract to supply *chunam* to the East India Company for its building works. *Chunam* was a form of plaster made from sea-sand and shell-lime, and was manufactured particularly in a district called the Sunderbund Woods. Early in 1771 the partners set off on a tour to inspect 'every place where our people are employed, that we may oblige them to do their Duty and see that they neither Cheat us, nor are cheated themselves by their Overseers. We shall probably be a Month or Six Weeks before we return to Calcutta, as the circuit we have to go is nearly fifteen hundred Miles.'[19]

On his return Hancock sent a graphic account to Philadelphia of his labours on her behalf:

Imagination can scarcely form an Idea of a more dismal Place than the Sunder-bunds: They begin just below Culpee and extend Southerly to the Sea, to the Eastward they are terminated by Luckypore; so that their Extent is greater than all England. The whole is divided by a prodigious Number of Rivers into Islands, some large and some small; all entirely covered with Jungles so thick that you can not see two feet into them, except in some few Places where the Salt-makers have cleared the Ground for the space of fifty or an hundred Yards. Through all these Woods, there is no fresh Water but at two Places. The only Animals are the Rhinoceros, Tygers of a very large Size, Deer & Wild Hogs. The Rivers abound with Fish. In the Sunderbunds are neither Houses nor Hutts, therefore the People who are employed in making Salt or Chunam are obliged before Sunset to remove in their Boats from the Shore into the Middle of the Rivers; where they are not perfectly safe, for the Tygers sometimes Swim off and take them out of their Boats. We have unfortunately lost eight Men by these terrible Beasts. All those Rivers which run directly to the Sea are very large, from eight to twenty Miles over, some few of those which run only from one great River to another are so very narrow that a Tyger can leap from the Shore into a boat in the Middle of the River, & in general the Mud of these Stinks very much.[20]

Another venture arose in 1772: 'You will be surprised to hear that I am become a Carpenter and a Blacksmith; your Rank is certainly greatly lowered but you will be of more real Value thereby. To explain my meaning

I must tell you that I have contracted with the Company for three years to make their Gun Carriages and to do all the Carpenter's business at the New Fort.'[21] But by the end of 1773 the *chunam* contract had failed, inasmuch as Lacam had managed cleverly to oust him from their partnership, so that Hancock bore a loss of Rs. 7,300 and Lacam continued alone to make a subsequent profit;[22] and also: 'By my other Contract I can neither gain nor lose, for the Company have put an entire Stop to their Works, you see how little Industry and Application can avail when Fortune or whatever else you please to call it is against a Man.'[23]

Throughout all these difficulties Hancock constantly sent home to Philadelphia supplies of the Indian foods she had grown to like during her sojourn there – a bag of leaves for curries, pickled mangoes, pickled limes, chillies, balychong spice and cassoondy sauce – together with as much of her favourite scent as he could acquire, the precious attar of roses from Patna or Echharabad. He also maintained a supply of fine Indian fabrics – soosy quilts and palampores for bed-linen, and seersuckers, sannow, doreas, muslin, dimity, atlas, Malda silks, chintz and flowered shawl that would make up into underwear and dresses for both Philadelphia and Betsy. He procured silks from Cossimbazar and silk handkerchiefs from Pullicat, and every so often would ask Philadelphia to share some of these goods with other members of the family, so that during Jane's childhood her father may still have been wearing neck-cloths made of Indian muslin, or her mother a Pullicat handkerchief, bringing an exotic touch to the otherwise homespun Hampshire rectory.

In Hancock's absence his wife and daughter lived at various addresses in the smart West End of London – Bolton Street, Hertford Street, Manchester Square – and also tried to spend the summer and autumn months in a cottage at Byfleet, Surrey, until driven away by riverside floods. From time to time they visited the Walters in Kent and the Austens in Hampshire, especially when Mrs Austen needed help during her later confinements. Philadelphia was in attendance for Henry's birth in 1771, and for that of Cassandra in 1773.[24] In 1770, after one of Philadelphia's flying visits, Mrs Austen wrote with dry amusement to Mrs Walter:

Sister Hancock staid with us only a few days, she had more Courage than you had and set out in a Post Chaise with only her little Bessy, for she brought neither Clarinda or Peter [Indian servants] with her, but believe she sincerely repented, before she got to her Journey's end, for in the middle of Bagshot Heath the Postilion discover'd She had dropped the Trunk from off the Chaise. She immediately sent him back with the Horses to find it, intending to sit in the Chaise till he return'd, but was soon out of patience and began to be pretty much frighted, so began her

Walk to the Golden Farmer about two miles off, where she arrived half dead with fatigue, it being in the middle of a very hot day. When she was a little recover'd she recollected she had left all the rest of her things (amongst which were a large parcel of India Letters, which she had received the night before, and some of them she had not read) in the Chaise with the Door wide open – She sent a man directly after them and got them all safe and after some considerable time the Driver came with the Trunk, and without any more misfortune got to Bolton Street about Nine o'clock – she is now settled in her Cottage, her direction is at Byfleet, near Cobham, Surrey – The Letters brought good accounts both of My Brother Hancock and Mr Hastings.[25]

Philadelphia did her best to be a conscientious and helpful wife, as Hancock acknowledged, but her impulsive and rather scatter-brained nature was a source of constant exasperation to him, and he often reproached her in his letters for sending things he did not want and then forgetting to provide the information or items which he had specifically requested. He had had to send back her miniature by Smart, as it was in danger of being spoilt by the Indian climate, and had requested that Smart should conserve it and then return it to him, but this was one of his requests that went unheeded.[26] Philadelphia persisted in sending him such things as waistcoats embroidered by herself, which he thought were too incongruously fine for an ailing elderly man like himself to wear; religious books which he had neither time nor desire to read; reading lamps that were useless without glass shades; and currant jelly that arrived full of maggots. She also took to heart her husband's comments about his frugal lifestyle and strenuous endeavours to make money on her behalf, and in turn tried to assure him that she was not living extravagantly; it must then have been equally exasperating for her to receive further reproaches from Hancock for what he considered to be ill-judged economies on her part.

On one topic they were in agreement, and that was the subject of Betsy's education. Hancock constantly reminded Philadelphia to see that Betsy had the best masters available to teach her writing, arithmetic, music and dancing, that she should have a Kirkman harpsichord to play and a pony to ride, and that she should also learn French, perhaps by visiting France or having a French companion. On the other hand, he sometimes feared that such an expensive education might in later life make Betsy discontented with her lot, and as early as 1769 put this problem to Warren Hastings for advice.[27] Hastings replied with kind encouragement:

Make no Change in the Plan you have already laid down. Neither French nor Dancing will disqualify a Woman for filling the Duties of any Sphere in Life. Her own Natural Understanding & gentle Disposition improved by the Precepts of such a Mother as few Children are blest with will fit her Mind to be satisfied with any Lot that she may meet with & to become it. But God forbid she should be disqualified for a better Way of Life because it is Possible she may not have a Fortune equal to it. A frugal Style of, & an early Practice in Economy will be a sufficient Precaution. – I cannot say all I will upon this Subject. My own Prospects and my Life are precarious, and it will require some years for me to get much above the world, but if I live & meet with the success which I have a Right to hope for, she shall not be under the Necessity of marrying a Tradesman, or any Man for her Support. I would not say thus much, but that I wish in every respect to dispell your Apprehensions.[28]

By 1772 Hastings had prospered sufficiently to fulfil this half-made promise, and Hancock was able to tell Philadelphia: 'A few days ago Mr Hastings, under the polite Term of making his God daughter a present, made over to me a Respondentia Bond for forty thousand Rupees to be paid in China; I have given directions for the amount, which will be about five thousand Pounds, to be immediately remitted home to my Attorneys.'[29] Early in 1775 Hastings increased the amount to £10,000, and a trust was set up in Philadelphia's name, with George Austen and John Woodman as her Trustees. The income would be nearly £400 a year, and the capital sum would provide a sufficient dowry for Betsy to make a good marriage.[30]

During these lonely years in India Hancock had perpetually suffered from a variety of painful and debilitating ailments, and this second kind gesture on the part of Warren Hastings came only just in time to relieve his mind of its constant worry as to what would happen to his family after his death. His last brief note to his wife was written in August 1775, and he died in November of that year and was buried in the Great Burying-Ground at Chowringhee.[31] News of his death did not reach Philadelphia until the summer of 1776, when luckily Mr and Mrs Austen were staying with her in London and so were immediately at hand to support her under the shock.[32] Hancock had made his Will in December 1774, naming Warren Hastings and another Indian friend, Edward Baber, as his executors and trustees; he made the specific request that Betsy should have the 'miniature picture of her Mother painted by Smart and set in a ring with diamonds round it which I request she will never part with as I intend it to remind her of her mother's virtues as well as of her person'.[33] His affairs were however in such confusion that it was another year before Mrs Hancock was in a position to know that her annual income would in future be about £600, the bulk of this sum being the interest from Hastings's trust fund.[34] She had already discovered that this would be inadequate for life in London, so decided to fulfil her husband's wish that Betsy – or rather Eliza, as the elegant young lady now preferred to be called – should acquire French culture, and mother and daughter, with their Indian maid Clarinda, set off for the Continent late in 1777. They went first to Germany and Belgium, spending the summer of 1778 in Brussels, and in the autumn of 1779 settled in Paris.[35]

Precisely how they managed to obtain introductions to French society is not known, but a group of letters exists, written by Eliza to her Kentish cousin Phylly Walter, from which it is clear that she and her mother had soon moved into far higher circles than any to which her devoted father could ever have aspired on her behalf.

We were a few days ago at Versailles & had the honor of seeing their Majesties & all the royal family dine & sup. The Queen is a very fine woman, she has a most beautiful complexion, & is indeed exceedingly handsome, she was most elegantly dressed, she had on a corset & Petticoat of pale green lutestring, covered with a transparent silver gauze, the petticoat & sleeves puckered & confined in different places with large bunches of roses, & an amazing large bouquet of white lilac. The same flower, together with gauze, feathers, ribbon & diamonds intermixed with her hair. Her neck was entirely uncovered & ornamented by a most beautiful chain of diamonds, of which she had likewise very fine bracelets, she was without gloves, I suppose to shew her hands & arms, which are without exception the whitest & most beautiful I ever beheld. The King was plainly dressed, he had however likewise some fine diamonds.[36]

Eliza did not become too fashionable to forget her Hampshire relations, and with this same letter, written in the summer of 1780, sent 'my picture in miniature done here to my Uncle G: Austen . . . It is reckoned here like what I am at present. The dress is quite the present fashion & what I usually wear.'[37] The miniature shows a piquante little face, with large dark eyes like her mother's, framed by romantically dishevelled powdered curls entwined by a blue ribbon, her white dress trimmed with ribbons of the same blue.[38] A year or two later Eliza had another miniature done, at Phylly's request, in the back of which she placed some of her dark-brown hair, with the words 'Amoris et Amicitiae' – 'Of Love and Friendship'.[39]

At some time during 1780–1 Eliza met a dashing young Captain in the Queen's Regiment of Dragoons, Jean-François Capot de Feuillide. He was about ten years older than she was, and came from Nérac in the province of Guienne, bordering on Gascony, in the south-west of France. His father had a small estate near Nérac, but Jean-François had left home to join the French army in 1769, and had the reputation of being one of its finest officers. It seems that the friendship with the Hancocks was attended with some degree of exaggeration on both sides, inasmuch as the Captain claimed to be the *Comte* de Feuillide; while Eliza, for her part, was evidently not unwilling that her friends in French society should think she was 'immensément riche', as befitted anyone connected with the 'fameux lord Hastings, gouverneur de l'Inde'.[40] In any event, by August 1781 Eliza had engaged herself to Jean-François, with the full approval of Mrs Hancock but with the strong disapproval of her trustees John Woodman and Mr Austen. Woodman told Warren Hastings of their worries in the matter:

Mrs & Miss Hancock are yet in France & likely to continue there the young Lady being on the point of Marriage with a French Officer which Mrs Hancock writes is of good family with expectation of good Fortune but at present but little. Her Letter was to Mr Austen & Self on the Subject and she seems inclined to give up to them the Sum which was settled on her for Life, and wants the Money to be transferred into the French Funds which we have thought prudent for her sake to decline and Mr Austen is much concerned at the connection which he sais [*sic*] is giving up all their friends their Country, and he fears their Religion.[41]

By December 1781 the marriage had taken place, and Woodman grumbled again to Hastings:

I wrote Mrs Hancock . . . who is in France, where I believe she intends to end her Days, having married her Daughter there to a Gentleman of that Country, I am afraid not very advantageously, although she sais it is entirely to her satisfaction, the Gentleman having great connections, and expectations. Her Uncle Mr Austen, and Brother don't approve of the Match, the latter is much concern'd at it; they seem already desirous of draining the Mother of every shilling she has.[42]

It is not known when Eliza discovered that her husband was not truly entitled to call himself a Comte, nor when he found out that she and her mother had only £600 a year between them; however, for the first few years at least their marriage was a happy one, and Eliza wrote enthusiastically and perhaps a little boastfully to Phylly Walter:

The man to whom I have given my hand is everyways amiable both in mind & person. It is too little to say he loves, since he literally adores me; entirely devoted to me, & making my inclinations the guide of all his actions, the whole study of his life seems to be to contribute to the happiness of mine. My situation is everyways agreeable, certain of never being separated from my dear Mama whose presence enhances every other blessing I enjoy, equally sure of my husband's affections, mistress of an easy fortune with the prospect of a very ample one, add to these the advantages of rank & title, & a numerous & brilliant acquaintance, amongst whom I can flatter myself I have some sincere friends, & you will unite with me in saying I have reason to be thankful to Providence for the lot fallen to my share.[43]

In the same letter she mentions how gay the season has been, on account of the birth of the Dauphin and of the festivities which marked that event.

Eliza was, however, intelligent and observant as well as pretty and vivacious, and her letters contain pertinent information, not mere frivolous gossip.

The gay world have lately been taken up with Longchamps, a kind of fashion which I will endeavour to give you some account of. Longchamps is a monastery situated in the Bois de Boulogne, a delightful wood I have already mentioned to you, in the environs of Paris. It was formerly the custom to go thither to hear vespers the three last days of Passion Week, but Devotion has given place to vanity. Every Body now goes to Longchamps not to say their Prayers but to shew their fine Cloaths & fine Equipages. They do not even enter the convent but content themselves with parading in the Avenue that leads to it in the stile of the coaches in Hyde Park of a Sunday: their Appearance is however much finer for the number & magnificence of the Carriages are incredible. Most People have new & elegant ones on this occasion with four or six fine horses, as many Lacqueys as possible behind, sometimes to the number of eight, & often running footmen. The <u>Elegants</u> or fashionable young men are in general either on horseback or in open carriages. The Queen & Royal Family are generally there, & what much contributed to the <u>beauty of the Shew</u> this year, several of the Princesses made their appearance in open Calashes drawn by six horses. The most elegant were the Dutchess de Chartres Cousin to his Majesty & the Princess de Lamballe whose natural beauty does not want all the additions it had received on this occasion, for all the Ladies are very much dressed. You may imagine that the <u>Coup d'oeil</u> of the whole must be striking.[44]

On 2 March 1784 one of the pioneers of ballooning, Jean-Pierre Blanchard (1753–1809), attempted to make an ascent from the Champ-de-Mars, and Eliza reported the event to Phylly in her letter a few weeks later:

I gave you some account of the Globes or <u>Ballons</u> in my last. The attention of the public has been once more awakened by an improvement attempted in this discovery by a M. Blanchard who undertook by means of wings & a rudder to direct the course of the <u>Ballon</u>. On the Day appointed for the experiment a most prodigious concourse assembled to witness it, but alas the obstinacy of one individual soon overset their expectations. It had been agreed that M. Blanchard & a Benedictine Monk should ascend with the Globe in order to regulate its motions, but at the instant they were seating themselves in the car fixed under this machine for the purpose of their conveyance, one of the young Men belonging to the <u>Ecole militaire</u> (or military academy) insisted on being of the party, nor could the strenuous opposition he met with prevail on him to relinquish his design; a violent scuffle ensued & the wings & rudder were soon demolished. M. Blanchard had however the courage notwithstanding the shattered condition of his vehicle to set out alone for the aerial regions; he ascended to the height of 1500 fathoms & returned from thence in perfect health & safety to the astonishment of most of the spectators.[45]

Later in 1784 M. de Feuillide took Eliza south to Guienne to meet his family for the first time – he had a widowed mother, brother Gabriel, sisters Dorothée and Augustine – and to start work on his own project for improving his estate and finances. He had obtained a royal grant of an area of marshland at Gabarret, not far from Nérac, which could be held tax-free for twenty years provided works of reclamation were undertaken and the land brought into cultivation. M. de Feuillide, who was certainly an enterprising and efficient man, set his labourers to work digging a vast canal with associated feeder ditches across the marsh, and as the waters gradually drained away and the land dried out began also to build houses and cottages for himself and his workers. His own house, called simply Le Marais, was to be a small but elegant country villa; in the meantime, he rented the nearby Chateau de Jourdan, and it was from here that Eliza wrote to Phylly in the summer of 1785:

I have without doubt already mentioned to You a Donation made by the King to Mons. de Feuillide & his heirs for ever, of 5000 Acres of Land little distant from his Paternal Estate, at that time & for many preceding Ages entirely covered with Water. Very considerable & expensive Works carried on for eighteen Months past, have entirely drained this large extent of Ground & nothing can equal the Public Surprise at the accomplishment of what was deemed impracticable; at the same time I have the Pleasure of seeing My Husband looked upon as the Benefactor of a whole Province, from the Salubrity its Air has acquired by being freed from the pernicious exhalations of such an extent of stagnant Water, very advantageously replaced by a fertile plain not less agreeable to the view than I flatter myself it will be profitable to [its] owners.[46]

Eliza remained in Guienne for another year or so, and no doubt she and her mother sent to the Austens in Steventon letters equally interesting as these addressed to the Walters in Kent. James Austen was certainly filled with enthusiasm for a trip abroad to stay with the de Feuillides, and his plans in this respect must have been the talking-point in the rectory for many weeks in advance.

CHAPTER 4

Childhood at Steventon, 1775–86

For the first three and a half years of her life Jane was the baby of the rectory family, and it is not surprising that she and Cassandra should have become inseparable companions, being as they were the only two little girls in a house full of boys – whose numbers indeed increased still further as time passed. On 23 June 1779 Mrs Austen, at the age of forty, gave birth to her sixth son and last child, Charles John; he was privately baptised the same day and publicly christened on 30 July, when his godparents were John Cope Freeman of Abbots Langley, Hertfordshire (Mr Austen's maternal first cousin), Mrs Jane Knight of Godmersham (the unmarried daughter of Thomas Knight of Godmersham, but of a sufficient age to warrant the courtesy title of 'Mrs') and James Stuart of Brewer Street, London (presumably a family friend). Cassandra and Jane now had a baby all of their own to play with, and in later years used to refer to Charles as 'our own particular little brother', deliberately misquoting Fanny Burney's *Camilla*, in which the heroine is referred to as 'my own particular little niece'.[1]

Even as Mr Austen's last son arrived in the family, his first was on the verge of leaving home and entering the wider world beyond Steventon. James, a gentle and studious boy, had benefited so much from his father's tuition in the classics as to be able to matriculate at St John's College, Oxford, on 3 July 1779, at the precociously early age of fourteen.[2] At this college he could claim the privileged entry of Founder's Kin, through his mother's ancestry on the Perrot side of her family; and upon arrival in Oxford he was honoured with an invitation to dine with his dignified great-uncle the Master of Balliol. 'Being a raw undergraduate, unaccustomed to the habits of the university, he was about to take off his gown, as if it were a great-coat, when the old man, then considerably turned eighty, said, with a grim smile, "Young man, you need not strip, we are not going to fight."'[3]

Edward, Henry and Frank were still at home and needing classmates to help them compete in their studies, so from about 1778 onwards, after William Vanderstegen had matriculated, Mr Austen concentrated much more seriously on increasing the number of his pupils, both to educate alongside his own sons and to provide some further income to meet the expenses of a growing family – at this date it seems that he charged approximately £35 p.a. per pupil to cover tuition, board and lodging.[4] By 1779 there were four other boys living in the rectory – Fulwar Craven Fowle, Gilbert East, Frank Stuart and one or other of the Deane boys, George or Henry, the sons of Henry Deane of Reading. Gilbert East was the son of Sir William East of Hall Place, Hurley, Berkshire, and at the age of fifteen was not at all of a studious nature; Mrs Austen sent him one of her amusing doggerel verses, pointing out that he had been away from Steventon for nine weeks and kept postponing his return – she feared he was not reading Latin at home but going out dancing, as they all knew he was a very good dancer, but he must not neglect his studies for social pleasures and so should come back to study again with Fowle, Stuart, Deane, Henry and Ned.[5]

It would seem that the frivolous Gilbert did return to Steventon in response to Mrs Austen's plea, for he certainly acquired sufficient education to enable him to go up to Oxford in 1783 and his grateful father presented the Austens with a picture by way of thanks.[6] Frank Stuart was presumably the son of the James Stuart whom Mr Austen had chosen as godfather for Charles; he seems to have been a jealous boy, for he 'accused [Mrs Austen] of partiality in writing verses for F. C. Fowle & not for him'. Mrs Austen accordingly wrote another poem exclusively for him – though it may not have been entirely to his liking, as she reproached him gently but firmly for his sulky looks and hinted that Fulwar was the better scholar of the two and therefore the more deserving of praise.[7] Frank Stuart left the rectory in 1782 but apparently did not go on to any university thereafter, which perhaps bears out Mrs Austen's assessment of his intellectual abilities.

Neither Frank Stuart nor the Deane boy (who probably stayed on at Steventon until 1786) seems to have kept in touch with the Austens in later life, but Fulwar Craven Fowle (1764–1840) and his younger brothers Tom (1765–97), William (1767–1801) and Charles (1770–1806), were destined to become very closely connected with the Austens. These four boys were the sons of the Revd Thomas Fowle (1727–1806), vicar of Kintbury in Berkshire and one of Mr Austen's university friends.[8] The quiet James Austen, who had inherited his mother's talent for versifying, much admired the more dominant Fulwar and in 1780 dedicated to him a poem entitled: 'An Epistle to Fulwar Craven Fowle Esqr. supposed Secretary of State in the reign of Geo. 4th, by J. Austen as a Country Curate' – imagining that, in future days when their careers had widely diverged, Fulwar might remember how he and James had enjoyed rambling and swimming together in the

Hampshire/Berkshire countryside.[9] As it happened, James's predictions were only partly fulfilled – he himself certainly remained a country parson all his days, though as vicar and rector rather than starveling curate – but so also did Fulwar Fowle, who matriculated in 1781, graduated in 1785, succeeded his father as vicar of Kintbury in 1798 and resided there till his death in 1840.

This year of 1779 was to prove a memorable one too for Edward Austen, though no one at that time could have guessed what the outcome of a casual encounter would be, nor how important an effect it would have upon the future lives of his brothers and sisters. Mr Austen's distant cousin Thomas Knight II of Godmersham[10] married on 8 May 1779 Catherine Knatchbull, of an old-established Kentish family, and their wedding tour included a call at Steventon so that he could introduce her to his Hampshire relatives. Here they saw Edward, then aged about twelve, and took him along with them for the rest of their tour. They evidently enjoyed his company and when, after a year or two of married life, it became clear that they were fated to remain childless, they decided to adopt Edward and make him their heir. Henry Austen, a bright little eight-year-old when the Knights first visited Steventon, never forgot the circumstances of the adoption, and many years later told his niece Anna Lefroy how it had come about, though he could not at that time (*c.* 1848) recall the precise dates of the events involved.

Mr and Mrs Knight from Godmersham came to Steventon Parsonage in their way to some place where they were intending for a time to remain. They took the child [Edward] with them by way of amusement, returning him to his home after a few weeks absence. It may be supposed that they were first attracted by his personal beauty, but no particular consequences at that time ensued, or seem to have been expected from this mark of preference for one little boy. Some time afterwards, probably more than a year, further advances were made (though not understood as such) in the way of adoption – A letter arrived from Godmersham begging that little Edward might be allowed to spend his holydays [*sic*] there – and proposing to send for him. His Father was not however inclined to consent to Mr Knight's request, looking only to the consequences of so many weeks idleness, and a probable falling behind in the Latin Grammar – but whilst he hesitated a few simple words from his Wife gently turned the scale – 'I think, my Dear, you had better oblige your cousins, and let the Child go' – And accordingly go he did, riding all the way on the Pony which Mr Knight's Coachman, himself on horseback, had led from Godmersham for his use. It seems a long journey for so young a boy to perform in such manner, even at the most leisurely rate of travelling, Godmersham being situated in East Kent, 10 miles to the south of Canterbury, but I tell the tale as it was told to me. Edward Austen returned from Godmersham ostensibly as much Edward Austen as ever, & remained for some years as such under the care of his natural Parents. – By degrees however, it came to be understood in the family that Edward was selected from amongst themselves as the adopted son & Heir of Mr Knight; and in further course of time he was taken more entire possession of, & sent to study in some German University.[11]

It seems that 1783 was the year in which adoption was finally agreed upon, as a silhouette bearing that date was painted by William Wellings to commemorate the event. It depicts Mr Austen formally presenting his son to Mrs Knight, while Mr Knight, leaning on the back of his sister Jane's chair, looks on approvingly.[12] It was probably also at this time that the Knights commissioned a portrait of Edward, which shows him as a chestnut-haired solemn-faced schoolboy, very neat and trim in a blue jacket and large frilly white shirt.[13]

Mr Austen was in the happy position of receiving kindnesses from both sides of his family, and although at this period he was probably in closer touch with the Knights, he did not forget his benevolent uncle Francis Austen. However, the latter was now well advanced in years, and obviously it would be very difficult for him to make the long journey from Kent to Steventon, where the rectory was in any case full of children and pupils, with room for guests only briefly at Christmas and midsummer.[14] It was therefore the young couple who visited their uncle from time to time in his large seventeenth-century town house in Sevenoaks High Street, The Red House. In 1776 Mr and Mrs Austen probably took James and Edward to be introduced to their father's benefactor,[15] and in 1780 it was the turn of Henry Austen, aged nine, to accompany his parents into Kent to meet his eighty-two-year-old great-uncle:

All that I remember of him is, that he wore a wig like a Bishop, & a suit of light gray ditto, coat, vest & hose. In his picture over the chimney the coat & vest had a narrow gold lace edging, about half an inch broad, but in my day he had laid aside the gold edging, though he retained a perfect identity of colour, texture & make to his life's end – I think he was born in Anne's reign, and was of course a smart man of George the First's. It is a sort of privilege to have seen and conversed with such a model of a hundred years since . . . A very pleasing amiable woman [his wife] was; I remember her about 1780, & thought her a great deal handsomer than her Daughter who always lived with her & my [great-]uncle till her death.[16]

The picture of Francis Austen to which Henry referred was probably painted *c.* 1750 at the time of his marriage, and portrays a burly middle-aged man, every inch the successful lawyer and powerful local dignitary – heavy-lidded eyes glancing shrewdly sideways, uncompromising jaw and tight-lipped mouth.[17]

Mrs Austen's Leigh relatives also took a kindly interest in her young family, and when her cousin the Revd Thomas Leigh of Adlestrop journeyed from Gloucestershire to Hampshire or London he was careful to note in his personal account books the tips which he distributed to the children in Steventon Rectory as he called there en route.[18] In December 1774 'Jemmy Austen' received half a guinea, in August 1779 the 'Master Austens' had 10s. to share amongst themselves, and in April 1781 the entry reads: 'Gave ye Austens 10s.6d.' On Mr Leigh's return journey the following month 'Neddy Austen' is the only one of the family who is mentioned, and he received 5s. all to himself. Mr Leigh's wife, Mary, was very proud of her ancestors,[19] and in 1788 finished writing a family history which she had compiled for the benefit of her nephew, James Henry Leigh, heir of the eldest branch of the Adlestrop Leighs. It may be that she had the 1781 visit to Steventon in mind when she recorded:

[Cassandra] wife of the truly respectable Mr Austen, has eight children – James, George, Edward, Henry, Francis, Charles, Cassandra, and Jane. With his sons (all promising to make figures in life) Mr Austen educates a few youths of chosen friends and acquaintances. When among this liberal society, the simplicity, hospitality, and taste which commonly prevail in affluent families among the delightful valleys of Switzerland ever recurs to my memory.[20]

In 1781 the pupils at Steventon, in addition to Stuart, East and Deane, were probably Tom Fowle, the second son of the Kintbury family, and George Nibbs, son of the James Langford Nibbs who was James Austen's godfather; these latter two boys both went up to Oxford in 1783, and Mr Nibbs, like Sir William East, also presented Mr Austen with a picture as a token of his gratitude for the care and tuition of his son.[21]

Although the Revd Thomas Leigh seems at this period to have noticed only the boys of the Austen family, Cassandra received her share of special attention from Mrs Austen's sister, Mrs Cooper. After leaving Southcote in 1771 Dr Cooper had settled in the West Country; he had acquired from Wells Cathedral the prebend of Holcombe Burnell in Devon,[22] and also had the livings of two little villages in Wiltshire, Hill Deverill and Whaddon.[23] He and his family lived in style at Bath, first of all at No. 12 in the newly built Royal Crescent, and then round about 1780–1 moved to No. 14 Bennett Street, opposite the Upper Rooms and so right at the centre of social life.[24] Here the Coopers invited Cassandra to visit them, and it was one of these visits which gave rise to the earliest mention of Jane in family tradition:

Cassandra in her childhood was a good deal with Dr & Mrs Cooper in Bath –
She once described to me her return to Steventon one fine summer evening. The
Coopers had sent or conveyed her a good part of the journey, but my Grandfather
had to go, I think as far as Andover to meet her – He might have conveyed himself
by Coach, but he brought his Daughter home in a Hack chaise; & almost home
they were when they met Jane & Charles, the two little ones of the family, who
had got as far as New down to meet the chaise, & have the pleasure of riding home
in it.[25]

This anecdote probably dates to the summer of 1782, when Jane would be
six and a half and so independent enough to scamper away unescorted,
dragging her little brother Charles, then aged just three, along with her.

In December 1782 occurred the first presentation of the amateur
theatricals – very fashionable at this period – that were to become a feature of Steventon rectory life during the next few years. James, now nearly
eighteen, produced *Matilda*, a tragedy by Dr Thomas Francklin, which
provided five acts of ranting blank verse, and added to it his own versified
prologue and epilogue, the former being spoken by Edward and the latter
by Tom Fowle.[26] *Matilda* was supposedly a costume drama, being set at the
time of the Norman Conquest; it threatened passion, murder and suicide
until, with a sudden collapse into happy-ending bathos, the wicked brother
meekly repented and the lovers were united. Cassandra may have had the
small part of Bertha, the heroine's friend, but it is unlikely that little Jane
was anything other than a fascinated spectator. Family tradition records
that the plays were presented either in the rectory dining-room or else in
the barn across the road; as the cast of *Matilda* numbers only six speaking
parts, it is probable that on this occasion the performance was indoors.
Either now or for some later production, James also organised the painting
of a 'set of theatrical scenes', which survived for many years.[27]

The following year, 1783, brought to the Steventon family life changes
which, though unremarkable at first, proved more significant as the years
went by. In January their neighbour, the Revd Dr Russell, the wealthy,
jovial and hospitable rector of Ashe, died at the advanced age of eighty-
seven; he had been the incumbent there since 1729 and had outlived two
wives in the meantime. His third wife, the mother of one hopelessly plain
spinster daughter, Mary, moved to Alresford, a small, pleasant market-town
about fifteen miles away to the south, not far from Winchester. There,
not long afterwards, the unprepossessing but rich Miss Russell was wooed
and married for her money by the charming young spendthrift George
Mitford, and their daughter Mary Russell Mitford, the future authoress,
was born in Alresford in 1787. Mrs Mitford did not lose touch with the

neighbours of her girlhood, and years later transmitted to her daughter some memories – understandably jealous ones – about Jane Austen's youthful prettiness.[28]

The presentations of both Ashe and Deane had been bought by Francis Austen of Sevenoaks so that his nephew could have whichever living first fell vacant; as George Austen now held Deane, his uncle sold the presentation of Ashe to another rich, kind uncle, Benjamin Langlois, for precisely the same reason – to provide for *his* nephew, the Revd I. P. George Lefroy. The Langlois and Lefroy families were of Huguenot origin and had been settled in Kent for some generations, but maintained business interests in Europe. Mr Langlois had been attached to the British Embassy in Vienna, and on his return to England had become an MP and Under-Secretary of State. He had an address in Cork Street, Burlington Gardens, London, but for the last years of his life came to live with his nephew in Hampshire.[29] Both uncle and nephew were well-educated men with a cosmopolitan polish, and it was this worldly and intellectual family who now took up residence in Ashe Rectory in May 1783. In 1778 George Lefroy had married Anne Brydges, of Wootton Court, Kent;[30] they brought with them to Hampshire two young children and had several more as the years passed. 'He was very fond of society, and she was a beautiful and talented woman, of pleasing address and considerable conversational powers, known to the neighbourhood around as "Madam Lefroy". He rebuilt a great part of the Rectory, and together they exercised a good deal of hospitality, and took for the time the lead in the neighbourhood.'[31] They were sufficiently well off, unlike the Austens, not to need to take pupils, so Madam Lefroy busied herself instead for the good of the parish by teaching the village children to read and write and make straw plait for bonnets and hats – then a profitable cottage industry – and when Jenner's discovery of the efficacy of vaccination against smallpox came to be generally accepted, she personally vaccinated all her husband's parishioners.[32] From 1783 onwards the Lefroys and Austens became ever more closely connected, first by friendship and subsequently by marriage.

However, in the spring of 1783 the Austens' immediate concern was not so much with their new neighbours as with the education of their daughters, now aged ten and seven; and according to family tradition the sisters, accompanied by their cousin, Jane Cooper, aged twelve, were sent to Oxford to be tutored by Mrs Ann Cawley, the sister of Dr Cooper. Mrs Cawley was the widow of a Principal of Brasenose College, and is said to have been a stiff-mannered person, unlike her amiable brother. While the little girls were in Oxford, it seems that James, who was still in residence at St John's and full of intellectual enthusiasm on their behalf, took his sisters sight-seeing through more 'dismal chapels, dusty libraries, and greasy halls' than Jane at least could bear to remember.[33]

With their daughters safely under Mrs Cawley's care, Mr and Mrs Austen set off at Easter 1783 for a short tour into Kent to visit their relatives,[34] and on this occasion took with them Francis William, aged about nine, as well as his elder brother, Henry. Francis was a small, tough little boy, as Jane afterwards recalled: 'Fearless of danger, braving pain, / And threaten'd very oft in vain'[35] – and had already made a name for himself in the family by his initiative in horse-dealing. All the Austen boys enjoyed foxhunting – gobbling a hasty breakfast in the kitchen in the early morning and then rushing off after hounds, in a scrambling sort of way, upon any pony or donkey that they could procure, or, in default of such luxuries, on foot. Such haphazard arrangements did not suit the practical and efficient Francis, so when only seven years old he bought on his own account – presumably with his father's permission – a pony for £1.11s.6d.; hunted it, jumping everything that the pony could get its nose over; and at the end of two years sold it again for £2.12s.6d. It was a bright chestnut and he called it 'Squirrel', though his elder brothers, to plague him, called it 'Scug'. Mrs Austen's well-worn, red woollen wedding-dress finally finished its useful life by being cut up into a jacket and breeches for Francis to wear in the hunting-field.[36] On this 1783 trip to Kent, Francis's self-control was unexpectedly tested in a way that he remembered to the end of his very long and distinguished life. The Austens went to Tonbridge to see their cousins the Revd Henry Austen and his three children – Elizabeth Matilda (1766–1855), Harriet Lennard (1768–1839) and Francis Edgar (1774–1804). Kentish Francis, who was almost exactly the same age as his Hampshire cousin, asked the latter

if I knew what 'wiring' was, and on my professing ignorance, he very deliberately ran a pin a considerable way into my leg, for which his sister Harriet gave him a scolding. He was at that time a day scholar at Tonbridge School, and therefore was only at home with intervals between school hours so that I had not much opportunity of being enlightened by his practical jokes.[37]

Later in 1783 Mrs Cawley moved from Oxford to Southampton, taking the three little girls with her, and here Jane's life very nearly came to a premature end. From 1770 onwards the town had been subjected to almost continual military activity associated with the French wars and the American War of Independence. In August 1783 troops returning from Gibraltar were quartered in Southampton and brought with them typhus fever as a result of their sea voyage in cramped and insanitary conditions;

within a few weeks the town's death-rate showed an alarming rise.[38] Both the Austen girls were infected, but Mrs Cawley did not think their illness sufficiently serious to warrant writing to Steventon. Luckily, Jane Cooper, as the eldest of the three, took it upon herself to call to the family for help, upon which Mrs Austen and Mrs Cooper set off at once for Southampton and took their daughters away.[39] Jane Austen was very ill and nearly died; but tragically Mrs Cooper also caught the fever, and after her return home to Bath died there on 25 October 1783 and was buried in Dr Cooper's church at Whaddon a few days later: 'Her form the Beauties of her mind express'd, / Her mind was Virtue by the Graces dress'd.'[40] Poor Dr Cooper was heartbroken and could not bear to continue living in Bath; he sub-let his house in Bennett Street,[41] resigned his Wiltshire livings and fled back to the Thames Valley countryside of his youth, moving in 1784 to the vicarage of Sonning, Berkshire,[42] where there were no memories of his beloved wife to haunt him. He never remarried – and indeed did not himself live much longer – but spent the last few years of his life devotedly rearing his two children, Edward and Jane. He gave his Austen nieces small tokens of jewellery by which to remember their aunt – Cassandra had a 'ring representing a sprig of Diamonds, with one Emerald' and Jane had a headband, which she later wore when she went to balls.[43]

It must have taken some time for the Austens to recover from the combined shocks of their daughters' dangerous illness and the death of Mrs Cooper, and it is not surprising that no amateur theatricals took place over the winter of 1783–4. For the present, Cassandra and Jane stayed at home, presumably being taught by their mother as best she could in the midst of her domestic duties. Two of Jane's childhood books still survive – *The history of Goody Two-Shoes*, and *Fables choisis*, which latter little textbook of French grammar was given to her on 5 December 1783.[44] Like Catherine Morland, she probably read John Gay's *Fables* and from these learned to recite 'The Hare and many Friends', as well as 'The Beggar's Petition' from Dr Moss's *Poems on Several Occasions*; she acquired miscellaneous information from Ann Murry's *Mentoria: or, The Young ladies instructor*, and from her brother Edward's gift of Dr Percival's *A Father's Instructions to his Children, consisting of Tales, Fables and Reflections; designed to promote the love of virtue, a taste for knowledge, and an early acquaintance with the works of Nature*,[45] and she also owned the literary anthology *Elegant Extracts*.[46]

By the summer of 1784 the social requirements of mourning for a close relative were sufficiently fulfilled to permit the family to produce their next dramatic entertainment, and Sheridan's modern comedy *The Rivals* was performed in July 'by some young Ladies & Gentlemen at Steventon'.

James as usual wrote a prologue and epilogue in verse, the former spoken by thirteen-year-old Henry, and the latter by the actor who played Bob Acres – perhaps James himself, preserving a modest anonymity in his record of the occasion.[47] As the play requires about a dozen characters, it may be that the Cooper cousins were invited to participate, or perhaps the Digweeds up the lane at the manor-house joined in. There were four Digweed boys – John, Harry, James and William – born between 1766 and 1776, and so much of an age with the Austen children. Jane, now eight and a half, might have been able to take the part of the pert maidservant Lucy. *The Rivals* is the only one of the plays performed at Steventon which has survived the ensuing 200 years still to be enjoyed by present-day audiences. It is noticeable that after *Matilda* no other tragedy was ever chosen for the family production; and it is also evident that the Austens were not in the least prudish, for some of the comedies performed in succeeding years, dealing as they did with the eternal battle between the sexes, were quite outspoken in their plot and dialogue.

It seems that by now Mr Austen's income was reasonably good, because entries in his bank account suggest that in the summer of 1784 he bought a chariot – a small carriage drawn by two horses and carrying three passengers – for the benefit of his wife and daughters.[48] This year he also paid £11.9s.0d. to Claude Nattes – presumably the artist better known as John Claude Nattes (*c.* 1765–1822) and later to become famous as a water colourist[49] – who had possibly been staying at the Rectory to give drawing lessons to the children. In later years Henry was reputed to be the artist of the family, and some of Cassandra's sketches still survive, while of Jane it was said: 'She had not only an excellent taste for drawing, but, in her earlier days, evinced great power of hand in the management of the pencil.'[50]

However, Cassandra, at least, needed more education than could be found for her at home, and in the spring of 1785 it was decided that she should go to the Abbey House School in Reading. At first it was planned that only Cassandra should go, but Jane could not bear the idea of being separated from her sister:

My Grandmother talking to me once [of] bygone times, & of that particular time when my Aunts were placed at the Reading Abbey School, said that Jane was too young to make her going to school at all necessary, but it was her own doing; she *would* go with Cassandra; 'if Cassandra's head had been going to be cut off, Jane would have her's cut off too'[51]

– so as the Austens were affectionate and understanding parents, both the girls, now aged twelve and nine respectively, were sent off to Reading, despite the fact that this would mean doubling the fees Mr Austen had to pay. Jane's book *Mentoria*, given to her on 29 June 1785, may perhaps have been one of the texts used at the school.[52] Their cousin, Jane Cooper, was also at the Abbey House and, as she was older than Cassandra, was probably sent there in advance of them.

The Abbey House School had been in existence for some considerable number of years, and was by now renowned throughout the south of England as a place where the daughters of the gentry and professional classes could 'be sent to be out of the way, and scramble themselves into a little education, without any danger of coming back prodigies'.[53] It took its name from the fact that part of its premises included the inner gateway of Reading Abbey, which was all that remained intact of the many buildings that had once made up the enormous twelfth-century Cluniac monastery.[54] The other part of the school occupied a large brick house attached to the eastern side of the gateway; this house had a 'beautiful old-fashioned garden, where the children played under tall trees in hot summer evenings', and an embankment at the bottom of the garden provided a viewpoint from which they could look down upon the romantic ruins of the rest of the Abbey.[55] The gateway itself was outside the house's garden walls and stood upon the Forbury – this had once been the precinct in front of the great west door of the Abbey church, but was now a rough open field on the edge of the town, where the boys from Dr Valpy's grammar school played and where the inhabitants of Reading held fairs and markets.

When Jane and Cassandra arrived at the Abbey House, the headmistress was a Mrs La Tournelle, assisted by her younger partner, Miss Pitts. Mrs La Tournelle's name was actually Sarah Hackitt, 'but having early in life been engaged as a French teacher, her employers thought it right to introduce her into the school under a foreign name. She accordingly took that of La Tournelle, and her real name was probably known only to a few of her numerous friends.'[56] She was a stout middle-aged woman, 'very active, although she had a cork leg; how she had lost its predecessor she never told'. Her domain was a wainscotted parlour, hung round with chenille pieces representing tombs and weeping willows; a screen in cloth-work stood in a corner, and there were several miniatures over the lofty mantelpiece.[57]

She never had been seen or known to have changed the fashion of her dress; her white muslin handkerchief was always pinned with the same number of pins, her muslin apron always hung in the same form; she always wore the same short sleeves, cuffs and ruffles, with a breast bow to answer the bow on her cap, both being flat with notched ends.[58]

She could not speak a word of French, but whenever she had an opportunity of holding forth, she spoke of plays and play-acting, and green-room anecdotes, and the private life of actors . . . She was only fit for giving out clothes for the wash, making tea, ordering dinner and, in fact, doing the work of a housekeeper.'[59]

Mrs La Tournelle and Miss Pitts employed two or three other school-mistresses, and by their united efforts the girls learned writing, spelling, French, history and geography, needlework, drawing, music and dancing, and presumably some elementary arithmetic as well. The school was well equipped with teaching aids – globes, a magic lantern with historical plates, excellent charts and maps, and also 'Scenes for Theatrical Exhibitions', are mentioned amongst its effects.[60] The masters from Dr Valpy's school on the other side of the Forbury used to call to give tutorials to the older girls, so probably they were responsible for the more academic instruction. The hours of study were not exacting, and provided the girls attended for morning prayers and at mealtimes, and said their appointed lessons, they were then free to spend the rest of the day chatting with their particular friends anywhere in the house or garden as they pleased. The Austen girls were happy there, for a few years later Jane wrote to Cassandra: 'I could die of laughter at it, as they used to say at school.'[61]

In October 1785 the girls' kind old cousin, the Revd Thomas Leigh, called in on them as he journeyed from Adlestrop to Mill Hill via Nettlebed and Egham, and tipped them half a guinea apiece.[62] There is also the family tradition that Edward Austen, accompanied by his cousin, Edward Cooper, came and took their respective sisters out in a party to dine at one of the Reading inns – perhaps the Crown in Crown Street or the Bear in Bridge Street, as these were the best hostelries of the time. This example of youthful independence and merrymaking shocked the Victorian generations of the family: 'It is true Edward Cooper was Jane Cooper's brother, and Edward Austen was brother to our Aunts, but it was a strange thing to allow.'[63]

It was possible for girls to stay on at the Abbey House School until well into their teens, but it seems that the Austens found they could not afford to keep both their daughters there for so many years – like Mr Austen, Mrs La Tournelle charged about £35 p.a. per pupil[64] – and the girls were brought back to Steventon for good before the end of 1786.[65] Thereafter the remainder of Jane's education was acquired at home, and for the rest of her life she never again lived anywhere beyond the bounds of her immediate family environment.

CHAPTER 5

Family life, 1786–92

The next few years saw Jane develop from a precociously bright little girl into a highly intelligent, articulate young woman, pretty as well as witty, devoted to her family and already studying the characters of the other inhabitants of her Hampshire world with the dispassionate interest of a natural-born psychologist. No letters of hers survive before 1796, but her first attempts at literary composition and the information available from other sources enable a fairly complete picture of her adolescence to be built up. This period also saw the close-knit family circle first contract, as some members died and Jane's brothers one by one left home, and then expand again as marriages created new family circles; by moving into these, Jane gained insights into several very different aspects of society, all of which would eventually be reflected in her works.

James, having gone up to Oxford so young, had already taken his Bachelor of Arts degree in 1783, but stayed on for several more years as a Fellow of St John's, organising the Steventon amateur theatricals when he returned home in the vacations and writing more poetry in addition to the theatrical prologues and epilogues. There was never any question but that he would enter the church, like his father before him, and he was ordained deacon at Christchurch, Oxford, by the newly-appointed Bishop of St David's, on 19 December 1787.[1] He was the quietest and most scholarly of the Austen sons, and a miniature painted in his early manhood shows him as much resembling his uncle Mr Leigh-Perrot, with large grey eyes, a gentle mouth, and a thoughtful, rather hesitant expression.[2] Many years later, after James's death in early middle age, Mrs Austen shrewdly assessed the characters and abilities of her two elder sons, in a letter to Mrs Leigh-Perrot: '[Edward] . . . has a most active mind, a clear head, & a sound Judgement, he is quite a man of Business. – That my dear James was not – Classical Knowledge, Literary Taste, and the power of Elegant Composition he possessed in the highest degree; to these [Edward] makes no pretentions. <u>Both</u> equally good amiable and sweet-temper'd.'[3]

James was throughout his life devoted to the natural beauties of the countryside and in his younger days was a keen rider to hounds. Although so studious, he was still boy enough, when up at Oxford, to throw aside his books and yield to temptation:

> For there in early days, a truant oft
> From Alma Mater's discipline & rule,
> In spite of imposition, & the frown
> Of angry Dean, or Tutor grave & wise,
> I've dashed through miry field, & boggy lane,
> Led by the musical & cheering notes
> Of the loud echoing pack, full many a mile.[4]

By 1785 he was in a mild way starting to fall in love, and relieved his feelings by writing a sonnet to Lady Catherine Powlett (daughter of the 6th Duke of Bolton, of Hackwood Park, near Basingstoke), in which he declared her to be a modern reincarnation of Venus, walking no longer in 'fair Idalia's love-devoted shades' or 'Paphos' blooming grove', but in Hampshire's springtime woodlands instead.[5]

He was also anxious to travel, and hoped to arrange a visit in the spring of 1786 to see his cousin Eliza de Feuillide, now living with her husband in Guienne and writing to England with news of the improvements they were carrying out on their estate. However, in January 1786 Eliza discovered that she was pregnant, and James's plans had to be delayed in consequence. As Eliza told Phylly Walter: 'should a Son be in store for M. de Feuillide he greatly wishes him to be a native of England for he pays me the Compliment of being very partial to my Country; but I own I have some repugnance to undertaking so long a journey in a situation so unfit for travelling'.[6] To make matters worse, M. de Feuillide was unable to accompany Eliza to England, due to his involvement with his land reclamation works,[7] and in the end she and Mrs Hancock left home without him in May 1786. Either Eliza had miscalculated her pregnancy, or else the long journey up from the south of France brought on a premature delivery, because in fact her son was born at Calais on 25 June.[8] He was named Hastings, Eliza possibly having an eye to the chance that her godfather, Warren Hastings, might set up another trust fund for her baby in return for this compliment. Despite the fact that Eliza was now in England, M. de Feuillide seems to have had no objection to receiving his wife's cousin in her absence, and it was agreed that James should go to France later in 1786. He stayed on the Continent for about a year, also visiting Spain and Holland during his travels.[9]

Edward by now was spending more of his time with his adoptive family in Kent, and instead of going to Oxford like his brother was sent by the

Knights on the Grand Tour. He set off early in 1786 and stayed abroad for four years, visiting Switzerland, Dresden and Rome.[10] In Switzerland he formed part of the 'Neufchatel Set' of young Englishmen which included Sir Henry Campbell and the first Lord Stanley of Alderley;[11] and he stayed in Dresden for a year, possibly studying at the university there, and was received at the court of Saxony.[12] While in Rome he had his portrait painted, full-length in oils, against a background of classical ruins, the temple of Minerva Medica;[13] he had the same serious look as in his boyhood, but was now of a florid complexion and much fuller in the face – indeed, with more than a hint of a double chin. Another representation of him, a miniature by Sir William Ross decades later,[14] shows that underneath this puppy-fat lay the same high cheekbones and beaky nose that several other members of the family had inherited. Upon his return to England at the end of 1790, Edward went to live permanently at Godmersham, so that he could learn how to manage the large estates that would one day be his.

Henry was therefore the eldest of the Austen sons still at home, and it was fully expected that he too would take Holy Orders.

My Uncle Henry Thomas Austen was the handsomest of his family, and, in the opinion of his own Father, also the most talented. There were others who formed a different estimate, and considered his abilities greater in shew than in reality, but for the most part he was greatly admired. Brilliant in conversation, and like his Father, blessed with a hopefulness of temper, which, in adapting itself to all circumstances, even the most adverse, seemed to create a perpetual sunshine of the mind. The Race is not however always to the swift – it never has been – and though so highly gifted by Nature, my Uncle was not prosperous in life.[15]

Henry had been tall for his age throughout his childhood, and at the age of seventeen was taller than his father.[16] He had the same peculiarly bright hazel eyes as Mr Austen;[17] and a miniature painted in middle life shows these eyes gazing alertly from a keen, bony face dominated by the Leigh nose inherited from his mother, and with a hint of a smile lurking round the firm mouth.[18] From the Austen side Henry seems to have inherited also the same strain of impetuosity that had manifested itself in his aunt, Mrs Hancock, an impatience which particularly appeared during travel:

He is said to have been driving on one occasion with a relation in one of the rough country lanes near Steventon when the pace at which the postchaise was advancing did not satisfy his eager temperament. Putting his head out of the window, he cried out to the postillion, 'Get on, boy! get on, will you?' The 'boy' turned round in his saddle, and replied: 'I *do* get on, sir, where I can!' 'You stupid fellow!' was the rejoinder, 'Any fool can do that. I want you to get on *where you can't.*'[19]

Very different in temperament was the cool, resolute Francis – small, curly-haired and nicknamed 'Fly' by the family due to his restless energy[20] – with the courage and abilities that would eventually take him to the rank of Admiral of the Fleet. In his old age he started writing his memoirs, couched in the third person and looking back dispassionately on his youthful self as on the activities of some other schoolboy:

He was educated at home under the immediate superintendence of his father who was admirably calculated to the instruction of youth as he joined to an unusual extent of classical learning and a highly cultivated taste for literature in general, a remarkable suavity of temper and gentleness of manners. Under his paternal roof he made considerable progress in the usual scholastic exercises (although never remarkable for facility in acquiring languages) until he decided on the Navy for his profession.[21]

Neither the Austens nor the Leighs had any naval traditions or connections; however, just as Mr Austen and his wife had recognised and understood the firmness of Jane's own decision to accompany her sister to school, so now they recognised Francis's determination to go to sea, and entered him at the Royal Naval Academy in Portsmouth in April 1786, just before his twelfth birthday.[22] At this training establishment the sons of naval officers received free board and tuition, but for Frank Mr Austen had to pay annual fees of £25 as well as the cost of his maintenance, estimated to be about £50 p.a.[23]

When Jane and Cassandra returned home from school in the autumn of 1786, their daily companions were therefore Henry and little Charles, and the two or three pupils then in residence at the rectory. The Deane boy, George or Henry, had matriculated in May 1786 and no more was heard from him; but the good-natured, ugly John Willing Warren, son of Mr Peter Warren, of Mildred Court, Cornhill, London, who had come some time in the 1780s and who also went up to Oxford in 1786, remained a friend for life and is mentioned in several of Jane's letters.[24] The other boys present at this period were probably William and Charles Fowle, the third and fourth sons of the vicar of Kintbury, following to Steventon in the wake of their elder brothers, Fulwar and Tom.[25] William went later to the United Hospitals Medical School and then to Edinburgh and Leyden Universities, acquiring a medical degree in 1791, while Charles chose the law and entered Lincoln's Inn in 1790.[26] Charles in particular seems to have been a great friend of Jane, and there are some suspiciously flirtatious references to him in her early letters.[27]

At Christmas 1786 the Austens held a family gathering at Steventon, and on the last day of the old year Mrs Austen wrote to her niece, Phylly Walter, then living at Seal, near Sevenoaks, Kent, giving a bright vignette of life in the rectory on that winter evening more than two centuries ago:

We are now happy in the company of our Sister Hancock Madame de Feuillide & the little Boy; they came to us last Thursday Sennet [21 December] & will stay with us till the end of next Month. They all look & seem to be remarkably well, the little Boy grows very fat, he is very fair & very pretty; I don't think your Aunt at all alter'd in any respect, Madame is grown quite lively, when a child we used to think her too grave. We have borrowed a Piano-Forte, and she plays to us every day; on Tuesday we are to have a very snug little dance in our parlour, just our own children, nephew & nieces, (for the two little Coopers come tomorrow) quite a family party, I wish my <u>third niece</u> could be here also; but indeed, I begin to suspect your Mother never intends to gratify that wish. You might as well be in Jamaica keeping your Brother's House, for anything that we see of you or are like to see. Five of my Children are now at home, Henry, Frank, Charles & my two Girls, who have now quite left school; Frank returns to Portsmouth in a few days, he has but short holidays at Christmas. Edward is well & happy in Switzerland. James set out for La Guienne, on a visit to the Count de Feuillide, near Eight weeks ago, I hope he is got there by this time and am impatient for a Letter; he was wind-bound some weeks in the little Island of Jersey or he would have got to the end of his long Journey by the beginning of this Month. – Every one of our Fireside join in Love, & Duty as due and in wishing a happy 87 to our dear Friends at Seal –[28]

This visit by Mrs Hancock and Eliza was the first they had made to Steventon since the autumn of 1786, when Jane had been still a baby, and they now brought with them as a present for her eleventh birthday a set of Arnaud Berquin's little books *L'ami des enfans*.[29] Jane was much impressed by Eliza's charm and cosmopolitan vivacity, and this initial childish admiration grew into a steady and affectionate adult friendship that lasted to the end of Eliza's life.

Now that the girls were permanently at home again, the remainder of their education had to depend upon their immediate family, augmented by association with the surrounding circle of Hampshire friends and neighbours. Mr Austen allowed himself the luxury of buying books, and by 1801 had amassed his own library of some 500 volumes,[30] which were all available for his children to study. Family tradition recalled that James had a large share in directing Jane's reading and forming her taste. Henry remembered that 'at a very early age she was enamoured of Gilpin on the Picturesque . . . Her reading was very extensive in history and belles lettres; her memory extremely tenacious. Her favourite moral writers were Johnson in prose, and Cowper in verse.'[31] Jane's own copy of volume two of *Rasselas* survives, with her name written on the title-page in a juvenile hand, showing that she had made early acquaintance with Johnson's work.[32] She read Fielding and knew *Tom Jones* well, but preferred Richardson's *Sir Charles Grandison*, her copy of which she read over and over again, so that 'all that was ever said or done in the cedar parlour, was familiar to her; and the wedding days of Lady L. and Lady G. were as well remembered as if they had been living friends'.[33] It seems that Mrs Austen subscribed to the journal *The Mirror*, since Jane was able to refer to issue No. XII of this, Saturday 6 March 1779, as an appropriate lesson for Catherine Morland when she returned home from her visit to Northanger Abbey.[34] The family were all 'great Novel-readers & not ashamed of being so',[35] and even Jane's very earliest literary compositions show acquaintance with contemporary bestsellers.[36] She also read William Hayley's *Poems and plays*, and in one of the latter, *The Mausoleum* (a comedy, despite its title), found the memorable name 'Lady Sophia Sentiment', which she appropriated for her own use a little later on.[37] She became able to read French with ease, and no doubt practised conversation with Eliza when the latter paid visits to Steventon, but apparently could never speak it fluently.[38]

As for other languages, she heard her father teaching Latin to his sons and pupils using Pote's *Eton Latin Grammar*, and with the boys learned one of the first rules: 'Propria, quae maribus tribuuntur, mascula dicas' (Proper names, which are assigned to the male kind, you may call masculines);[39] she understood enough to be able to inscribe 'Ex dono mei Patris' in the manuscript volume Mr Austen gave her in 1790, that now known as *Volume the Second*.[40] She also learned a little Italian, probably in conjunction with music and singing lessons, using Veneroni's *The complete Italian Master*.[41] Mrs Austen's girlhood music books were brought out again for the use of her daughters, and several other volumes, containing both printed and manuscript songs and music, were compiled by Jane during the 1780s and 1790s. From Mrs Austen's letter of 31 December 1786, it would seem that a pianoforte had then been only borrowed for the period of the Christmas family gathering, but thereafter one was acquired on a more permanent basis and Jane received music lessons until at least 1796.[42]

Goldsmith's four-volume *The History of England, from the earliest times to the death of George II*, was a Steventon schoolroom textbook, and volume one has some dates marked in the margins, starting with '23rd August' at page 15, suggesting that so many pages were read as a daily or weekly task.[43] That Jane enjoyed history is evident by the close attention she paid to Goldsmith's narrative, and the marginal comments which she could not resist making. As befitted a descendant of the 'Loyal Leighs', she was a vehement defender of the Stuarts, from Mary Queen of Scots onwards, and the pages of volumes three and four are peppered with her exclamations of praise for them and condemnation of their enemies.[44] She read Whitaker's *Mary Queen of Scots Vindicated*, and sided delightedly with him as a defender of Mary's memory.[45] Other marginalia in Goldsmith show that in her teens she was staunchly anti-Whig and anti-Republican, and although in adulthood the party politics of the day seem to have occupied very little of her attention, she probably always retained these early views, for 'she seldom changed her opinions either on books or men'.[46] Jane's copy of *Elegant Extracts* also bears her marginal comments praising Mary and denigrating Queen Elizabeth I.[47]

It was at this period of her life that Jane was befriended by the charming and intelligent Madam Lefroy of Ashe. In 1786 Madam Lefroy's younger brother, (Sir) Egerton Brydges, left Kent and came to Hampshire with his sister, Charlotte, in order to be near the Lefroys; he rented Deane parsonage from Mr Austen and stayed there for two years.[48] (James Austen promptly forgot the charms of Lady Catherine Powlett, and wrote sonnets to Miss Charlotte Brydges instead.)[49] In later life Egerton Brydges achieved some renown as an antiquarian bibliographer and genealogist, but in 1786 he was a conceited, neurotic young intellectual, despising the Kentish and Hampshire country squires and masochistically pleased to think they reciprocated his dislike. The best side of his character was shown in his love for his sisters, and of Madam Lefroy he wrote:

She had an exquisite taste for poetry, and could almost repeat the chief English poets by heart, especially Milton, Pope, Collins, Gray, and the poetical passages of Shakespeare; and she composed easy verses herself with great facility . . . The charm of her first address was magical; her eyes were full of lustre; and the copiousness and eloquence of her conversation attracted all ears and won all hearts . . . She was spotless; and her heart was the seat of every affectionate and moral virtue . . . The nearest neighbours to the Lefroys were the Austens of Steventon. I remember Jane Austen, the novelist, a little child; she was very intimate with Mrs Lefroy and much encouraged by her.[50]

Probably Jane had first been invited to Ashe Rectory as a playmate for little Jemima Lucy Lefroy, four years her junior, but her own quick wits and literary interests had evidently soon endeared her to Mrs Lefroy as a personal, even if very youthful, friend. Jane in her turn looked on Madam Lefroy as 'a perfect model of gracefulness and goodness'.[51] With such encouragement, it is not surprising that Jane too studied the 'chief English poets' and could quote appropriately from them for use in *Northanger Abbey* a few years later.[52]

Apart from reading, much of the girls' time would have been devoted to learning how to sew and embroider neatly, and Jane became a 'great adept' at satin-stitch in particular.[53] Like all little girls of the period, she probably stitched a sampler, and perhaps used for it the verse to which she referred in *Northanger Abbey*:

> Despair of nothing that you would obtain
> Unwearied diligence your point will gain
> Great blessings ever wait on virtuous deeds
> And tho' a late a sure reward succeeds.[54]

In later years Jane and Cassandra were able to pay dressmakers to make up their chosen fabrics into gowns,[55] but in the Steventon days the girls must have had to learn very early in life how to help their mother sew their own dresses as well as cravats and shirts for their father and brothers. Needlework then formed so large a part of female duties that it was unnecessary to specify it as being *needle* work – to say that a girl or lady was 'working' could only mean that she was sewing. However, once the day's lessons and 'work' were over, Jane probably shared with Catherine Morland the joys of rolling down the green slope at the back of the house, running about the countryside and playing baseball and cricket with the boys.

The letters of Eliza de Feuillide and Phylly Walter are the main sources of information about the Austen family for the period 1787–8. After returning to London from Steventon in the New Year of 1787, Eliza entered as enthusiastically into the life of high society in England as she had into that in France, renting a smart house in Orchard Street for the purpose; she invited Henry Austen to stay with her there during April, and although Henry was then only a lanky boy of sixteen and Eliza a sophisticated society matron of twenty-six, it is probable that their mutual attraction, which was to culminate in their marriage ten years later, dated from this period.[56]

During September Eliza and her mother visited Tunbridge Wells and swept up Phylly Walter from her quiet home at Seal to join them in the gaieties of the summer season at the Wells. The two young women had not seen each other since 1777, and Phylly was amazed at the cheerful frivolity of the life to which Eliza had grown accustomed during the intervening years. She wrote to her brother, James Walter, in Lincolnshire in tones half-envious and half-shocked, detailing the pleasures which seemed so extravagant to her but so commonplace to her cousin. Eliza and Mrs Hancock hardly ever travelled in any other way than by 'an elegant coach & four', and their days in Tunbridge Wells were passed in dancing, party-going and play-going, strolling on the Pantiles or round the Rocks, and hunting through all the milliners' shops for the newest hats. Eliza had requested the local theatrical troupe to perform Mrs Cowley's *Which is the Man?* and Garrick's *Bon Ton* for her amusement on Saturday evening, 8 September, and the house had been crowded out for these two comedies. Phylly much admired Mrs Hancock's character: 'I do not know a fault she has – so strictly just & honorable in all her dealings, so kind and obliging to all her friends and acquaintance, so religious in all her actions, in short I do not know a person that has more the appearance of perfection' – but was equivocal in her feelings towards Eliza:

The Countess has many amiable qualities, such as the highest duty, love and respect for her mother: for whom there is not any sacrifice she would not make, & certainly contributes entirely to her happiness: for her husband she professes a large share of respect, esteem and the highest opinion of his merits, but confesses that Love is not of the number on her side, tho' still very violent on his: her principles are strictly just, making it a rule never to bespeak anything that she is not quite sure of being able to pay for directly, never contracting debts of any kind. Her dissipated life she was brought up to – therefore it cannot be wondered at.

Eliza had already been in touch with the Austens regarding plans for their festivities at Christmas 1787–8, by which time James would be home from his foreign travels and able to organise theatricals again, and Phylly continued:

They go at Xmas to Steventon & mean to act a play Which is the Man? and Bon Ton. My uncle's barn is fitting up quite like a theatre, & all the young folks are to take their part. The Countess is Lady Bob Lardoon [*sic*] in the former and Miss Tittup in the latter. They wish me much of the party & offer to carry me, but I do not think of it. I should like to be a spectator, but am sure I should not have courage to act a part, nor do I wish to attain it.[57]

Sure enough, a few weeks later Eliza reminded Phylly:

You know we have long projected acting this Christmas in Hampshire & this scheme would go on a vast deal better would you lend your assistance. You may remember when you was at Tunbridge my expressing a very earnest & a very natural wish to have you with me during the approaching festival, & on finding there were two unengaged parts I immediately thought of you, & am particularly commissioned by My Aunt Austen & her whole Family to make the earliest application possible, & assure you how very happy you will make them as well as myself if you could be prevailed on to undertake these parts & give us all your company . . . Your accommodations at Steventon are the only thing My Aunt Austen & myself are uneasy about, as the House being very full of Company, she says she can only promise you 'a place to hide your Head in' but I think you will not mind this inconvenience . . . I assure you we shall have a most brilliant party & a great deal of amusement, the House full of Company & frequent Balls. You cannot possibly resist so many temptations, especially when I tell you your old Friend James is returned from France & is to be of the acting party.[58]

However, Phylly made excuses for herself and refused the invitation, which called forth a quick rejoinder from Eliza, surprised that her meek country cousin should diverge from the course of action decreed for her:

I received your Letter Yesterday My Dear Friend & need not tell You how much I am concerned at your not being able to comply with a request which in all probability I shall never have it in my power to make again. The not leaving your Mother alone is certainly very essential, but would it not be possible to engage some Friend or Neighbour to come & stay with her during so short an absence? . . . I will only allow myself to take notice of the strong reluctance You express to what You call <u>appearing in Publick</u>. I assure You our performance is to be by no means a publick one, since only a selected party of Friends will be present . . . You wish to know the exact Time which we should be <u>satisfied with</u>, & therefore I proceed to acquaint You that a fortnight from New Years Day <u>would do</u>, provided however You could bring yourself to act, for My Aunt Austen declares 'She has not room for any <u>idle young</u> people'.[59]

But Phylly stuck to her initial decision not to participate, and the Christmas theatricals this year took place without her. Although Eliza had been fancying herself in the leading female roles in *Which is the Man?* and *Bon Ton*, for some reason these plays were not after all performed, the one chosen instead being Mrs Centlivre's well-loved old 1714 comedy of *The Wonder – a Woman keeps a secret!* The setting of this was sixteenth-century Portugal, which gave scope for a plot in which stern fathers could threaten their daughters with arranged marriages or banishment to nunneries, while the daughters schemed to marry the men of their choice. The heroine, Donna Violante, is successful in keeping secret the hiding-place of her friend, Donna Isabella, until such time as the happy ending can be attained after five acts of near-calamities, thus proving herself to be 'The Wonder' of the title. James, back from his ordination in Oxford, as usual wrote prologue and epilogue for the performances on 26 and 28 December 1787; the epilogue was 'Spoken by a Lady in the character of Violante', and Eliza must have enjoyed uttering the declaration of female emancipation that James provided for her:

> But thank our happier stars, those days are o'er,
> And woman holds a second place no more.
> Now forced to quit their long held usurpation,
> These men all wise, these Lords of the Creation!
> To our superior rule themselves submit,
> Slaves to our charms, & vassals to our wit;
> We can with ease their every sense beguile,
> And melt their resolutions with a smile.[60]

A week or so later, in the New Year, the Steventon house-party performed *The Chances*, a comedy set in sixteenth-century Naples and adapted by Garrick from the much older play originally written by John Fletcher. The plot once again dealt with the confusions of disguised ladies and jealous gallants, and Eliza's role was probably that of Second Constantia.

This year 1788 was the climax of the Steventon theatricals, for plays were presented every few months. After Eliza had returned to London, James's next choice was Henry Fielding's burlesque *The Tragedy of Tragedies, or, The Life and Death of Tom Thumb the Great*, which had parodied 'the conventionally extravagant and unreal tragedy of the contemporary stage'[61] when it was first written in 1731, and had remained popular ever since. It had all the panoply of classic tragedy – the conquering hero returning in triumph, princesses contending for his love, despotic royal parents – but Tom Thumb, as his name implies, is a dwarf, the captive queen Glumdalca a giantess, and the royal parents a ridiculous, quarrelsome pair of drunks. The play ends with a ludicrous massacre as all the characters one by one kill each other. There would have been no part for Eliza in such pantomime knockabout farce, but perhaps little Charles, aged nine, was Tom Thumb and tall Henry disguised himself as Glumdalca – Cassandra and Jane might then have been Queen Dollalolla and Princess Huncamunca respectively. The play was 'acted to a small circle of select Friends' on 22 March 1788, and James spoke his own prologue, in which he drew upon his recent foreign travels to inform his audience as to the various ways in which the French, Spanish and Dutch amused themselves as compared to the English.[62] Some time later in 1788 the family put on 'a private Theatrical Exhibition', but James's prologue for this gives no precise date nor any indication of the play performed – perhaps on this occasion the participants wrote all the entertainment themselves.

In the summer of 1788 Henry was planning to travel to France with Eliza and her mother when they returned later in the year, but was 'sadly mortified at one of the Fellows of St John's choosing to marry or die, which vacancy he is obliged to fill up'[63] – so instead he matriculated at St John's on 1 July. James was licensed to his first curacy, that of Stoke Charity, a little village a few miles north of Winchester, on 14 July,[64] but remained at his college rather than reside in his Hampshire parish. Eliza passed through Oxford in August, and told Phylly:

My cousin James met us there ... We visited several of the Colleges, the Museum etc. & were very elegantly entertained by our gallant relations at St John's, where I was mightily taken with the Garden & longed to be a <u>Fellow</u> that I might walk in it every Day, besides I was delighted with the Black Gown & thought the Square Cap mighty becoming. I do not think you would know Henry with his hair powdered & dressed in a very <u>tonish</u> style, besides he is at present taller than his Father.[65]

Also in July 1788 Mr and Mrs Austen paid another of their family visits to Mr Francis Austen at The Red House in Sevenoaks, this time taking Cassandra, aged fifteen and a half, and Jane, aged twelve and a half, to introduce them to their aged great-uncle and his family. His eldest son, Francis Motley, had by now provided him with eleven grandchildren, of whom the eldest three or four (Francis Lucius (1773), Thomas (1775), Jane (1776) and John (1777)) were probably called over to meet their young cousins. Mr Francis Austen was then over ninety, and since the death of his wife (Jane's godmother) in January 1782 his widowed niece Mrs Elizabeth Fermor had kept house for him,[66] but he was not so old as to be incapable of arranging a dinner party for his guests, to which the Walters were invited. Some days later Phylly wrote to her brother with news of this family reunion, a letter which gives one of the few early references to Jane as an individual:

Yesterday I began an acquaintance with my 2 female cousins, Austens. My uncle, aunt, Cassandra & Jane arrived at Mr F. Austen's the day before. We dined with them there. As it's pure Nature to love ourselves I may be allowed to give the preference to the Eldest who is generally reckoned a most striking resemblance of me in features, complexion & manners. I never found myself so much disposed to be vain, as I can't help thinking her very pretty, but fancied I could discover <u>she</u> was not so well pleased with the comparison – which reflection abated a great deal of the vanity so likely to arise, & so proper to be supprest. The youngest (Jane) is very like her brother Henry, not at all pretty & very prim, unlike a girl of twelve: but it is hasty judgement which you will scold me for. My aunt has lost several fore-teeth which makes her look old: my uncle is quite white-haired, but looks vastly well: all in high spirits & disposed to be pleased with each other . . . I continue to admire my amiable likeness the best of the two in every respect: she keeps up conversation in a very sensible & pleasing manner. Yesterday they all spent the day with us, & the more I see of Cassandra the more I admire [her] – Jane is whimsical & affected.[67]

On their way back to Hampshire in August the Austens spent a day or two in London and dined in Orchard Street with Eliza and Mrs Hancock, then busy packing up with a view to returning to France the following month. 'What did you think of my Uncle's looks?' – Eliza enquired later of Phylly – 'I was much pleased with them, and if possible he appeared more amiable than ever to me. What an excellent & pleasing man he is; I love him most sincerely as indeed I do all the family. I believe it was your first acquaintance with Cassandra and Jane.'[68] It would seem from Phylly's comments that while Cassandra had already reached near-maturity, poor Jane was still at the ugly duckling stage of being neither child nor woman, and it is interesting to learn that her likeness to Henry, which Mr Austen had noticed at her birth, still persisted. So far as is known, this trip was Jane's first visit to both Kent and London.

The end of 1788 saw the first major gap appear in the Steventon family, when Francis finished his technical studies at the Academy in Portsmouth and left with a glowing report to the Lords of the Admiralty from the Governor, Henry Martin:

I beg leave to observe to their Lordships that this Young Gentleman has completed his plan of Mathematical learning in a considerably shorter time than usual, his assiduity indeed has been uncommon, and his conduct during the whole time he has been at the Academy, has been in all respects so properly correct, that I have never had a complaint or one unfavourable report of him from any Master or Usher altho' he has a lively and active disposition.[69]

Francis was now classified as a Volunteer and joined the frigate HMS *Perseverance*, under Captain Isaac Smith, for a year's practical training in seamanship, after which he would be rated as Midshipman. He sailed for the East Indies on 23 December 1788, taking with him a long letter from Mr Austen full of fatherly advice, both practical and moral, for his future career as a naval officer.[70] Francis cherished this letter, and at his death at the age of ninety-one it was found – water-stained, singed at the edges and frayed by constant reading – amongst his private papers. Mr Austen assured him that he could 'depend on hearing from some of us at every opportunity' – but bearing in mind the hardships and dangers of naval life the Steventon family must often have wondered, as they wrote their letters, if they would ever see Francis again. He himself recalled: 'Our youth, although rather small of stature, of a vigorous constitution and possessing great activity of body, was not long in acquiring a competent knowledge of the practical parts of seamanship to which he was urged by the natural energies of his mind and a general thirst for knowledge.'[71] He became Midshipman on 22 December 1789 and remained on HMS *Perseverance* until 5 November 1791, after which he moved to HMS *Minerva*. He received his promotion to Lieutenant on 28 December 1792 while still in the East Indies, and did not return to England until the end of 1793.

CHAPTER 6

First compositions, 1787–92

According to Jane's own memories, 1787 was the year in which she started to devote her spare time to writing,[1] and several of her early essays in literary composition – now known as the *Juvenilia* – were copied out by her as a 'collected edition' into three manuscript books, *Volume the First, Volume the Second* and *Volume the Third*.[2] A few of the pieces are specifically dated, and most of the others can be placed in approximately chronological order by internal evidence or allusions to family events. Only two, 'Amelia Webster' and 'Edgar and Emma', have no indication at all of dating and have to be guessed at as being the first of her efforts thought worthy of preservation. The playlet 'The Mystery', dedicated to her father, may have formed part of the 'private Theatrical exhibition' in 1788, and the family trip to Kent in July and August 1788, with its return via London, probably inspired the London setting of 'The Beautifull Cassandra', as well as teasing Cassandra with a description of how she had *not* behaved whilst there. 'Sir William Mountague' mentions a date of Monday, 1 September, which quite genuinely occurred in 1788, and Jane may have chosen this deliberately in order to lend a spurious air of veracity to the story, which was dedicated to little Charles; the 'Memoirs of Mr Clifford' is the second piece dedicated to Charles and probably followed soon after 'Sir William Mountague'. This too has the apparent veracity given by the use of local place-names and leaves the hero stranded at Mr Robins's establishment which, as Charles would know, was the Crown Inn at Basingstoke.[3]

The Cooper cousins came to Steventon for Christmas 1788–9, and in February 1789 Eliza wrote from France to Phylly Walter: 'I suppose You have had frequent accounts from Steventon, & that they have informed you of their theatrical Performances, The Sultan and High Life below Stairs, Miss Cooper performed the part of Roxelana [*sic*] & Henry the Sultan, I hear that Henry is taller than ever.'[4] *The Sultan* was a two-act farce by Isaac Bickerstaffe, first performed in London in 1775 but only recently published in 1784, in which a dauntless English girl, Roxalana, persuades the Turkish

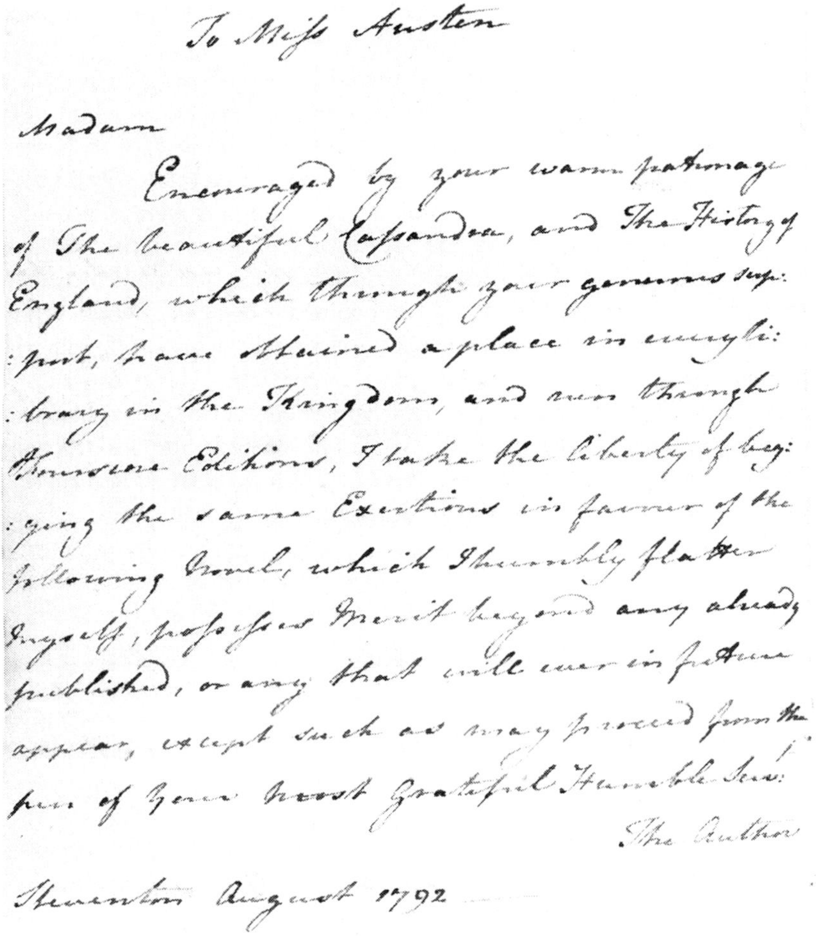

To Miss Austen

Madam

Encouraged by your warm patronage of The beautiful Cassandra, and The History of England, which through your generous support, have obtained a place in every library in the Kingdom, and run through Numerous Editions, I take the liberty of begging the same Exertions in favour of the following Novel, which I humbly flatter Myself, possesses Merit beyond any already published, or any that will ever in future appear, except such as may proceed from the pen of Your most Grateful Humble Serv:

The Author

Steventon August 1792

Plate 4 Manuscript page from *Volume The Third* of the *Juvenilia*, 1792.

Emperor by her teasing wit and charm to disband his harem and make her his one and only Empress. James's epilogue was spoken by Jane Cooper in the character of Roxalana, and was another provocative declaration of woman's superiority over man.[5] *High Life Below Stairs* was also a short farce, written by the Revd James Townley in 1759, in which a household of lazy servants behave like their absent masters – flirting, drinking, gambling and quarrelling. Jane probably wrote and dedicated 'Henry and Eliza' to her cousin Jane Cooper during this Christmas period; and as her playlet 'The

Visit', dedicated to James, contains a quotation from *High Life Below Stairs*, this suggests that it too was written early in 1789.[6]

This winter season of 1788–9 saw the last of the amateur theatricals at Steventon rectory, for James, the family's actor-manager, now had other literary interests in view. With Henry beside him in Oxford to provide assistance, James was planning to publish a weekly magazine, *The Loiterer*. Its motto was 'Speak of us as we are', and the contents were to provide a 'Rough, but not entirely inaccurate Sketch of the Character, the Manners, and the Amusements of Oxford, at the close of the eighteenth century'. 'In after life he used to speak very slightingly of this early work, which he had the better right to do, as, whatever may have been the degree of their merits, the best papers had certainly been written by himself.'[7] Henry contributed several papers, and the remainder came from their cousin, Edward Cooper, now up at Queen's College, and other undergraduate friends.[8] The first issue was published on 31 January 1789, and so must have been a main topic of discussion amongst the Steventon family party that Christmastime. Issue No. IX, published on Saturday, 28 March 1789, contains a burlesque letter to the editor, complaining about the lack of feminine interest, and in particular the lack of sensational fiction, in the issues to date. This letter is signed 'Sophia Sentiment' – the name taken from Hayley's *The Mausoleum* – and the tone of the burlesque is so much in keeping with Jane's juvenilia as to make it a reasonable assumption that she also wrote this offering for her brother's magazine.[9] It is significant that it was only this issue, No. IX, which was advertised in the *Reading Mercury*, the local newspaper which circulated in North Hampshire; it could be that James arranged for the advertisement to be placed where he knew his little sister would read it and so enhance the pleasure she must have felt on seeing her first words in print.[10] *The Loiterer* ran for sixty issues, finishing only in March 1790 when James finally left Oxford.[11]

In the spring of 1789 Mr Austen let Deane parsonage again, vacant since Egerton Brydges's return to Kent the previous year. The advertisement in August 1788 in the *Reading Mercury* described it as a 'neat brick dwelling-house', with four living-rooms and four bedrooms, as well as all the necessary store rooms and servants' quarters, plus a large garden, coach-house and stabling for six horses, and made it sound far more desirable than the later family memories of a 'low damp place with inconvenient rooms'.[12] However, as the house was empty for six months or more, it may be that enquirers did indeed notice and were put off by these defects in the property. Mr Austen's next tenants were the newly widowed Mrs Lloyd (1728–1805) and her two daughters Martha (1765–1843) and Mary (1771–1843), who until now had been living at Enborne, near Newbury, Berkshire, where the Revd Noyes Lloyd had been rector until his death at the end of January 1789.[13] Mrs Lloyd's second daughter, Eliza (1768–1839), had recently married her cousin, Mr Austen's old pupil, Fulwar Craven Fowle, and it was possibly through this chain of connection rather than by the advertisement that the Lloyds came to hear of the vacant house at Deane. Martha Lloyd was aged about twenty-three and Mary eighteen, so they were both rather older than the Austen girls, now sixteen and thirteen respectively; however, they soon became firm friends, and within a few months Jane dedicated 'Frederic and Elfrida' to Martha as 'a small testimony of the gratitude I feel for your late generosity to me in finishing my muslin Cloak'.[14]

As their acquaintance deepened, Jane and Cassandra learned from the Lloyd girls the strange family story of their grandmother, 'the cruel Mrs Craven' – 'a most courteous and fascinating woman in society', but with 'a stern tyrannical temper'[15] and the determination to acquire the wealth that her ne'er-do-well husband, Charles Craven, could not provide. Even while her husband was still alive, she had charmed the rich Mr Jemmet Raymond of Barton Court, Kintbury, into making her his heiress, and had then married Mr Raymond within a few months of Mr Craven's unlamented death. Once mistress of Barton Court, she had persuaded – or perhaps somehow compelled – her son, John Craven, to marry her new husband's half-sister, 'a young woman of weak intellect' but with a good fortune and more in prospect; and her docile daughter Jane was married off to Mr Fowle, the vicar of Kintbury – a marriage which luckily turned out well. The other three Craven daughters, less docile and more un-happy, took advantage of their mother's absence to run away from home and marry wherever they could. One married a yeoman farmer in Gloucester-shire, the second could do no better than take his horse-dealer friend; but the third, Martha Craven, did better than her sisters, by becoming the wife of Mr Lloyd, who was a beneficed clergyman of respectable character and good position, although towards the end of his life he 'became a sad ner-vous invalid, generally keeping much in his own room and some days equal to nothing'.[16] The Lloyds lived at Deane until January 1792, when they moved to Ibthorpe, about sixteen miles away from Steventon and not far from Andover. This move did not end their friendship with Cassandra and Jane, and in years to come both Martha and Mary were destined to marry into the Austen family.

Jane's next literary productions were two items to be sent out to Francis, now far away at sea – 'The Adventures of Mr Harley' and 'Jack and Alice'.[17] These were probably written early in 1790 but, as they are dedicated to him

as a Midshipman aboard HMS *Perseverance*, must in any event fall within
the period from 22 December 1789 to 5 November 1791.[18] Her 'novel in a
series of Letters', 'Love and Freindship', the first item to be transcribed into
her father's gift of *Volume the Second*, is dated at the end as being finished
on Sunday, 13 June 1790, and is dedicated to 'Madame la Comtesse de
Feuillide'; it is likely that Eliza was then staying at Steventon again prior
to visiting Margate later that year.[19] It was probably also in 1790, now
that Jane was in her fifteenth year, thinking of love and friendship and
perhaps beginning to 'curl her hair and long for balls',[20] that she could not
resist the temptation of filling in mock marriage entries for herself on the
printed specimen page at the beginning of the marriage register then in
use in Steventon church. For the banns entry she created a 'Henry Frederic
Howard Fitzwilliam, of London'; for the marriage entry changed him to
'Edmund Arthur William Mortimer, of Liverpool'; and finally decided that
her mythical husband would be plain 'Jack Smith' and herself 'Jane Smith
late Austen'.[21]

Her ideas of love and romance acquired a more realistic basis in 1791,
when Edward became the first of the Austen sons to marry. Amongst
the Godmersham neighbours he had met the thirteen-strong family of
Sir Brook Bridges of Goodnestone Park, Wingham, and his choice had
fallen upon the third daughter, Elizabeth (1773–1808). She and her sisters
were all graceful, brown-haired beauties, who had been educated in London
at the 'Ladies Eton', the boarding school in Queen Square, Bloomsbury,
run by the Misses Stevenson exclusively for the daughters of the nobility
and gentry. The academic content of the curriculum was minimal and the
pupils learned little more than French, music and dancing, while strong
emphasis was placed on social etiquette – an old coach was kept propped
up in a back room so that the girls could practise the art of getting in and
out of it in a modest and elegant manner.[22] Edward's engagement to Elizabeth Bridges was announced on 1 March 1791,[23] and during the year her
two elder sisters Fanny and Sophia also became engaged. Fanny married
first, becoming Mrs Lewis Cage of Milgate, and then on 27 December 1791
there was a double wedding at Goodnestone when Elizabeth married Edward Austen and Sophia married William Deedes of Sandling.[24] Edward
and Elizabeth started their married life at Rowling, a small country house
provided for them by the Bridges family not far from Goodnestone, and
their first four children were born there. Jane's tale 'The Three Sisters' was
dedicated to Edward, and burlesqued the matrimonial plans of the Bridges
girls by those of three quarrelling sisters who had certainly never learned
any good manners or social graces.[25]

James was the next of the brothers to settle in life; he was the least ambitious and most home-loving of them all, so after being priested at Oxford in the summer of 1789 had moved back to his familiar Hampshire home territory the following spring, when he became curate of Overton, the nearest little town to Steventon.[26] Here he lived in the 'very small vicarage house',[27] and indulged his love of foxhunting by going out with the Kempshot pack under the mastership of Mr William Poyntz. At this date Kempshot Park was leased by the Prince of Wales (later Prince Regent and George IV) and Mr Poyntz's diary shows several occasions when James was out in the field alongside the Prince and his courtiers.[28] It was probably thanks to their common interest in hunting that the hearty young sportsman Mr William John Chute of The Vyne presented James to the vicarage of Sherborne St John in September 1791.[29] James was conscientious in riding from Overton to Sherborne St John every Sunday to do duty there, and it may be for this reason that the Austens arranged for the two handicapped members of the family, Thomas Leigh and young George Austen, to be boarded out together in the care of the Culham family, cottagers in the neighbouring village of Monk Sherborne. It would then be easy for James to call upon the Culhams at regular intervals to pay for his relatives' upkeep.[30]

It was also while James was living in Overton that he became acquainted with General Edward Mathew and his family, who had recently returned from the West Indies and were living in the old Manor House at nearby Laverstoke.[31] General Mathew had been in the army all his life, serving bravely with the Coldstream Guards in Europe in the mid-eighteenth century, becoming equerry to George III from 1762–76, seeing further fierce action in the American War of Independence, and finally being made Commander-in-Chief of the Windward and Leeward Islands and Governor of Grenada for the last ten years of his active service. The General 'was in his own house and family a despot whose will no-one could venture to dispute', but although autocratic and hot-tempered was kind-hearted and very generous.[32] His wife, Lady Jane Bertie, was a daughter of the 2nd Duke of Ancaster and sister of the 3rd Duke. The Mathews had three daughters, of whom the second, Anne (1759–95), was by now turned thirty but still unmarried. She had 'large dark eyes, & a good deal of nose',[33] and was 'tall and elegant, somewhat pale, with most beautiful eyes . . . remarkably small-boned and slight'.[34] Anne Mathew must have seen in James Austen her last chance of matrimony, and he had a weakness for elegant, aristocratic young women. The General and Lady Jane 'could not have considered the young curate a good match for their daughter, though as his uncle Mr Leigh-Perrot had no children and he was his father's eldest son, it was possible that he might some day have a comfortable income'[35] – but for Anne's sake they gave their consent to the marriage, and made her an allowance of £100 a year. From the Leigh family James received the vicarage of Cubbington in Warwickshire;[36] this raised his funds to about £200 a year, so on a joint annual income of £300 they were married at Laverstoke on 27 March 1792, Mr Austen taking the service,[37] and lived for a few months at Court House, Overton,[38] until moving back to Deane parsonage later in 1792. Here they immediately spent £200 in completely refurnishing the house,[39] and thereafter Anne kept her own closed carriage and James had a pack of harriers: 'It is scarcely necessary to add that the income was insufficient.'[40]

The youngest of the boys, Charles, left home in July 1791, when at the age of twelve he followed in Francis's footsteps and entered the Royal Naval Academy at Portsmouth.[41] It is possible that the Austens made the occasion of his journey there the basis for a family holiday trip to the Hampshire seaside, for Eliza, writing some weeks later to Phylly Walter, agreed with her: 'as to Cassandra it is very probable as You observe that some Son of Neptune may have obtained her Approbation as She probably experienced much homage from these very gallant Gentlemen during her Aquatic Excursions. I hear her Sister & herself are two of the prettiest Girls in England.'[42] Such an expensive trip could have been undertaken thanks to the last act of kindness on the part of Francis Austen of Sevenoaks; he died on 21 June 1791 at the great age of ninety-three, and when his Will was proved the following month it was found that he had bequeathed £500 to each of his nephews.[43] This was probably the largest lump sum Mr Austen had ever received, and on the strength of it he risked a little gamble by spending £26.4s.0d. buying shares in Government lotteries. The following year he did win a quarter of a prize, but as this amounted to only £5.0s.0d. the gamble turned into a loss, and there is no record that he was ever again tempted to try his luck in this manner.[44]

Now that his sons had all left home Mr Austen could allow himself to relax gradually from his tutorial work, and from 1791 to 1796 there were only three or four boys boarding at the rectory at different periods – Richard Buller, William Stephen Goodenough, and two others whose names have not been preserved.[45] Richard Buller was the son of the Revd Dr William Buller, then a Prebendary of Winchester Cathedral and living at No. 3 The Close,[46] but soon to be appointed Bishop of Exeter. Richard, aged about fourteen when he came to Steventon, seems to have been a sickly boy[47] who may have needed special care and attention, for his father paid Mr Austen on average £150 a year for his board and tuition; by comparison the bills of William Goodenough, (the son of Mr Stephen Goodenough of Winterborne Stoke, Wiltshire), and those of the third and fourth boys, amounted to only about £65 each annually.[48] Richard and William did not share the family's enjoyment of the 'scrooping' sound of the weathercock on its pole in the garden, and their complaints in this respect led Mrs Austen to compose another of her cheerful rhymes on their behalf, addressed to Mr Austen as 'The humble petition of Rd. Buller and W. Goodenough' –

> Dear Sir, we beseech & intreat & request
> You'd remove a sad nuisance that breaks our night's rest
> That creaking old weathercock over our heads
> Will scarcely permit us to sleep in our beds.
> It whines & it groans & makes such a noise
> That it greatly disturbs two unfortunate boys
> Who hope you will not be displeased when they say
> If they don't sleep by night they can't study by day . . .[49]

These boys both went up to Oxford early in 1795; Goodenough does not seem to have kept in touch with the Austens, but Buller remained a devoted friend until his early death in 1806, and is mentioned several times in Jane's letters.[50] Payments for the final pupil cease after the summer of 1796.[51]

The decrease in size of the household meant that there was more elbow-room available in the rectory for the permanent inhabitants, and

one of the Bed chambers, that over the Dining room, was plainly fitted up, & converted into a sort of Drawing room; but this transformation did not occur till my Grand Father & Grand Mother had reared a goodly family of children . . . not probably till my two Aunts, Cassandra and Jane . . . were living at home as grown up young ladies. This room, the Dressing room, as they were pleased to call it, communicated with one of smaller size where my two Aunts slept; I remember the common-looking carpet with its chocolate ground that covered the floor, and some portions of the furniture. A painted press, with shelves above for books, that stood with its back to the wall next the Bedroom, & opposite the fireplace; my Aunt Jane's Pianoforte – & above all, on a table between the windows, above which hung a looking-glass, 2 Tonbridge-ware work boxes of oval shape, fitted up with ivory barrels containing reels for silk, yard measures, etc. I thought them beautiful, & so perhaps in their day, & their degree, they were. But the charm of the room, with its scanty furniture and cheaply papered walls, must have been, for those old enough to understand it, the flow of native homebred wit, with all the fun & nonsense of a clever family who had but little intercourse with the outer world.[52]

Mr Austen's account with the local house-furnishing firm in Basingstoke shows that the wallpaper was blue, the curtains blue-striped, and the press with its bookshelves painted chocolate to match the carpet.[53]

Jane now had a corner of the house which she could consider her study, and her writing proceeded apace. On 26 November 1791 she finished and dedicated to Cassandra 'The History of England from the reign of Henry the 4th to the death of Charles the 1st' – a gleeful parody of Goldsmith's *History of England*, complete with most unlikely portraits of the monarchs to head each chapter; these were drawn and painted by Cassandra, who copied some of the comic faces from printed engravings.[54] 'Evelyn' may have been written immediately afterwards, as it is dedicated to Mary Lloyd and the Lloyds' departure from Deane was imminent; Mr Austen needed to have his other parsonage back in order to provide a home for James and his future wife Anne Mathew, as James was going to act as his father's curate. As a farewell present, Jane made for Mary Lloyd a very small bag of white cotton with gold and black zigzag stripes, which contained a little rolled-up housewife, furnished with minikin needles and fine thread. In the housewife was a tiny packet containing a folded scrap of paper, on which Jane wrote:

> This little bag I hope will prove
> To be not vainly made –
> For, if you thread & needle want
> It will afford you aid.
> And as we are about to part
> 'Twill serve another end,
> For when you look upon the bag
> You'll recollect your friend. – Jany. 1792.[55]

The Christmas of 1791–2 was saddened, however, by the anticipation of Mrs Hancock's death. She and Eliza had come back from France in the summer of 1789, and after staying probably first at Steventon and then for a few months in Margate for the benefit of little Hastings's health,[56] had returned to live in Orchard Street, London, in the spring of 1791. Soon afterwards she had developed symptoms of cancer of the breast, and by the October of that year it was clear that she could not survive much longer. Eliza nursed her with cheerful devotion, but in the privacy of her letters to Phylly Walter spoke miserably of the inexorable progress of her mother's illness. Phylly, still half-envious, wrote to James Walter in tones of smug piety:

Poor Eliza must be left at last friendless & alone. The gay and dissipated life she has long had so plentiful a share of has not ensur'd her friends among the worthy: on the contrary many who otherwise have regarded her have blamed her conduct and will now resign her acquaintance. I always felt concerned and pitied her thoughtlessness. I have frequently looked forwards to the approaching awful period, and regretted the manner of her life, & the mistaken results of my poor aunt's intended, well-meant kindness; she will soon feel the loss & her want of domestic knowledge. I have just wrote to assure her she may command my services.[57]

All through 1791 Eliza had been hoping that her husband would be able to join her,

but the turn which the affairs of France have taken will not allow him to quit the Continent at this Juncture . . . my spouse who is a strong Aristocrate or Royalist in his Heart has joined this latter party who have taken refuge in Piedmont and is now at Turin where the French Princes of the Blood are assembled and watching some favorable opportunity to reinstate themselves in the Country they have quitted, I am no politician but think they will not easily accomplish their purpose . . .[58]

and later on: 'from the present appearance of things France will probably be engaged in a War which will not admit of an Officer whose services will certainly be required, quitting the Country at such a period'.[59] It was not until early in 1792 that he managed to visit England, probably only just before Mrs Hancock's death on 26 February. Following her burial in the churchyard at Hampstead – then still a separate village to the north of London – on 6 March,[60] M. de Feuillide took Eliza to Bath for a fortnight's recuperation and then proposed remaining in London with her for some time,

but he soon received Accounts from France which informed him that having already exceeded his Leave of Absence, if he still continued in England he would be considered as one of the Emigrants, & consequently his whole property forfeited to the Nation; Such Advices were not to be neglected and M. de F. was obliged to depart for Paris, but not however without giving me hopes of his return in some Months, that is to say when the state of Affairs will let him, for at present it is a very difficult Business for a military man especially, to obtain Leave to absent himself.[61]

Eliza went to Steventon in August to be comforted by Mr Austen:

in my opinion his Likeness to My beloved Mother is stronger than ever, Often do I sit and trace her Features in his, till my Heart overflows at my Eyes, I always tenderly loved my Uncle, but I think he is now dearer to me than ever, as being the nearest and best beloved Relative of the never to be sufficiently regretted Parent I have lost –

and to find companions in her two young cousins:

Cassandra & Jane are both very much grown (The latter is now taller than myself) and greatly improved as well in Manners as in Person both of which are now much more formed than when You saw them, They are I think equally sensible, and both so to a degree seldom met with, but still My Heart gives the preference to Jane, whose kind partiality to me, indeed requires a return of the same nature.[62]

Mrs Hancock's death was not the only bereavement suffered by the Austens in 1792, and only a week or two after Eliza's arrival they had to give shelter to another orphaned niece, Jane Cooper. Dr Cooper's health had likewise been failing fast in recent months, and in the summer he and his two children set off on what was hoped might be a restorative holiday. Their kind old friends, the Lybbe-Powys family, went with them, as Mrs Lybbe-Powys recorded:

On Monday the 25 of June 1792 Mr Powys myself and Caroline went in the Evening from Fawley to Docr. Coopers at Sonning intending to set off ye next morning by slow journeys for the Isle of Wight, it had been fixt for the Lakes but the Drs health was so indifferent we had persuaded him fr. going so far, but as he ever found himself better by change of Air, he was very desirous of taking some journey.[63]

Following their arrival on the Island they dined on 2 July with Admiral Sir Hyde Parker and his family at Knighton House, and there met Captain Thomas Williams, RN, commander of HMS *Lizard*. Captain Williams attached himself firmly to their party and acted with all the speed and determination of Admiral Croft[64] – by the time the Powys and Cooper families started homewards at the end of July he and Jane Cooper were engaged and their wedding day fixed.[65]

The party stayed the night of 7 August at the Wheatsheaf Inn at the corner of Popham Lane, and the next day all the Austens joined them there for breakfast before they set off again for Sonning and Fawley.[66] Mrs Lybbe-Powys summed up the trip sadly:

a most pleasant Tour which we should all have enjoyed in a much greater degree, had we not visibly seen poor Docr. Coopers health daily declining though ye journey seem'd to have been of service, as often as he changed the Air, but at last we thought him too far gone, to be at any great distance from home, and intreated to return, which he always seem'd unwilling to do, perhaps thinking it might be less anxiety to his Children, if he had died at any other place, as never were Father or Children more fond of or attentive to each others Happiness.[67]

Their return was only just in time, for Dr Cooper died at Sonning vicarage on 27 August, requesting in his Will that he should be buried at Whaddon beside his wife; Jane Cooper's wedding therefore had to be postponed, and in the meantime she too went to live with the Austens.[68] Captain Williams arrived at Steventon to claim his bride in December and the marriage took place on 11 December, the service being taken by Mr Austen's old pupil, Tom Fowle – now in Holy Orders like his father and elder brother – and with Edward Cooper, Cassandra and Jane as witnesses.[69] The Leighs of Adlestrop gave the bride a cloak worth £5.16s.8d.,[70] and the newly married couple set off for the Isle of Wight, where Captain Williams's mother had a cottage at Ryde.[71]

While Eliza was staying at Steventon, she wrote to Phylly at the end of October 1792:

I can readily believe that the Share of Sensibility I know You to be possessed of would not suffer You to learn the tragical Events of which France has of late been the theatre without being much affected, My private Letters confirm the Intelligence afforded by the public Prints and assure me that nothing we there read is exaggerated, M. de F. is at present in Paris, He had determined on coming to England, but finds it impossible to get away.[72]

After this letter there is a gap of two years in Eliza's surviving correspondence, and the only trace of her movements during this period is that in March 1794 she was back in London and reading a report, in one of the news-sheets which circulated amongst the French *émigrés* in England, that her husband had been condemned to death.[73] This news had crossed the Channel quickly, and was quite correct. In February 1794 M. de Feuillide was arrested at his lodgings, No. 15 rue Grenelle-St Honoré, Paris, on the charge of suborning witnesses in favour of the Marquise de Marboeuf. The Marquise had been accused of conspiring against the Republic in 1793, one of the chief counts against her being that she had laid down certain arable land on her estate at Champs, near Meaux, in lucerne, sainfoin and clover, with the object of producing a famine. The Marquise, by way of defence, printed a memorial of her case, stating among other things that she had not done what she was accused of doing, and that further, even if she had, she had a perfect right to do what she liked with her own property. M. de Feuillide attempted to bribe a certain man named Morel, one of the Secretaries of the Committee of Public Safety, to do away with evidence likely to incriminate the Marquise and even to give evidence in her favour. Morel accepted the bribes and then betrayed de Feuillide to the Committee, the result being that the Marquise and M. de Feuillide were both guillotined, the latter on 22 February 1794.[74]

The next definite news of Eliza is contained in her letter of September 1794, in which she states that she has been staying with friends in Washington, County Durham, since July of that year.[75] Whatever may have happened to her during these two years, the cruel death of her husband brought the horrors of the French Revolution straight into the peaceful Steventon rectory, and left Jane with a loathing of republican France for the rest of her life.[76]

During this year of family upheavals, Jane's next story was probably 'Lesley Castle', dedicated to Henry, as its first letter bears the date of 3 January 1792 and the others supposedly continue until 13 April. Following this came 'Catherine, or The Bower', dedicated to Cassandra, in August 1792, which contains a passage concerning an impoverished girl's trip to Bengal in search of a husband – an obvious reflection of the facts of Mrs Hancock's life, which Jane's parents perhaps felt could be more freely discussed now that she was dead. Jane acquired her next manuscript book, *Volume the Third*, on 6 May 1792, as she noted on the first leaf – inside the front cover Mr Austen pencilled: 'Effusions of Fancy by a very Young Lady consisting of Tales in a Style entirely new', and into this book she transcribed both 'Evelyn' and 'Catherine'. The 'Collection of Letters', dedicated to Jane Cooper, was probably written during the autumn of 1792 while she was staying at Steventon in the months immediately prior to her marriage.

After the death of the patriarchal Francis Austen of Sevenoaks in 1791 the Hampshire Austens had very little further contact with his descendants, although letters were occasionally exchanged between them when family weddings or deaths occurred, and years later Jane noticed that her cousin Colonel Thomas Austen had been appointed Aide de Camp to the Lord Lieutenant of Ireland.[77] Francis Motley Austen sold The Red House and his own house at Lamberhurst and bought instead the Kippington estate on the outskirts of Sevenoaks, where he settled down to rear his large family and live the life of a rich country gentleman, busying himself with social activities rather than with the work of his father's legal firm. When the Austens visited Kent from this time onwards, it would be to see the Knights at Godmersham or Edward and Elizabeth at Rowling, and the first record in this respect is that of Cassandra staying with the newly weds at Rowling in the summer of 1792. As soon as she returned to Hampshire, she and Jane went off to visit the Lloyds at Ibthorpe,[78] and Jane made her début into society from there that autumn when she danced at Enham House, near Andover (the home of Anne Mathew's sister Mrs Dewar), and met the two 'vulgar, broad featured' Misses Cox whom she recognised years later at another dance; she also went to a ball at Hurstbourne Park, and saw several 'fat girls with short noses', who proved to be the daughters of Mr Atkinson, the rector of Knight's Enham.[79] Once back at Steventon, there were assembly balls at Basingstoke Town Hall every month during the winter season,[80] besides private parties and dances given by the neighbouring Hampshire families; and when weather conditions permitted longer journeys to be taken, she could look forward to visiting the Leighs at Adlestrop, the Lybbe-Powys family and other connections in Oxfordshire, her mother's old friend Mary Newell (now Mrs Birch) who lived in the Windsor neighbourhood, where 'everybody is rich',[81] as well as going to Rowling and meeting all Edward's Kentish friends and in-laws. Jane, then, like thousands of other young ladies, now had nothing to do but live 'to be fashionable, happy, and merry'.[82]

CHAPTER 7

The young Jane, 1792–6

What was Jane like, in looks and character, as she reached the age of seventeen and stepped into the adult world? Unfortunately, although several likenesses of the various Austen sons exist, professionally executed, the only authentic representation of Jane's features is the watercolour sketch of her made by Cassandra later in life, probably *c.* 1810. This is accurate enough to show that she bore a strong resemblance to her father and several of her brothers, but it cannot be considered as a true portrait – her affectionate niece, Anna, indeed, called it 'so hideously unlike'.[1] Several verbal descriptions of Jane are on record, but these again relate to the later years of her life, post 1800; however, as they all agree with each other, it seems reasonable to assume that her appearance did not alter very much during her adult life, and that Anna's words, for example, could apply to Jane equally at seventeen or at twenty-seven:

The Figure tall & slight, but not drooping; well balanced, as was proved by her quick firm step – Her complexion of that rather rare sort which seems the peculiar property of light brunettes – A mottled skin, not fair, but perfectly clear & healthy in hue; the fine naturally curling hair, neither light nor dark; the bright hazel eyes to match, & the rather small but well-shaped nose. One hardly understands how with all these advantages she could yet fail of being a decidedly handsome woman.[2]

The hazel eyes, Anna added elsewhere, were 'something like' those of Mr Austen.[3]

Jane's brother Henry, in his 'Biographical Notice' of 1817, wrote in a more formal and high-flown style:

Of personal attractions she possessed a considerable share. Her stature was that of true elegance. It could not have been increased without exceeding the middle height. Her carriage and deportment were quiet, yet graceful. Her features were separately good. Their assemblage produced an unrivalled expression of that cheerfulness, sensibility, and benevolence, which were her real characteristics. Her complexion was of the finest texture. It might with truth be said, that her eloquent blood spoke through her modest cheek. Her voice was extremely sweet. She delivered herself with fluency and precision. Indeed she was formed for elegant and rational society, excelling in conversation as much as in composition.[4]

Anna noticed the depth of her nature:

Her unusually quick sense of the ridiculous inclined her to play with the trifling commonplaces of every day life, whether as regarded people or things; but she never played with its serious duties or responsibilities – when grave she was very grave. I am not sure but that Aunt Cassandra's disposition was the most equally cheerful of the two. Their affection for each other was extreme; it passed the common love of sisters, and it had been so from childhood.[5]

Family remembrance summed up the differences between the two:

They were not exactly alike. Cassandra's was the colder and calmer disposition; she was always prudent and well judging, but with less outward demonstration of feeling and less sunniness of temper than Jane possessed. It was remarked in her family that 'Cassandra had the *merit* of having her temper always under command, but that Jane had the *happiness* of a temper that never required to be commanded.'[6]

The vivacity that delighted her family was less appreciated by the plain, dumpy Mrs Mitford, now the mother of one short, fat, little girl, who saw Jane at some time between 1792 and 1795, probably at a Basingstoke assembly ball, and jealously thought her 'the prettiest, silliest, most affected, husband-hunting butterfly she ever remembered'.[7]

As far as marriage was concerned, it already seemed that Cassandra for one need have no fear of dwindling into a lonely old maid, since it was about now that she became engaged to her childhood friend, Mr Austen's former pupil, Tom Fowle – perhaps he took the opportunity to propose to Cassandra when he stayed at Steventon to perform the marriage service for Jane Cooper and Captain Thomas Williams in December 1792. Tom had obtained from his kinsman the 1st Earl of Craven the rectory of Allington, near Amesbury, in Wiltshire, but as this was only a very small living he could not yet afford to get married. However, Lord Craven had also promised him one or other of the Shropshire livings that were in his gift, whenever one should fall vacant – West Felton, Onibury, and Wistanstow[8] – and Cassandra, no doubt with her parents' example in mind, was content to sew her trousseau and wait till such time as Tom could provide a home for her. James too was looking forward to the day when he would perform the marriage ceremony between his sister and his boyhood friend.[9]

Jane became an aunt for the first time when Edward's eldest daughter Fanny Catherine was born at Rowling on 23 January 1793 – Lady Bridges provided a vast collection of 'Child-Bed Linen' for Elizabeth and the baby, that cost over £40.[10] Nearer home, at Deane, James's wife Anne was suffering

Plate 5 Revd George
Austen; silhouette, *c.* 1800?

Plate 6 Mrs George
Austen; silhouette, *c.* 1800?

Plate 7 James (1765–1819),
miniature *c.* 1790?

Plate 8 Edward (1767–1852),
portrait, *c.* 1788.

Plate 9 Henry (1771–1850),
miniature *c.* 1820?

Plate 10 Cassandra (1773–1845),
silhouette, n.d.

Plate 11 Francis (1774–1865),
miniature, 1796.

Plate 12 Charles (1779–1852),
portrait, *c.* 1809.

Plate 13 Jane Austen (1775–1817), watercolour by Cassandra, *c.* 1810?

Plate 14 Watercolour miniature made from Cassandra's painting, by James Andrews of Maidenhead, *c.* 1869.

Plate 15 Steel-engraved version of Andrews's miniature, by Lizars, as used in the *Memoir*, 1870.

through her first pregnancy: 'She is so much incommoded by her present Situation as to be confined to her Bed for whole Days'[11] – but Jane Anna Elizabeth arrived safely on 15 April 1793, probably thanks to the practical help of her efficient grandmother: 'Mrs Austen rose from her bed in the middle of the night, and walked by the light of a lantern a mile and a half of a muddy country lane to attend her [daughter-in-law], and to usher into the world a new grandchild . . .'[12] This baby, known always as Anna, spent much of her early life in close touch with her Austen grandmother and young aunts, and it is her memories, recorded in later years, which provide a good deal of such biographical information about Jane as is available. Her baptismal party at Laverstoke the following month was a lavish affair; the godparents were the 5th Duke and Duchess of Ancaster (Anna's great-uncle and -aunt), and General Mathew, 'a very generous and freehanded man who carried his money literally and metaphorically loose in his pocket and gave to everyone that asked without deigning to look whether the coin bestowed was a guinea or a shilling',[13] gave twenty guineas to be divided between the nurse and the maid-servants. 'The consequence was that the Nurse was very dissatisfied that she had not more – had five only been given she would have been thankful.'[14]

Jane took her new responsibilities as an aunt suitably solemnly, and sent to baby Fanny five short pieces of nonsense (those of the *Juvenilia* now known collectively as 'Scraps'), purporting to be her 'Opinions and Admonitions on the conduct of Young Women'; and for baby Anna wrote two more 'Miscellanious [*sic*] Morsels', dedicating them to her on 2 June 1793, 'convinced that if you seriously attend to them, You will derive from them very important Instructions, with regard to your Conduct in Life'.[15] Later in the year, following France's declaration of war against Britain in February 1793, one of the General's old friends, General Cornelius Cuyler, hurriedly raised a new regiment for overseas service, the 86th Regiment of Foot; and General Mathew purchased the chaplaincy of the regiment as a sinecure for his son-in-law James Austen, reckoning it would add something to the young family's income even after a deputy had been paid.[16]

James obviously never intended that his military chaplaincy should take him abroad on active service, but the outbreak of war changed the course of Henry's life. He had graduated at Oxford the previous year, but 'not being old enough for ordination, and the political circumstances of the time 1793 calling on every one not otherwise employ'd to offer his services in the general defence of the Country',[17] he took a lieutenant's commission in the Oxfordshire Militia and remained so engaged till 1800. Militia regiments were not expected to go abroad to fight, but were intended as home defences should invasion take place – which on at least two occasions during the Napoleonic Wars, was deemed very likely to occur. It may be that Eliza de Feuillide had been teasing Henry about a suitable choice of profession for a young man in a time of national danger, for while she was staying at Steventon in the autumn of 1792, she wrote to Phylly:

Henry is now rather more than Six Foot high I believe, He also is much improved, and is certainly endowed with uncommon Abilities, which indeed seem to have been bestowed, tho' in a different way, upon each Member of this Family – As to the Coolness which You know had taken place between H. and myself, it has now ceased, in consequence of due acknowledgments on his part, and we are at present on very proper relationlike terms, You know that his Family design him for the Church.[18]

The Oxfordshire Militia spent some time quartered in East Anglia, moving between Great Yarmouth, Norwich and Ipswich so as to be ready to defend the vulnerable coastline in that area, but Henry also managed to retain his Fellowship at St John's College until 1798 and obtained sufficient leave of absence from his military duties to enable him to visit Oxford, Steventon, London and Kent throughout his years of service without any apparent difficulty.

Another family wedding occurred early in 1793, when Mrs Austen's nephew, Edward Cooper, married Caroline Lybbe-Powys on 14 March – 'a match that gave all her friends the highest satisfaction, as there cannot be a more worthy young man' – his new mother-in-law wrote happily in her diary.[19] Edward, now a Fellow of All Souls, obtained the curacy of Harpsden from his college, following in the footsteps of his grandfather, the Revd Thomas Leigh, so that Mrs Austen was able to visit again the home of her girlhood as her nephew's guest. Mrs Lybbe-Powys went to stay with her daughter later in the year when Edward first preached at Harpsden, and noted that a 'very excellent sermon he gave us'.[20] In later years Edward published several volumes of sermons, which Jane did not much care for but which were reprinted and admired well into the nineteenth century.[21]

Although James was content to employ a curate for his Warwickshire living of Cubbington, and so far as is known never set foot in that parish,[22] he was a most conscientious vicar of Sherborne St John and rode over nearly every week to do Sunday duty, usually staying to dine with Mr Chute at The Vyne afterwards. Thus it was that when Mr Chute married the shy, artistic little Miss Elizabeth Smith in London on 15 October 1793 and brought her home to Hampshire that same day, the Austens were amongst the first of the neighbours to make the bride's acquaintance.[23] Nearly forty years into the future James's son would marry Mrs Chute's niece, but as yet James was only an impecunious country vicar and Mrs Chute the mistress of a fine mansion and estate with every expectation of a prosperous family life ahead of her, so that no such thought of marital alliance could ever then have crossed their minds.

The winter of 1793 brought happiness to Steventon rectory in the return of Francis from his service in the Far East after an absence of five years, during which he had grown from an untried boy of fourteen into a successful young officer, already distinguished by his promotion to Lieutenant at the age of eighteen. He had several months' shore leave before taking up his next posting to the sloop HMS *Lark* in March 1794, so it was probably he who was available to escort his sisters to Southampton in December 1793 to stay with their relations, the Butler-Harrison family. The Austens' cousin, Elizabeth Matilda Austen of Tonbridge, had married in 1789 the wealthy John Butler-Harrison II, who lived at St Mary's, a rural suburb outside the old city walls of Southampton. Tradition on her side of the family recalled that she 'was one of the most beautiful women in Kent, & on her way to Chawton (a family place in Hants) to be married, her carriage was escorted as far as the boundaries of Kent by the young men of the county on horseback'.[24] Since then Mr Butler-Harrison had been Sheriff of Southampton in 1790 and would be twice elected Mayor, in 1794 and 1811. By now they had two children and were expecting a third, but this did not deter them from inviting their Hampshire cousins to stay, and one Tuesday evening in December Jane and Cassandra danced happily at the Assembly Ball in the Dolphin Inn, as Jane remembered years later when she was once again in Southampton.[25] Elizabeth Matilda Butler-Harrison was born on 17 December and Jane was one of her godparents when she was christened the following month.[26]

There are no precise dates available for Jane's activities during 1794, but at midsummer she and Cassandra evidently visited Adlestrop, for the Revd Thomas Leigh noted in his private account book on 2 July that he had passed over £1.16s.6d. to his wife to give to Cassandra.[27] The Leighs' neighbour and distant cousin Mrs Chamberlayne of Maugersbury House met the Austens during this visit, and thought they were 'very charming young women'.[28] On a hot day later in the year the sisters travelled to Kent to stay with Edward, stopping at the Bull in Dartford on the first stage of their journey and suffering bad butter at the breakfast they ate there.[29] There was now another baby at Rowling, a brother for little Fanny, as Edward's first son, Edward the younger, had been born on 10 May. It was probably during this visit that Jane met and briefly cherished a girlish passion for young Mr Edward Taylor of Bifrons, near Patrixbourne, who had such 'beautiful dark eyes';[30] she also met Lady Pym Hales with her two youngest daughters, Caroline and Harriet, and Marianne Bridges, one of Edward's many sisters-in-law, who was the invalid of the family and died a few years later.[31]

On 23 October 1794 the Austens' benefactor, Thomas Knight II, had a stroke and died suddenly at his Hampshire estate of Chawton, at the comparatively early age of fifty-eight. 'His carriage and address were those of the man of fashion, and his temper serene, accompanied with a friendly disposition, equally candid and sincere.'[32] His estates were of course left to his widow for her lifetime, but he demonstrated his confidence in the Austen family not only by making Edward his heir, as had always been promised, but by providing in his Will that, should Edward's line fail, the estates should continue to descend to each of the other Austen sons in succession. For the immediate moment he also left £50 apiece to Cassandra and Jane, which was probably the largest sum either of them had so far ever possessed, as their father could allow them only £20 a year each for their personal expenses and even this small sum was paid in quarterly instalments.[33] Another of Mr Knight's kinsmen, the Revd John Rawstorne Papillon of Acrise, was given first refusal of the rectory of Chawton at the next vacancy, with the provision that if he did not wish to accept this promise of a living, it should then be offered to Henry Austen. Henry, although now with his regiment in East Anglia, was by no means averse to returning to his original idea of ordination, and at his request Edward offered up to £1,200 to buy Mr Papillon's refusal in advance of the vacancy occurring. However, the Papillon family did not choose to oblige Henry in this respect, and when the then rector of Chawton, Revd John Hinton, died in 1802, John Papillon took over.[34] By one of life's little ironies, years later Henry was for a short time curate to Mr Papillon in this very living, but never acquired it for himself.[35]

There is no definite information as to the progress of Jane's literary composition since the summer of 1793, when on 3 June she dedicated the last item of her collected *Juvenilia* – two verses of a mock 'Ode to Pity' – to Cassandra,[36] and her journeyings about during 1793 and 1794 may have left her little time for creative writing apart from the necessary letters to the various members of her family, especially Frank and Charles, who were now both away at sea. Charles left the Naval Academy in September 1794 and shipped as a Midshipman aboard HMS *Daedalus*, under the command of his cousin's husband Captain Thomas Williams; and Frank was still in the sloop HMS *Lark* in home waters, beating about the Downs and the North

Sea and growing restless for the lack of opportunity for advancement. Mr Austen therefore sought the help of the family's old friend, Warren Hastings, to get Frank moved into a larger ship with more chance of active service:

I have had the favour of both your letters, & must ever acknowledge myself much your debtor, for the friendly manner in which you have undertaken our cause, & the application you have made in behalf of my Son. – As to the event of it I am not very sanguine, convinced as I am that all Patronage in the Navy rests with Ld. Chatham; however as it may be of material service to us to have a warm Friend at the Board, I am very thankful you have procured us one in Adml. Affleck. If I mistake not he had formerly some acquaintance with my family, & perhaps his recollection of that may be an additional motive with his regard for you to endeavour to assist us. Should we not succeed in our first object of getting him promoted, it might forward his views to have him removed to a Flag Ship on a more probable Station; & this is a circumstance you might, if you had no objection, suggest to the Admiral when you meet him [in] Town. And here I must not omit to inform you that we have by the Application of a Friend gained, as we hope, another Ld. of the Admiralty, Mr Pybus, in our interest, a circumstance you will mention or not as you think proper. I shall not trouble you with anything further on this subject than to assure I should not have introduced my son to your notice, had I not been convinced that his merits as a Man & A Sailor will justify any recommendations.[37]

Warren Hastings had now been enduring for years his trial before the House of Lords since his impeachment by the Whigs in 1787 on charges of cruelty and extortion during his term of office as Governor of Bengal. The Leighs and Austens had never for a moment doubted that Hastings was innocent of the charges, and were grieved to think of their friend's mental suffering as the trial dragged on from year to year. Phylly Walter was staying with Eliza in London in April 1788, and told her brother:

I have once been to the Trial which, because an uncommon sight, we fancied worth going to, and sat from 10 till 4 o'clock, compleatly tired, but I had the satisfaction of hearing all the celebrated orators, Sheridan, Burke & Fox. The first was so low we cd. not hear him, the 2nd so hot and hasty, we cd. not understand, & the 3rd was highly superior to either as we cd. distinguish every word, but not to our satisfaction as he is so much against Mr Hastings whom we all here wish so well.[38]

In 1790 Mrs Leigh of Adlestrop thanked him for finding time in the midst of all his 'matters of the first import' to provide her with a reading list:

– And now I will go & lay up yr. Letter in lavender: – who has not posthumous (if not present) vanity? perhaps in Centuries to come, when Party & prejudice are no more, it will appear favorable for <u>Somebody</u>, that that Great Man (as he will then be term'd) honor'd with notice his most obliged & obedient humble Servant M. Leigh.[39]

When Hastings was finally overwhelmingly acquitted in 1795 there was but one feeling in the family; they all admired him as a high-minded patriot, a warm and disinterested friend and a scholar whose approbation was an honour. The Revd Thomas Leigh wrote: 'we beg you to be assur'd yt. amist ye flood of congratulations flowing in upon you, none will be accompanied wh. more heartfelt sincerity than those wch. you receive fm. Adlestrop',[40] and Henry Austen, whose enthusiastic temperament was reflected in his literary style, begged

to offer you the warm & respectful congratulations of a heart deeply impressed with a sense of all you have done & suffered. Permit me to congratulate my Country; & myself as an Englishman; for right dear to every Englishman must it be to behold the issue of a contest where forms of judicature threaten'd to annihilate the essence of justice.[41]

Following her completion of *Volume the Third* of the *Juvenilia*, Jane's literary projects were assuming a more adult style, although the process of selection and elimination both in subject and method was not yet finalised. It is probable that *Lady Susan* was written next, as a first attempt to deal with a serious theme – but one which proved difficult to handle when bound by the constraints of an epistolary novel, and therefore had to be wound up with a summary and ironic conclusion. This conclusion indeed may have been added at a later date, perhaps when Jane made a fair copy of the original text at some time in or after 1805.[42] On 5 December 1794 Mr Austen purchased in Basingstoke 'a Small Mahogany Writing Desk with 1 Long Drawer and Glass Ink Stand Compleat' for 12s.;[43] this seems to be an accurate description of the desk owned by Jane which survives as a family heirloom,[44] and it is tempting to think that it was given to her as a nineteenth birthday present. If so, she may have used it during 1795 when she embarked upon her first full-length project – *Elinor and Marianne*, the prototype *Sense and Sensibility*. Family tradition recalled that this too was written in letters, and read aloud in this form; in the final version the sisters are never apart at all, but it is possible to envisage a different structure of the plot whereby letters could have passed between the various characters and carried the course of action along with them.[45] However, to convert *Elinor and Marianne* later on into the straightforward narrative of *Sense and Sensibility* must have involved Jane in considerable difficulty and labour, and so decided her against using the epistolary style for any further novels. Her knowledge of the London scene necessary for the central part of the story was evidently gained from contact with Eliza; by 1795 the latter was probably living in London again and Jane may well have visited her there and seen for herself the fashionable promenade in Kensington Gardens, or Gray's the jewellers in Sackville Street, with some foolish young man fussing over his choice of a toothpick-case. It is also very likely that Eliza stayed at Steventon again during the summers of 1795 and 1796, though documentary evidence for this supposition is lacking.

The winter of 1794–5 was exceptionally severe, with a cold spell lasting from December until March,[46] and the eventual thaw brought floods to Steventon. The Austens' neighbour, Mrs Bramston of Oakley Hall, wrote to a friend:

as you live on the top of a hill, I will not ask you how you like floating on the Waters, & as we live on the Side of a one, I cannot tell you from Experience, but our neighbours say they rather like the Ground floor than the upper apartments, Mr Austens family did not descend for two days, Mr James Austen lost 2 fat pigs, one poor farmer had but 60 Ewes, & above 20 were drownd, Corn carried out of the Barns, & numberless Accidents did the sudden thaw create.[47]

Mr Austen was obliged to spend more than £11 early in April buying new carpets for his sodden ground floor rooms.[48]

Perhaps the long, cold winter had weakened James's wife, Anne, for she suddenly collapsed and died at Deane on 3 May 1795:

she dined with her husband in perfect health apparently, but was taken ill immediately afterwards. It was supposed she had eaten something that disagreed with her and an emetic was given. The doctor was sent for, but I am not sure that he arrived in time to see her alive as she lingered only a few hours; he told her husband he knew there was some internal adhesion of the liver and he thought it had probably been ruptured and so caused her death.[49]

She had been 'a very tender mother, and the poor little girl [Anna, aged just two] missed her so much, and kept so constantly asking and fretting for "Mamma" that her father sent her away to Steventon to be taken care of and consoled by her aunts Cassandra and Jane'.[50] Anna spent most of the next two years at Steventon until her father's remarriage in 1797, and the Austens bought a little cherrywood chair for her particular use, costing half-a-crown.[51] General Mathew continued to pay James the £100 a year that had been Anne's allowance, so that it could now be spent upon Anna's maintenance and education; he was very proud of his pretty little granddaughter, who had inherited her mother's beautiful eyes,[52] and on one occasion while she was at Steventon he swooped down upon the rectory – evidently while Mr and Mrs Austen were not there – and 'chose to take her out to a dinner party regardless of the unsuitableness of her age, or the pleasure of his host and hostess; and her Aunts did not venture to remonstrate'.[53]

Frank was transferred to the 32-gun HMS *Andromeda* in May 1795 – presumably through the influence of either Admiral Affleck or Mr Pybus – but in the meantime, while still aboard the *Lark*, he took part in the evacuation of British troops from Ostend and Nieuwport in this arctic winter of 1794–5. The expeditionary force had had to be rescued following the collapse of the Dutch kingdom and the declaration of a new Batavian republic which allied itself with revolutionary France. The *Lark* was also one of the squadron despatched across the North Sea to bring Princess Caroline of Brunswick from Cuxhaven to England for her ill-fated marriage to the Prince of Wales. Perhaps Frank caught a glimpse of this blonde, buxom hoyden as she disembarked at Gravesend on 5 April, and was able to tell his sisters that she wore a muslin dress with a blue satin petticoat and a black beaver hat with blue and black feathers.[54]

In the autumn of 1795 Frank moved again, to the 98-gun HMS *Glory*, which was one of the convoy commanded by Admiral Sir Hugh Christian escorting General Sir Ralph Abercromby's 19,000-strong force to the West Indies, where the French were instigating and assisting the slaves to rebel against British rule. The expedition was delayed by lack of men and equipment and when it did sail from Portsmouth in November it was delayed still further by hurricanes in the Channel which caused many casualties to ships and men. Amongst the troops involved were The Buffs (3rd Foot), of which regiment the Lloyds' kinsman young Lord Craven had recently purchased the colonelcy – as his mother, the 'Beautiful Lady Craven', said, he had 'all the military furor of the times upon him'.[55] Lord Craven asked Tom Fowle to accompany him as his private chaplain; and Tom, not daring to offend his patron by citing his engagement to Cassandra Austen as a reason for refusing, accepted the offer, and hurriedly made his Will in October 1795 before joining the Craven entourage.[56] Although The Buffs sailed with the main fleet in November, Lord Craven did not accompany his men but followed later in his own private yacht, thus luckily missing the calamitous storms. Tom wrote to Jane on 8 January 1796, telling her that they planned to sail from Falmouth on Sunday, 10 January if the wind were favourable. As Jane wrote blithely to Cassandra four days later: 'By this time therefore they are at Barbadoes I suppose.'[57]

Jane had every reason to feel blithe during this winter of 1795–6, for she was now enjoying the admiration of several young men – there was a rich Mr Heartley, the well-connected but spendthrift Revd Charles Powlett from Winslade, and her father's old pupil, John Willing Warren, now a Fellow of

Oriel, who was staying at Steventon for this Christmas holiday period. Some people, at least, thought Warren must be in love with her, but Jane herself did not believe that this was so. Charles Fowle, the youngest of the four Fowle sons, was on very friendly terms with her, but now that Cassandra was engaged to Tom Fowle, Jane viewed Charles more as a brother than a potential admirer. She was at present more interested in the admiration she was receiving from a visitor to the immediate neighbourhood, another Tom – Tom Lefroy, staying at Ashe rectory with his uncle the Revd George Lefroy. For him, Jane's feelings were poised on the knife-edge between flattered amusement and the exciting apprehension of possible romantic commitment, and this ambivalence is reflected in the first two of her extant letters, those which she wrote to Cassandra during January 1796. At that time Cassandra was staying with the Fowles at Kintbury to take leave of *her* Tom before he departed with Lord Craven, and had been with them for some weeks, so had not herself met the Lefroys' nephew.

Tom Lefroy (1776–1869) was very slightly younger than Jane, a fair, serious young man, destined by his family for the Bar. He was the eldest son of Colonel Anthony Peter Lefroy, late of the 9th Light Dragoons and now retired to an estate in Limerick, and his education and future legal career were being mapped out and paid for by old Mr Benjamin Langlois. Col. Lefroy had a large family, and whilst Mr Langlois was not averse to providing financial support to his Irish nephew as well as to his Hampshire one, it was understood that Tom, at least, was expected to 'rise into distinction and there haul up the rest'.[58] So far he had fulfilled expectations and dutifully acquired his degree at Trinity College, Dublin, in 1795, but his health and eyesight then gave cause for concern and it was decided he should go to Ashe for a holiday before starting his legal studies. Great-uncle Benjamin considered that Tom had 'everything in his temper and character than can conciliate affections. A good heart, a good mind, good sense and as little to correct in him as ever I saw in one of his age.'[59]

It was this shy, intelligent young stranger who was staying at Ashe rectory in the winter of 1795–6, and with whom Jane danced and flirted at three balls, in a manner that called forth Cassandra's elder-sisterly reproaches:

You scold me so much in the nice long letter which I have this moment received from you, that I am almost afraid to tell you how my Irish friend and I behaved. Imagine to yourself everything most profligate and shocking in the way of dancing and sitting down together. I can expose myself, however, only once more, because he leaves the country soon after next Friday, on which day we are to have a dance at Ashe after all. He is a very gentlemanlike, good-looking, pleasant young man, I assure you. But as to our having ever met, except at the three last balls, I cannot say much; for he is so excessively laughed at about me at Ashe, that he is ashamed of coming to Steventon, and ran away when we called on Mrs Lefroy a few days ago.[60]

Tom and his young cousin, J. H. George Lefroy, made the usual courtesy call at Steventon the morning after the latest ball – that at Manydown on 8 January – and Jane decided that Tom's one fault was that 'his morning coat is a great deal too light'.[61] However, she was looking forward to the next ball at Ashe on 15 January because, as she teased the prudent Cassandra: 'I rather expect to receive an offer from my friend in the course of the evening. I shall refuse him, however, unless he promises to give away his white Coat.' Jane added, with something of a swagger, a message for Mary Lloyd, then also staying at Kintbury with her cousins and perhaps inclined to be a little envious of Jane's social success:

Tell Mary that I make over Mr Heartley & all his Estate to her for her sole use and Benefit in future, & not only him, but all my other Admirers into the bargain wherever she can find them, even the kiss which C. Powlett wanted to give me, as I mean to confine myself in future to Mr Tom Lefroy, for whom I do not care sixpence. Assure her also as a last & indubitable proof of Warren's indifference to me, that he actually drew that Gentleman's picture for me, & delivered it to me without a Sigh.

This letter was finished on the morning of 15 January, and Jane's last flippant comment was: 'At length the Day is come on which I am to flirt my last with Tom Lefroy, & when you receive this it will be over. – My tears flow as I write, at the melancholy idea.'[62]

There is no further information as to what happened at Ashe on the evening of 15 January, and it is highly unlikely that Tom proposed or that Jane ever really believed he would do so. However, Mr and Mrs Lefroy had seen enough of their mutual attraction to take fright at the idea of an engagement between so youthful and penniless a pair, and Tom was sent off rapidly to London to live under the watchful eye of his great-uncle Benjamin while he studied at Lincoln's Inn. The Lefroy parents were vexed with him, and told their sons that Tom was to blame for paying attentions to Jane when he knew full well that he was in no position to think of marriage; and years later George and his younger brother Edward Lefroy recalled how '[their] Mother had disliked Tom Lefroy because he had behaved so ill to Jane Austen, with sometimes the additional weight of the Father's condemnation . . .'[63] Although Tom stayed at Ashe again in the autumn of 1798,[64] no meetings with the Austens took place during this visit, and it was not until Madam Lefroy called at Steventon parsonage in mid-November that Jane had any further news of him: 'I was too proud to make any enquiries; but on my father's afterwards asking where he was, I learnt that he was gone back to London in his way to Ireland, where he is called to the Bar and means to practise.'[65] Tom became a very successful barrister, married a college friend's sister in 1799 and lived to a great age, ending his career as the austere and venerable Lord Chief Justice of Ireland, head of a large family and owner of a rich estate in County Longford.[66] Although he was very happy in his marriage, he never forgot Jane Austen, and 'to the last year of his life she was remembered as the object of his youthful admiration –',[67] when he told a nephew that he had had a 'boyish love' for her.[68] As for Jane, it sounds as if she had grown fonder of Tom than she cared to admit at the time; but this disappointment was only temporary and by no means one which blighted her life, for a few months later she started writing that happiest of all her novels – the work that was eventually published in 1813 under the title of *Pride and Prejudice*.

CHAPTER 8

Later years at Steventon, 1796–9

After Jane's brief Christmas-holiday romance and Cassandra's sad but hopeful farewell to Tom Fowle, the next news of the sisters is that they stayed with their Cooper cousins at Harpsden during April 1796 and dined with the Lybbe-Powys family and other Oxfordshire neighbours during this visit.[1] The Coopers by now had the first two of their eventual family of eight children and Henry Austen was godfather to their eldest son, Edward Philip.[2]

As for Henry himself, it seemed that he would soon bring another daughter-in-law into the Austen family, for at some time early in 1796 he became engaged to Miss Mary Pearson, daughter of Captain Sir Richard Pearson, RN, one of the officers of the Greenwich Hospital for Seamen. He obtained her miniature and showed it proudly to his parents, and Mrs Austen was pleased to think that Miss Pearson was a very pretty girl. James too had recovered from the shock of his sudden bereavement the previous year and was thinking of remarriage. He had gone with Jane to the ball at Manydown and while she was flirting with Tom Lefroy he chose Alethea Bigg as his partner, and Jane thought he deserved 'encouragement for the very great improvement which has lately taken place in his dancing'.[3] Before that, however, James had been casting his eyes towards the more familiar charms of Eliza de Feuillide, who apparently visited Steventon once again at this time.

There is a gap in Eliza's letters to Phylly Walter from October 1792 until September 1796, and consequently detailed knowledge of her movements during these four years is lacking. The only definite information available is that she was in London in March 1794,[4] and in the summer went to stay with her friend Mrs Egerton, whose husband Charles was the incumbent of Washington, County Durham. From there she wrote to her godfather, Warren Hastings, on 19 September, thanking him for forwarding a foreign letter:

On seeing a foreign Post Mark I flattered myself with receiving some important information, and was much disappointed to find myself addressed from Corunna by a Person to whom I am almost a Stranger, and who writes merely to request my endeavors to obtain an english Passport. In Answer to your kind enquiries concerning my Health, I have the satisfaction of saying, that I find myself much the better for the Northern Air of which I have now made some trial, having been at this place, that is to say on the borders of Northumberland ever since July; I purposed returning to London some time next Month, but Mr & Mrs Egerton, the Friends to whom I have already paid so long a visit, kindly insist on my not leaving them till after Christmas.[5]

It would seem from this letter that Eliza was even then uncertain as to the precise fate of her husband, though it is unlikely that she could have had any real expectation he was still alive. It appears that she visited Steventon again, probably in the summer of 1795 and, according to family tradition, flirted with both James and Henry Austen – to such an extent, indeed, that the impetuous young Henry proposed to her, and had to be kindly refused.[6] By September 1796 Eliza was once more in the social whirl, writing from Tunbridge Wells to Phylly and begging the latter to join her for a further holiday at Brighton before she went back to London later in the autumn.[7] She had certainly been toying with the idea of marrying James Austen, for she told Phylly in December 1796:

I am glad to find you have made up your mind to visiting the Rectory, but at the same time, and in spite of all your conjectures and belief, I do assert that Preliminaries are so far from settled that I do not believe the parties ever will come together, not however that they have quarrelled, but one of them cannot bring her mind to give up dear Liberty, and yet dearer flirtation – After a few months stay in the country She sometimes thinks it possible to undertake sober Matrimony, but a few weeks stay in London convinces her how little the state suits her taste – Lord S-s' card has this moment been brought me which I think very ominous considering I was talking of Matrimony, but it does not signify, I shall certainly escape both Peer & Parson.[8]

By this time, in fact, although Eliza did not yet know it, James had grown tired of being kept dangling by her and had turned his attentions elsewhere, with a more satisfactory outcome as far as he was concerned.

At midsummer 1796 news was received of a thrilling naval action in which Charles had participated, under Captain Thomas Williams in the 32-gun frigate HMS *Unicorn*. While cruising off the Scilly Isles on 8 June they had intercepted three French ships; one of these, the 44-gun *La Tribune*, tried to escape, but the *Unicorn* kept up a running fight for ten hours before closing for a brief and decisive battle, in which *La Tribune* was dismasted and captured. The chase had extended over 210 miles and Capt. Williams's crew had suffered no injury, despite the fact that the *Unicorn* was out-gunned by *La Tribune*. As soon as the *Unicorn* returned to port with her prize, Capt. Williams received the honour of knighthood, so that Mrs Austen's niece was now Lady Williams and Jane was moved to refer to her cousin's husband as 'his royal Highness Sir Thomas Williams', in one of her letters written a few weeks later in September.[9]

Jane was then staying at Rowling, having arrived there in August after travelling from Steventon via London in the company of Edward and Frank, who was once again on shore leave awaiting a new posting.[10] On the journey down to Kent she had stopped off at Greenwich, at Henry's request, to meet Mary Pearson, and Henry was anxious that she should return the same way and take Miss Pearson with her to Steventon to introduce her to the rest of the family. Jane was of course happy to oblige Henry if she could, but warned Cassandra:

If Miss Pearson should return with me, pray be careful not to expect too much Beauty. I will not pretend to say that on a first veiw, she quite answered the opinion I had formed of her. – My Mother I am sure will be disappointed, if she does not take great care. From what I remember of her picture, it is no great resemblance.[11]

The weeks at Rowling passed away very comfortably in fine September weather – almost too fine for Jane's taste: 'What dreadful Hot weather we have! – It keeps one in a continual state of Inelegance.'

There was much contact with Edward's in-laws, the large Bridges family, including an impromptu dance at Goodnestone on 3 September, and other social calls were exchanged, as Jane reported to Cassandra in her four letters surviving from the period of this visit. These letters show that even at the age of twenty Jane had already developed her power of shrewd social observation and the ability to record her perceptions in terse elliptical comments which, like Japanese *haiku* verses, simultaneously inform and yet intrigue the reader still further. 'Lady Hales, with her two youngest daughters, have been to see us. Caroline is not grown at all coarser than she was, nor Harriet at all more delicate.'[12] 'We have been very gay since I wrote last; dining at Nackington, returning by Moonlight, and everything quite in Stile, not to mention Mr Claringbould's Funeral which we saw go by on Sunday.' On the way to Nackington she was reminded of her visit two years ago and the charms of Mr Edward Taylor:

We went by Bifrons, & I contemplated with a melancholy pleasure, the abode of Him, on whom I once fondly doated . . . Miss Fletcher and I were very thick, but I am the thinnest of the two – She wore her purple Muslin, which is pretty enough, tho' it does not become her complexion. There are two Traits in her Character which are pleasing; namely, she admires Camilla, & drinks no cream in her Tea.[13]

Fanny Burney – or Madame d'Arblay as she then was – had advertised her new novel *Camilla* for subscription in 1795 and it is possible that the Austens' cousins, the Cookes of Great Bookham, who were neighbours of the d'Arblays when the latter were living there from 1793 to 1797, had canvassed their connections to obtain subscribers. Jane's name appears on the list, the subscription being one guinea for the five volumes of the work, and following its publication on 1 July 1796 she had been enjoying it very much, as is shown by her references to it in these letters of September 1796 and also by the marginal comment she made in her copy; indeed, years later she was still of the opinion that the character of Sir Hugh Tyrold was extremely well drawn, and that Madame d'Arblay was the very best of English novelists.[14]

Jane whiled away some more of her time by sewing shirts for Edward, playing with his children – there was now a third baby, George, born in November 1795, who was her especial favourite during his infancy – and practising her music, so as not to fall behind in her studies and disappoint her tutor, Mr Chard, when she returned home. The visit ended in some disarray, however, as Frank was suddenly told of his appointment to a new 32-gun frigate just launched at Deptford, HMS *Triton*, and had to leave Rowling almost immediately upon receipt of this news.[15] It seems probable that Edward took Jane home to Steventon at the end of the month, but there is no further information as to whether Miss Pearson went with them. If she did, her introduction to the Austen family cannot have proved successful, for within a few weeks she broke off her engagement to Henry. He went to London and sought sympathy from Eliza, who told Phylly:

Our Cousin Henry Austen has been in Town he looks thin & ill – I hear his late intended is a most intolerable Flirt, and reckoned to give herself great Airs – The person who mentioned this to me says She is a pretty wicked looking Girl with bright Black Eyes which pierce thro & thro, No wonder the poor young Man's heart could not withstand them.[16]

James, meanwhile, having given up hope of winning Eliza, had been dividing his attentions between two Marys – Mary Harrison of Andover on the one hand and the family's old friend, Mary Lloyd, on the other. Jane was equally happy with the idea of either of the two as a new sister-in-law, and wrote from Kent to Cassandra: 'Let me know . . . which of the Marys will carry the day with my Brother James.'[17] Mary Lloyd came to stay for several weeks at Steventon in the autumn, and this close contact enabled James to come to a decision, for he proposed to her in November. Mrs Austen was delighted and wrote a warm letter of welcome:

Mr Austen & Myself desire you will accept our best Love, and that you will believe us truly sincere when we assure you that we feel the most heartfelt satisfaction at the prospect we have of adding you to the Number of our very good Children. Had the Election been mine, you, my dear Mary, are the person I should have chosen for James's Wife, Anna's Mother, and my Daughter; being as certain, as I can be of anything in this uncertain World, that you will greatly increase & promote the happiness of each of the three. Pray give our Love to Mrs Lloyd & Martha, & say, we hope they are as well pleas'd with, and as much approve of, their future Son & Brother, as we with, & of, our Daughter. I look forwards to you as a real comfort to me in my old age, when Cassandra is gone into Shropshire, & Jane – the Lord knows where. Tell Martha, she too shall be my Daughter, she does me honor in the request – and Mr W: shall be my Son if he pleases – don't be alarm'd my dear Martha, I have kept & will keep your secret as close if I had been entrusted with it; which I do assure you I never was, but found it out by my own Sprack Wit – but as we are now all of one family there is no occasion I should keep it any longer a secret from herself.[18]

It is interesting to note that, while Mrs Austen evidently had no doubt in her own mind that Cassandra would live peacefully with Tom Fowle in one of Lord Craven's Shropshire parishes, she recognised that there was some unique quality in her younger daughter which seemed to prevent so easy a forecast of her future life being made.

Eliza, who had no jealousy in her nature, was also delighted to hear of James's engagement, and as usual discussed this event with Phylly:

Has Cassandra informed You of the Wedding which is soon to take place in the family? James has chosen a second Wife in the person of Miss Mary Floyd [*sic*] who is not either rich or handsome, but very sensible & good humoured – you have perhaps heard of the family for they occupied my Uncle's house at Deane six or seven years since, and the eldest [*sic*] Sister is married to Mr Fulwar Fowle who is Brother to Cassandra's intended: Jane seems much pleased with the match, and it is natural she should, having long known & liked the Lady.[19]

James and Mary were married in her home parish of Hurstbourne Tarrant on 17 January 1797:

> Cold was the morn, & all around
> Whitened with new fallen snow the ground,
> Yet still the sun with cheering beam,
> Played on the hill, & vale, & stream,
> And almost gave to winter's face
> Spring's pleasing cheerfulness & grace . . .,[20]

and after having to leave Deane parsonage when James brought his first wife there, Mary now returned to be its mistress as his second wife. On 22 February James took Mary to The Vyne to introduce her to Mr and Mrs Chute, and the latter wrote to her sister:

This morning was absolutely devoted to receiving company . . . first Mr and Mrs James Austen, a bridal visit; she is perfectly unaffected, and very pleasant; I like her. Was it not for the smallpox which has scarred and seamed her face dreadfully, her countenance would be pleasing; to my near-sighted eyes at a little distance she looked to advantage . . .[21]

Although the Austens were genuinely pleased that James should marry again, it was recognised that

this marriage [was] a more imprudent one than the first, for the very small fortune the lady possessed she insisted should be spent in paying the gentleman's debts, and he had nothing to settle on her to provide for a second family unless his uncle Mr Leigh Perrot did something for him. I do not think the wedding could have taken place had not General Mathew been willing to continue the 100£ a year he had allowed his daughter as a maintenance for his poor little Grandchild.[22]

James and Mary eventually had two children – James Edward (1798–1874) and Caroline Mary Craven (1805–80) – and Caroline recalled:

The intimacy with the Mathews continued more than might have been expected, under the circumstances, for the General was one of my brother's godfathers. My mother was a frequent guest at Clanville, and was treated with great consideration by General Mathew, but said she never could get over the fear of him; he was a man whose word was undisputed law to his whole family.[23]

No letters of Jane's survive between 18 September 1796 and 8 April 1798, and the family chronicle for this period has to be compiled from other sources. A brief memorandum scrap, made many years later by Cassandra,[24] shows that Jane started writing *First Impressions* (the prototype *Pride and Prejudice*) in October 1796 and continued work on this until August 1797. So far as is known, this was her first attempt at writing a full-length novel in a straightforward narrative form and it was originally rather longer than *Pride and Prejudice*, for she 'lopt and cropt' the text when finally revising it for publication.[25] Like all her other works, Jane read this one aloud to the family, thinking that little Anna, then aged three and a half and playing about in the room, would not bother to listen.

Listen however I did with so much interest, & with so much talk afterwards about 'Jane & Elizabeth' that it was resolved for prudence sake, to read no more of the story aloud in my hearing. This was related to me years afterwards, when the

Novel had been published; & it was supposed that the names might recall to my recollection that early impression.[26]

As Jane used family Christian names for several of her characters, it could well have puzzled and shocked the Austens' neighbours if Anna had babbled out that Jane loved Mr Bingley but Elizabeth had been snubbed at a dance by Mr Darcy.

But in the middle of the family's amusement with *First Impressions* and their satisfaction at James's marriage, came news that changed the course of Cassandra's life. She would now never live in Shropshire as Mrs Austen had so confidently predicted, for instead of Tom Fowle's long-awaited return from the West Indies, they heard that he had died of yellow fever off St Domingo in February 1797 and had been buried at sea. On 3 May Eliza wrote to Phylly:

I have just received a letter from Steventon where they are all in great Affliction (as I suppose You have heard) for the death of Mr Fowle, The Gentleman to whom our Cousin Cassandra was engaged – He was expected home this Month, from St Domingo where he had accompanied Lord Craven, but Alas instead of his arrival news were received of his Death – This is a very severe stroke to the whole family, and particularly to poor Cassandra for whom I feel more than I can express – Indeed I am most sincerely grieved at this Event & the Pain which it must occasion our worthy Relations – Jane says that her Sister behaves with a degree of resolution & Propriety which no common mind could evince in so trying a situation.[27]

Lord Craven is reported to have said afterwards that had he known of Tom's engagement he would never have allowed him to go to so dangerous a climate. Poor Tom had done the best he could for his fiancée before setting off on his last journey, by leaving her his limited savings of £1,000; if invested in Government stocks this sum could provide Cassandra with an income of about £35 a year which, while not enough to live on, would at least make her slightly less dependent upon family charity should she remain unmarried.

Cassandra's lot in life did indeed turn out to be spinsterhood; without in any way becoming a melancholy recluse, she evidently felt that no other man could replace Tom in her affections, so that although she continued to take her place in society and go to dances with Jane, the family gradually came to realise that she preferred to stay single. From now on all Cassandra's attentions were given to her immediate family circle – taking over more of the household responsibilities as her mother grew older, frequently visiting Edward and his rapidly increasing family in Kent, and acting as the recipient and inspiration of Jane's chatty, witty letters whenever the sisters were

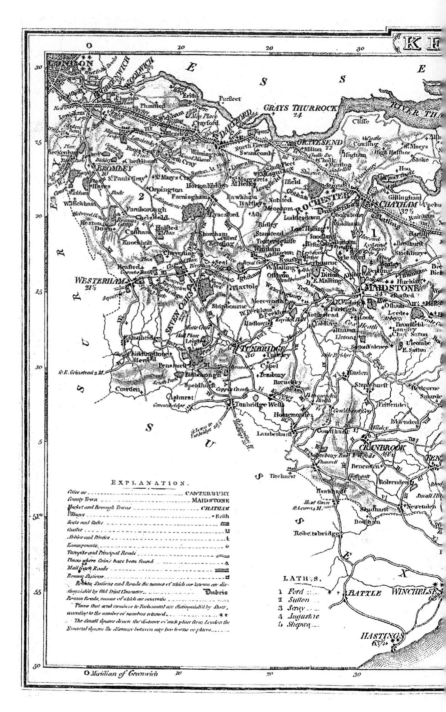

Plate 16 Map of Kent, taken from *A Journey round the Coast of Kent*
(L. Fussell, London, 1818).

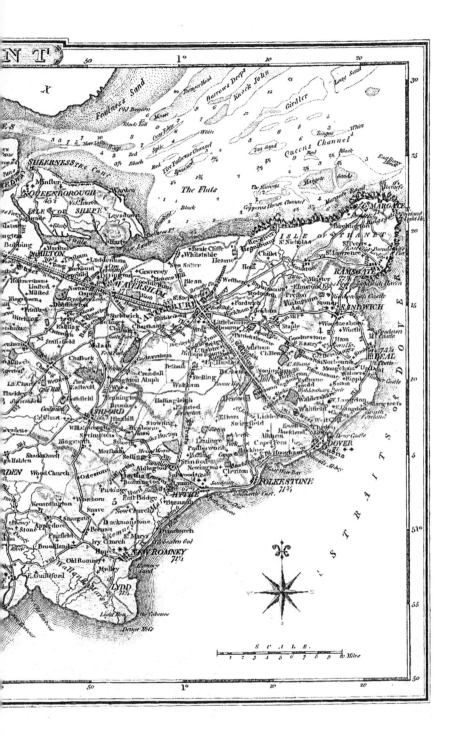

separated. As the years passed Cassandra and Jane drew ever more closely together in spirit – 'They seemed to lead a life to themselves within the general family life, which was shared only by each other. I will not say their true, but their <u>full</u>, feelings and opinions were known only to themselves. They alone fully understood what each had suffered and felt and thought.'[28]

Cassandra's bereavement must have caused some delay in Jane's work on *First Impressions*, but when it was eventually finished in August 1797 the family liked it so much that Mr Austen thought it should be published. He therefore wrote on 1 November to the London publisher Thomas Cadell:

I have in my possession a Manuscript Novel, comprised in three Vols. about the length of Miss Burney's Evelina. As I am well aware of what consequence it is that a work of this sort should make it's first Appearance under a respectable name I apply to you. Shall be much obliged therefore if you will inform me whether you chuse to be concerned in it; What will be the expence of publishing at the Author's risk; & what you will venture to advance for the Property of it, if on a perusal, it is approved of? Should your answer give me encouragement I will send you the Work.

Across the top of this letter is Cadell's brief note: 'declined by Return of Post.'[29]

As Jane was very modest in her own assessment of her work, she probably had never seriously expected, despite her family's praise, that her book would be accepted for publication; so this refusal in no way discouraged her from her next project – that of rewriting *Elinor and Marianne* into *Sense and Sensibility*. This she immediately embarked upon, in November 1797 according to Cassandra's recollection;[30] the task must have occupied her until well into the following year, for she was almost at once interrupted when Mr Leigh-Perrot came to Steventon to escort his sister and nieces to Bath, as Mrs Austen felt her health would benefit by taking the waters. This is Jane's first recorded visit to Bath, but it is possible she had gone there in earlier years; although Dr Cooper had left Bath in 1783 following his wife's death, the Leigh-Perrots had begun to pay visits to the spa for the sake of their health,[31] and on one occasion at least had lodged in Bond Street for six months, so a similar invitation to the Austens may have been extended then.[32] The National Portrait Gallery in London has a silhouette of a girl or young woman which by reason of its provenance seems quite likely to be that of Jane Austen,[33] and it may have been executed by a Bath artist[34] either during this present visit or a little later when Jane was actually living in Bath. In 1797 the Leigh-Perrots were lodging in Paragon Buildings, where the Austens arrived on a gloomy November afternoon and stayed for about a month. Jane was able to tell Eliza that this visit had proved very beneficial to Mrs Austen, and when she went home she took with her Mr Leigh-Perrot's gift of Hume's *History of England* from his own library.[35]

On returning home for Christmas, the Austens received news that may not have been entirely unexpected – that Henry and Eliza de Feuillide were engaged. It transpired that he had first proposed to her in 1795, at which time she had rejected him; and his short-lived engagement to Mary Pearson may have been an attempt to break away from the fascination his cousin held for him. Eliza, for her part, was by no means certain that she wished to marry again; but Phylly had noticed that Henry's name kept cropping up in her correspondence and prophesied that marriage would follow. In July 1797 Eliza had been evasive on the subject:

As to your enquiry concerning another youth, I have to say that I believe his Match with a certain Friend of ours, which I know You looked upon as fixed, will never take place – For my own part I think the young Man ill used but the Lady is so well pleased with her present situation that She cannot find in her Heart to change it, and says in her giddy way that independance and the homage of half a dozen are preferable to subjection and the attachment of a single individual . . . I am more & more convinced that She is not at all calculated for sober Matrimony.[36]

However, during August and September Eliza removed her funds from the trusteeship of Mr Austen and Mr Woodman and took them into her own hands, and then on 26 December 1797 wrote to her godfather:

As I flatter myself You still take an interest in my welfare, I think it incumbent on me to acquaint You with a circumstance by which it must be materially influenced. I have consented to an Union with my Cousin Captn Austen who has the honor of being known to You. – He has been for some time in Possession of a comfortable Income, and the excellence of his Heart, Temper, & Understanding, together with his steady attachment to me, his Affection for my little Boy, and disinterested concurrence in the disposal of my Property, in favor of this latter, have at length induced me to an acquiescence which I have withheld for more than two years.[37]

The marriage took place on 31 December 1797 in London at Marylebone parish church, and Eliza went off with Henry to follow the drum – or rather, to enjoy the social life in which the Oxfordshire Militia engaged while they were stationed in East Anglia.[38] Mr Austen was evidently very pleased by his son's choice, and made a gift of £40 to the regimental funds so that the other officers could join in the wedding festivities.[39]

When the news of this wedding became known in the Steventon neighbourhood, it coincided with Mr Austen's purchase of a new carriage, or else the repainting of his old one, and in later years Anna recorded some local gossip on the subject:

About the time of Mr Henry Austen's marriage with his first Wife his Father set up a carriage which, not unnaturally, bore on its pannels [*sic*] the family crest: namely, a Stag on a Crown Mural. The latter circumstance was accounted for, in his own way, by a neighbouring Squire, who reported that 'Mr Austen had put a coronet on his carriage because of his son's being married to a French Countess –'[40]

This Christmas of 1797 might have proved a romantic one for Jane as well, for Madam Lefroy – perhaps trying to make amends for nipping in the bud the flirtation with Tom Lefroy the previous year – had been doing a little matchmaking for her young friend with a more eligible gentleman. This year she invited to Ashe the Revd Samuel Blackall (1771–1842), a tall, learned young Fellow of Emmanuel College, Cambridge – older than Tom, and with every expectation of acquiring a rich college living in the not too distant future. There is no evidence as to what she told Jane about him beforehand, but she seems to have assured Mr Blackall that Mr Austen's younger daughter was well worth his consideration as a suitable wife. Unfortunately, although Mr Blackall was basically good-humoured and kind-hearted (and a year or two later two little girls in Cambridge liked him well enough to invite him to their Twelfth Night tea-party and to send him a Valentine thereafter),[41] he was unskilled at courtship and his pompous manner and loud didactic conversation, so far from attracting Jane, seem to have reduced her to stunned silence. His visit in 1797 was apparently only brief and Madam Lefroy urged him in the following months to come again for the Christmas of 1798, to which he replied: 'It would give me particular pleasure to have an opportunity of improving my acquaintance with that family [the Austens] – with a hope of creating to myself a nearer interest. But at present I cannot indulge any expectation of it.' Jane was sardonically grateful for this news:

This is rational enough; there is less love and more sense in it than sometimes appeared before, and I am very well satisfied. It will all go on exceedingly well, and decline away in a very reasonable manner. There seems no likelihood of his coming into Hampshire this Christmas, and it is therefore most probable that our indifference will soon be mutual, unless his regard, which appeared to spring from knowing nothing of me at first, is best supported by never seeing me. Mrs Lefroy made no remarks on the letter, nor did she indeed say anything about him as relative to me. Perhaps she thinks she has said too much already.[42]

Mr Blackall had certainly impressed his egocentric personality on Jane's memory, though not in the way he could have wished; for when he eventually did marry a Miss Susannah Lewis in 1813, she commented to Frank:

I should very much like to know what sort of a Woman she is. He was a peice of Perfection, noisy Perfection himself which I always recollect with regard. – We had noticed a few months before his succeeding to a College Living, the very Living which we remembered his talking of & wishing for; an exceeding good one, Great Cadbury in Somersetshire. – I would wish Miss Lewis to be of a silent turn & rather ignorant, but naturally intelligent & wishing to learn; – fond of cold veal pies, green tea in the afternoon, & a green window blind at night.[43]

In the spring of 1798 the threat of a full-scale invasion of England became very real, because Napoleon's army was encamped along the French coast and propaganda statements were being issued itemising the vast quantities of soldiers and armaments which would soon be transported across the Channel.[44] The English Government therefore passed the Defence of the Realm Act in April 1798, the purpose of which was to evaluate the country's resources in terms of the local manpower, weaponry, equipment and stores that might be available to resist such an attack. Mr Austen, aided by one of the literate villagers, completed the official form regarding his parish of Steventon; this shows that out of the total population of approximately 150, there were 39 able-bodied men, but armed only with their agricultural implements, to defend the remaining non-combatants, or else to assist with their evacuation in the 12 wagons and five carts to which the 34 draft horses could be harnessed.[45]

Nevertheless, until such an invasion actually occurred, there was no reason why life in the English countryside, even in those counties bordering the Channel, should not continue in its normal routine, and it does not appear that the Austens allowed their activities to be curtailed or disarranged in any way. Jane's work on *Sense and Sensibility* was temporarily interrupted again at Easter 1798 when Mr William Hampson Walter, who had been senile for the past year, died peacefully at his home in Kent. Cassandra – who by now had become the family scribe – was away from Steventon, so it fell to Jane to write the formal letter of condolence from the Austens to Phylly Walter.[46] Mr Walter's death came as no surprise, but later in the year a calamity occurred – on 9 August Mrs Austen's niece, Lady Williams, was driving herself through Newport in the Isle of Wight when a runaway dray-horse crashed into her little light whiskey. She was thrown out and died a few hours later without regaining consciousness. Apart from her visits to Steventon before her marriage, Jane Williams had kept affectionately in touch with the Austens thereafter, staying with them again while Sir Thomas was away at sea in September 1796, and her death must have been a severe shock to them, especially to Jane and Cassandra, who were her friends and contemporaries.[47] However, as no letters of Jane's survive between those of 8 April and 24 October 1798, her reactions to this tragic accident are unknown.

The Austens indeed may not have received the sad news until several days after the event, for during August they travelled to Kent to make their first recorded visit to Godmersham, where Edward had recently removed from Rowling. The previous autumn the widowed Mrs Knight had decided that she wished Edward to enter into possession of her late husband's estates during her lifetime, instead of waiting to inherit after her death. On first learning of her intentions Edward demurred:

I am confident we should never be happy at Godmersham whilst you were living at a smaller and less comfortable House – or in reflecting that you had quitted your own favourite Mansion where I have so often heard you say your whole Happiness was center'd, and had retired to a residence and Style of Living to which you have been ever unaccustomed, and this to enrich us.

Mrs Knight, however, had carefully considered the matter before making her intentions known, and his letter only confirmed her resolution that she was acting correctly:

From the time that my partiality for you induced Mr Knight to treat you as our adopted Child, I have felt for you the tenderness of a Mother, & never have you appeared more deserving of affection than at this time; to reward your merit, therefore, & to place you in a situation where your many excellent qualities will be call'd forth & render'd useful to the neighbourhood, is the fondest wish of my heart. Many circumstances attached to large landed Possessions, highly gratifying to a Man, are entirely lost on me at present; but when I see you in the enjoyment of them, I shall, if possible, feel my gratitude to my beloved Husband redoubled, for having placed in my hands, the power of bestowing happiness on one so very dear to me.[48]

Mrs Knight therefore retired to White Friars, a large old house in Canterbury, retaining an income of £2,000 a year from the Godmersham property, and Edward and his family took up residence there instead. The Austens had probably visited Godmersham on occasions during the lives of Mr Knight and his father, but as Cassandra and Jane and their parents drove up to the house in late August 1798 they could for the first time see Edward step forward to receive them as its owner.

Godmersham was and is a handsome Palladian mansion, of red brick with ashlar dressings, about eight miles from Canterbury and set in a landscaped park in the Stour valley with wooded downland rising behind it. Mr Thomas Brodnax-May-Knight had built the centre block, seven bays wide, in 1732, and not long before his death in 1781 had added lower two-storeyed wings

Plate 17 Godmersham Park, north front.

to the left and right of the main building. The eastern wing contained 'a most excellent library', and from the rear of the house could be seen 'delightful prospects of the hill and pleasure grounds';[49] on the hill was placed a summer-house in the form of a Doric Temple, with its associated Temple Walk, another summer-house was a Gothic Seat or Hermitage, the River Walk had its Bathing House, and a narrow path sheltered by tall lime trees led through the park to the little flint-built Norman church of St Lawrence.[50] Inside the house the best rooms were the hall and drawing-room, which were splendidly decorated with white-painted plasterwork and carving and marble chimney-pieces – but the cost of creating these rooms seems to have been in excess even of Mr Knight's finances, for the remainder of the house was more simply furnished. Jane's letters mention the uses and decorations of some of the other rooms, but these are not now identifiable due to structural alterations in the intervening years.[51]

As the sisters were staying at Godmersham together, no letters are available to provide precise information as to the events of August and September, but later in the year Jane referred to having attended balls at Ashford which she had not much enjoyed due to the crowded room and hot weather.[52] It seems probable that during these leisurely summer days she finished rewriting *Sense and Sensibility* and then, recalling her visit to Bath the previous year, embarked upon *Northanger Abbey*. The heroine's name was originally planned to be 'Susan', and the novel was known to the family simply by this title; later on she became 'Catherine' Morland, but the final title was not given until publication many years later. Cassandra's memorandum states 'North-hanger Abby [*sic*] was written about the years 98 & 99',[53] and at the end of October Jane specifically mentions that her father was reading the newly published *The Midnight Bell* by Francis Lathom, one of the 'horrid' novels that Isabella Thorpe recommends to Catherine Morland.[54]

During the Austens' visit a fifth baby was born to Edward and Elizabeth – William, on 10 October, the first of their children to be born at Godmersham – and when Mr and Mrs Austen and Jane set off for Hampshire on 24 October Cassandra stayed behind in order to tend Elizabeth and run the household while she recovered from the birth. Cassandra did not return to Steventon until March 1799, and ten of Jane's letters survive of those written to her during this six months' separation. The Austens travelled home via Sittingbourne, Dartford, Staines and Basingstoke, and unluckily the swaying and jolting of the coach during the three-day journey proved too much for Mrs Austen's constitution; upon reaching home she took to her bed with what Mr Lyford the Basingstoke surgeon thought must be incipient jaundice: 'He wants my mother to look yellow and to throw out a rash, but she will do neither.'[55] Jane too, therefore, had to act as nurse and housekeeper for five weeks before her mother was sufficiently recovered to take her place at the family dining-table again, so naturally her letters during November 1798 are much concerned with the details of her mother's health.[56]

To add to her problems, she could not ask for assistance with nursing Mrs Austen from the relations closest to hand at Deane, for Mary Lloyd's first child was expected very soon; the monthly nurse was in residence and Mary's old friend Miss Debary of Hurstbourne Tarrant had come to supervise the household.[57] On 18 November Jane was able to finish off a letter to Cassandra with the good news: 'I have just received a note from James to say that Mary was brought to bed last night, at eleven o'clock, of a fine little boy, and that everything is going on very well'[58] and a week later she added: 'I had only a glimpse of the child, who was asleep; but Miss Debary told me that his eyes were large, dark, and handsome.'[59] So did Jane announce, all unwittingly, the birth of her future biographer, James Edward Austen-Leigh, who in 1870 was to publish the *Memoir* of his aunt from which all later biographical works have stemmed. He was christened at Deane on New Year's Day 1799, and Jane herself made the entry in the parish register.[60] He was known in the family as 'Edward' to distinguish him from his father, but in some of Jane's earlier letters had to be further distinguished as 'Little' Edward to avoid confusion with his uncle and cousin of the same name.

James Austen's second marriage was to prove, over the years, something of a mixed blessing to his family, and Mrs Austen's anticipation of universal happiness was not entirely fulfilled. He himself was very happy with Mary Lloyd and wrote poems in her praise: 'Anxious and earnest to fulfil / The claims of Mother, friend & wife' – persuading himself in the end that he had never loved anybody else except her;[61] but poor Mary, it seems, could never forget that he had not only been married previously to Anne Mathew but had also wanted to marry Eliza de Feuillide, and it was noticed in the family that to the last days of her life Mary continued to dislike and speak ill of Eliza.[62] These memories, coupled with the consciousness of her pockmarked, ruined face and her worries over their limited income, left her with underlying feelings of jealous insecurity that on occasion made her irritatingly tactless and officious. Jane and Cassandra in particular, who had liked Mary as a friend, found her less likeable as a sister-in-law, and in some of Jane's letters there are references to her written in a distinctly exasperated tone.[63]

The relationship between Mary Lloyd and Anna was also strained; James, presumably afraid of upsetting Mary by appearing to give too much attention to the child of his first marriage, went to the opposite extreme and almost ignored Anna. She had still some shadowy recollection of her own mother

as a tall and slender lady dressed in white; but from her father she never even heard her name, not a word as to look or character or habits or of her love for her child . . . [her stepmother] was a clever cheerful hospitable woman, generous where money was concerned though a careful & excellent manager. She was also warm hearted & would take any trouble for her friends. But her manner was abrupt & sharp, & she had a tartness of temper from which even her own children occasionally suffered. She did not love her stepdaughter, & she slighted her, she made her of no estimation, & the last & least in her father's house. She was very far indeed from being the cruel stepmother of fiction, & perhaps in truth of former times, but certainly it never entered into her imagination that she was to make no difference between her and her own children . . . I do not suppose her father was consciously unkind to her, but his heart was entirely absorbed in his two younger children, especially his son . . . for his motherless child with all her loveliness, intelligence and generosity of temper, he had not affection enough to care to do her justice. She was however a most dutiful daughter and she never spoke of him but with affection, and of her stepmother but with respect.[64]

James and Mary lived at Deane parsonage from 1797 until the spring of 1801, and Anna's earliest memories of her Austen aunts date to these years at the turn of the century.

I recollect the frequent visits of my two Aunts, & how they walked in wintry weather through the sloppy lane between Steventon & Dean [*sic*] in pattens, usually worn at that time even by Gentlewomen. I remember too their bonnets: because though precisely alike in colour, shape & material, I made it a pleasure to guess, & I believe always guessed right, which bonnet & which Aunt belonged to each other – Children do not think of Aunts, or perhaps of any grown up people as young; yet at the time to which I now refer my Aunts must have been very young women – even a little later, when I might be 9 or 10 yrs. old [i.e., *c.* 1802–3] I thought it so very odd, to hear Grandpapa speak of them as 'the Girls'. 'Where are the Girls?' 'Are the Girls gone out?'[65]

Anna also remembered that her Aunt Jane 'was especially kind, writing for her the stories she invented for herself long ere she could write and telling her others of endless adventure and fun which were carried on from day to day or from visit to visit'.[66]

Cassandra and Jane were now obliged to pay their visits on foot again, for new taxes meant that the family chariot had become too expensive to use, and it was put into store before the winter of 1798.[67] Mr Austen's income from his parishes and the sale of his farm produce fluctuated unpredictably from year to year, and since he had ceased taking pupils his only other fixed income was rather less than £100 a year deriving from dividends and a small pension from the Hand-in-Hand Society.[68] However, he continued to buy books – Cowper's works, Boswell's *Tour to the Hebrides* and *Life of Johnson*, and *Arthur Fitz-Albini*, a novel just published by their one-time neighbour Egerton Brydges, by which Mr Austen was disappointed as it was so poorly written.[69] Jane too thought it was very bad taste on Egerton's part to mock his Kentish neighbours by writing derogatory pen-portraits of them. Mrs Austen's cousin, Mrs Cooke of Bookham, was also dabbling in literature, and her novel *Battleridge, an historical tale founded on facts* appeared early in 1799.[70] Mrs Austen, for her part, may have subscribed to a new journal, *The Lady's Monthly Museum*, for in its first and second volumes (1798–9) there appeared a series of moralising essays called 'Effects of Mistaken Synonymy', in one of which the neat phrase 'Sense and Sensibility' was printed as a full headline.[71] Wherever Jane happened to see this journal, it must at once have struck her that the phrase would make a far more relevant and memorable title for her lately finished novel than the purely neutral one of the heroines' names, *Elinor and Marianne*.

Her work on *Northanger Abbey* in the autumn of 1798 probably had
to be laid aside whilst tending her mother, and apart from news of
Mrs Austen's health Jane's letters to Cassandra at the end of the year were
much concerned with the careers of her sailor brothers. Charles, after his
success in the *Unicorn* in 1796, had followed Captain Sir Thomas Williams
into the 44-gun *Endymion*, and had then been promoted to a lieutenancy
in the little 16-gun *Scorpion*. He had now been on the *Scorpion* for two
years and, like Frank before him, was anxious to join a larger ship where
there would be more chance of active service; Frank, for his part, had been a
lieutenant for six years and was hoping for promotion. Mr Austen therefore
sought patronage for his sons through another useful family connection –
James's father-in-law, General Mathew, had a niece who was the wife of
Admiral Gambier. The Admiral in turn consulted Lord Spencer, First Lord
of the Admiralty; and on 28 December Jane dashed off a hurried joyful
note: 'Frank is made. – He was yesterday raised to the Rank of Commander, & appointed to the Petterel Sloop, now at Gibraltar . . . Lieut: Charles
John Austen is removed to the Tamer [*sic*] Frigate – this comes from the
Admiral . . . I cannot write any more now, but I have written enough to
make you very happy . . .'[72]

Frank was then away in the Mediterranean but Charles, in home waters,
managed to get leave and visited Steventon and the Fowles at Kintbury in
January 1799 before joining HMS *Tamar* at Deal. Now nearly twenty, he
had grown tall and handsome – Madam Lefroy thought him handsomer
than Henry – and had adopted the modern style of cutting his hair short
and wearing it unpowdered, a departure from tradition of which his brother
Edward rather disapproved.[73] To Jane's disappointment he was unable to
reach Steventon in time to accompany her to Lady Dorchester's ball at
Kempshot on 8 January, and had to leave again only a few days later.[74]

This series of Jane's letters ends with that of 21 January 1799 and, as
referred to therein, Cassandra probably came back from Godmersham in
March, for when Mr and Mrs Chute dined at Steventon on 26 March they
found both Jane and Cassandra at home; in return Jane – but for some
reason apparently not Cassandra – dined at The Vyne on 19 April.[75] The
following month Edward, who had been unwell the previous winter and
feared he was beginning to develop gout, came to Steventon with Elizabeth
and their two eldest children, and while Cassandra stayed at home with
Mr Austen, Mrs Austen and Jane joined his party and went on to Bath,
arriving there on the overcast wet afternoon of Friday, 17 May. Edward had
rented No. 13 Queen Square, and Jane sat down at once to tell Cassandra
about it:

We are exceedingly pleased with the House; the rooms are quite as large as we expected, Mrs Bromley [the landlady] is a fat woman in mourning, & a little black kitten runs about the Staircase . . . I like our situation very much – it is far more chearful than Paragon, & the prospect from the Drawingroom window at which I now write, is rather picturesque, as it commands a perspective veiw of the left side of Brock Street, broken by three Lombardy Poplars in the Garden of the last house in Queen's Parade.[76]

The family party stayed in Bath until the end of June, and Jane's four surviving letters tell of Edward's health: 'He drinks at the Hetling Pump, is to bathe tomorrow, & try Electricity on Tuesday';[77] of the latest fashions in millinery: 'Flowers are very much worn, & Fruit is still more the thing. – Eliz: has a bunch of Strawberries, & I have seen Grapes, Cherries, Plumbs & Apricots – There are likewise Almonds & raisins, french plumbs & Tamarinds at the Grocers, but I have never seen any of them in hats';[78] of walks in the countryside: 'We took a very charming walk from 6 to 8 up Beacon Hill, & across some fields to the Village of Charlcombe, which is sweetly situated in a little green Valley, as a Village with such a name ought to be';[79] and of dining with Edward's Kentish neighbour, Mr Evelyn of St Clere, then lodging in Queen's Parade. Mr Evelyn had 'all his life thought more of Horses than of anything else',[80] and on his advice Edward now bought an expensive pair of black coach-horses. Jane's uncle and aunt are only briefly mentioned in these four letters, for Mr Leigh-Perrot's gout was now chronic and at this time he was mostly housebound with his feet wrapped in flannel. The couple had given up hiring temporary lodgings and were now permanently renting No. 1 Paragon Buildings,[81] dividing their time between Bath and Scarlets. Jane called at Paragon on 16 June, and perhaps it was on this occasion that Mr Leigh-Perrot gave her from his own library Bell's *Travels from St Petersburg* and Goldsmith's *An history of the Earth*, as well as *Orlando Furioso* and Thomson's poetical works.[82] It seems that the trip to Bath did benefit Edward, for following his return to Kent no other illness of his is ever mentioned in Jane's letters.

In the first half of this year there occur in Jane's correspondence the earliest brief references to her adult literary work, showing that since its completion in August 1797 *First Impressions* had become an established favourite in the family circle. While Cassandra was at Godmersham in January Jane acknowledged a request from her: 'I do not wonder at your wanting to read *first impressions* again, so seldom as you have gone through it, & that so long ago'[83] and six months later from Bath she teasingly told her sister: 'I would not let Martha read First Impressions again upon any account, & am very glad that I did not leave it in your power. – She is very cunning, but I see through her design; – she means to publish it from Memory, & one more perusal must enable her to do it. –'[84] This visit to Bath provided Jane with further local colour for *Northanger Abbey*, which was presumably finished about midsummer 1799, before the family began a round of holiday visits to their various cousins – the Cookes at Great Bookham, the Leighs at Adlestrop and the Coopers at Harpsden.[85]

Their stay at the latter place, in August to September, was by way of leavetaking, for the Coopers were on the verge of departing for Staffordshire. Earlier in the year the Hon. Mary Leigh of Stoneleigh had offered the family living of Hamstall Ridware to Edward Cooper:

Yesterday came a letter to my mother from Edward Cooper to announce, not the birth of a child, but of a living; for Mrs Leigh has begged his acceptance of the Rectory of Hamstall-Ridware in Staffordshire, vacant by Mr Johnson's death. We collect from his letter that he means to reside there, in which he shows his wisdom. Staffordshire is a good way off; so we shall see nothing more of them till, some fifteen years hence, the Miss Coopers are presented to us, fine, jolly, handsome, ignorant girls. The living is valued at 140£ a year, but perhaps it may be improvable.[86]

Mrs Lybbe-Powys looked after her four grandchildren while Edward and Caroline went up to furnish their new home, and the Coopers finally moved north in October 1799.[87]

After their summer journeyings, the Austens were at home again for the seasonal festivities during the autumn and winter of 1799–1800; and thanks to Mrs Austen's penchant for versifying, there exists a verbal snapshot of the assembly ball held at Basingstoke on Thursday, 7 November 1799. The little poem was written down years later by Mrs Austen's granddaughter Anna, who described it as being 'Sent by Mrs Austen to one of her Daughters staying from home', though unfortunately she does not specify whether it was Jane or Cassandra who was the absentee. Certainly, two members of the Austen family attended the ball – perhaps James and Mary Lloyd, or possibly James escorting one of his sisters – and Mrs Austen, after hearing all the details of the evening from her children, converted them into rhyme, for the benefit of her other daughter:

> I send you here a list of all
> The company who graced the ball
> Last Thursday night at Basingstoke;
> There were but six and thirty folk,
> Altho' the Evening was so fine.
> First then, the couple from the Vine;
> Next, Squire Hicks and his fair spouse –

They came from Mr Bramston's house,
With Madam, and her maiden Sister;
(Had she been absent, who'd have miss'd her?)
And fair Miss Woodward, that sweet singer,
For Mrs Bramston liked to bring her;
With Alethea too, and Harriet
They came in Mrs Hicks' chariot;
Perhaps they did, I am not certain.
Then there were four good folk from Worting:
For with the Clerks there came two more
Some friends of theirs, their name was Hoare.
With Mr, Mrs, Miss Lefroy
Came Henry Rice, that pleasant boy;
And lest a title they should want,
There came Sir Colebrook and Sir Grant.
Miss Eyre of Sherfield and her Mother;
One Miss from Dummer and her brother,
The mother too as chaperon;
Mr and Mrs Williamson;
Charles Powlett and his pupils twain;
Small Parson Hasker, great Squire Lane;
And Bentworth's rector, with his hat,
Unwillingly he parts from that.
Two Misses Davies with two friends –
And thus my information ends.
P.S. It would have been a better dance
But for the following circumstance –
The Dorchesters, so high in station,
Dined out that day, by invitation,
At Heckfield Heath with Squire Le Fevre;
Methinks it was not quite so clever
For one Subscriber to invite
Another, on the Assembly night;
But 'twas to meet a General Donne
His Lordship's old companion;
And as the General would not stay
They could not fix another day.[88]

This letter shows very clearly the quantity and quality of the society with whom the Austens mixed in the Steventon neighbourhood, and those families who were absent on that occasion are mentioned elsewhere as being present at other Basingstoke assemblies or private balls – Lord Portsmouth from Hurstbourne, Lord Bolton from Hackwood, the Mildmays of Dogmersfield, Portals of Freefolk, Jervoises of Herriard, Bigg-Withers of Manydown, as well as the Austens' immediate neighbours the Harwoods of Deane and the Holders of Ashe Park.

Following the Lloyd family's departure from Deane, Jane and Cassandra had found other close friends in Elizabeth, Catherine and Alethea Bigg, the three younger daughters of Mr Lovelace Bigg-Wither of Manydown Park.[89] Manydown was an old manor house near Worting, on the Basingstoke/Andover road, owned by the Bishopric of Winchester, and of which the Wither family had been tenants for centuries; Jane and Cassandra often visited here and the names of their friends appear frequently in Jane's letters. Elizabeth became Mrs Heathcote and was the mother of Sir William Heathcote of Hursley Park (who remembered seeing Jane at a Twelfth Night party when he was a little boy), and Catherine married rather late in life the Revd Herbert Hill, uncle of the Poet Laureate Robert Southey. Some of Jane's later letters mention visits to Catherine at Streatham, then a separate village to the south of London, where Mr Hill became rector in 1810. Alethea never married and was probably for that reason all the closer to the Steventon sisters, and one of the latest of Jane's extant letters is addressed to her. The youngest of the large family was the only surviving son and heir, Harris, a tall, stammering, rather sickly youth,[90] whom his anxious father did not dare send away to school.[91] The family were not present at Basingstoke on this particular occasion, and Mrs Chute ('the couple from the Vine') noted in her diary that the ball was only 'thinly attended'.[92]

CHAPTER 9

The Leigh-Perrots and Bath, 1799–1801

Mrs Austen's brother and sister-in-law, Mr and Mrs Leigh-Perrot, had for many years now led a prosperous and uneventful life at Scarlets, their small country house at Hare Hatch, near Wargrave, in Berkshire, enjoying the respect and friendship of a large circle of acquaintances. Among those who sooner or later were neighbours of the Leigh-Perrots were Richard Lovell Edgeworth (amateur scientist and father of the novelist Maria Edgeworth), who acknowledged the help he received from Mr Leigh-Perrot in his experiments of telegraphing from Hare Hatch to Nettlebed by means of windmills;[1] and Thomas Day, author of the one-time famous moral story for children, *Sandford and Merton*. A more disreputable acquaintance was the notorious young Earl of Barrymore, who for a short period lived in Wargrave and built there an extravagant private theatre; in this, apart from dramatic productions, he held lavish parties to which all the surrounding nobility and gentry were invited. In January 1790 the Earl gave a fancy-dress masked ball and firework display, and Mr Leigh-Perrot went dressed as a 'Counsellor', while his wife was 'a strikingly elegant Pilgrim, in an Irish stuff bound with ermine, and a rich diamond cross in her high-crowned hat'.[2]

Mr Leigh-Perrot was an intelligent man with an enquiring mind, and his abilities would have stood him in good stead had he been obliged to adopt any profession; he was also of a kind and affectionate disposition, combining an easy temper with ready wit and much resolution of character. His wife did not have the same amiability of nature, but was nevertheless highly respected; she was very shrewd where financial matters were concerned, had a great idea of the claims of family ties and a keen sense of justice as between herself and others. The couple were completely devoted to each other and seemed to have no regrets at being childless, their only worries being their own increasing ill-health as time went by – Mrs Leigh-Perrot became rather deaf and developed bronchitis, and her husband suffered from gout, for which visits to Bath were prescribed. Although they entered

Plate 18 Portrait miniature, attributed to Jeremiah Meyer, of Mrs Leigh-Perrot, ?1764.

Plate 19 Portrait miniature by John Smart of Mr Leigh-Perrot, 1764.

into the social life of Bath while they were there, they much preferred their Berkshire home, as Mrs Leigh-Perrot wrote many years later in her widowhood: 'being full half the Year in Bath we wished to enjoy Scarlets the other half without Company, & we were too happy in each other, to allow us to think our retired half year the least dull . . . whilst I had him, He was the whole World to me'.[3]

Just before Jane left Bath in June 1799, she told Cassandra: 'Last Sunday We all drank tea in Paragon; my Uncle is still in his flannels, but is getting better again.'[4] By August Mr Leigh-Perrot was sufficiently recovered from this latest gouty attack to be walking about once more in the town with his wife, and on 8 August was in the Pump Room at midday for his medicinal drink while his wife bought some black lace to trim a cloak. For this purpose she went to a haberdasher's shop known as Smith's, on the corner of Bath and Stall Streets, where she had enquired the day before as to their latest stocks of lace. Although she did not know it, the shop was in financial straits – Smith and his wife had separated, he had absconded and been declared bankrupt and the business was now managed by Smith's sister-in-law, Elizabeth Gregory, under the control of William Gye and Lacon Lamb, the trustees for Smith's creditors. Gye had a printing business in Westgate Buildings, Bath, and was himself of doubtful reputation; it seems that he and Miss Gregory, together with her lover, Charles Filby, whom she officially employed as her shop-assistant, decided on the night of 7 August to blackmail Mrs Leigh-Perrot when she called again to buy the lace in which she had expressed interest. On 8 August, therefore, as she bought the black lace she wanted, a card of *white* lace was included in her parcel; when the couple walked past the shop again half an hour later, Miss Gregory came out, asked Mrs Leigh-Perrot if she had any white lace in her possession and, on being shown the unopened parcel, removed from it the card of white lace and returned to her shop. Filby then ran after the Leigh-Perrots and asked for their name and address, which he was given. The couple were rather puzzled and annoyed by the episode, but assumed that some genuine mistake had occurred in the shop, and had no inkling that anything was amiss until four nights later, when they received an anonymous note addressed to 'Mrs Leigh-Perrot, Lace dealer: Your many visiting Acquaintance, before they again admit you into their houses, will think it right to know how you came by the piece of Lace stolen from Bath St., a few days ago. Your Husband is said to be privy to it.'[5]

Meanwhile Miss Gregory and Filby, after consultation with Gye, went to the Bath magistrates and laid a charge against Mrs Leigh-Perrot of stealing lace to the value of 20s.; and on Wednesday evening 14 August the highly embarrassed Mayor and magistrates, to whom she was well known socially, formally committed her to the Somerset County Gaol at Ilchester, to await trial at Taunton Assizes the following March. As the lace was valued at more than 1s., the crime of which she was accused was that of grand larceny, which at that date was punishable by death; in practice, however, if she were found guilty, she would probably be reprieved and instead transported to Botany Bay for a term of fourteen years. Upon arrival at Ilchester the Leigh-Perrots were lodged in the gaol-keeper's own house – which, while sparing them the indignity of sharing barred cells with genuine criminals, still left them in extreme discomfort. 'Governor' Scadding, as he was known locally, had a wife and five young children including a new baby, and his small house in the centre of the prison buildings was cramped, dirty and noisy. An attempt to obtain bail was refused, so the couple had to resign themselves to a seven-months' wait in squalid conditions until the end of March 1800.

It is not known when Mrs Leigh-Perrot found time or spirits to inform the Austens of her plight, for it was not until mid-September 1799 that she wrote to her Cholmeley cousins in Lincolnshire to tell them what had happened during the past month. In October and November she gave them more information:

One of my greatest Miseries here (indeed my very first) is the seeing what my dearest Husband is daily going through – Vulgarity, Dirt, Noise from Morning till Night. The People, not conscious that this can be Objectionable to anybody, fancy we are very happy, and to do them justice they mean to make us quite so[6] . . . this Room joins to a Room where the Children all lie, and not Bedlam itself can be half so noisy, besides which, as not one particle of Smoke goes up the Chimney, except you leave the door or window open, I leave you to judge of the Comfort I can enjoy in such a Room . . . No! my Good Cousin, I cannot subject even a Servant to the suffering <u>we</u> daily experience . . . My dearest Perrot with <u>his</u> sweet composure adds to <u>my</u> Philosophy; to be sure he bids fair to have his patience tried in every way he can. Cleanliness has ever been his greatest delight and yet he sees the greasy toast laid by the dirty Children on his Knees, and feels the small Beer trickle down his sleeves on its way across the table unmoved . . . <u>Mrs Scadding's Knife well licked to clean it from fried onions</u> helps me now and then – you may believe how the Mess I am helped to is disposed of – here are <u>two dogs and three Cats</u> always <u>full as hungry</u> as myself.[7]

Due to their own family commitments the Cholmeleys were unable to travel south to visit her, and in the meantime the Austens had decided that their sympathy would best be demonstrated by providing Mrs Leigh-Perrot with congenial female companionship, a decision which was mentioned by Mr Mountague Cholmeley in his letter of 11 January 1800:

You tell me that your good sister Austen has offered you one, or both, of her Daughters to continue with you during your stay at that vile Place, but you decline the kind offer as you cannot procure them Accommodation in the House with you, and you cannot let those Elegant young Women be your Inmates in a Prison nor be subject to the Inconveniences which you are obliged to put up with . . .[8]

The Cholmeleys and Austens tried instead to sustain their relatives by constant correspondence; and on 4 January 1800 Mr Leigh-Perrot presented a seed-pearl necklet to his wife as a token of his affection, with a note tucked into the case that read:

> My dearest Wife
> With thee no Days can Winter seem,
> Nor Frost nor Blast can Chill;
> Thou the soft Breeze, the Chearing Beam,
> That keeps it Summer Still.
> yours Faithfully
> lovingly & Wholly
> James Leigh Perrot.[9]

After their committal to Ilchester Mr Leigh-Perrot received two anonymous letters, the first from a servant at the Greyhound Inn in Bath and the second from one of Gye's own employees, warning that Gye was the originator of the blackmail plot and Filby his willing accomplice, and that the plotters met at the Greyhound to discuss tactics:

considerably are they disappointed that no Offer from you has been made to buy off the Witnesses against your innocent and highly injured Lady; they have tried to find some safe Method of proposing this themselves, but are afraid of each other. They are circulating the most false and injurious calumnies to prejudice Mrs Perrot in the Eye of the World; but they find she has too many Friends for this purpose to succeed to their utmost wish . . .

Another letter written about this time must have given much pleasure to the Leigh-Perrots:

White Hart, Bath. Honored Sir – You may have forgot your old postillon Ben Dunford but I shall never forget yours & my Mistresses great Goodness to me when I was taken with the small pox in your sarvice. You sent me very careful to Mothers & paid a Nurse & my Doctor, & my Board for a long time as I was bad, & when I was too bad with biles all over my Head so as I could not go to sarvice for a many weeks you maintaned me. the Famaly as I lives with be going thro Bath into Devonshere & we stops 2 days at the Inn and there I heard of the bad trick as those bad Shopkeepers has sarved my Mistress and I took the libarty of going to your House to enquire how you both do and the Housekeeper said She sent a pasel to You every Week and if I had any thing to say She coud send a letter. I hope Honored Sir you will forgive my taking such libarty to write but I wish any body could tell me how to do you & Mistress any good. I woud travel Night & Day to sarve you both. I be at all times with my humble Duty to Mistress & you Honored Sir your dutyfull Sarvant Ben Dunford.[10]

Other friends of the Leigh-Perrots wrote from Bath with sympathy and encouragement,[11] while those who did not know them repeated the rumours circulated by the blackmailers – the Revd Mr Holland, vicar of Over Stowey deep in rural Somerset, wrote in his diary on 22 March 1800:

At Stowey met Mr Symes the lawyer. He told me that Mrs Parrot [*sic*] had bought off her prosecutor. Alas, alas that money should be able to screen a person from Justice in this Kingdom so remarkable for good laws and uncorrupted Judges. She was accused of stealing lace out of a shop in Bath, is a person of considerable fortune and has a poor Jerry Sneak of a husband who adheres to her through all difficulties.[12]

As the dreary winter months passed and the time of the Assizes drew nearer, the Austens too had family problems, as Mrs Leigh-Perrot told the Cholmeleys:

My dear Affectionate Sister Austen, tho' in a state of health not equal to trials of any kind, has been with the greatest difficulty kept from me. In a letter from her a day or two ago I had the pain to hear of her Valuable Son James having had his Horse fall with him by which his Leg was broken. This is a loss indeed because he has been a perfect Son to me in Affection, and his firm Friendship all through this trying Business had taught me to look to him and his Wife (a Relation of Lord Craven's well bred and sensible) to have come to us at the Assizes. Now I can neither ask Mother or Wife to leave him nor could I accept the Offer of my Nieces – to have two Young Creatures gazed at in a public Court would cut one to the very heart.[13]

It seems that the Leigh-Perrots' other nephew, Edward Cooper, was not so sympathetic as the Austens, or else he may have written letters of 'cruel comfort',[14] for he fell out of his aunt's favour at this time and remained unforgiven for the following thirty years.[15]

The trial took place at Taunton on Saturday 29 March 1800, in the Great Hall of the old castle buildings, before a crowded court. The criminal law of England, as it then existed, made it very difficult for Mrs Leigh-Perrot to prove her innocence; she could not give evidence on oath on her own behalf, her husband was not allowed to give evidence for her and her counsel were not allowed to address the jury on her behalf but could only examine and cross-examine witnesses. Mr Leigh-Perrot had engaged the best counsel and secured his most influential acquaintance as witnesses to his wife's good character, but he was aware that if they encountered an unsympathetic jury it would be quite possible for an adverse verdict to be given. According to family tradition, he had decided that if this happened, and the sentence were transportation, he would sell his property and accompany his wife to Australia.

Miss Gregory, Filby and a junior shop-girl, Sarah Raines, told their well-rehearsed tale for the prosecution – Filby now claiming that he had *seen* Mrs Leigh-Perrot pick up the card of white lace from a box on the counter – and in response to this Mrs Leigh-Perrot was allowed to do no more than assure the jury that she was innocent of the charge. However, her lawyers were able to cast doubts on Filby's honesty and character; other witnesses testified that extra items besides their proper purchases had been included in their parcels from the shop; three Bath tradesmen spoke of Mrs Leigh-Perrot's integrity in her dealings with them; and eleven of the couple's long-standing friends from Berkshire and Bath attested to her high moral standards. The judge's summing-up lasted nearly an hour, and after a consultation of less than fifteen minutes the jury returned a verdict of 'Not Guilty', which was greeted immediately by claps of approval from the spectators. 'The trial lasted seven hours, and the scene at the acquittal was extremely affecting. The agitation and embraces of Mr and Mrs Perrot may be more easily conceived than described.'[16]

The couple returned to Bath the next day, not arriving till late at night, and in letters to her Cholmeley cousins during the following week Mrs Leigh-Perrot described the aftermath of the affair:

before 10 on Monday Morning our anxious Friends began coming in . . . my whole time has been taken up in kissing and Crying . . .[17] To be sure (as a kind Friend told us) I stand some chance of being killed by Popularity – tho' I have escaped from Villainy . . . That these Wretches had marked me for somebody timid enough to be Scared and Rich enough to pay handsomely rather than go through the terrible Proceedings of a public Trial nobody doubts; and by timing it when I had only my Husband with me they were sure that I could have no Evidence against them. Surely our boasted Laws are strangely defective – owing to this Circumstance I find no Punishment from me can attach to this Villain – and had he gone off the very day before the Trial, we should have lain under the Stigma of having bought him off without a possibility of Clearing ourselves[18] . . . my dear and Affectionate Sister Austen is impatient for our going into Hampshire, but I cannot go just yet. I shall not feel quite easy till our heavy charges are known and paid.[19]

As well as enduring seven months of semi-confinement the Leigh-Perrots had to pay nearly £2,000 for the expenses involved in defending themselves against this cunning plot. Her letter of 14 April 1800 is the last from

Mrs Leigh-Perrot in the series relating to her trial, so the date of her visit to Steventon remains unknown; the reporter present in the court-room at Taunton had noted that she was 'very pale and emaciated',[20] so she may well have stayed several weeks in Hampshire during the summer to recuperate.[21]

Apart from these references to the Austens in connection with Mrs Leigh-Perrot's ordeal, there is very little news of the Steventon family's movements during the first half of this year, as Jane's letters do not begin again until the end of October. One glimpse of the sisters occurs, however, in a letter dated 7 January 1800 from their neighbour, Mrs Bramston of Oakley Hall, who tells her correspondent that the Miss Austens are to dine with her on Thursday, 9 January and go on to the Basingstoke assembly ball afterwards.[22]

Frank and Charles were both now in the thick of active service in the Mediterranean, and the rectory inhabitants anxiously awaited the arrival of short hurried notes from them, passed back to England at irregular intervals with other naval or military despatches. Following Frank's promotion to Commander at the end of 1798, he had taken over the *Peterel* sloop at Gibraltar on 27 February 1799, and since then had been cruising about in coastal waters with the task of intercepting any vessel that crossed his path. If the stranger were friendly, news and assistance could be exchanged, while enemy ships could be attacked. By the summer of 1799 the Royal Navy was all over the Mediterranean, blockading Genoa and Malta, in possession of Minorca and patrolling the Egyptian and Syrian coasts, while Nelson was stationed at Palermo. The French armies in Italy and Egypt were therefore equally unable to receive reinforcements or to return to France. Frank was able to capture nearly forty small foreign ships of varying descriptions as they crept along the coast between Marseilles and Genoa including, in April 1799, a fishing-boat which turned out to be carrying enemy officers and $9,000 in specie – from this alone his share of the prize-money was $750. In June 1799 he participated in Lord Keith's capture of the French Rear-Admiral Perrée and his squadron near Toulon; and the next year, in March 1800, he intercepted three French ships just outside Marseilles. Although within point-blank shot of the shore batteries, he succeeded in driving two of them upon the rocks and capturing the third, the brig *La Ligurienne*, without the loss of a single man of his own crew. When the news of this daring and successful exploit reached the Admiralty, Frank was promoted Post-Captain on 13 May 1800, but owing to the difficulty of communicating with vessels on active service the Steventon family knew the good news long before he did. In August 1800 he was with Sir Sidney Smith's squadron blockading Alexandria, and here was able to burn a Turkish

80-gun warship, which had run aground near the island of Aboukir, in order to prevent her falling into French hands. The Turkish Capitan-Pasha was so pleased by this that he presented Frank with a handsome sabre and pelisse. It was not until October 1800, when the *Peterel* put in at Rhodes, that Frank learned of his promotion and handed over command of his sloop to the Captain Inglis who had been sent out to succeed him.[23]

Charles, for his part, joined the frigate *Tamar* as second lieutenant in December 1798, but almost immediately thereafter transferred to the *Endymion* and so returned to be under the command of Sir Thomas Williams. The *Endymion* was serving in the western Mediterranean and in 1799 and 1800 was engaged in attacking Spanish gunboats off Algeciras and capturing privateers, including one, *La Furie*, from which Charles's share of the prize-money was £40. When the *Scipio*, with a crew of 140, was captured in a violent gale, Charles, with no more than four of his own men to assist him, took control of this prize. The *Endymion* returned to Gosport in the early autumn of 1800, and while Charles was awaiting fresh sailing orders Jane's sisterly duty was to make him some new shirts, sending them to him by half-dozens as they were finished.[24]

After the negative information that Cassandra and Jane did not go to Ilchester or Taunton in the spring of 1800, the next positive news of them is that during September they were present at a ball somewhere in Hampshire at which they saw their acquaintance, Mrs Blount, with her 'broad face, diamond bandeau, white shoes, pink husband, & fat neck'.[25] The following month Edward and his eldest son – young Edward, now aged six – came to Steventon and returned to Godmersham via Chawton and London taking Cassandra with them; her visit to Kent, including a three-week stay in London upon the return journey, meant that she was absent from home until the end of February 1801, but only eleven letters survive out of the many that Jane must have written to her during this five months' separation. She kept Cassandra in touch with the usual cheerful daily routine at Steventon and the visits paid to neighbours within walking distance: 'At Oakley Hall we did a great deal – eat some sandwiches all over mustard, admired Mr Bramston's Porter & Mrs Bramston's Transparencies, & gained a promise from the latter of two roots of hearts-ease, one all yellow & the other all purple, for you.'[26] 'We had a very pleasant day on Monday at Ashe; we sat down 14 to dinner in the study, the dining room being not habitable from the Storm's having blown down its chimney.'[27] This same storm, on Sunday, 9 November, blew down two elms in front of Steventon rectory, the maypole with its 'scrooping' weathercock at the back of the house, and a further four elms in the garden and field beyond.[28] Mr Austen had been planning to replant this latter area with thorns and lilacs on one side and beech, ash and larch on the other, but following the storm was not so sure:

A new plan has been suggested concerning the plantation of the new inclosure on the right hand side of the Elm Walk – the doubt is whether it would be better to make a little orchard of it, by planting apples, pears & cherries, or whether it should be larch, Mountain-ash & acacia. – What is your opinion? – I say nothing, & am ready to agree with anybody.[29]

The winter-season balls at Basingstoke had started again:

Did you think of our Ball on thursday evening [30 October], & did you suppose me at it? – You might very safely, for there I was. – On wednesday morning it was settled that Mrs Harwood, Mary & I should go together, & shortly afterwards a very civil note of invitation for me came from Mrs Bramston, who wrote I beleive as soon as she knew of the Ball. I might likewise have gone with Mrs Lefroy, & therefore with three methods of going, I must have been more at the Ball than anybody else . . . The Portsmouths, Dorchesters, Boltons, Portals & Clerks were there, & all the meaner & more usual &c. &c.'s. . . . You were enquired after very prettily, & I hope the whole assembly now understands that you are gone into Kent, which the families in general seemed to meet in ignorance of. – Lord Portsmouth surpassed the rest in his attentive recollection of you.[30]

Three weeks later Jane was dancing again at Lord Portsmouth's own ball at Hurstbourne Park, accompanied by Charles, who had ridden up from Gosport on a hired hack especially for the occasion.[31]

Another of Mr Austen's old pupils, Richard Buller, had become vicar of Colyton in South Devon and recently married Miss Anna Marshall, but retained very fond memories of his years at Steventon, and wrote to the family at this time.

I have had a most affectionate letter from Buller; I was afraid he would oppress me by his felicity & his love for his Wife, but this is not the case; he calls her simply Anna without any angelic embellishments, for which I respect & wish him happy – and throughout the whole of his letter indeed he seems more engrossed by his feelings towards our family, than towards her, which you know cannot give any one disgust. – He is very pressing in his invitation to us all to come & see him at Colyton, & my father is very much inclined to go there next Summer. – It is a circumstance that may considerably assist the Dawlish scheme. – Buller has desired me to write again, to give him more particulars of us all.[32]

At the end of November Jane went to stay with Martha Lloyd at Ibthorpe, where she had 'the pleasure of thinking myself a very welcome Guest, & the pleasure of spending my time very pleasantly', despite the wet weather which made it 'too dirty even for such desperate Walkers as Martha & I to get out of doors'. She told Cassandra: 'Martha has promised to return with me, & our plan is to have a nice black frost for walking to Whitchurch, & there throw ourselves into a postchaise, one upon the other, our heads hanging out at one door, & our feet at the opposite.'[33] But while Jane was away, the latent strain of impetuosity in the Austens suddenly manifested itself in her father; and family tradition says that as she and Martha arrived from Ibthorpe early in December they were met in the rectory hall by Mrs Austen, who greeted them with: 'Well, girls, it is all settled, we have decided to leave Steventon in such a week and go to Bath' – and to Jane the shock of this intelligence was so great that she fainted away. Mary Lloyd, who was also present to greet her sister, remembered that Jane was 'greatly distressed'.[34]

No letters to Cassandra survive for the month of December 1800, which suggests that she destroyed those in which Jane gave vent to feelings of grief and perhaps even resentment at being so suddenly uprooted from her childhood home without any prior consultation by her parents as to her own opinions in the matter – Cassandra too had presumably been left in ignorance of this decision. 'My Aunt was very sorry to leave her native home, as I have heard my Mother relate.'[35] '[She] loved the country and her delight in natural scenery was such that she would sometimes say she thought it must form one of the joys of heaven.'[36] To make holiday visits to the town was one thing, but to exchange permanently the homely but comfortable rectory and the fields and woodlands of Hampshire for a tall narrow terrace house in one of Bath's stone-paved streets must have been nearly as dismaying a prospect to Jane as that of incarceration in the Ilchester gaoler's house had been for Mrs Leigh-Perrot. So hasty, indeed, did Mr Austen's decision appear to the Leigh-Perrots that they suspected the reason to be a growing attachment between Jane and William Digweed, one of the four brothers at Steventon manor house. There is not the slightest evidence of this supposition in Jane's letters, although on occasion she teasingly suggested that another of the brothers, the Revd James Digweed, must be in love with Cassandra, especially when he gallantly declared that the two elms blown down in the storm had fallen from grief at her absence;[37] in any case, to marry into the Digweed family would have been by no means unsuitable for either of the Austen daughters. It seems most probable that Mr Austen's age and Mrs Austen's continuing ill-health were the deciding factors for retirement: 'Bath it was supposed would suit her case, and it was a place that she liked.'[38]

By January 1801 Jane had recovered her composure, and the six letters written in the New Year are in her usual style of cheerful irony. Her one-time admirer the Revd Charles Powlett had married Miss Anne Temple in November 1796, at which time 'his wife [was] discovered to be everything that the Neighbourhood could wish her, silly & cross as well as extravagant'.[39] Jane and Martha now met her at Deane, apparently for the first time since the marriage: 'Mrs Powlett was at once expensively & nakedly dress'd; we have had the satisfaction of estimating her Lace & her Muslin; & she said too little to afford us much other amusement'[40] – but she did refer to her husband as her 'Caro Sposo',[41] a touch of affectation that Jane did not forget.[42] Mr Powlett, for his part, seems to have been equally bored with the entertainment provided by James and Mary, and unappreciative now of the company of Jane and Cassandra, for he entered curtly in his diary: 'we dined and slept at J. Austen's, dies perdita!'[43]

The plans for the retirement to Bath naturally figure largely in these letters:

I get more & more reconciled to the idea of our removal. We have lived long enough in this Neighbourhood, the Basingstoke Balls are certainly on the decline, there is something interesting in the bustle of going away, & the prospect of spending future summers by the Sea or in Wales is very delightful. – For a time we shall now possess many of the advantages which I have often thought of with Envy in the wives of Sailors or Soldiers. – It must not be generally known however that I am not sacrificing a great deal in quitting the Country – or I can expect to inspire no tenderness, no interest in those we leave behind.[44]

Mrs Leigh-Perrot was delighted that her relatives were coming to Bath:

This morning brought my Aunt's reply, & most thoroughly affectionate is it's tenor. She thinks with the greatest pleasure of our being settled in Bath . . . She is moreover very urgent with my mother not to delay her visit in Paragon if she should continue unwell . . . At present, & for many days past my mother has been quite stout, & she wishes not to be obliged by any relapse to alter her arrangements.[45]

There was much discussion amongst themselves as to locations for house-hunting: the family were united in their dislike of Axford Buildings; Mrs Austen hankered after Queen Square and knew that Cassandra would wish to avoid Trim Street; Mr Austen favoured the environs of Laura Place, but Jane thought the houses there would be too expensive. She herself liked the idea of Charles Street – 'the buildings are new, & it's nearness to Kingsmead fields would be a pleasant circumstance',[46] or else 'It would be very pleasant to be near Sidney Gardens! – we might go into the Labyrinth every day.'[47] There was also the question of how many servants they could afford to keep:

My Mother looks forward with as much certainty as you can do, to our keeping two Maids – my father is the only one not in the secret. – We plan having a steady Cook, & a young giddy Housemaid, with a sedate, middle aged Man, who is to undertake the double office of Husband to the former & sweetheart to the latter. – No Children of course to be allowed on either side.[48]

It was agreed that James and his family would move into Steventon rectory so that he could act as his father's curate, and the Austens had next to decide what they would take to Bath, and how the remainder of the household goods could best be disposed of. The ladies of the neighbourhood soon bought up Mrs Austen's poultry-yard – her 'Bantam-cocks and Galinies',[49] and Mr Bayle, the cabinet-maker and auctioneer from Winchester, valued the furniture at more than £200, in addition to which Mr Austen intended to sell his library of more than 500 volumes.[50] 'My father is doing all in his power to encrease his Income by raising his Tythes &c., & I do not despair of getting very nearly six hundred a year.'[51] Out of this James would have to be paid for his curacy of Steventon, and also another curate would have to be found for Deane, at a stipend of £50 a year. Madam Lefroy's daughter, Jemima Lucy, was now engaged to the recently ordained young Mr Henry Rice, and he it was who accepted the position, marrying Jemima Lucy later in the year. Jane prophesied rather acidly: 'It will be an amusement to Mary to superintend their Household management, & abuse them for expense.'[52] It seems that Jane suspected Mary Lloyd had been instrumental in persuading Mr Austen to make his sudden decision to retire while his daughters were away from home, and was both hurt and surprised at the way in which James and his wife were so rapidly cuckooing their parents out of the rectory:

My father's old Ministers are already deserting him to pay their court to his Son; the brown Mare, which as well as the black was to devolve on James at our removal, has not had patience to wait for that, & has settled herself even now at Deane . . . everything else I suppose will be seized by degrees in the same manner.[53]

James and Mary were planning a small family party at Ibthorpe in mid-January to celebrate the fourth anniversary of their wedding, and Jane said tersely to Cassandra: 'I was asked, but declined it.'[54]

At the end of January Jane went to stay at Manydown for about a month, and while she was there Edward brought Cassandra back to London, where she stayed with Henry and Eliza for three weeks. Henry had just recently resigned his commission in the Oxfordshire Militia, and instead set himself up as an army agent and banker, with his office in Cleveland Court, St James's.[55] He and Eliza were now living at No. 24 Upper Berkeley Street, off Portman Square, and the last of Jane's letters of this series was sent from Manydown to Cassandra at that address. She was able to pass on the good news that Charles was nearly home again – the *Endymion* had been becalmed off Plymouth when he wrote, but he hoped to dock in Portsmouth within a day or two and would go straight to visit Henry thereafter. His latest voyage had been to Lisbon, taking abroad the King's sixth son, Prince Augustus (later created Duke of Sussex), for the sake of his health – the Prince was a lifelong sufferer from asthma and needed to spend the winters in a warmer climate. 'Charles spent three pleasant days in Lisbon. – They were very well satisfied with their Royal Passenger, whom they found fat, jolly & affable . . . [Charles] received my letter, communicating our plans, before he left England, was much surprised of course, but is quite reconciled to them, & means to come to Steventon once more while Steventon is ours.'[56]

Cassandra returned home during February, and the months of March and April were spent in making the final preparations for leaving Steventon. Jane acted temporarily as her father's parish clerk, writing up a few entries of baptism and burial in the Steventon and Deane registers;[57] and passed on to little Anna her own childhood books *Mentoria* and *Elegant Extracts*.[58] Edward and Elizabeth paid a farewell visit during April, and Frank too returned from the Mediterranean just in time to join his family at Steventon before their move took place. At the beginning of May 1801 Mrs Austen and her daughters left their old home and went to Ibthorpe, while Mr Austen and Frank went to London and then on to Godmersham; the three-day sale of the contents of Steventon rectory began on 5 May, and the auctioneer's advertisements in the *Reading Mercury* show that Jane had to abandon her pianoforte by Ganer and 'a large collection of music by the most celebrated composers'.[59] On Monday, 4 May, leaving Cassandra behind them for the time being, Jane and her mother travelled in a single day from Ibthorpe to Bath, where they stayed with the Leigh-Perrots at No.1 Paragon.[60]

CHAPTER 10

Bath and the West Country, 1801–4

During the separation of Jane and Cassandra the letters begin again, but only four survive out of the seven or eight written in May 1801. Jane was trying to reconcile herself to the idea of living in a town and to appreciate the benefits that urban life could afford; but the difficulty of finding a new home as comfortable as Steventon rectory had been and the boredom of being obliged to attend Mrs Leigh-Perrot's small and very dull evening parties whilst they were staying in Paragon depressed her greatly. The only relief she could find for her feelings was in writing twice-weekly to Cassandra. Mrs Austen had not been upset by the journey to Bath and was suffering from nothing more than a slight cold instead of her usual feverish or bilious complaints; but her aunt had a violent cough and was 'deafer than ever'; and her uncle, although he had 'quite got the better of his lameness', could still only walk slowly with the aid of a stick and so provided no company for 'desperate walkers' such as Jane.[1]

Her first letter was begun on 5 May, the day following her arrival:

The first veiw of Bath in fine weather does not answer my expectations; I think I see more distinctly thro' Rain. – The Sun was got behind everything, and the appearance of the place from the top of Kingsdown, was all vapour, shadow, smoke & confusion. – I fancy we are to have a House in Seymour St or thereabouts. My Uncle & Aunt both like the situation –. I was glad to hear the former talk of all the Houses in New King St as too small; – it was my own idea of them . . . When my Uncle went to take his second glass of water, I walked with him, & in our morning's circuit we looked at two Houses in Green Park Buildings, one of which pleased me very well . . . The only doubt is about the Dampness of the Offices, of which there were symptoms.[2]

Mr Philips, the proprietor of this house, No. 12, was quite prepared to raise the kitchen floor to please potential new tenants, 'but all this I fear is fruitless – tho' the water may be kept out of sight, it cannot be sent away, nor the ill effects of its nearness be excluded.'[3] The houses in New King Street turned out to be even smaller than Jane had imagined, and the only

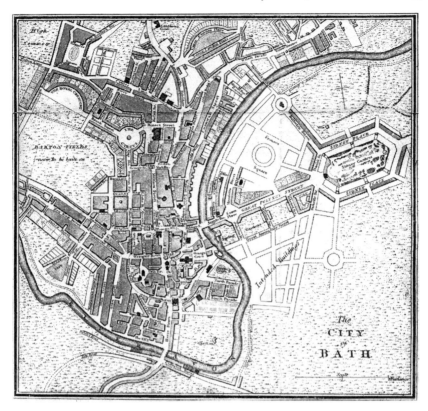

Plate 20 'The City of Bath', from *A Guide to all the Watering and Sea Bathing Places*, c. 1820.

one available in Seymour Street was also uninviting when inspected, so the accommodation problem was still unresolved when she wrote her last letter of this series on 26 May.

In the meantime, Mrs Leigh-Perrot's friends had been calling and Jane met again the sisters' old acquaintance and distant cousin, Mrs Chamberlayne, who 'remembers us in Gloucestershire when we were very charming young women'.[4] Mrs Chamberlayne had at least the merit of being fit and active even if rather dull, and she accompanied Jane on a fast walk to Weston one hot day and then to Lyncombe and Widcombe on another, before their transient friendship terminated with the Chamberlaynes' departure from Bath – 'I respect Mrs Chamberlayne for doing her hair well, but cannot feel a more tender sentiment.'[5] Jane wrote crossly:

Another stupid party last night; perhaps if larger they might be less intolerable, but here there were only just enough to make one card table, with six people to look over, & talk nonsense to each other. Ly. Fust, Mrs Busby & a Mrs Owen sat down with my Uncle to Whist within five minutes after the three old <u>Toughs</u> came in, & there they sat with only the exchange of Adm: Stanhope for my <u>Uncle</u> till their chairs were announced.[6]

Admiral Stanhope, like the Chamberlaynes, was another distant cousin of Mr Leigh-Perrot, and in fact there were quite a number of Leigh relations living in or visiting Bath at the time, who came to call upon the Austens in the following weeks, though Jane does not seem to have been particularly impressed by any of them.[7]

On Monday, 11 May the Leigh-Perrots took Jane to the penultimate ball of the season at the Upper Rooms where, although there were very few dancers, she found some interest in talking to her brother Edward's Kentish friend, the horse-loving, irascible old Mr Evelyn, and in watching from afar her own kinswoman, the Hon. Mary Cassandra Twisleton. Miss Twisleton's erstwhile husband, Captain Edward Ricketts, RN, had divorced her in 1799 for adultery with Captain Richard Head Graves of the Lancashire Volunteers; the illicit romance had taken place at Portchester and Titchfield, and the scandal had consequently reverberated round Hampshire.[8]

I am proud to say that I have a very good eye at an Adultress, for tho' repeatedly assured that another in the same party was the <u>She</u>, I fixed upon the right one from the first. – A resemblance to Mrs Leigh was my guide. She is not so pretty as I expected; her face has the same defect of baldness as her sister's, & her features not so handsome; – she was highly rouged, & looked rather quietly & contentedly silly than anything else.[9]

Jane tried to amuse herself by pretending to Cassandra that she was flirting with Mr Evelyn, but the joke misfired and she had to withdraw her teasing exaggeration when faced by Cassandra's prudent anxieties:

I assure you inspite of what I might chuse to insinuate in a former letter, that I have seen very little of Mr Evelyn since my coming here; I met him this morning for only the 4th time, & as to my anecdote about Sidney Gardens, I made the most of the Story because it came in to advantage, but in fact he only asked me whether I were to be at Sidney Gardens in the evening or not.

He did, however, invite her to come for a drive in his fast four-horse phaeton, an invitation which she was inclined to accept: 'I really beleive he is very harmless; people do not seem afraid of him here, and he gets Groundsel for his birds & all that' and in fact on the following day, 'We went to the top of Kingsdown & had a very pleasant drive.' When she came in to Paragon after this jaunt, she found on the table a letter from Charles, just returned to Portsmouth from his latest voyage, with the good news that his share of the prize-money from the capture of the privateer *La Furie* would amount to £40,

but of what avail is it to take prizes if he lays out the produce in presents to his Sisters. He has been buying Gold chains & Topaze Crosses for us; – he must be well scolded . . . He will receive my yesterday's letter to day, and I shall write again by this post to thank & reproach him. – We shall be unbearably fine.[10]

At the end of May Mr Austen travelled back from Godmersham and collected Cassandra from Kintbury en route, so that by the beginning of June the family were finally assembled in Bath. Their house-hunting ended when one of them noticed an advertisement in the *Bath Chronicle* of 21 May: 'The lease of No. 4 Sydney Place, three years and a quarter of which are unexpired at Midsummer. The situation is desirable, the Rent very low, and the Landlord is bound by covenant to paint the two first floors this summer. A premium will therefore be expected. For particulars apply to Messrs. Watson and Foreman, Cornwall Buildings, Bath.' This house, facing Sydney Gardens, was just the location where Jane had hoped they might settle; at £150 p.a. the rent was affordable; and while the landlord redecorated the premises the Austens went further into the West Country for one of the seaside holidays that she had earlier been anticipating.[11]

After these letters during May 1801, there is a gap in Jane's surviving correspondence until the one isolated letter of 14 September 1804, so that her movements during the intervening period can only be deduced from hints and glimpses found in other sources. In January 1801 the Austens had been thinking of going to Sidmouth in the coming summer,[12] and in the absence of any evidence to the contrary they presumably fulfilled this plan. From there it would be easy to visit the neat little stone-built town of Colyton, a few miles eastward along the Devon coast, where Mr Austen's former pupil Richard Buller had been the incumbent since 1799 and occupied a large Tudor vicarage in which to receive his guests, in accordance with his invitation issued to the Austens in November 1800.[13] By the end of September 1801 the family were back in Hampshire, staying with James and Mary at Steventon; Jane and Cassandra spent a day at Ashe rectory with Madam Lefroy, and the Lefroys then dined at Steventon to take leave of the Austens before they returned to Bath on Monday, 5 October.[14]

A letter from Eliza de Feuillide to Phylly Walter, dated 29 October 1801, confirms that the seaside holiday had been quite prolonged: 'I conclude that you know of our Uncle & Aunt Austen and their daughters having spent the summer in Devonshire – They are now returned to Bath where they are superintending the fitting up of their new house.'[15] Sydney Place was at that time on the outskirts of Bath, on the edge of open countryside; an easy walk along the wide, handsome Great Pulteney Street and over Pulteney Bridge led to the centre of the town, while No. 4 itself overlooked Sydney Gardens, where public concerts and other entertainments were held on gala nights. The gardens also included a miniature maze or 'labyrinth', as Jane had earlier reminded Cassandra, that provided a walk of nearly half a mile.

After Eliza's reference to the Austens, there is no further news of them until the spring of the following year, when Mrs Lybbe-Powys came to Bath for the season and noted briefly in her diary contacts with them in February and March.[16] In April 1802 James and Mary visited Bath for a few weeks, bringing Anna with them, now aged just nine; she was very fond of her grandparents and to the end of her life never forgot how they both

seemed to enjoy the cheerfulness of their Town life, and especially perhaps the rest which their advancing years entitled them to, which, even to their active natures, must have been acceptable. I have always thought that this was the short Holyday [*sic*] of their married life . . . My Grand Father as a young man was considered extremely handsome – so I have been told, and he was still handsome when advanced in age – At the time when I have the most perfect recollection of him he must have been getting on hard, as people say, for 70. His hair in its whiteness might have belonged to a much older man; it was very beautiful & glossy, with short curls above the ears . . . I can well remember at Bath, where my Grand Father latterly resided, what notice he attracted, when on any public occasion he appeared with his head uncovered.[17]

At some time the previous year – probably while he was visiting London and Godmersham – Mr Austen had had his miniature painted, and this representation of his features bears out Anna's description of him.[18] During this period of their retirement Mr and Mrs Austen also had their silhouettes painted, and that of Mrs Austen clearly shows the beaky Leigh nose of which she was so proud.[19]

At the end of March 1802 the Treaty of Amiens was signed, which brought about a short cessation of hostilities between Great Britain and France. Napoleon used the treaty as a breathing-space in which to re-equip the French armed forces, but nearly half the British soldiers and sailors were immediately demobilised. Charles Austen left the *Endymion* and joined his family in Bath, and was thus able to accompany them on their summer holidays this year. No precise dates are known, but the Austens certainly went to Dawlish, for in 1814 Jane recalled that 'The Library [at Dawlish] was particularly pitiful & wretched 12 years ago.'[20] There is the tradition that a visit was made to Teignmouth, where the family stayed at a house called 'Great Bella Vista'; as Dawlish is so close to Teignmouth it is probable that this was also part of the 1802 holiday.[21] Later in the summer the Austens went to Wales – Tenby and probably Barmouth as well [22] – and from there Mr and Mrs Austen and Charles travelled back to Hampshire, arriving at Steventon on 14 August. Frank, who had been appointed Captain of the 98-gun HMS *Neptune* only as recently as August 1801, was now at Portsmouth preparing for his ship to be paid off, and on 23 August his parents, together with James and Mary, visited him there to inspect his fine vessel. Cassandra and Jane were not participants in this seaside trip and may perhaps have been with the Fowles at Kintbury or the Lefroys at Ashe, for they did not arrive at Steventon until 1 September. Two days later Charles accompanied them to Godmersham, where they all stayed for several weeks; Edward now had seven children, for since Jane's visit in 1798 his second and third daughters, Lizzy and Marianne, had been born in 1800 and 1801 respectively. Charles brought his sisters back to Steventon on 28 October, and on 25 November Jane and Cassandra moved on to visit their old friends, Catherine and Alethea Bigg, at Manydown, intending to stay with them two or three weeks.[23]

However, only one week later, on Friday, 3 December, Mary Lloyd was surprised to see a carriage draw up unexpectedly outside Steventon rectory, containing her sisters-in-law and their two friends. To her further surprise, a scene of tearful and affectionate farewells took place in the hall, and as soon as the carriage had gone Cassandra and Jane declared it was absolutely necessary for them to return to Bath the next day, and that James must conduct them there. Saturday was of course a most inconvenient day for a single-handed parson to leave his parish and arrange for the Sunday duty to be taken at such short notice; but the sisters refused to remain until Monday, nor would they give any reason for this refusal, so that James was therefore obliged to yield and to go with them to Bath. Eventually the explanation was given – on the evening of 2 December Harris Bigg-Wither had asked Jane to marry him and she had accepted, but then on the following morning had changed her mind and withdrawn her consent.

In later years Mary Lloyd passed on this tale to her daughter Caroline, who pondered about the matter:

Mr Wither was very plain in person – awkward, & even uncouth in manner – nothing but his size to recommend him – he was a fine big man – but one need not look about for secret reason to account for a young lady's _not_ loving him – a great many would have taken him _without_ love – & I beleive the wife he did get was very fond of him, & that they were a happy couple – He had sense in plenty & went through life very respectably, as a country gentleman – I _conjecture_ that the advantages he could offer, & her gratitude for his love, & her long friendship with his family, induced my Aunt to decide that she would marry him <u>when</u> he should ask her – but that having accepted him she found she was miserable & that the place & fortune which would certainly be <u>his</u>, could not alter the <u>man</u> – She was staying in his <u>Father's</u> house – old Mr Wither was then alive – To be sure she should not have said yes – over night – but I have always respected her for the courage in cancelling that yes – the next morning – All worldly advantages would have been to her – & she was of an age to know <u>this</u> quite well – My Aunts had very small fortunes & on their Father's death they & their Mother would be, they were aware, but poorly off – I beleive most young women so circumstanced would have taken Mr W. & trusted to love after marriage.[24]

Mary Lloyd much regretted Jane's decision, as she thought the match would have been a most desirable one.[25]

It seems that afterwards Jane referred to this embarrassing event in some letters to Cassandra which the latter subsequently destroyed, but not before a much younger niece, Catherine Hubback (Frank's fourth daughter, 1818–77), had read them. She recalled: 'I gathered from the letters that it was in a momentary fit of self-delusion that Aunt Jane accepted Mr Wither's proposal, and that when it was all settled eventually, and the negative decisively given she was much relieved. I think the affair vexed her a good deal, but I am sure she had no attachment to him.'[26] Harris Bigg-Wither consoled himself two years later by marrying Miss Anne Howe Frith from the Isle of Wight, and went to live with her at Wymering, near Cosham, Hants, not returning to Manydown until he inherited the estate after his father's death in 1813. It is not known whether Jane ever saw him again, but her friendship with his sisters continued unaltered until her death.

Mrs Lybbe-Powys's diary once again makes mention of the Austens being in Bath in February 1803;[27] and it seems probable that this was the spring when Anna too visited Bath again and met her great-uncle, the 5th Duke of Ancaster, and his only grandson, her young cousin, Brownlow Charles Colyear.

I remember the last Duke and Duchess of Ancaster and being presented to the former (who was my God Father) in the Pump Room at Bath, being then about 10 years of age. My Grandmother Austen with whom I was staying took upon herself this introduction, after which I was invited once or twice to spend the day in Gt. Pulteney Street, where the Duke had a house . . . This Duke & Duchess . . . had had one child, a Daughter, who married a handsome agreable but dissipated Irish Peer [Lord Milsington], & died early leaving one Son. This child was brought up by the Ancasters. He was rather younger than myself, but I well recollect spending a day with them at Bath, & giving him his first lesson in dancing.[28]

Apart from these references, nothing else is known of the elder Austens' movements this year until the end of the summer; in the meantime Henry and Eliza took advantage of the Peace of Amiens to go to France in the hope of recovering some of the de Feuillide property. Eliza was no longer the mother of the heir, for poor little Hastings after many years of ill-health had finally dwindled away to an early death in the autumn of 1801;[29] but as the widow of M. de Feuillide she could rightfully expect to have a share in his estate in Guienne. Henry too was considering increasing his business affairs by becoming an importer of French wines, and had moved his office from Cleveland Court to Cannon Row, very close to the Houses of Parliament – perhaps anticipating that many MPs might become his customers.[30] They set off probably in the late summer of 1802, taking with them as travelling companion an old friend, Mrs Marriott,[31] but it seems unlikely that Eliza made any headway in her claim to some of the de Feuillide property. Henry returned to England in the spring of 1803,[32] and on 16 May that year Napoleon suddenly broke the Peace of Amiens and renewed the war between Great Britain and France. Orders were given for all English travellers to be detained; but as Eliza's French was so perfect she passed everywhere for a native, and was thus able to give all the orders for a hurried return journey, which saved herself and Mrs Marriott from an internment of eleven years' duration.[33]

The outbreak of war naturally meant that both Frank and Charles returned to active service; Charles took up his post again as first lieutenant of the *Endymion* and served aboard her with distinction until he was promoted in October of the following year to the command of the sloop HMS *Indian*. Frank received new and different orders from the Admiralty:

Whereas it has been judged expedient for the more effectually preventing the landing of an Enemy in this Country, that the Inhabitants of the Towns and Villages on the Coast, who shall voluntarily offer themselves for its protection, shall be enrolled in their respective Districts, under the name of Sea-Fencibles; and whereas we think fit to appoint you to command all such Men as shall enroll themselves under the description above-mentioned; – *From Sandown exclusive to the No. Foreland inclusive* – You are hereby required and directed to repair forthwith to *Ramsgate*, and take upon you the command of all such Men as may from time to time enroll themselves within the said District, for the Defence of the Coast, accordingly.

Frank arrived in Ramsgate in July 1803 and stayed there organising his sea-fencibles until the spring of 1804, when he returned to sea as captain of the 50-gun HMS *Leopard*, stationed off Boulogne. While he was living in Ramsgate he became noted for his quietly devout behaviour – '*the* officer who knelt in church'[34] – and his period of service here also marked a turning-point in his life, for he became acquainted with Mr John Gibson and his family, who had a comfortable house in the High Street.[35] The eldest daughter, Mary, (1785–1823), was a fair-haired, cheerful girl, not yet twenty but practical and resilient, and Frank soon decided that she was the right wife for him. They became officially engaged in 1804 and hoped to be married as soon as he had gained a little more prize-money.

Jane's other two brothers were also involved in the preparations at this time for the strengthening of local defences against the threatened invasion of England. In Hampshire the parishes of Ashe, Deane, Steventon and Hannington combined to subscribe for the formation of a troop of volunteers; the Lefroys, Digweeds, Harwoods, Bramstons and Portals all helped, and James Austen together with John Harwood went riding round the four parishes collecting the names of men willing to serve.[36] In Kent, Edward Knight formed his local villagers into the Godmersham & Molash Company of the East Kent Volunteers, wearing a uniform of red coat, blue breeches, and red sash; with Edward as their Captain, his men took their turn with other volunteer companies for guard duty at the Kentish ports and main towns.[37]

In 1803 another, and on this occasion a contemporary, chronicler of the Austen family's activities appears on the scene – Edward's eldest daughter, Fanny, only just ten years old but very self-possessed and mature for her age, and fluent with her pen. 'Godmersham was fast filling with a numerous and joyful race of children; all born to bask in the brightest sunshine that fond & wealthy Parents could spread around them.'[38] Fanny, as the first daughter followed by four sons, spent a great deal of time in her mother's company and soon learned how to play her own part in Kentish society. She enjoyed receiving letters and, unlike most children, also enjoyed writing them, so seized upon every opportunity to find a suitable correspondent. Her first governess, Miss Dorothy Chapman, left Godmersham early in 1803, and for more than fifty years thereafter Fanny kept in touch with her, providing her with information about the Godmersham family in particular and the rest of the Austens in general. On 9 September 1803 she told Miss Chapman: 'we expect Grandpapa & Grandmama [Austen], Saturday, & from that time our House will be full'.[39] Fanny did not specify whether her Aunt Jane was also of the house-party, but Egerton Brydges recorded her presence in Kent that year:

When I knew Jane Austen I never suspected that she was an authoress; but my eyes told me that she was fair and handsome, slight and elegant, but with cheeks a little too full. The last time I think that I saw her was at Ramsgate in 1803; perhaps she was then about twenty seven years old. Even then I did not know that she was addicted to literary composition.[40]

On their return journey to Somerset during October, both Cassandra and Jane stopped off at Ashe to see Madam Lefroy, as they had done in 1801.[41] As soon as they reached Bath, it seems likely that they set off again for an autumn holiday in Lyme Regis, for in 1808 Jane recalled seeing a fire in that town which, according to local records, broke out in one of the central streets on 5 November 1803 and destroyed a number of houses on the north-eastern side of Lyme.[42] The mild climate of the West Country would make a November holiday quite feasible, and certainly in *Persuasion* it is during that month that the Musgrove party pay their visit.

In January 1804 Mr and Mrs Lybbe-Powys paid their annual visit to Bath, and as usual called upon the Austens as soon as they arrived.[43] Nothing further would be known about the family before Jane's letter of 14 September were it not for another source of information that commenced in this New Year. As a Christmas present for 1804 Elizabeth Austen gave Fanny a little diary – *The Ladies Complete Pocket Book* – and, with the meticulous attention to detail that seems to have been an Austenian trait, she soon fell into the habit of making daily entries, even if only of a few words. She kept such diaries ever afterwards until she was too old and frail to continue writing, and they exist in an unbroken run from 1804 to 1872. Those covering the years 1804–17 frequently mention her Aunt Jane and other members of the Austen family, and her letters to Miss Chapman of the same period expand the brief diary entries and sometimes provide further details. In mid-March of this year Fanny was able to tell Miss Chapman: 'Grandmama Bridges is perfectly well & so is Grandmama Austen now, but she has been very ill.'[44] It seems that Dr William Bowen was called in to attend to Mrs Austen, for upon her recovery from this illness she wrote her humorous verses entitled 'Dialogue between Death and Mrs A.':

> Says Death, 'I've been trying these three weeks and more
> To seize on old Madam here at Number Four,
> Yet I still try in vain, tho' she's turned of three score;
> To what is my ill success owing?'
> 'I'll tell you, old Fellow, if you cannot guess,
> To what you're indebted for your ill success –
> To the prayers of my husband, whose love I possess;
> To the care of my daughters, whom Heaven will bless,
> To the skill and attention of Bowen.'[45]

When Mrs Austen was sufficiently fit to travel – probably in the mid-summer of 1804 – the family gave up the last three months of the lease of No. 4 Sydney Place and set off for a tour of the Devon and Dorset seaside resorts, accompanied on this occasion by Henry and Eliza.[46] Henry had moved his office again, from Cannon Row to Albany in Piccadilly, and had taken into partnership one of his old friends from the Oxfordshire Militia, Henry Maunde;[47] he had also moved his home from Upper Berkeley Street to No. 16 Michael's Place, a terrace which overlooked the fields and market gardens of Brompton, then still a separate village on the outskirts of London.[48] At some time in the late summer the party arrived in Lyme Regis, and it seems probable that they lodged first at Pyne House, No. 10 Broad Street. During one of their walks in the countryside Cassandra made a watercolour sketch of Jane, seen from behind, 'sitting down out of doors, on a hot day, with her bonnet strings untied.'[49]

Early in September the party divided, and Henry and Eliza went to Weymouth, taking Cassandra with them. Jane and her parents stayed in Lyme and moved into smaller lodgings thereafter – perhaps into Hiscott's boarding house further up Broad Street, the site of the present Three Cups hotel.[50] Her only letter surviving from this year is that of 14 September, written when Cassandra was just leaving Weymouth to go on to Ibthorpe, where Martha was tending old Mrs Lloyd, now very feeble.

We are quite settled in our Lodgings by this time as you may suppose, & everything goes on in the usual order. The servants behave very well, & make no difficulties, tho' nothing certainly can exceed the inconvenience of the Offices, except the general Dirtiness of the House & furniture & all its Inhabitants . . . I endeavour as far as I can to supply your place & be useful & keep things in order; I detect dirt in the Water-decanters as fast as I can, and give the Cook physic, which she throws off her Stomach. I forget whether she used to do this, under your administration . . . The Ball last night was pleasant, but not full for Thursday . . . Nobody asked me the two first dances – the two next I danced with Mr Crawford – & had I chosen to stay longer might have danced with Mr Granville . . . or with a new, odd looking Man who had been eyeing me for some time, & at last without any introduction asked me if I meant to dance again. – I think he must be Irish by his ease, & because I imagine him to belong to the Honble. Barnwalls, who are the son & son's wife of an Irish Viscount – bold, queerlooking people, just fit to be Quality at Lyme . . . I need not say that we are particularly anxious for your next Letter, to know how you find Mrs Lloyd & Martha. – Say Everything kind for us to the latter, – The former I fear must be beyond any remembrance of, or from, the Absent.[51]

Jane and her parents remained in Lyme some weeks longer, and probably visited Richard Buller again at Colyton during this period. Either this year or previously they certainly also visited Charmouth, Up Lyme and Pinny, for the beautiful summer scenery of these places made such an impression on Jane that she described it in *Persuasion* with greater fullness and enthusiasm than she ever displayed when sketching in the topography of her other novels. The family, including Cassandra, returned to Bath on 25 October 1804 and, after all, rented a house in Green Park Buildings – No. 3, on the east side; perhaps the benefits of being on the edge of the city, with part of Kingsmead field between the two terraces of Green Park Buildings East and West, and a fine view of Beechen Cliff across the Avon, outweighed their previous fears of damp kitchens and consequent 'putrid fevers'.[52]

There is a family tradition that during one of these seaside holidays between 1801–4 Jane met the only man whom she could seriously have wished to marry, had fortune been kinder to her. Cassandra knew the details of this brief episode, but in her later life passed on to Caroline Austen merely the barest outline of what had happened years before. In 1870 Caroline wrote out the account, for her brother's use in preparing the second edition of his *Memoir:*

All that I know is this. At Newtown, Aunt Cassandra was staying with us [Caroline and her mother, Mary Lloyd – they lived at Newtown, near Newbury, Berkshire, from 1825 to 1836] when we made acquaintance [during 1828] with a certain Mr Henry Edridge, of the Engineers. He was very pleasing and very good-looking. My aunt was very much struck with him, and I was struck by her commendation; she so rarely admired strangers. Afterwards, at another time – I do not remember exactly when [probably early 1829] – she spoke of him as of one so unusually gifted with all that was agreeable, and said that he reminded her strongly of a gentleman whom they had met one summer when they were by the sea – I think she said in Devonshire; I don't think she named the place, and I am sure she did not say Lyme, for that I should have remembered – that he seemed greatly attracted by my Aunt Jane – I suppose it was an intercourse of some weeks – and that when they had to part (I imagine he was a visitor also, but his family might have lived near) he was urgent to know where they would be the next summer, implying or perhaps saying that he should be there also, wherever it might be. I can only say that the impression left on Aunt Cassandra was that he had fallen in love with her sister, and was quite in earnest. Soon afterwards they heard of his death. Mr Henry Edridge also died of a sudden illness [on 6 November 1828] soon after we had seen him at Newtown, and I suppose it was that coincidence of early death that led my aunt to speak of him – the unknown – at all. I am sure she thought he was worthy of her sister, from the way in which she recalled his memory, and also that she did not doubt, either, that he would have been a successful suitor.

Caroline's statement, imprecise though it is, is the fullest and earliest account available and, bearing in mind her reputation in the family for having a wonderfully accurate and retentive memory, must be considered reliable, stemming as it does from the unimpeachable authority of Cassandra herself. In the absence of any further evidence from outside sources, however, Jane's stillborn romance can only remain 'nameless and dateless'.[53]

Following her rapid production of *Sense and Sensibility, First Impressions* and *Susan* (to give them the titles by which they were then known to the family) between 1795–9, the following three or four years of Jane's life seem to have been quite devoid of literary composition. This barren period has been accounted for in several ways – as arising from grief at leaving Steventon, or at the abrupt termination of her seaside romance, or to want of a settled home. It is probable that each factor contributed to Jane's inability to compose afresh before 1804. However, during 1802 or early 1803 she found the heart – perhaps encouraged by Henry – to return to *Susan* and make a second copy of the manuscript, adding as she did so a reference to Maria Edgeworth's latest novel, *Belinda*, published in 1801, at the end of chapter v. Whether she made any other alteration is not known, but in the spring of 1803 Henry's lawyer and agent William Seymour sold this manuscript on Jane's behalf to a London publisher, Benjamin Crosby & Son, of Stationer's Hall Court, for £10, with a stipulation for early publication.[54] Crosby did in fact advertise *Susan* in *Flowers of Literature* vol. 1 (for 1801 and 1802, published in 1803), as being 'In the Press', but never thereafter produced it.[55] It seems probable that upon further consideration he felt it would be impolitic for him to do so; he was thoroughly committed to publishing just such 'Gothic Romances' as were ridiculed by this unknown authoress, so that if he were to bring out *Susan* he ran the double risk of, on the one hand, offending his established authors and, on the other, of losing money if the new book were ignored by unsympathetic critics and so failed to sell.

But the task of copying out *Susan*, mechanical though it was, must have reawakened Jane's zest for creation, all the more so following the encouragement of Crosby accepting her manuscript for publication. Presumably it was well into 1803 – perhaps even early 1804 – before she realised that 'early publication' was unlikely to occur, and it seems she was too modest to press Crosby on the point, even via Mr Seymour. Nevertheless, in the meantime, according to family tradition, she had composed the plot of another full-length novel (at that stage untitled but now known as *The Watsons*) and started her first draft of it.[56] She wrote about 17,500 words before the end of 1804; but two sad events in quick succession once again diverted her mind and discouraged her from original composition.

CHAPTER II

Bath and Southampton, 1804–8

On 16 December 1804 Jane celebrated her twenty-ninth birthday in Bath, and on that same day in Hampshire Madam Lefroy rode out from Ashe Rectory, accompanied as usual by her servant, to shop in Overton. She met James Austen in the town, and observed to him that the horse she was riding was so stupid and lazy she could scarcely make him canter.

My father rode homeward, she staying to do some errands in Overton; next morning the news of her death reached Steventon. After getting to the top of Overton Hill, the horse seemed to be running away – it was not known whether anything had frightened him – the servant, unwisely, rode up to catch the bridle rein – missed his hold and the animal darted off faster. He could not give any clear account, but it was supposed that Mrs Lefroy in her terror, threw herself off, and fell heavily on the hard ground. She never spoke afterwards, and she died in a few hours . . .

and on 21 December James buried her.[1] Jane's immediate reaction to the tragic news is unknown, but on the anniversary four years later she wrote her longest and most serious set of verses in memory of this dear friend of childhood days, still grieving bitterly at her loss.[2]

Only a few weeks later, however, she suffered an even greater loss, for on 21 January 1805 her father died after a very brief illness. To Jane fell the task of informing her brothers; James at Steventon was the nearest and he arrived early the following morning. Henry was paying his usual New Year visit to Godmersham when the news was received there, and left at once for Bath, though Edward was unable to accompany him.[3] Charles, aboard HMS *Indian*, was now far away at Halifax, Nova Scotia; and Jane addressed Frank's letter to HMS *Leopard* at Dungeness:

I have melancholy news to relate, & sincerely feel for your feelings under the shock of it. – I wish I could better prepare You for it. – But having said so much, Your mind will already forestall the sort of Event which I have to communicate. – Our dear Father has closed his virtuous & happy life, in a death almost as free from suffering as his Children could have wished. He was taken ill on Saturday morning, exactly in the same way as heretofore, an oppression in the head with fever, violent tremulousness, & the greatest degree of Feebleness . . . Heavy as is the blow, we can already feel that a thousand comforts remain to us to soften it. Next to that of the consciousness of his worth & constant preparation for another World, is the remembrance of his having suffered, comparatively speaking, nothing. – Being quite insensible of his own state, he was spared all the pain of separation, & he went off almost in his Sleep. – My Mother bears the Shock as well as possible; she was quite prepared for it, & feels all the blessing of his being spared a long Illness . . . Adieu my dearest Frank. The loss of such a Parent must be felt, or we should be Brutes. – I wish I could have given you better preparation – but it has been impossible.[4]

This letter, however, crossed in the post with one from Frank to Cassandra, sent when he was setting sail for Portsmouth. Jane therefore had to write a second letter to await his arrival at Portsmouth, in much the same terms but adding: 'It has been very sudden! – within twenty four hours of his death he was walking with only the help of a stick, was even reading! . . . His tenderness as a Father, who can do justice to? . . . The Serenity of the Corpse is most delightful! – It preserves the sweet, benevolent smile which always distinguished him.'[5] The funeral took place on 26 January at Walcot church – scene of Mr Austen's marriage in 1764 – where he was buried in the crypt with, later on, a simple ledger stone placed over the vault.[6] Afterwards Mrs Austen picked out two little items of his personal effects that she felt Frank would value – a pocket compass/sundial and a pair of scissors – and Jane offered these to him in her letter of 29 January.[7]

This bereavement now placed Mrs Austen and her daughters in straitened circumstances. Mr Austen's Will, made in 1770 and never altered thereafter, was simplicity itself – he left everything to his wife and she was to be the sole executrix[8] – but most of his income had been derived from the livings of Steventon and Deane, and his small annuity from the Hand-in-Hand Society died with him. Fortunately, her sons were only too willing to help her, and they rapidly agreed amongst themselves their respective contributions. Frank had just heard that he was appointed to the 80-gun HMS *Canopus*, and on the strength of this wrote to Henry offering £100 p.a. towards their mother's upkeep. Henry, impulsive as ever, could not bear to keep this a secret and on 28 January told him:

It was so absolutely necessary that your noble offer towards my Mother should be made more public than you seem'd to desire, that I really cannot apologize for a partial breach of your request. With the proudest exultations of maternal tenderness the Excellent Parent has exclaimed that never were Children so good as hers. She feels the magnificence of your offer, and accepts of half. I shall therefore honor her demands for 50 pounds annually on your account. James had the day before yesterday communicated to me & Her his desire to be her Banker for the same annual assistance, & I as long as I am <u>an Agent</u> shall do as he does. – If Edward does the least he ought, he will certainly insist on her receiving a £100 from him. So you see My Dear F., that with her own assured property, & Cassandra's, both producing about £210 per ann., She will be in the receipt of a clear £450 pounds per Ann. – She will be very comfortable, & as a smaller establishment will be as agreeable to them, as it cannot but be feasible, I really think that My Mother & Sisters will be to the full as rich as ever. They will not only suffer no personal deprivation, but will be able to pay occasional visits of health and pleasure to their friends.[9]

James also wrote to Frank about their mother:

Her future plans are not quite settled, but I believe her summers will be spent in the country amongst her Relations & chiefly I trust among her children – the winters she will pass in comfortable lodgings in Bath. It is a just satisfaction to know that her Circumstances will be easy, & that she will enjoy all those comforts which declining years & precarious health call for. You will I am sure forgive Henry for not having entirely complied with your request for secrecy upon one very important subject in your letter . . . You would indeed have had a high gratification could you have witnessed the pleasure which our Dear Mother experienced when your intention was communicated to her.[10]

From Henry's letter, however, it can be seen that while Cassandra had a small personal income (the interest on the £1,000 that Tom Fowle had left her), Jane had nothing at all that she could call her own. Furthermore, she was now totally dependent upon her brothers not only financially but also to a large extent socially, for she could not travel on a journey of any distance unless one of them was available to accompany her.

Early in February Frank had a month's leave before moving to HMS *Canopus*; he took his fiancée Mary Gibson to the theatre in London and carried away some happy romantic memory about which he lovingly teased her later in the year –

the evening was not quite so productive of pleasure to me as the last theatrical representation I had witnessed, which was at Covent Garden some time in the beginning of February last when I had the honor of being seated by a fair young lady with whom I became slightly acquainted the preceding year at Ramsgate. Do you happen to recollect anything of that evening? I think you do and that you will not readily forget it.[11]

Mrs Austen gave up the Green Park Buildings house at the end of March 1805 and with her daughters moved into lodgings at 25 Gay Street, halfway up the hill leading to the Circus and not far from the Royal Crescent. Almost immediately after this move, Cassandra had to go to Ibthorpe to help Martha Lloyd nurse Mrs Lloyd, 'who from repeated paralytic seizures had been failing in mind and body for some time past'.[12] She did not return until mid-May, but only two letters from Jane survive out of the several written during this six weeks' separation. The weather was very fine, and life in Bath followed its usual placid course, the days spent walking in the town and countryside with friends and relations – their Cooke cousins were presently staying in Alfred Street – and the evenings exchanging visits to drink tea. Jane also of course wrote to her brothers:

I was not able to go on yesterday, all my Wit & leisure were bestowed on letters to Charles & Henry . . . I wrote to Henry because I had a letter from him, in which he desired to hear from me very soon. – His to me was most affectionate & kind, as well as entertaining; – there is no merit to him in that, he cannot help being amusing . . . One thing more Henry mentions which deserves your hearing; he offers to meet us on the Sea-coast if the plan, of which Edward gave him some hint, takes place. Will not this be making the Execution of such a plan, more desirable & delightful than Ever. – He talks of the rambles we took together last Summer with pleasing affection.[13]

Cassandra's news was that Mrs Lloyd was now comatose, and Jane replied:

Poor woman! May her end be peaceful & easy, as the Exit we have witnessed! . . . If there is no revival, suffering must be all over; even the consciousness of Existence I suppose was gone when you wrote. The Nonsense I have been writing in this & in my last letter, seems out of place at such a time; but I will not mind it, it will do you no harm, & nobody else will be attacked by it.[14]

On 16 April Mrs Lloyd died as peacefully as Jane had hoped, and her thoughts were now with the living: 'Your account of Martha is very comfortable indeed, & now we shall be in no fear of receiving a worse. This day, if she has gone to Church, must have been a trial of her feelings, but I hope it will be the last of any acuteness',[15] and before Cassandra returned to Bath Mrs Austen and Jane perhaps sent her some little verses to cheer up Martha, who, while busy settling her mother's affairs, had the needless annoyance of her mourning-wear being delayed. Jane offered the 'Lines supposed to have been sent to an uncivil Dressmaker':

> Miss Lloyd has now sent to Miss Green,
> As on opening the box, may be seen,
> Some yards of a Black Ploughman's Gauze,
> To be made up directly, because
> Miss Lloyd must in mourning appear
> For the death of a Relative dear –

Miss Lloyd must expect to receive
This license to mourn & to grieve,
Complete, ere the end of the week –
It is better to write than to speak.

and Mrs Austen provided 'Miss Green's reply':

I've often made clothes
For those who write prose,
But 'tis the first time
I've had orders in rhyme.
Depend on't, fair Maid,
You shall be obeyed;
Your garment of black
Shall sit close to your back,
And in every part
I'll exert all my art;
It shall be the neatest
And eke the completest
That ever was seen –
Or my name is not Green![16]

As Martha was now almost alone in the world, it was agreed that she should presently come to live with Mrs Austen and her daughters – a partnership which succeeded so well that it lasted for more than twenty years, ending only after the death of Mrs Austen in 1827.

This year the Austen ladies started their family holiday early in June, travelling to Godmersham via Steventon. Mary Lloyd was imminently expecting her second child and, at twelve, Anna was too young to be helpful on such an occasion. She therefore joined her grandmother and aunts and arrived with them at Godmersham on 19 June, where on the following day good news was received, as Fanny noted in her diary: 'We heard that Aunt James Austen was safely brought to bed of a daughter whose name is to be Caroline Mary Craven.' Many years later Caroline, like her half-sister Anna, was able to provide reminiscences of her aunt Jane which their brother James Edward used when composing his *Memoir*.

Fanny also recorded in her diary the children's games in which the adults too participated:

Wednesday 26th June: Aunts and Grandmama played at school with us. Aunt Cassandra was Mrs Teachum the Governess Aunt Jane, Miss Popham the Teacher Aunt Harriet, Sally the Housemaid, Miss Sharpe, the Dancing master the Apothecary and the Serjeant, Grandmama Betty Jones the Pie woman, and Mama the Bathing woman. They dressed in Character and we had a most delightful day – After dessert we acted a Play called 'Virtue Rewarded'. Anna was Duchess St Albans, I was the Fairy Serena and Fanny Cage a Sheperdess [*sic*] 'Mona'. We had a Bowl of Syllabub in the evening.

In July some of the Bridges in-laws joined the house-party, and three years afterwards Jane remembered how 'animated' she and Cassandra had been when talking with Harriet Bridges and the Godmersham governess, Anne Sharp.[17] Although Miss Sharp left Godmersham a few months later, early in 1806, the friendship which Jane had formed with her at this time continued for the rest of her life, and after Jane's death Miss Sharp kept in touch with Mrs Austen and Cassandra into the 1820s.[18] There was another happy day for the children on 30 July: 'Aunts Cassandra and Jane, Anna, Edward, George Henry William and myself acted "The spoilt child" and "Innocence Rewarded", afterwards we danced and had a most delightful evening.'

It may have been during this visit to Godmersham, or possibly on some previous occasion between 1800 and 1805, that Jane wrote the miniature play *Sir Charles Grandison* for a similar family performance, with or without some degree of help from Anna.[19]

Fanny's diary shows that Mrs Austen and Anna left Godmersham on 31 July but Cassandra and Jane stayed on, dining out frequently and going to the balls in Canterbury during the mid-August Race Week – Henry made one of his flying visits to join in these latter festivities, much to Fanny's admiration. Later in August Cassandra and Jane alternated in paying short visits to Lady Bridges at Goodnestone, which gave rise to Jane's letters of 24, 27 and 30 August during the sisters' separation, keeping Cassandra in touch with the daily events at each of the family homes. One of the younger sons of the Bridges family, Edward (1779–1825), was still single and living at Goodnestone, and Jane wrote ironically: 'It is impossible to do justice to the hospitality of his attentions towards me; he made a point of ordering toasted cheese for supper entirely on my account.'[20] There is another gap in Jane's correspondence after 30 August 1805, but it seems possible that Edward Bridges proposed or attempted to propose to her some time later in the year, a proposal which she had no difficulty in politely rejecting.[21]

After Jane's return to Godmersham early in September, Edward and Elizabeth went to London for a week, spending their time in shopping, play-going and sight-seeing for Fanny's benefit, and dining with Henry and Eliza at Brompton and No. 1 The Courtyard, Albany – the latest location for Henry's office. During this time Jane and Cassandra stayed with Elizabeth's sister Mrs Deedes, at the Deedes' country house a few miles away at Sandling, near Folkestone.

By mid-September the house-party was reassembled at Godmersham, and on 17 September they set off for Worthing to join Mrs Austen and Martha Lloyd, who were already in lodgings there. The next day Fanny noted: 'I went with G. Mama in the morning to buy fish on the beach & afterwards with Mama & Miss Sharpe to Bathe where I had a most delicious dip . . . We dined at 4 & went to a Raffle in the evening, where Aunt Jane won & it amounted to 17s. . .' Fanny and her parents returned home a few days later, but Mrs Austen and her daughters, together with Martha, stayed in Worthing until at least early November, possibly being joined by Henry, and may have remained there over Christmas, as the next definite news of their movements is not until January 1806.[22] Perhaps it was during these autumn evenings that Jane made a fair copy of her early work *Lady Susan*, adding its 'Conclusion' as she did so; but to *The Watsons*, put aside so soon after its inception, she never returned.

Meanwhile, Frank had been helping to make naval history aboard his new command. In March 1805 Nelson wrote: 'I hope to see [Captain Austen] alongside a French 80-gun ship, and he cannot be better placed than in the *Canopus*, which was once a French Admiral's ship, and struck to me. Captain Austen I knew a little of before; he is an excellent young man.'[23] Admiral Louis hoisted his flag in the *Canopus* and soon became second-in-command to Nelson, and Frank, as his flag-captain, took part in the chase after Villeneuve to the West Indies and back. September was then spent in blockading Cadiz; and, after Nelson's arrival from England in the *Victory* on 28 September, the *Canopus* was ordered to 'complete supplies' at Gibraltar. After this followed an order to Admiral Louis to give protection as far as Cartagena to a convoy proceeding to Malta. On receiving the news that the enemy fleet was coming out of Cadiz, the *Canopus* made haste to rejoin the main fleet, in spite of contrary winds, with the apprehension of being too late for the imminent battle.

In a letter commenced on 15 October and continued in his spare moments until 4 November, Frank told Mary Gibson: 'I do not profess to like fighting for its own sake, but if there has been an action with the combined fleets I shall ever consider the day on which I sailed from the squadron as the most inauspicious one of my life'. On 27 October he added:

Alas! my dearest Mary, all my fears are but too fully justified. The fleets have met, and, after a very severe contest, a most decisive victory has been gained by the English . . . but I am truly sorry to add that this splendid affair has cost us many lives, and amongst them the most invaluable one to the nation, that of our gallant, and ever-to-be-regretted, Commander-in-Chief, Lord Nelson, who was mortally wounded by a musket shot, and only lived long enough to know his fleet successful . . . to lose all share in the glory of a day which surpasses all which ever went before, is what I cannot think of with any degree of patience; but, as I cannot write upon that subject without complaining, I will drop it for the present, till time and reflection reconcile me a little more to what I know is now inevitable.[24]

On 3 January 1806 Jane and Martha arrived at Steventon and, as befitted a family with naval interests, Jane gave little James Edward, now aged eight, *The British Navigator, or, A collection of voyages made in different parts of the world.*[25] Cassandra and Mrs Austen arrived a week later, the latter starting the New Year with a reasonable £68 in hand.[26] The Steventon family had just suffered a bereavement, as Anna's grandfather General Mathew had died on 26 December 1805, an event which caused James financial worries for some time. Although the General had been personally appointed by George III to his Governorship of Grenada and command of the Leeward Islands, the payment of his salary had never been officially ratified by the Exchequer, and now upon his death the Exchequer claimed back from his estate the sum of £24,000 – not only the original salary but compound interest upon it as well – and the new Whig Government insisted upon the exaction of this amount. This meant in turn that the annual £100 given by the General to James on Anna's behalf ceased, and that her eventual inheritance of her mother's portion of the estate was diminished by £1,000.[27] But what Fortune took away with one hand it seemed she was prepared to return with the other; the Austens' old friend Mr Fowle, then rector of Hamstead Marshall, died in February 1806 and Lord Craven, as patron, asked James to take over the living for a few years until the young man whom he intended to appoint should come of age for ordination. However, James was a man of strict principle and felt that to accept the living temporarily on such terms smacked of simony, and would be against the wording of the declaration which he would have to make upon acceptance. After a week's deliberation he rejected the offer, much to Mary Lloyd's annoyance, since the living was worth about £300 a year and this would have made a very welcome addition to James's income, depleted as it was by the loss of General Mathew's allowance.[28]

On 29 January Mrs Austen left Steventon, taking Anna with her, and found temporary lodgings in Bath in Trim Street, while looking for accommodation to rent on a more permanent basis. Jane and Cassandra went for three weeks to Manydown, returning to Steventon in late February and finally joining their mother in Bath in mid-March. Here they arrived to find an unexpected pleasure – a legacy from Mrs Lillingston, one of Mrs Leigh-Perrot's circle of Bath friends, who had died at the end of January.

She had made Mr Leigh-Perrot her executor and also left bequests to himself, his wife and his nieces – Jane and Cassandra each received £50, an amount which proved more than sufficient to cover Jane's personal expenses for the entire year following.[29]

After his disappointment at missing Trafalgar, Frank was to some extent consoled by taking part in Sir John Duckworth's cruise to the West Indies and in the victory over the French at St Domingo on 6 February 1806. He wrote to Mary Gibson the next day to assure her of his safety, and in the following weeks, as the squadron sailed homewards with three prizes, the officers received votes of thanks from the President and Council of St Kitts Nevis and from the House of Commons.[30]

By April Mrs Austen was getting exasperated at her failure to find suitable accommodation and wrote to Mary Lloyd from 'Trim Street Still' on 10 April:

> I had a letter the other day from Edwd. Cooper, he wrote to congratulate us on Frank's Victory and safety, and to invite us to Hamstall in the ensuing Summer, which invitation we seem disposed to accept . . . We are disappointed of the Lodgings in St James's Square, a person is in treaty for the whole House, so of course he will be prefer'd to us who want only a part. – We have look'd at some others since, but don't quite like the situation – hope a few days hence we shall have more choice, as it is supposed many will go from Bath when this gay week is over.[31]

Although Mrs Austen could not have guessed it when she wrote, Frank's recent victory at sea proved the indirect solution to her accommodation problem. When he docked at Plymouth early in May, Lloyd's Patriotic Fund presented him with a silver vase valued at £100 as a memento of St Domingo, and he also received a gold medal as he left the *Canopus*. This accession of honours and prize-money evidently encouraged him to think that he could now afford to marry Mary Gibson, and so the date of 24 July was chosen. It was probably also his idea that, as he would no doubt be appointed to another ship within a few months, his bride would be happier living in company than on her own, following his departure again to sea; so it was arranged that Mrs Austen and her daughters would move to Southampton – at that time a fairly fashionable watering-place[32] – and that Mary Gibson would live with them. They would all then be very close to the great Portsmouth dockyard, where Frank was bound to call from time to time no matter which ship he was aboard. As he himself put it: 'He fixed his abode at Southampton making one family with his mother and sisters, a plan equally suited to his love of domestic society and the extent of his income which was somewhat restricted.'[33]

On 2 July 1806 Mrs Austen, with her daughters and Martha Lloyd, left Bath for the last time, to the great relief of both Cassandra and Jane – two years later Jane was still recalling their 'happy feelings of Escape!'[34] Their immediate destination was Clifton, and here Martha left them to go on to Harrogate. She had been hoping to be escorted there by an old acquaintance, Mr Best, but this year for some reason he was reluctant to make the journey, a situation that prompted one of Jane's wittiest doggerel poems:

> Oh! Mr Best, you're very bad
> And all the world shall know it;
> Your base behaviour shall be sung
> By me, a tuneful poet.
>
> You used to go to Harrogate
> Each summer as it came,
> And why, I pray, should you refuse
> To go this year the same?

– and so on for several more stanzas, ending up with praise of Martha's merits as a travelling companion:

> Take her, & wonder at your luck,
> In having such a Trust.
> Her converse sensible & sweet
> Will banish heat & dust . . .[35]

Frank married Mary Gibson in Ramsgate on 24 July as planned, and the young couple went to Godmersham for a prolonged honeymoon. From Clifton Jane wrote to little Fanny and sent her some verses imaginatively describing their bridal trip, as if spoken by Fanny herself:

> See they come, post haste from Thanet,
> Lovely couple, side by side;
> They've left behind them Richard Kennet
> With the Parents of the Bride!
>
> Canterbury they have passed through;
> Next succeeded Stamford-bridge;
> Chilham village they came fast through;
> Now they've mounted yonder ridge.
>
> Down the hill they're swift proceeding,
> Now they skirt the Park around;
> Lo! The Cattle sweetly feeding
> Scamper, startled at the sound!

Run, my Brothers, to the Pier gate!
Throw it open, very wide!
Let it not be said that we're late
In welcoming my Uncle's Bride!

To the house the chaise advances;
Now it stops – They're here, they're here!
How d'ye do, my Uncle Francis?
How does do your Lady dear?[36]

Now that Jane had two sisters-in-law called Mary, it became her custom to refer to them in her letters as 'Mrs J. A.' and 'Mrs F. A.' in any context where ambiguity might arise; and to their nephews and nieces they were known as 'Aunt James' and 'Aunt Frank'.

The Austens did not stay long at Clifton, and by the end of the month were at Adlestrop rectory, the home of Mrs Austen's cousin, the Revd Thomas Leigh, and part of the estate of Adlestrop House where the younger Mr James Henry Leigh and his family lived. Since their last visit here Revd Thomas Leigh had commissioned Humphrey Repton in 1802 to carry out his ideas for improvements to the estate – he had enclosed the village green and planted out the cottages, moved the entrance to the rectory and opened up the back of the house, and made a new garden that merged with his nephew's grounds:

a lively stream of water has been led through a flower garden, where its progress down the hill is occasionally obstructed by ledges of rock, and after a variety of interesting circumstances it falls into a lake at a considerable distance, but in full view both of the mansion and the parsonage, to each of which it makes a delightful, because a natural, feature in the landscape.[37]

For his services Repton charged a fee of five guineas a day, as Mr Leigh evidently informed his cousins in the course of showing them round his improvements.

The Austens did not, however, stay long at Adlestrop either, for on 5 August they set out, together with Mr Leigh, his sister Elizabeth, his lawyer Mr Joseph Hill and all the house-party, to go to Stoneleigh Abbey in Warwickshire. This sudden journey was the result of some rather peculiar family circumstances, the origin of which dated back twenty years. In 1786 the last Lord Leigh of Stoneleigh had died unmarried, leaving his property to his sister, the Hon. Mary Leigh, for her life, and thereafter, according to the odd wording of his Will, 'unto the first and nearest of his kindred, being male and of his blood and name, that should be alive at the time'. All the Leighs of the Stoneleigh branch had died out, and an heir had therefore to be sought amongst their remote cousins, the Adlestrop Leighs. In ordinary circumstances the heir would have been James Henry Leigh, who was the head of this branch; but by the wording of Lord Leigh's Will all those of an older generation, who were thus 'the first and nearest of his blood and name', appeared to take precedence of the natural heir. Ever since 1786 the Adlestrop Leighs had been discussing amongst themselves how this strange situation was to be settled, and some of the men who descended in the female line had even changed their names back to 'Leigh' in the hope that this would give them a claim.

On 2 July 1806 the Hon. Mary Leigh died in London;[38] and as the eldest Leigh at this time was Revd Thomas, his lawyer advised that he should take immediate possession to forestall any other claimants – hence the hasty trip from Adlestrop to Stoneleigh. This visit, and the whole question of the succession to Stoneleigh, was of especial interest to the Austens, for it seemed likely that Mr Leigh-Perrot would have a life-interest in the estate after Revd Thomas Leigh, if he survived him. It was, however, obviously most in accordance with the desire of the testator that the estate should descend by the usual rules of primogeniture to James Henry Leigh; so Mr Leigh-Perrot eventually resigned his claim to the estate in exchange for a capital sum of £24,000 and an annuity of £2,000, which latter lasted until the death of his widow in 1836.[39]

Stoneleigh Abbey had been founded as a Cistercian monastery in 1155, and following the Dissolution the site passed into the hands of the Leigh family in 1561. They then built a new house, utilising the stones of the old Abbey and part of its foundations, and early in the eighteenth century the third Lord Leigh remodelled the west wing into a new principal front, leaving the remainder of the Elizabethan building unaltered. It was this newer west wing that Mrs Austen described in her letter of 13 August 1806 to Mary Lloyd:

And here we all found ourselves on Tuesday (that is yesterday sennight) Eating Fish, venison & all manner of good things, at a late hour, in a Noble large Parlour hung round with family Pictures – every thing is very Grand & very fine & very Large – The House is larger than I could have supposed – we can now find our way about it, I mean the best part, as to the offices (which were the old Abby [*sic*]) Mr Leigh almost dispairs [*sic*] of ever finding his way about them – I have proposed his setting up directing Posts at the Angles – I expected to find everything about the place very fine & all that, but I had no idea of its being so beautiful, I had figured to myself long Avenues, dark rookeries & dismal Yew Trees, but here are no such melancholy things; The Avon runs near the house amidst Green Meadows, bounding [*sic*] by large and beautiful Woods, full of delightful Walks . . . I will now give you some idea of the inside of this vast house, first premising that there are 45 windows in front, (which is quite strait with a flat Roof) 15 in a row – you go up a considerable flight of steps (some offices are under the house) into a large Hall, on the right hand, the dining parlour, within that the Breakfast room, where we generally sit, and reason good, tis the only room (except the Chapel) that looks towards the River, – on the left hand the Hall is the best drawing room, within that a smaller, these rooms are rather gloomy, Brown wainscoat & dark Crimson furniture, so we never use them but to walk thro' them to the old picture Gallery; Behind the smaller drawing Room is the State Bed chamber with a high dark crimson Velvet Bed, an <u>alarming</u> apartment just fit for an Heroine, the old Gallery opens into it – behind the Hall & Parlour a passage all across the house containing 3 staircases & two small back Parlours – there are 26 Bed Chambers in the new part of the house, & a great many (some very good ones) in the Old . . . Our Visit has been a most pleasant one, we all seem in good humour, disposed to be pleas'd, endeavor to be agreable, and I hope succeed – Poor Lady Saye & Sele, to be sure, is rather tormenting, tho' some times amusing, and affords Jane many a good laugh – but she fatigues me sadly on the whole . . .[40]

The tiresome Dowager Lady Saye and Sele was a Leigh cousin and mother of the adulterous Mary Cassandra Twisleton whom Jane had observed in Bath; her other daughter, Julia Judith, was the wife of James Henry Leigh. Twenty years before, Fanny Burney had been rendered speechless in the face of Lady Saye and Sele's relentless, ridiculous chatter, and her intelligence had evidently not increased with age.[41] Mrs Austen concluded: 'Tomorrow we depart, Hamstall is 38 miles from hence. We have seen the remains of Kenilworth Castle, which afforded us much entertainment, I expect still more from the sight of Warwick Castle, which we are going to see to-day.'

From Stoneleigh the Austens went on to see Edward Cooper and his family at Hamstall Ridware, just over the border into Staffordshire: 'a beautifully situated parsonage house on a considerable eminence, back'd with fine woods, seen at a distance from the road to this happy village',[42] where the church, St Michael's, was 'a very neat old Spire Building of stone, having two side Ailes [*sic*] Chancel &c. and makes a magnificent appearance as a Village Church'.[43] Edward Cooper had recently published some of his sermons,[44] and his eldest son, Edward Philip, now aged nearly twelve, was precociously imitating his father in this respect and lording it over his younger brothers and sisters in a way that met with Jane's disapproval. When he was sent to school at Rugby in 1809, she commented: 'it will be a great change, to become a raw school boy from being a pompous Sermon-Writer, & a domineering Brother. – It will do him good I dare say.'[45] The Austens stayed at Hamstall Ridware for about five weeks before returning to Hampshire; unfortunately during this period Edward's eight children

Plate 21 Southampton – early nineteenth-century engraving of the medieval city walls as seen from the tidal inlet of Southampton Water.

all developed whooping cough, and Jane succumbed to the infection a few weeks later.[46]

The Austens arrived early in October at Steventon, where Frank and Mary Gibson had been staying since mid-September, and on 10 October they all left Steventon together to start their new life in Southampton.[47] They took lodgings there – the location of which remains unidentified – while looking for a more permanent home. The approach of Christmas brought movement to the family circle again – Martha Lloyd went to the Fowles at Kintbury and Cassandra went to Godmersham, and as their absence meant there were spare beds in the lodgings, James and Mary and their toddler Caroline came to Southampton for the New Year. This visit was not one of unmixed enjoyment for Jane, who had to bear the brunt of the entertaining; the weather was in general too bad for exercise and James, who hated to be confined indoors, was bored and restless; Mary Gibson was already pregnant and suffering fainting fits in consequence; and Mary Lloyd was uninterested in any of the books Jane had chosen for the family's evening pastime of reading aloud. Some letters to Cassandra are missing for the period from the end of December to early January 1807, and by her letter of 7 January Jane was looking forward with relief to the departure of the Steventon group. 'When you receive this, our guests will be all gone or going; and I shall be left to the comfortable disposal of my time, to ease of mind from the torments of rice puddings and apple dumplings, and probably to regret that I did not take more pains to please them all.'[48] It was probably during this visit that Jane wrote two little plays giving in amusing fashion instructions on baby-care, a topic about which Mary Gibson was then understandably anxious. The composition of these little works would have afforded an opportunity for Mary Lloyd to join in by proffering practical advice and information, and so provide an occupation of reasonably common interest for all the ladies during the long winter evenings.[49]

Apart from these family visitors, Southampton residents were starting to call upon the Austens, not always to Jane's pleasure.

Our acquaintance increase too fast. [Frank] was recognised lately by Admiral Bertie, and a few days since arrived the Admiral and his daughter Catherine to wait upon us. There was nothing to like or dislike in either. To the Berties are to be added the Lances, with whose cards we have been endowed, and whose visit Frank and I returned yesterday . . . We found only Mrs Lance at home, and whether she boasts any offspring besides a grand pianoforte did not appear. She was civil and chatty enough, and offered to introduce us to some acquaintance in Southampton, which we gratefully declined . . . They live in a handsome style and are rich, and she seemed to like to be rich, and we gave her to understand that we were far from being so; she will soon feel therefore that we are not worth her acquaintance.[50]

After the departure of James and his family, no more letters from Jane to Cassandra survive until that of 8 February 1807; it would seem that, despite the optimism expressed by James and Henry in their correspondence with Frank after Mr Austen's death, Jane was suddenly very depressed by the limitations of the life imposed on her mother and herself by their bereavement and diminished income, and Cassandra probably destroyed the letters in which Jane gave vent to these gloomy feelings, as well as those written over the Christmas period in which she may have voiced exasperation concerning James and his wife.

By February matters were improving, for the family had taken a lease of 'a commodious old-fashioned house in a corner of Castle Square . . . [it] had a pleasant garden, bounded on one side by the old city walls; the top of this wall was sufficiently wide to afford a pleasant walk, with an extensive view, easily accessible to ladies by steps'.[51] The far side of the city wall was washed by the tides of Southampton Water, and beyond lay the wooded slopes of the Isle of Wight – known locally simply as 'the Island'. The approach to Castle Square was unfortunately through some very narrow, dirty lanes,[52] but the Square itself was occupied 'by a fantastic edifice, too large for the space in which it stood, though too small to accord well with its castellated style, erected by the second Marquis of Lansdowne'.[53] In Cassandra's absence Jane and Mrs Austen were replanning the garden of their new home:

Our Garden is putting in order, by a Man who bears a remarkably good Character, has a very fine complexion & asks something less than the first. The Shrubs which border the gravel walk he says are only sweetbriar & roses, & the latter of an indifferent sort; – we mean to get a few of a better kind therefore, & at my own particular desire he procures us some Syringas. I could not do without a Syringa, for the sake of Cowper's Line. – We talk also of a Laburnam. – The Border under the Terrace Wall, is clearing away to receive Currants & Gooseberry Bushes, & a spot is found very proper for Raspberries.[54]

It was a wet day as Jane wrote, but Frank had been to church and brought back with him Catherine, the ten-year-old daughter of his friend Capt. Foote, RN, for a day's visit, and Jane added:

she is now talking away at my side & examining the Treasures of my Writing-desk drawer; – very happy I beleive; – not at all shy of course . . . Our little visitor has just left us, & left us highly pleased with her; – she is a nice, natural, openhearted, affectionate girl, with all the ready civility which one sees in the best Children of the present day; – so unlike anything that I was myself at her age, that I am often all astonishment & shame.

James was due to come to Southampton again during February, a prospect which Jane did not now relish:

I am sorry & angry that his Visits should not give one more pleasure; the company of so good & so clever a Man ought to be gratifying in itself; – but his Chat seems all forced, his Opinions on many points too much copied from his Wife's, & his time here is spent I think in walking about the House & banging the Doors, or ringing the Bell for a glass of Water.[55]

There is another gap in Jane's letters after this of 8 February, which suggests that in later years Cassandra censored further criticisms of James following his next visit.

On 20 February Jane started another letter, expecting it to be the last before Cassandra returned; but before she could finish it she received one from her sister with the news that she would not be back until the end of March or early April. Apart from the disappointment over Cassandra's delayed return, however, Jane was looking forward to seeing Martha again within the next few days; also the cleaning and furnishing of the Castle Square house was proceeding apace and they hoped to move in on or about

9 March. 'We hear that we are envied our House by many people, & that the Garden is the best in the Town.'[56] Cassandra was finally brought away from Godmersham by Henry in mid-March, and probably spent a few days in London with him and Eliza before returning to Southampton early in April. He had just recently taken another of his Oxfordshire Militia friends into partnership, Mr James Tilson of Watlington Park, and had moved his offices from Albany to No. 10 Henrietta Street, Covent Garden.[57]

No sooner had the family moved into the Castle Square house than on 23 March Frank received his next appointment – the command of HMS *St Albans*, for convoy duty to and from South Africa, China and the East Indies. By 4 April he was aboard at Sheerness and busy fitting-out for the long voyage ahead, which meant he was absent from Southampton for the birth of his first child on 27 April – poor Mary Gibson had a painful confinement and was 'most alarmingly ill' for some days, but thereafter made a good recovery, and the baby was 'a fine little girl, named Mary Jane, & called by both names'.[58] Frank set off in the *St Albans* from Sheerness on 21 May and arrived at Spithead a few days later, so was no doubt able to attend Mary Jane's christening at All Saints, Southampton, on 31 May.[59] He had another month of home life before setting sail for the Cape of Good Hope on 30 June.

It was now Charles's turn to provide his family with good news. Since 1804 he had been engaged in the unpleasant and unprofitable duty of enforcing the right of search on the Atlantic seaboard of America, to ensure that neutral countries such as America were not trading with France. While stationed at Bermuda he had met the Chief Justice, Mr James Christie Esten, and the latter's young sister-in-law Miss Frances Fitzwilliam Palmer. Fanny Palmer and her sister Mrs Esten were the daughters of a former Attorney-General of Bermuda, Mr John Grove Palmer, who had now retired to his London home at 22 Keppel Street, Bloomsbury. Fanny (1790–1814) was pink, plump and had beautiful, rich golden hair that was Charles's especial delight.[60] They became engaged in the spring of 1806 and were married in Bermuda on 19 May 1807, when she was just seventeen.[61] It was however to be another four years before Charles returned to England to introduce his wife and the two little girls who by then had been born to them – Cassandra Esten in 1808 and Harriet Jane in 1810.

Following Frank's departure at the end of June, Mary Gibson went to Ramsgate and to Godmersham, and while she was away Edward Cooper brought his three eldest children to Southampton to see the Austens, arriving there on 10 August. The Godmersham family were also thinking of a summer holiday; in April Edward had visited Hampshire to inspect his other estate at Chawton, just vacated by the latest tenant Mr Coulthard, and had followed this up by a further visit in mid-June to Chawton and to Southampton to say goodbye to Frank. Plans had evidently been made then for a family gathering later in the year, so now Edward brought the elder members of his family to Chawton Great House at the end of August, and as soon as the Coopers left Southampton after a fortnight's stay, Mrs Austen and her daughters went to Chawton and James brought his family there as well.[62]

Although Edward had inherited Chawton simultaneously with Steventon and Godmersham, he himself had always lived in Kent and not paid much attention to his Hampshire properties, being content to leave Steventon in the hands of the Digweed family as permanent tenants, leasing Chawton for short terms to various gentlemen who, for whatever reason, did not possess their own estates, and visiting Hampshire only twice a year to check on the management of the properties. This visit in 1807 was the first time, therefore, that young Fanny had seen the house, so she hastened to tell Miss Chapman about it:

This is a fine large old house, built long before Queen Elizabeth I believe, & here are such a number of old irregular passages &c &c that it is very entertaining to explore them, & often when I think myself miles away from one part of the house I find a passage or entrance close to it, & I don't know when I shall be quite mistress of all the intricate, & different ways. It is very curious to trace the genealogy of the Knights & all the old families that have possessed this estate, from the pictures of which there are quantities, & some descriptions of them have been routed out, so that we are not at a loss for amusement. There are quantities of Trees about the house (especially Beech) which always makes a place pretty, I think.[63]

The older part of Chawton House was of flint and stone, dating to the first half of the sixteenth century but possibly incorporating medieval foundations, and in the middle of the seventeenth century two red-brick gabled wings had been added, necessitating extra staircases and awkward passages, as Fanny had noticed. There was an immense hall and a gallery supposed to be haunted, the walls were hung with tapestry instead of paper, and the open fireplaces still had fire-dogs instead of grates.[64] On this occasion the house-party stayed ten days, exploring the rambling house and its estate, calling on neighbours and tenants in the village and shopping in Alton, and young Edward was taken to start his first term at Winchester.

It was probably during this holiday period that Mrs Austen, Cassandra, Jane and Edward's wife, Elizabeth sat down together and each composed their set of 'Verses to Rhyme with "Rose"', which are undated but cannot be later than September 1807.[65] When the Austen ladies returned to

Southampton on 11 September Edward and his family followed them there, and Fanny's diary records the events of the next few days: strolling to the Polygon, a smart new residential development outside the old city walls, after church on Sunday, a visit to the theatre on Monday evening, a water-trip to Hythe to meet Charles's mother-in-law, Mrs Palmer, who was also on holiday in Hampshire with her second daughter, Harriet, and walking in the High Street in the late summer evenings with Aunts Cassandra and Jane. Henry rushed down from London and organised a picnic in the romantic ruins of Netley Abbey and a drive through the New Forest to Lyndhurst and Lymington. Edward and his family, accompanied by Henry, returned to Chawton in mid-September and were back at Godmersham early in October.[66]

There is no further news of Mrs Austen and her daughters for the rest of this year, but at the end of December Jane noted at the back of her diary her cash account for 1807. She had started the year with £50.15s.6d. (the bulk of this sum perhaps being Mrs Lillingston's legacy) and ended it with £6.4s.6d. in hand. The 'waterparties and plays' enjoyed during September had cost 17s.9d., and a 'journey' – presumably that to Chawton – £1.2s.10d. The largest item of expenditure was £13.19s.3d. on 'Cloathes & Pocket', followed by 'Washing' at £9.5s.11½d. 'Presents' accounted for £6.4s.4d., 'Charity' for £3.10s.3½d., and 'Letters & Parcels' cost £3.17s.6½d. Her personal luxury was £2.13s.6d. for 'Hire Piano Forte'.[67]

CHAPTER 12

Southampton and Chawton, 1808–9

No letters of Jane's survive for the first half of 1808, and it appears that during most of this period she and Cassandra were together paying visits in Hampshire and Berkshire; in January and February they alternated between Steventon and Manydown, before going on to Kintbury at the end of February.[1] At Manydown their old friends Catherine and Alethea Bigg were still unmarried, but the third daughter, Elizabeth, Mrs Heathcote, was now a young widow and had returned to her father's house with her only child, William, born in 1801. William was a clever, handsome little boy, who grew up to be the schoolmate and lifelong friend of Jane's nephew, James Edward; many years later he 'remembered being at a Twelfth-day party where Jane Austen drew the character of Mrs Candour, and assumed the part with great spirit',[2] and it seems likely that the party concerned took place during this visit in January 1808.

On 25 February Jane and Cassandra went from Steventon to Kintbury, a few miles over the Berkshire border, to stay with the Fowle family. Kintbury was a quiet agricultural village, built on the chalky banks of the little Kennet river; James Austen had courted Mary Lloyd there while she was staying with her sister, Mrs Fowle, and wrote some of his verses in fond remembrance of the scene:

> Where sloping uplands catch the sun's first beam,
> Where winding through the meadows Kennet's stream
> Reflects in outline true, but tints less bright
> The grey church tower, tall tree & mansion white
> . . . The river's bank, the causeway's shaded walk . . .[3]

On the other side of the Kennet was the estate of Barton Court, now owned by the MP for Berkshire, Mr Charles Dundas, and where the Lloyd girls' grandmother, the 'cruel Mrs Craven', had ended her days rich in worldly goods after her marriage to the previous owner, Mr Jemmet Raymond. In Kintbury church stands a large marble monument bearing the busts of

Mrs Craven and her second husband; if this representation of her is accurate, the strong determined features shown would seem to confirm the ruthless nature which family tradition records.[4]

Of the four Fowle sons who had once been Mr Austen's pupils, only the eldest, Fulwar, now remained. Not long after Tom's death at St Domingo, the third son William, who had become a military physician, went with the army to Egypt and died there in 1801; and Jane's particular friend, the youngest son, Charles, had suddenly fallen ill in 1805 and died early in 1806. Fulwar, although he had never become Secretary of State – as James Austen had admiringly suggested, when they were boys together in 1780 – had made quite a name for himself locally. In addition to his pastoral duties as vicar of Kintbury, thanks to the several invasion emergencies during these wartime years he had become Lieutenant-Colonel of a large company of riflemen that formed part of the Berkshire Volunteers, and was personally congratulated by George III at a review of these volunteer troops on Bulmarsh Heath, near Reading, in June 1805, when the King said: 'I knew that you were a good clergyman and a good man; now I know that you are a good officer.' On another occasion George III was reported as saying of Fulwar: 'He is the best preacher, the best officer and the best rider to hounds in all my royal county of Berkshire.'[5] Fulwar was now the father of six children; his eldest son, Fulwar William (1791–1876), was destined for the church and his second son, another Tom, was already out in the world as a promising midshipman under Charles Austen's command on the sloop HMS *Indian* at Bermuda.[6] In 1838 Fulwar William gave a description of Jane Austen as he remembered her from the days of his youth: 'she was pretty – certainly pretty – bright & a good deal of color in her face – like a doll – no that wd. not give at all the idea for she had so much expression – she was like a child – quite a child very lively & full of humor – most amiable – most beloved –'[7]

After this visit to Kintbury the next news of Jane is that she and Henry spent the night of 15 May at Steventon en route for London.[8] Here she stayed with him in his house at Brompton until mid-June, and saw the ladies going to Court on 4 June for the King's birthday celebrations. In the meantime James took Anna to Southampton to stay with Mrs Austen and Cassandra, and then brought Mary Lloyd and his two younger children in his new chaise to London to stay at the Bath Hotel in Arlington Street. Jane joined them there early in the morning of 14 June, and while James went ahead by public coach she and Mary set off for Godmersham in their own carriage with the children at a more leisurely pace. Jane's first surviving letter from this year, which she commenced on 15 June, told Cassandra of the journey into Kent and the happy reception at their destination:

Our two brothers were walking before the house as we approached, as natural as life. Fanny and Lizzy met us in the Hall with a great deal of pleasant joy . . . Elizabeth, who was dressing when we arrived, came to me for a minute attended by Marianne, Charles, and Louisa, and, you will not doubt, gave me a very affectionate welcome. That I had received such from Edward also I need not mention; but I do, you see, because it is a pleasure.[9]

Edward's family now numbered ten and Elizabeth was once again pregnant, with the baby expected in September; Jane thought she did not look very well and, as the family were for the moment without a resident governess, relieved her of some of her maternal duties by helping to teach the little ones their lessons. It may be that Jane found the children were reading Charlotte Smith's *Minor Morals, interspersed with sketches of Natural History, Historical Anecdotes, and Original Stories*, and took the opportunity to copy out from this the poem 'Kalendar of Flora' – a list of seasonal wild flowers – for the benefit of Cassandra, the florist of the Austen family.[10]

This visit by James and Mary to Godmersham was 'for the first time these 10 years', as Fanny noted in her diary, and they were 'much struck with the beauty of the place.'[11] James Edward enjoyed playing with his cousins Lizzy and Charles, but little Caroline found the boisterous Godmersham children rather too much for her.

I remember the Godmersham visit well, in many little points; and I don't think I <u>was</u> very happy there, in a strange house. I recollect the model of a ship in a passage, and my cousins' rabbits out of doors, in or near a long walk of high trees. I have been told it was the lime-tree walk. As I never visited the place again, the very little that I <u>do</u> remember, must date from that time.[12]

Three weeks passed away 'quite a la Godmersham', receiving and paying calls amongst the Kentish circle, in 'Elegance & Ease & Luxury', and Jane also spent a day or two with Mrs Knight in Canterbury, finding her 'as gentle & kind & friendly as usual', though in rather poor health. 'I cannot help regretting that now, when I feel enough her equal to relish her society, I see so little of the latter.'[13] Jane gave a copy of one of her own favourites, Cowper's *Poems*, to Fanny on 29 June, but perhaps it did not appeal equally to the latter, for she made no mention of the gift in her diary.[14] Henry paid another of his flying visits from London to join the house-party for the first week of July, and he and James went to Deal to welcome Frank, who had just arrived there in the *St Albans* after his latest trip, convoying home ships of the East India Company.

James took his family back to Steventon on 7 July, and the following day Edward escorted Jane to Southampton, spending a night at Guildford en route. Mrs Austen went to Steventon for the second half of July, and in her absence Cassandra and Jane entertained Catherine and Alethea Bigg in the Castle Square house. Catherine was now engaged to the Revd Herbert Hill, uncle of the poet Robert Southey; Mr Hill was considerably older than herself and had been for many years chaplain to the British trading settlement at Oporto, Portugal, until the threat of French invasion brought him back to England in the summer of 1801.[15] Jane hemstitched some pocket handkerchiefs for Catherine, as a wedding present, and on 26 August added a little verse to go with them:

> Cambrick! with grateful blessings would I pay
> The pleasure given me in sweet employ.
> Long may'st thou serve my friend without decay,
> And have no tears to shed but tears of joy.

This verse embodied Jane's second thoughts on the subject, because she also retained the text of her first, equally charming, composition:

> Cambrick! Thou'st been to me a Good,
> And I would bless thee if I could.
> Go, serve thy Mistress with delight,
> Be small in compass, soft & white;
> Enjoy thy fortune, honour'd much
> To bear her name & feel her touch;
> And that thy worth may last for years,
> Slight be her Colds & few her Tears.[16]

In the summer of 1808 another phase of the long-drawn-out struggle against Napoleon commenced – the Peninsular War, when the Portuguese and Spanish rose against French domination and English troops were sent to help them regain their independence. Frank's next task, therefore, during July, was to take aboard Brigadier-General Anstruther and his staff and escort troopships out to the Portuguese coast, where they disembarked at Mondego Bay. On 21 August, as the *St Albans* stood off at sea, Frank 'observed an action between the English and French armies on the heights over Merceira' – this was the battle of Vimeiro, the first British victory of the campaign. The following day Frank picked up the wounded and the French prisoners, and by early September was back at Spithead, discharging the latter into the prison hulks anchored there. The *St Albans* then had to go to Great Yarmouth for servicing, and Mary Gibson followed Frank into lodgings in the town where, as Jane said: 'with fish almost for nothing, & plenty of Engagements & plenty of each other, [they] must be very happy'.[17]

The Steventon family visited Southampton again at the end of September, and it was possibly on this occasion that James Edward saw in Castle Square the unusual carriage affected by the Marchioness of Lansdowne, who was as eccentric a personality as her husband, the builder of the 'Gothic' castle.

The Marchioness had a light phaeton, drawn by six, and sometimes by eight little ponies, each pair decreasing in size, and becoming lighter in colour, through all the grades of dark brown, light brown, bay and chestnut, as it was placed farther away from the carriage. The two leading pairs were managed by two boyish postilions, the two pairs nearest to the carriage were driven in hand. It was a delight to me to look down from the window and see this fairy equipage put together; for the premises of this castle were so contracted that the whole process went on in the little space that remained of the open square.[18]

At Godmersham Elizabeth was now imminently expecting her eleventh baby, and Fanny wrote to Miss Chapman: 'Aunt Cassandra I am happy to say is coming to stay here some time, it will be a great comfort to me to have her assistance in the lessons during Mama's confinement, as well as her company.'[19] Cassandra arrived on 28 September, just a few hours too late to be present at the birth of Brook John, Edward's sixth son, but was able to write immediately to Jane with the good news that both mother and child were doing well.

Jane's letters of 1 and 7 October kept Cassandra in touch with Southampton life, especially the exciting occurrence of a fire that broke out in the High Street on the night of 4 October, which had reminded Jane of the previous occasion when they saw a fire in Lyme Regis. In these two letters also occur the first mentions of the Austens' intention to leave Southampton and move to Alton, a busy little town in Hampshire next door to Edward's Chawton estate. It seems that rents in Southampton were greatly increasing, and now that Frank had his own young family to support, Mrs Austen presumably felt she could not continue to accept £50 a year from him. In 1806 Henry had entered into another banking partnership, joining his London firm to that of Messrs Gray & Vincent in Alton, and with this local contact Jane and her mother were now expecting to 'hear of something perfectly unexceptionable there, through him'.[20]

There is also a hint that Jane had some slight embarrassment in thinking of Cassandra's being in contact with the Bridges family again: 'I wish you may be able to accept Lady Bridges's invitation, tho' *I* could not her son Edward's'[21] – and when Cassandra told her the following month that Edward Bridges was now engaged to Harriet Foote, Jane's congratulations seem to have a note of relief in them:

Your news of Edw: Bridges was <u>quite</u> news . . . I wish him happy with all my heart, & hope his choice may turn out according to his own expectations, & beyond those of his Family – and I dare say it will. Marriage is a great Improver – & in a similar situation Harriet may be as amiable as Eleanor. – As to Money, that will come you may be sure, because they cannot do without it. – When you see him again, pray give him our Congratulations & best wishes.[22]

In her letter of 7 October Jane told Cassandra:

I am greatly pleased with your account of Fanny; I found her in the summer just what you describe, almost another Sister, & could not have supposed that a neice would ever have been so much to me. She is quite after one's own heart; give her my best Love, & tell her that I always think of her with pleasure.

But before this letter reached Godmersham, Fanny had scrawled with a trembling hand in her diary on 10 October: 'Oh! the miserable events of this day! My mother, my beloved mother torn from us! After eating a hearty dinner, she was taken <u>violently</u> ill and <u>expired</u> (may God have mercy upon us) in ¹/₂ an hour!!!!' Edward's two eldest sons, young Edward and George, were now at Winchester College, so the Steventon family collected the boys at once for a few days' compassionate leave; the brief information of Elizabeth's death therefore reached Southampton via Steventon, to be followed by a letter direct from Cassandra with more details.

Henry went immediately to Godmersham to join in the mourning, and Jane's letters of 13 and 15 October were full of love and sympathy for the bereaved household.

We have felt, we do feel for you all – as you will not need to be told – for you, for Fanny, for Henry, for Lady Bridges, & for dearest Edward, whose loss & whose sufferings seem to make those of every other person nothing . . . My dear, dear Fanny! – I am so thankful that she has you with her! . . . You will know that the poor Boys are at Steventon, perhaps it is best for them . . . but I own myself disappointed by the arrangements; – I should have loved to have them with me at such a time . . . We need not enter into a Panegyric on the Departed – but it is sweet to think of her great worth – of her solid principles, her true devotion, her excellence in every relation of Life . . . That you are for ever in our Thoughts, you will not doubt. – I see your mournful party in my mind's eye under every varying circumstance of the day; – & in the Eveng. especially, figure to myself its sad gloom: – the efforts to talk, – the frequent summons to melancholy orders &

cares – & poor Edward restless in misery going from one room to the other, – & perhaps not seldom upstairs to see all that remains of his Elizabeth.

As Jane had wished, the two schoolboys did come to Southampton for a few days before finally returning to Winchester, and her letter of 24 October shows how she comforted and cheered them with walks or river trips during the day and parlour games in the evenings.[23]

There must be letters missing between those of 15 and 24 October, which would have contained Jane's first comments on the offer of a cottage at Chawton made by Edward to Mrs Austen. In the midst of his grief – probably in consequence of his loss – he wished to keep in closer touch with his mother and sisters, and gave them a choice between a house at Wye, near Godmersham, or one at Chawton. As they had already been considering going to Alton, Chawton was the obvious choice, and by November Henry was enthusiastically planning the move for them. Cassandra stayed on at Godmersham until the spring of 1809 to help Fanny, barely sixteen, shoulder the responsibilities so suddenly thrust upon her – to be companion to her father, mistress of a large household and surrogate mother to her ten younger brothers and sisters. 'Aunt Cassandra, who you most likely know to have been with us, ever since the day poor little John was born, has been the greatest comfort to us all in this time of affliction & will not leave us yet I hope', Fanny told Miss Chapman.[24]

The remaining six of this group of Jane's letters, written between December 1808 and January 1809, show that as she recovered her spirits she determined to crowd into her remaining months at Southampton as many engagements as possible. She and Martha went to one of the Assembly Balls at the Dolphin on 6 December – 'It was the same room in which we danced 15 years ago! – I thought it all over – & inspite of the shame of being so much older, felt with thankfulness that I was quite as happy now as then',[25] and also to that in celebration of the Queen's birthday, held on 18 January.

A larger circle of acquaintance & an increase of amusement is quite in character with our approaching removal . . . Every body is very much concerned at our going away, & every body is acquainted with Chawton & speaks of it as a remarkably pretty village, & every body knows the House we describe – but nobody fixes on the right.[26]

These pleasant daily occupations did not stifle Jane's deeper feelings, and on 16 December she wrote her most sad and serious verses, those to the memory of Madam Lefroy, beginning:

The day returns again, my natal day;
What mix'd emotions in my mind arise!
Beloved Friend, four years have passed away
Since thou were snatched for ever from our eyes.

The day commemorative of my birth,
Bestowing life, and light, and hope to me,
Brings back the hour which was thy last on earth,
O! bitter pang of torturing memory!

and continuing for a further eleven quatrains, recalling Madam Lefroy's years of friendship and kindness towards her.[27]

In January 1809 the weather in Southampton was mild but very wet and windy, preventing Jane and her mother from going to church for two consecutive Sundays,[28] so it may have been at this time Jane composed her 'Evening Prayers', which could be read aloud at home upon similar occasions.[29] Cassandra was beginning to think of returning to Hampshire in order to help wind up the Castle Square establishment – Mrs Austen planned to leave Southampton for good on 3 April and stay at Godmersham while the Chawton cottage was being refurbished – and Edward brought her back in mid-February. Upon her return she received a letter from Charles, written in Bermuda on Christmas Day 1808, proudly announcing the birth of his first child:

I am sure you will be delighted to hear that my beloved Fanny was safely deliver'd [of] a fine girl on the 22nd of December and that they are both doing remarkably [*sic*] well. The Baby besides being the finest that ever was seen is really a good looking healthy young Lady of very large dimensions and as fat as butter I mean to call her Cassandra Esten and beg the favour of you to be a Sponsor . . . The October and November mails have not yet reached us so that I know nothing about you of late . . .

an ignorance which led to his unwittingly painful postscript: 'I am very anxious to hear how Dear Elizabeth has got thro' her late confinement.'[30]

The family's departure from Southampton was delayed by Mrs Austen falling ill during March, and their arrival at Godmersham postponed yet again at the last minute, as Fanny told Miss Chapman on 20th April:

We expected to have had our Hampshire party long before this, but Grandmama has been delayed at Alton from illness; however she is now recovering, & able to move from the Inn to a cottage of Mrs F. Austens close to the town (where she is settled for the two years her husband expects to be absent. He is gone to China, & she is to be confined in June) but it is very uncertain whether she will be well enough to continue her journey, before their future residence at Chawton will be ready for them, & then I conclude they will not come at all, which will be a great disappointment for all parties.[31]

The Austens eventually arrived at Godmersham on 15 May and stayed until the end of June; Mrs Austen was probably still feeling weak, as Fanny does not mention her as participating in the family's social round, but Jane and Cassandra joined as usual in the daily occupations of trips to Canterbury and Goodnestone and neighbourhood visiting, which included a little domestic calamity at Wye on 12 June: 'Aunt Cassandra, Charles, Louisa & myself formed the party & getting out of the carriage at Mrs Cuthberts a gust of wind caught her (Aunt Cassandra's) white Pelisse & dashed it against the wheels in such a manner that she was covered with black mud . . .'[32]

The Godmersham house-party was increased by an unfamiliar guest when Eliza de Feuillide arrived from London on 22 June – the first visit she had made to Kent since November 1801,[33] and probably only occasioned now by the fact that she and Henry were in the process of moving from their house in Brompton to a larger one at No. 64 Sloane Street, a long smart avenue connecting the ancient, little Thames-side village of Chelsea to the main western approach road into London. Eliza's Parisian culture evidently made a strong impression on Fanny, as her diary entry for 15 July reads in part: 'Uncle & Aunt Henry Austen went away early ce matin. Quel horreur!!'

Just before leaving Southampton Jane had made a sudden despairing attempt to prod Crosby & Co. into publishing *Susan*; she wrote to them on 5 April, using the assumed name of 'Mrs Ashton Dennis', offering to supply a second copy of the manuscript if the one sold to them for £10 in 1803 had been lost, and pointing out that she was prepared to offer the novel to another publisher if they were no longer interested. Mr. Richard Crosby replied curtly by return of post that 'there was not any time stipulated for its publication, neither are we bound to publish it, Should you or anyone else [*sic*] we shall take proceedings to stop the sale. The MS shall be yours for the same as we paid for it.'[34] Jane's reaction to this bullying snub is unknown, but that the name 'Susan' was uppermost in her mind at this date is confirmed by another of Fanny's comments in her correspondence with Miss Chapman when, apropos suitable names for babies, she says: 'Robert is too hideous to be borne except by my two Aunts, Cassandra & Jane, who are very fond of both <u>Robert</u> and <u>Susan</u>!! did you ever hear of such a depraved taste? however it is not my fault.'[35] Jane soon received yet more discouragement, as an anonymous two-volume novel also called *Susan* was

Plate 22 Chawton Great House, west front.

published by John Booth in June 1809;[36] obviously her own story, if it were
ever to appear in print, would now have to have the heroine's name altered
throughout, as well as the title.

Mrs Austen and Jane left Godmersham on 30 June and a week later
Edward escorted Cassandra into Hampshire after them, so that on 7 July
1809 they entered what was to be the last home for all three of them, the
'corner house by the pond' on Edward's estate at Chawton.[37] The village
was situated in a slight valley about a mile to the south-west of Alton, the
nearest post-town, and one of the main coach roads from London passed
through it, dividing just outside the Austens' house – the right fork went to
Winchester and Southampton (the modern A31), the left to Fareham and
Gosport (the modern A32) – and a shallow but 'very considerable' pond
lay at the junction of these roads.[38] The manor house (known as the 'Great
House') was a few hundred yards further on down the Gosport road, set
on the slope of a wooded hill above the rather decrepit little church of
St Nicholas and commanding a view over the valley to the hill opposite,
which was crowned with a beech-wood called Chawton Park. The corner
house by the pond had originally been built as a roadside inn, but its latest
occupant was Mr Seward, Edward's agent or steward for the Chawton estate.
It was a late seventeenth-century building, L-shaped and two-storeyed, of

Plate 23 Chawton Cottage (Jane Austen's House Museum).

red brick with a tiled roof, and could muster six bedrooms as well as garrets above for storage or servants' rooms.[39]

James Austen's younger daughter, Caroline, often visited her grandmother and aunts at Chawton during the period 1809–45, and in the 1860s recorded her memories of life in 'the Cottage' (as it came to be called by the family) for her brother, James Edward, to use in his *Memoir* of their Aunt Jane.

The house was quite as good as the generality of Parsonage houses then – and much in the same old style – the ceilings low and roughly finished – some bedrooms very small – none very large but in number sufficient to accommodate the inmates, and several guests . . . The front door opened on the road, a very narrow enclosure of each side, protected the house from the possible shock of any runaway vehicle – A good sized entrance, and two parlours, called dining and drawing room, made the length of the house; all intended originally to look on the road – but the large drawing room window was blocked up and turned into a bookcase when Mrs Austen took possession and another was opened at the side, which gave to view only turf and trees . . . The dining room could not be made to look anywhere but on the road – and there my Grandmother often sat for an hour or two in the morning, with her work or her writing – cheered by its sunny aspect, and by the stirring scene it afforded her . . . A high wooden fence shut out the road (the Winchester road it was) all the length of the little domain, and trees were planted inside to form a shrubbery walk – which carried round the enclosure, gave a very sufficient space for exercise – you did not feel cramped for room; and there was a pleasant irregular mixture of hedgerow, and grass, and gravel walk and long grass for mowing, and orchard – which I imagine arose from two or three little enclosures having been thrown together, and arranged as best might be, for ladies' occupation – There was besides, a good kitchen garden, large court and many out-buildings, not much occupied – and all this affluence of space was very delightful to children, and I have no doubt added considerably to the pleasure of a visit – Everything indoors and out was well kept – the house was well furnished, and it was altogether a comfortable and ladylike establishment, tho' I beleive the means which supported it, were but small –[40]

Anna, more critical than Caroline, thought Edward should have done more for his mother and sisters and that the house was 'small & not very good', though the Austen ladies made it 'if not all that their home might & should have been, [still] such as fully satisfied the moderate desires of one, who had no taste for luxury or worldly state, and lived besides under the happy belief that what was decreed by those she loved must be wisest . . .'[41] The Chawton estate account book for 1808–19 shows that in 1809 Edward spent £45.19s.0d. on structural alterations to the Cottage and another £35.6s.5d. for plumbing works, while several of his labourers delivered and chopped firewood and trenched the garden for Mrs Austen on various dates during the second half of the year. Caroline recalled that a donkey-carriage was provided for her grandmother's use, and this presumably explains the entry on 29 December 1809 of £3.4s.6d. paid for hay and corn delivered to Mrs Austen's.[42]

At this date about 60 families lived in Chawton parish, giving a total of nearly 400 inhabitants, but the bulk of these were forestry or agricultural labourers employed either by Edward or by other local landowners. The current tenant of the Great House, since 1808, was Mr John Charles Middleton, a widower with six young children and a thin, effusive spinster sister-in-law, Miss Maria Beckford, to keep house for him. Behind the Cottage, in a larger house set back from the high road, lived the Prowtings, who became the Austens' closest friends in the village. Mr William Prowting was a magistrate and Deputy Lieutenant for the county and had two unmarried daughters, Catherine Ann and Ann Mary, both rather younger than the Austen sisters; in due course Jane developed the custom of walking from the end of the Cottage's garden across the intervening field to call on them, as the villagers living nearby came to notice.[43] In 1811 Ann Mary married Captain Benjamin Clement, RN, and the young couple moved across the road to live in another house owned by the Prowtings.[44]

At Chawton Lodge, a few yards further up the Winchester road, were Mr and Miss Hinton, two of the children of the previous rector of Chawton, the Revd John Hinton, who had died in 1802. The present rector was the Revd John Rawstorne Papillon – that same Mr Papillon who had refused to sell the reversion of the Chawton living to Henry Austen in 1794. Mr Papillon had rebuilt the rectory in 1803,[45] and now lived there with his spinster sister, Elizabeth; on hearing that the Austens were going to move to Chawton, Mrs Knight had told Cassandra that this bachelor rector might prove a very suitable husband for Jane, a suggestion to which the latter cheerfully replied: 'I am very much obliged to Mrs Knight for such a proof of the interest she takes in me – & she may depend upon it, that I will marry Mr Papillon, whatever may be his reluctance or my own. – I owe her much more than such a trifling sacrifice.'[46] Another neighbour was Miss Benn, the middle-aged, poverty-stricken sister of the Revd John Benn, rector of the adjacent parish of Farringdon; with a dozen children of his own to rear, Mr Benn could do little for her and Miss Benn was reduced to renting a ramshackle cottage from 'Old Philmore', one of the Chawton villagers[47] – an uncomfortable reminder to Jane and Cassandra that, but for their own brothers' financial support, such an existence could all too easily have been theirs.

In Alton itself Mary Gibson and baby Mary Jane had been living in Rose Cottage, Lenten Street, since April 1809 when Frank departed for China; and in 1811 Mr and Mrs Harry Digweed – one of the sons from Steventon Manor House who had recently married Jane Terry from Dummer – also moved to a house in Lenten Street.[48] Mrs Digweed was amiable but feather-brained, and afforded Jane much quiet amusement in this respect – 'Dear Mrs Digweed! – I cannot bear that she shd. not be foolishly happy after a Ball.'[49] Henry's bank, Austen Gray & Vincent, was at No. 10 Alton High Street (later moving to No. 34),[50] and he could now write to his family at less expense to them by enclosing his letters with the parcels of correspondence exchanged between the Hampshire branch and the London office, and they could of course reply in the same way.

As may be supposed a great deal of intercourse was kept up between Steventon & Chawton. Our Grandfather [James Austen] was a most attentive son & one of the pleasures of my mother's [Anna's] youth was sometimes riding with him to see her Grandmother & Aunts through the pretty cross roads & rough lanes inaccessible to wheels which lay between the two places.[51]

Mary Lloyd, with James Edward and Caroline, could pay visits by driving the long way round on the main roads via Basingstoke and Alton, as Caroline remembered:

My visits to Chawton were frequent – I cannot tell when they began – they were very pleasant to me – and Aunt Jane was the great charm – As a very little girl, I was always creeping up to her, and following her whenever I could, in the house and out of it – I might not have remembered this, but for the recollection of my Mother's telling me privately, I must not be troublesome to my Aunt – Her charm to children was great sweetness of manner – she seemed to love you, and you loved her naturally in return – This as well as I can now recollect and analyse, was what I felt in my earliest days, before I was old enough to be amused by her cleverness – But soon came the delight of her playful talk – Everything she could make amusing to a child – Then, as I got older, and when cousins came to share the entertainment, she would tell us the most delightful stories chiefly of Fairyland, and her Fairies had all characters of their own – The tale was invented, I am sure, at the moment, and was sometimes continued for 2 or 3 days, if occasion served –[52]

Anna, now in her teens, had the same memories as her younger sister in this respect:

Aunt Jane was the general favourite with children, her ways with them being so playful, & her long circumstantial stories so delightful! These were continued from time to time, & begged for of course at all possible or impossible occasions, woven, as she proceeded, out of nothing, but her own happy talent for invention. Ah! if but one of them could be now recovered![53]

Caroline recalled further:

As to my Aunt's personal appearance, her's was the first face that I can remember thinking pretty, not that I used that word to myself, but I know I looked at her with admiration – Her face was rather round than long – she had a bright, but not a pink colour – a clear brown complexion and very good hazle [sic] eyes – She was not, I beleive, an absolute beauty, but before she left Steventon she was established as a very pretty girl, in the opinion of most of her neighbours – as I learnt afterwards from some of those who still remained – Her hair, a darkish brown, curled naturally – it was in short curls round her face (for then ringlets were not). She always wore a cap – Such was the custom with ladies who were not quite young – at least of a morning but I never saw her without one, to the best of my remembrance, either morning or evening. I beleive my two Aunts were not accounted very good dressers, and were thought to have taken to the garb of middle age unnecessarily soon – but they were particularly neat, and they held all untidy ways in great disesteem.[54]

This description of Jane tallies well with her appearance in the only authentic portrait, the light watercolour sketch done by Cassandra which is now in the National Portrait Gallery, and it is therefore probable that this sketch, though undated, was executed round about 1810.[55]

In this summer of 1809, as Mrs Austen, now aged nearly seventy, settled in at the Cottage, she handed over the reins of domestic government to Cassandra and concentrated upon her own favourite pastimes of patchwork and gardening. In the former occupation her daughters also participated, as Jane reminded Cassandra: 'Have you remembered to collect peices for the Patchwork? – We are now at a stand still;'[56] and the latter was with her

no idle pastime, no mere cutting of roses & tying up of flowers. She dug up her own potatoes & I have no doubt she planted them, for the kitchen garden was as much her delight as the flower borders & I have heard my mother [Anna] say that when at work she wore a green round frock like a day labourer.[57]

Cassandra acted as scribe for the Cottage, and Fanny's diary shows that letters were exchanged between Kent and Hampshire every two or three weeks; also, as the Godmersham boys grew up, Edward sent them one after the other to Winchester and it became a regular practice for them to break their journey at the Cottage, carrying letters and parcels, at the beginning and end of each school term. Martha Lloyd shared the housekeeping with Cassandra, and her carefully compiled manuscript recipe book still survives to show the dishes which the family enjoyed.[58] Jane's task was to make the breakfast at 9 o'clock – 'that was her part of the household work – The tea and sugar stores were under her charge – and the wine – Aunt Cassandra did all the rest –'[59] 'It was a very quiet life according to our ideas but they were readers & besides the housekeeping our Aunts occupied themselves in working for the poor & teaching here & there some boy or girl to read & write.'[60] 'I did not often see my Aunt with a book in her hand, but I beleive she was fond of reading and that she had read and did read a good deal. I doubt whether she cared very much for poetry in general; but she was a great admirer of Crabbe.'[61] 'She thoroughly enjoyed Crabbe; perhaps on account of a certain resemblance to herself in minute and highly finished detail; and would sometimes say, in jest, that, if she ever married at all, she could fancy being Mrs Crabbe; looking on the author quite as an abstract idea, and ignorant and regardless of what manner of man he might be.'[62]

Before leaving Southampton Jane had planned to buy a pianoforte upon arrival at Chawton – 'as good a one as can be got for 30 Guineas – & I will practise country dances, that we may have some amusement for our nephews & neices, when we have the pleasure of their company'[63] – and this instrument was evidently soon acquired, for Caroline recalled:

Aunt Jane began her day with music – for which I conclude she had a natural taste, as she thus kept it up – tho' she had no one to teach; was never induced (as I have heard) to play in company; and none of her family cared much for it. I suppose, that she might not trouble them, she chose her practising time before breakfast – when she could have the room to herself – She practised regularly every morning – She played very pretty tunes, I thought – and I liked to stand by her and listen to them; but the music (for I knew the books well in after years) would now be thought disgracefully easy – Much that she played from was manuscript, copied out by herself – and so neatly and correctly, that it was as easy to read as print[64] . . . the song that I heard her sing oftenest, was a little French ditty in her MS book – The 2 first lines were, Que j'aime a voir les Hirondelles / Volent ma fenetre tous les jours – As a child, this was my favourite, & was what I asked for the oftenest.[65]

Several of Jane's music books still exist, and in them can be found other songs which the rising generation remembered hearing – a Scottish ballad, 'The Yellow Haired Laddie', a theatrical item, 'The Wife's Farewell', from the farce *Of Age Tomorrow*, and 'The Soldier's Adieu' by Dibdin. In this last, as she copied out the words 'Remember thou'rt a Soldier's Wife', Jane, as befitted a member of a naval family, carefully crossed out 'Soldier's' and wrote 'Sailor's' above the line instead.[66]

I don't beleive Aunt Jane observed any particular method in parcelling out her day but I think she generally sat in the drawing room till luncheon; when visitors were there, chiefly at work – She was fond of work – and she was a great adept at overcast and satin stitch – the peculiar delight of that day – General handiness and neatness were amongst her characteristics – She could throw the spilikens for us, better than anyone else, and she was wonderfully successful at cup and ball – She found a resource sometimes in that simple game, when she suffered from weak eyes and could not work or read for long together – . . . After luncheon, my Aunts generally walked out – sometimes they went to Alton for shopping – Often, one or the other of them, to the Great House – as it was then called – when a brother was inhabiting it, to make a visit – or if the house were standing empty they liked to stroll about the grounds – sometimes to Chawton Park – a noble beech wood, just within a walk – but sometimes, but that was rarely, to call on a neighbour – They had no carriage, and their visitings did not extend far – there were a few families living in the village – but no great intimacy was kept up with any of them – they were upon friendly but rather distant terms, with all –[67]

In the evening she would sometimes sing, to her own accompaniment, some simple old songs, the words and airs of which, now never heard, still linger in my memory.[68]

CHAPTER 13

First publication, 1809–12

Jane was now nearly thirty-four years old, and had entered the home which she was to occupy throughout the remaining eight years of her life – the home which she left only to die at Winchester in the summer of 1817. Into this period were to be crowded a large proportion of her most important literary work and all the contemporary recognition which she was destined to enjoy. The first six of these years, at least, until her health began to fail, must have been peacefully happy. She was back in her native Hampshire, living in a house very similar to the Steventon rectory, and with the freedom to walk out and enjoy the natural beauties of her brother's estate. As well as James visiting from Steventon, Edward stayed for longer periods at Chawton Great House and also lent it to Frank and Charles during their shore leaves, while Henry made frequent trips from London to the Alton branch of his bank and was very ready to take his sisters back with him to show them the sights of the metropolis and, presently, to help Jane transact her literary business. In the Cottage Jane had her mother, her lifelong friend, Martha, and above all her 'other self', Cassandra, with whom disagreement was impossible.

In the time of my childhood, it was a cheerful house – my Uncles, one or another, frequently coming for a few days; and they were all pleasant in their own family – I have thought since, after having seen more of other households, <u>wonderfully</u>, as the <u>family</u> talk had much of spirit and vivacity, and it was never troubled by disagreements as it was not their habit to argue with each other – There always was perfect harmony amongst the brothers and sisters, and over my Grandmother's door might have been inscribed the text, 'Behold how good and joyful a thing it is, brethren, to dwell together in unity'. There was firm family union, never broken but by death –[1]

In anticipation of the benefits which this move to Chawton would afford, Jane's spirits rose, and her pleasure was almost immediately increased when Mary Gibson at Rose Cottage gave birth safely to Frank's first son, Francis William the younger, on 12 July. The only other surviving letter from this period, that of 26 July 1809, is one of Jane's most cheerful and affectionate essays in doggerel verse – congratulating Frank on the arrival of his heir, teasing him with reminiscences of his own boyhood naughtiness and, as a postscript, assuring him how comfortable they were in their new home.[2]

There is now a gap in Jane's correspondence of nearly two years, and news of the Austen family in general and Jane's activities in particular during this period has to be found in other sources, of which the most helpful are Fanny's diaries. On 21 October 1809 Edward brought Fanny and his fifth son, little Charles, to stay at Chawton Cottage for three weeks and Fanny made several entries mentioning her two aunts, showing that both of them were at home at the time. Mrs Knight also wrote from Canterbury to Fanny on 26 October: 'I heard of the Chawton Party looking very comfortable at Breakfast, from a gentleman who was travelling by their door in a Post-chaise about ten days since. Your account of the whole family gives me the sincerest Pleasure, and I beg you will assure them all how much I feel interested in their happiness.'[3] During November Edward and his children returned to Godmersham via Steventon, and from there took Anna back with them for a visit that lasted until the following spring. Poor Anna, still only sixteen, was in disgrace at home for having engaged herself just recently to their neighbour, the Revd Michael Terry, one of the Dummer family. The reason for her parents' annoyance is not clear, for Mr Terry, though admittedly double Anna's age, was 'tall & good looking & well connected with the certainty of a comfortable family living';[4] but James and Mary Lloyd nevertheless refused to countenance such an engagement, and Anna's trip to Godmersham was evidently in the nature of a banishment.

So far as is known, this winter of 1809–10 was the last time Anna stayed in Kent, and her comments on the Godmersham family, although recorded many years later, must reflect the impressions she had gained during this and her previous visits. She remembered Elizabeth Austen as being

a very lovely woman, highly educated, though not I imagine of much natural talent. Her tastes were domestic, her affections strong, though exclusive, and her temper calculated to make Husband and children happy in their home. Indeed my Uncle's own disposition was so sweet and yielding, his whole character so opposed to contention of every kind that he could never have been, under any circumstances, an irritable or discontented man –[5]

and elsewhere she wrote:

I have intimated that of the two Sisters Aunt Jane was generally the favourite with children, but with the young people of Godmersham it was not so. They liked her indeed as a playfellow, & as a teller of stories, but they were not really fond of her. I believe that their Mother was not; at least that she very much preferred the elder Sister. A little talent went a long way with the Goodneston Bridgeses of that period, & <u>much</u> must have gone a long way too far.[6]

Perhaps Elizabeth, like Lady Middleton, thought that anyone who was fond of reading must be 'satirical',[7] and vaguely suspected that her witty, penniless young sister-in-law viewed the nobility and gentry of the Godmersham circle with some degree of irreverent amusement.

In the New Year of 1810 Mr Terry's sister, Charlotte, pleaded his cause and Fanny wrote to Cassandra to mediate on Anna's behalf, with the upshot that during March James Austen eventually gave his consent to an engagement and Mr Terry was allowed to call at Godmersham to see Anna; following this reconciliation she returned to Hampshire and in April went to stay at Dummer with her fiancé's family for three days. Unfortunately – or perhaps in the long run, fortunately – this 'further acquaintance convinced her of her mistake & her father put an end to the engagement. As a match it would have been about as suitable as one between Lizzie Bennet & Mr Collins, or between Emma Woodhouse and Mr Rushworth had they ever met –' so one of Anna's daughters wrote years later.[8] However, even the sympathetic Fanny was shocked at such inconstancy on Anna's part and her parents were still further displeased at the embarrassment she had caused them, so she was once again banished from Steventon – this time to Chawton Cottage, for nearly three months.[9] Jane was worried now and for some years to come, at the 'unsteadiness' of her niece's nature, fearing that it would lead to unhappiness;[10] and it may have been during this summer of 1810 that she wrote the 'Mock Panegyric on a Young Friend':

> In measured verse I'll now rehearse
> The charms of lovely Anna;
> And, first, her mind is unconfined
> Like any vast savannah.
>
> Ontario's lake may fitly speak
> Her fancy's ample bound;
> Its circuit may, on strict survey
> Five hundred miles be found . . .

and so on for a further five stanzas.[11] James Edward believed that 'all this nonsense was nearly extempore, and that the fancy of drawing the images from America arose at the moment from the obvious rhyme which presented itself in the first stanza'[12] – but nevertheless the poem, though witty and affectionate, does constitute a gentle warning against the excesses of unrestrained emotions.

Anna eventually returned to Steventon in mid-July, accompanied by Mrs Austen, and it seems probable that at the same time Jane and Cassandra went to stay at Manydown, coming from there to dine at Steventon during the first week in August. Young Fulwar William Fowle also called at Steventon rectory in August,[13] and it was perhaps this visit he remembered many years later when he added his reminiscences of Jane to those of the other members of her family: 'She was a very sweet reader. She had just finished the 1st Canto of Marmion, & I was reading the 2nd – when Mr W. Digweed was announced it was like the interruption of some pleasing dream . . .'[14] On *Marmion*'s first publication in the summer of 1808 Jane had not liked it very much, but in January 1809 she sent a copy out to Charles in the West Indies – 'very generous in me, I think' – and as time passed evidently learned to enjoy it.[15] Caroline too remembered that Jane

was considered to read aloud remarkably well. I did not often hear her but <u>once</u> I knew her take up a volume of Evelina and read a few pages of Mr Smith and the Brangtons [*sic*] and I thought it was like a play. She had a very good <u>speaking</u> voice – This was the opinion of her contemporaries – and though I did not <u>then</u> think of it as a perfection, or ever hear it observed upon, yet its tones have never been forgotten – I can recall them even now – and I <u>know</u> they <u>were</u> very pleasant.[16]

In October 1810 Edward and Fanny visited Hampshire again, staying first for a week at Steventon. Caroline was now old enough to take some notice of the comings and goings of her adult relatives, and recalled this and other similar visits:

My Uncle Edward . . . came to Chawton and Steventon generally twice a year to look after his affairs. He must have been more his own 'man of business' than is usual with people of large property, for I think it was his greatest interest to attend to his estates. In my recollection, he never hunted or shot . . . Of the five brothers, <u>he</u>, who had always had unlimited means for such indulgence, was the only one without a strong taste for field sports, and <u>he</u> cared not for them at all. He was very cheerful and pleasant, and had some of my Aunt Jane's power and good nature, of telling amusing stories to his nephews and nieces.[17]

Edward and his daughter moved on to Chawton Cottage and stayed there for three weeks during November, and Fanny again made some specific references in her diary to being in Aunt Jane's company at this period.

At Rose Cottage in Alton Frank was now back with his family, and Fanny noted that it was the first time she had seen him for four years. He had returned from China earlier than expected, arriving in home waters at the end of July 1810, when Mary Gibson had rushed off to stay with him in lodgings at Chatham. Soon afterwards he received formal thanks from the

Admiralty and the more tangible rewards of 1,000 guineas and silver-plate from the East India Company, for his success in convoying their ships to and from the Far East; while lying at anchor in the river of Canton, there had been quarrels between the English sailors and the Chinese inhabitants, and it was only by virtue of Frank's tact and firmness that the convoy had been able to leave China safely.[18] Charles too, although still far away in the West Indies, was able to write home with good news during 1810 – in February his second daughter, Harriet Jane, was born in Bermuda, for whom Jane and Henry were proxy godparents;[19] and in May he was promoted Post-Captain into the 74-gun HMS *Swiftsure*, flagship of Sir John Borlase Warren.

It is unfortunate that Jane and Cassandra were apparently not separated between July 1809 and April 1811, for in the absence of any letters during this period it cannot be known exactly when Jane returned at last to literary composition, nor why it was that she decided to offer her earliest novel for publication; perhaps the discouragement received in this respect in regard to *First Impressions* and *Susan* reminded her of the proverb 'third time lucky'. She picked up *Sense and Sensibility*, and made two little updating touches in the text – a reference to the twopenny postal service within London, and the addition of Scott's name as a popular poet alongside Cowper and Thomson [20] – but there the matter might have rested had it not been for the encouragement provided in her home circle. 'It was with extreme difficulty that her friends, whose partiality she suspected whilst she honoured their judgement, could prevail on her to publish her first work';[21] however, at some time over the winter of 1810–11 this manuscript was accepted by Thomas Egerton of Whitehall for publication upon commission (i.e., at the author's expense), even though Jane was so sure 'its sale would not repay the expense of publication, that she actually made a reserve from her very moderate income to meet the expected loss'.[22]

At the end of March 1811 Jane went to London to stay with Henry and Eliza at No. 64 Sloane Street in order to correct her proofs, while Cassandra went to Godmersham. Five letters survive of those written between April and June 1811, and in between news of Jane's activities in London is one reference to the progress of *Sense and Sensibility* through the press. The Cooke cousins were also staying in London, and Jane went with Mary Cooke to Bullock's Liverpool Museum of natural history exhibits at No. 22 Piccadilly and also to the Gallery of the British Institution in Pall Mall, at which latter place they saw Benjamin West's enormous new painting, *Christ Healing the Sick* – 'I had some amusement at each, tho' my preference for Men & Women, always inclines me to attend more to the company than the sight.'[23] On 23 April Eliza gave a large evening party, with professional musicians engaged for entertainment, at which Jane met many old friends and family connections: 'I was quite surrounded by acquaintance, especially Gentlemen; & what with Mr Hampson, Mr Seymour, Mr W. Knatchbull, Mr Guillemarde, Mr Cure, a Capt. Simpson, brother to the Capt. Simpson, besides Mr Walter & Mr Egerton, in addition to the Cookes & Miss Beckford & Miss Middleton, I had quite as much upon my hands as I could do.'[24]

In her letter written two days later, describing this occasion, she assured Cassandra:

No indeed, I am never too busy to think of S & S. I can no more forget it, than a mother can forget her sucking child; & I am much obliged to you for your enquiries. I have had two sheets to correct, but the last only brings us to W's [Willoughby's] first appearance [chapter IX of volume I]. Mrs K. [Knight] regrets in the most flattering manner that she must wait till May, but I have scarcely a hope of its being out in June. – Henry does not neglect it; he has hurried the Printer, & says he will see him again today. – It will not stand still during his absence, it will be sent to Eliza. – The Incomes remain as they were, but I will get them altered if I can. – I am very much gratified by Mrs K's interest in it; & whatever may be the event of it as to my credit with her, sincerely wish her curiosity could be satisfied sooner than is now probable. I think she will like my Elinor, but cannot build on any thing else.[25]

During this London visit Jane walked, dined and drank tea with various members of Henry's circle of friends – 'I find all these little parties very pleasant –'[26] and in particular liked Henry's banking partner Mr James Tilson and his wife Frances, with whom she corresponded from time to time. She was also very interested to drive out one evening to meet an émigré French family, the Comte d'Antraigues with his opera-singer wife and musical son, Julien, then lodging at No. 27 The Terrace, Barnes.

Monsieur the old Count, is a very fine looking man, with quiet manners, good enough for an Englishman – & I beleive is a Man of great Information & Taste. He has some fine Paintings, which delighted Henry as much as the Son's music gratified Eliza – & among them, a Miniature of Philip 5. of Spain, Louis 14's grandson, which exactly suited my capacity. – Count Julien's performance is very wonderful.[27]

Jane's impression that the Comte was a 'Man of great Information' was quite unwittingly all too accurate, for he was in fact a political intriguer and professional secret agent, working – sometimes simultaneously – for the French Royalists, Russia and Prussia, and possibly even against England as well. In July 1812, a little over a year after Jane met them, the Comte and his wife were murdered in their house at Barnes by a deranged Italian manservant who then committed suicide.[28]

Before returning to Hampshire Jane received a letter from Cassandra with the Kentish news, part of which called forth a wry smile in response. Amongst the guests talking to Jane at Eliza's musical evening had been Mrs Knight's brother, Mr Wyndham Knatchbull, whose opinions of the party had been passed on by her to Cassandra and so now back to Jane. 'I depended upon hearing something of the Eveng. from Mr W. K. – & am very well satisfied with his notice of me. "A pleasing looking young woman", – that must do; – one cannot pretend to anything better now – thankful to have it continued a few years longer!'[29] Jane was now in her thirty-sixth year, middle-aged by contemporary standards, so Mr Knatchbull's brief comment was still something of a compliment. Despite Mrs Knight's hope that Jane might find her match in Mr Papillon, it seems that she herself was now quite resigned to the state of spinsterhood, though not without some natural regrets at the passing of her youth. However, although Jane did not know it at the time, Henry's lawyer, William Seymour, also present and talking to her at this musical party, seems likewise to have considered her 'a pleasing looking young woman', and in the ensuing months began to think seriously of asking her to marry him.[30]

Early in May Jane left London, and on her homeward journey paid a short visit to her old friend, Catherine Bigg, now Mrs Hill and mother of a little boy, at Streatham, of which parish the Revd Herbert Hill had recently become rector. At Chawton she found only Mrs Austen and Anna, for Martha was also away in London and Cassandra was not due to return from Kent for some weeks. Jane's next three letters to Cassandra, during May and June, tell of Anna's amusements with the other girls in the neighbourhood – the Middletons at the Great House and the Benns at Farringdon Rectory – the progress of the newly planted fruit-trees, shrubs and flowers in the Cottage's garden, and the difficulty of trying to fit into the Cottage's limited accommodation the various guests whom they would like to entertain. Frank and Mary had moved from Rose Cottage to lodgings at Cowes in the Isle of Wight while waiting for his next appointment, but hoped to visit both Steventon and Chawton later in the summer – Mrs Austen was prepared to give up her own bedroom to them, but that still meant two maids and three children (Frank's second son, Henry Edgar, had been born in April) would have to be crammed into the spare room. The Cookes also wanted to call, and Jane herself wished to invite Miss Anne Sharp, the one-time governess at Godmersham with whom she and Cassandra had kept in touch.[31]

In the event, the Cookes cancelled owing to ill-health, and Frank and his family probably came during July, before he took up his next command of HMS *Elephant* at Portsmouth. Miss Sharp had to be postponed until early September, since before she could come Eliza de Feuillide made one of her rare trips into the country and stayed at the Cottage early in August, which overlapped with the happy event of Charles's return to England. On 18 August Cassandra wrote to their Kentish cousin Phylly Walter (now Mrs Whitaker, thanks to a recent, very belated, marriage):

We are now quite alone, but till very lately we have had our house almost running over. My Brother Charles & his Family spent one week with us during Eliza's visit & they all left us together last Thursday. After an absence from England of almost seven years you may guess the pleasure which having him amongst us again occasion'd. He is grown a little older in all that time, but we had the pleasure of seeing him return in good health & unchanged in mind. His Bermudan wife is a very pleasing little woman, she is gentle & amiable in her manners & appears to make him very happy. They have two pretty little girls. There must be always something to wish for, & for Charles we have to wish for rather more money. So expensive as every thing in England is now, even the necessaries of life, I am afraid they will find themselves very very poor.[32]

Later in the year Charles took his wife to Steventon, and little Caroline remembered: 'I was much charmed with both – but thought they looked very young for an uncle and aunt – tho' she must then have been the mother of two children. She was fair and pink, with very light hair, and I admired her greatly.'[33] Charles's next command was that of HMS *Namur*, the guard-ship stationed at the Nore, off Sheerness, and to save money his wife and children lived on board with him. 'We had doubted whether such a scheme would prove practicable during the winter, but they have found their residence very tolerably comfortable, & it is so much the cheapest home she could have that they are very right to put up with little inconveniences –' Cassandra told cousin Phylly the following spring.[34]

In Cassandra's August letter to Phylly there is no mention of the fact that Jane now had a novel nearing publication, and it seems that at this time the only people who knew of her authorship, apart from Mrs Austen, Cassandra and Martha, were her brothers and their wives, Mrs Knight, the family's patroness, the Leigh-Perrots, and Fanny, the eldest of the next generation. Frank's and Charles's children were of course too young to be concerned, but Anna, James Edward and Caroline were not let into the secret till some two years later, following the appearance of *Pride and Prejudice* as well as *Sense and Sensibility*. There is no information as to why the publication of the latter was delayed until nearly the end of 1811 despite the original intention for it to come out in May of that year, and the only other reference to it is in Fanny's diary – on 27 September she noted the receipt of a letter from Cassandra, and immediately afterwards, the next day, made the longer entry: 'Another letter from Aunt Cassandra to beg we would not mention that Aunt Jane Austen wrote "Sense & Sensibility"'. Perhaps it was frustration over this delay, or worry as to whether she might sustain a financial loss, which gave Jane the headaches that led her to compose, on 27th October 1811, the verses beginning 'When stretch'd on one's bed / With a fierce-throbbing head . . .'[35]

However, she did not have much longer to wait, for the first advertisement of publication appeared in *The Star* of 30 October 1811 and *The Morning Chronicle* of 31 October, and these newspapers repeated the advertisement, with varying forms of wording, several times during November. The work was published in the usual three volumes, price 15s., and the print-run was probably 750 or 1,000 copies. The title-page showed the book as being 'By A Lady', but some of the advertisements carelessly or possibly deliberately rearranged this wording and made it appear as 'By Lady –' or 'By Lady A –' Reviewers did not notice it until the spring of 1812, but it sold promptly and steadily, and by 24 November the Countess of Bessborough was already asking Lord Granville Leveson Gower: 'Have you read "Sense and Sensibility"? It is a clever novel. They were full of it at Althorp, and tho' it ends stupidly I was much amus'd by it –'[36]

The Royal Family were also reading it – the Duke of York, misled by the wording of the later advertisements, believed it was written by Lady Augusta Paget and, together with his praises, passed on this misinformation to his niece, Princess Charlotte. Charlotte, only child of the Prince Regent and that foolish, unhappy Caroline of Brunswick whom Frank Austen had assisted in escorting to England in 1795, was now a tomboyish sixteen-year-old trying hard to improve herself, and on 22 January 1812 she wrote: '"Sence and Sencibility" [*sic*] I have just finished reading; it certainly is interesting, & you feel quite one of the company. I think Maryanne [*sic*] & me are very like in disposition, that certainly I am not so good, the same imprudence, &c, however remain very like. I must say it interested me much.'[37]

Jane, of course, could not know of these immediately appreciative comments, and must have waited nervously during the next few months to see if she would be called upon to pay Egerton's losses should the book fail to sell. She spent a few days at Steventon at the end of November 1811 and no doubt the prospects of success or failure of this her first venture were then discussed with James and Mary. James in turn visited Chawton the following month, and it seems that as he passed through Alton he dropped into the post an anonymous note to his sister, in a disguised handwriting, containing a verse entitled

> To Miss Jane Austen the reputed Author of Sense and Sensibility a
>   Novel lately published:
> On such Subjects no Wonder that she shou'd write well,
> In whom so united those Qualities dwell;
> Where 'dear Sensibility', Sterne's darling Maid,
> With Sense so attemper'd is finely pourtray'd.
> Fair Elinor's Self in that Mind is exprest,
> And the Feelings of Marianne live in that Breast.
> Oh then, gentle Lady! continue to write,
> And the Sense of your Readers t'amuse & delight.
> A Friend.[38]

The first notice appeared in *The Critical Review* for February 1812, where the book was singled out for

particular commendation. . . . It is well written; the characters are in genteel life, naturally drawn, and judiciously supported. The incidents are probable, and highly pleasing, and interesting; the conclusion such as the reader must wish it should be, and the whole is just long enough to interest without fatiguing. It reflects honour on the writer, who displays much knowledge of character, and very happily blends a great deal of good sense with the lighter matter of the piece.

A shorter review in *The British Critic* for May 1812 called it 'a very pleasing and entertaining narrative'.[39] These favourable opinions ensured that by July 1813 every copy of the first edition had been sold, and Jane not only covered her expenses but made a profit into the bargain. 'She could scarcely believe what she termed her great good fortune when "Sense and Sensibility" produced a clear profit of about £150 [actually £140]. Few so gifted were so truly unpretending. She regarded the above sum as a prodigious recompense for that which had cost her nothing.'[40] A profit of £140 for a first novel was in fact quite reasonable for the period – Fanny Burney had received only £30 for *Evelina* in 1778, Maria Edgeworth £100 for *Castle Rackrent* in 1800 and Susan Ferrier would receive £150 for *Marriage* in 1818. The money was undoubtedly very welcome, but still more important from another point of view was the favourable reception of the work. Had it been a failure and an expense to its author, she would hardly have dared, nor could she have afforded, to make a second venture; on the success of *Sense and Sensibility*, therefore, depended the existence of *Pride and Prejudice*.

Cassandra's brief memorandum giving the dates of composition of Jane's novels starts off: 'First Impressions begun in Oct. 1796. Finished in Augt. 1797. Publish'd afterwards, with alterations & contractions, under the Title

of Pride & Prejudice.'[41] It has been noticed that *Pride and Prejudice* as it
now stands was written to fit the calendars of 1811 and 1812, so it would
seem likely that once *Sense and Sensibility* was safely going through the press
in Egerton's hands in the spring of 1811, Jane returned to *First Impressions*
and revised and shortened this manuscript with a view to offering it again
for publication if she could afford to do so. However, a novel entitled *First
Impressions*, by Margaret Holford, had been published in London by the
Minerva Press in 1800,[42] so it was necessary for Jane to find a different title
for her text. This she did, in the fifth volume of Fanny Burney's *Cecilia*,
where the phrase 'Pride and Prejudice' is repeated three times in quick
succession and given further prominence by being printed in capitals;[43]
the phrase also had the attraction of matching very well with 'Sense and
Sensibility'.

So far as is known, Jane spent 1812 almost entirely at home in Chawton,
and it is Fanny's diary for this year which once again provides the first
mention of her, in the spring. Edward paid one of his biannual visits to
Hampshire in April, bringing Fanny and her cousin, Fanny Cage, with
him, and as the Middleton family were still occupying the Great House, he
and the girls stayed at the Cottage for a fortnight; on 21 April Fanny noted
'Aunts Cassandra & Jane, Fanny [Cage] & I walked with Miss Middleton
to Farringdon & back.' Jane's earlier comment that she would play country
dances on the pianoforte to entertain her nephews and nieces was no idle
boast, for Fanny also noted in her diary on 16 April: 'Had a little dance in the
evening.' This year Fanny was starting to suffer the joys and anxieties of a
first romance, in the person of Mr John Pemberton Plumptre of Fredville,
one of her Kentish neighbours, and his name appears in her diary with
increasing frequency.

Mary Lloyd met Mrs Austen and Jane in Basingstoke on 9 June and
drove them back to Steventon for a fortnight's visit, one which Mrs Austen
made into a milestone in her life, for it was the last time she ever went
there.

I have heard that when she determined to go no more from her own house she
said her last visit should be to her eldest son – and that accordingly she came, and
made her farewell to the place where [the] most part of her own married life had
been spent. She kept her resolution, and as I believe, never again left Chawton for
a single night.[44]

At the same time, Henry took Cassandra with him to Godmersham; she
did not return to Hampshire until late July or early August, but no letters

survive of those which Jane must have written to her during this separation. On 25 June Jane and her mother returned to Chawton, bringing Anna with them for a visit that lasted three months. This was the beginning of the period of Anna's 'greatest share of intimacy' with her aunt: 'the two years before my marriage, & the two or three years after . . . when the original 17 years between us seemed to shrink to 7 – or to nothing'.[45] Of Jane's two eldest nieces Anna was brighter both in looks and intelligence than Fanny, but was also more mercurial and excitable than her rather staid and prosaic cousin, who had had responsibility thrust upon her so early in life. Both occupied a good deal of Jane's thoughts and affections, but Anna was the one who caused her the most amusement and also the most anxiety, as she seemed still an impulsive child when compared with the mature Fanny.

However, during this summer Jane found to her pleasure that Anna possessed something of the family talent for literary composition as well as a strong sense of the ridiculous, and with Jane's encouragement Anna now wrote a 'mock-heroic story . . . [which] had no other foundation than their having seen a neighbour passing on the coach, without having previously known that he was going to leave home –'[46] This coach, Falknor's daily service to Southampton, was given the suitably ominous Gothic title of 'The Car of Falkenstein', and the story remained a joke between aunt and niece for some months to come. Anna recalled:

It was my great amusement during one summer visit at Chawton to procure Novels from a circulating Library at Alton, & after running them over to relate the stories to Aunt Jane. I may say it was her amusement also, as she sat busily stitching away at a work of charity, in which I fear that I took myself no more useful part. Greatly we both enjoyed it, one piece of absurdity leading to another, till Aunt Cassandra fatigued with her own share of laughter wd. exclaim 'How <u>can</u> you both be so foolish?' & beg us to leave off –[47]

It was in searching this Library that my mother [Anna] came across a copy of *Sense and Sensibility* which she threw aside with careless contempt, little imagining who had written it, exclaiming to the great amusement of her Aunts who stood by 'Oh that must be rubbish I am sure from the title.'[48]

One book that Anna did borrow, however, was *Lady Maclairn, the Victim of Villainy*, a rambling repetitive tale by Mrs Hunter of Norwich, in which all the characters, male and female alike, were frequently to be found weeping or else burst into tears during conversation. After her return to Steventon at the end of September, Anna made some imaginative sketches of the places described in *Lady Maclairn*, and sent them to Jane accompanied by a letter purporting to be written by Mrs Hunter. James went to Chawton on 29 October 1812, and it seems likely that he took Anna's joke with him and brought back Jane's appropriately lachrymose response two days later:

Miss Jane Austen begs her best thanks may be conveyed to Mrs Hunter of Norwich for the Threadpaper which she has been so kind as to send her by Mr Austen, & which will be always very valuable on account of the spirited sketches (made it is supposed by Nicholson or Glover) of the most interesting spots, Tarefield Hall, the Mill, & above all the Tomb of Howard's wife, of the faithful representation of which Miss Jane Austen is undoubtedly a good judge having spent so many summers at Tarefield Abbey the delighted guest of the worthy Mrs Wilson. Miss Jane Austen's tears have flowed over each sweet sketch in such a way as would do Mrs Hunter's heart good to see; if Mrs Hunter could understand all Miss Jane Austen's interest in the subject she would certainly have the kindness to publish at least 4 vols. more about the Flint family, & especially would give many fresh particulars on that part of it which Mrs H. has hitherto handled too briefly; viz, the history of Mary Flint's marriage with Howard. Miss Jane Austen cannot close this small epitome of the miniature abridgment of her thanks & admiration without expressing her sincere hope that Mrs Hunter is provided at Norwich with a more safe conveyance to London than Alton can now boast, as the Car of Falkenstein which was the pride of that Town was overturned within the last 10 days.[49]

At some time in the autumn of 1812 Jane probably visited Henry in London, taking the manuscript of *Pride and Prejudice* with her, now emboldened to offer it to Egerton following the success of *Sense and Sensibility*. There is no documentary evidence for such a trip, but negotiations for publication would obviously take some days if not weeks, before Egerton agreed to accept it during November. It seems likely too that on her return from London Jane was accompanied home by her as yet undeclared admirer, William Seymour, for many years later he told a member of the Austen family that 'he had escorted [Jane Austen] from London to Chawton in a postchaise, considering all the way whether he should ask her to become his wife! He refrained however, and afterwards married twice.'[50]

In November Edward and Fanny called again at the Cottage, this time including Lizzy, now nearly thirteen, in the party, and cousin Mary Deedes as Fanny's companion; Jane referred to them as 'Edward & his Harem' when she wrote to Martha on 29 November following their departure. Mrs Knight, the family's kind and generous friend, who had been ailing for many years, had died in Canterbury on 14 October, and Edward and all his family now officially took the name of 'Knight' as he entered into his full inheritance. Fanny was annoyed, and scribbled in her diary: 'Papa changed his name about this time in compliance with the will of the late Mr Knight and we are therefore all <u>Knights</u> instead of dear old <u>Austens</u>

How I hate it!!!!!!' In her letter to Martha Jane mentioned the change and pledged herself: 'I must learn to make a better K.'

This letter of 29 November 1812 provides the only mention of *Pride and Prejudice* prior to its publication, as Jane informed Martha:

P. & P. is sold. – Egerton gives £110 for it. – I would rather have had £150, but we could not both be pleased, & I am not at all surprised that he should not chuse to hazard so much. – Its' being sold will I hope be a great saving of Trouble to Henry, & therefore must be welcome to me. – The Money is to be paid at the end of the twelvemonth.[51]

There is nothing to indicate exactly when Jane had finished revising her text, or when it had first been offered to Egerton, but it is not surprising that on this occasion, despite Jane's continuing modest estimation of her own literary worth, he had instantly recognised a potential best-seller and was anxious to secure the copyright for himself.

CHAPTER 14

Pride and Prejudice, *1813*

The year 1813 opened excitingly for Jane, as *Pride and Prejudice* was first advertised on 28 January in *The Morning Chronicle*, at 18s. the three volumes; the title-page described it as being 'by the Author of "Sense and Sensibility"', and it seems probable that no more than 1,500 copies were printed.[1] Luckily for posterity, Jane and Cassandra were separated on a number of occasions during 1813, and the eighteen letters which survive from this year make several references not only to *Sense and Sensibility* and *Pride and Prejudice*, but also to the progress of the next book, *Mansfield Park*.

Earlier in the month Cassandra had gone to Steventon, so Jane's letter to her of Friday, 29 January is full of exhilaration at being able to announce the first appearance of this, her favourite work:

I want to tell you that I have got my own darling Child from London; – on Wednesday I received one Copy, sent down by Falknor, with three lines from Henry to say that he had given another to Charles & sent a 3d by the Coach to Godmersham; just the two Sets which I was least eager for the disposal of. I wrote to him immediately to beg for my two other Sets, unless he would take the trouble of forwarding them at once to Steventon & Portsmouth – not having an idea of his leaving Town before to day; – by your account however he was gone before my Letter was written. The only evil is the delay, nothing more can be done till his return – Tell James & Mary so, with my Love. For your sake I am as well pleased that it shd. be so, as it might be unpleasant to you to be in the Neighbourhood at the first burst of the business . . . Miss Benn dined with us on the very day of the Books coming, & in the eveng. we set fairly at it & read half the 1st vol. to her – prefacing that having intelligence from Henry that such a work wd. soon appear we had desired him to send it whenever it came out – & I beleive it passed with her unsuspected. – She was amused, poor soul! that she cd. not help you know, with two such people to lead the way; but she really does seem to admire Elizabeth. I must confess that I think her as delightful a creature as ever appeared in print, & how I shall be able to tolerate those who do not like her at least, I do not know . . . The 2d vol. is shorter than I cd. wish – but the difference is not so much in reality as in look, there being a larger proportion of Narrative in that part. I have lopt & cropt so successfully however that I imagine it must be rather shorter than S. & S. altogether.[2]

A week later Jane continued:

Our 2d evening's reading to Miss Benn had not pleased me so well, but I beleive something must be attributed to my Mother's too rapid way of getting on – & tho' she perfectly understands the Characters herself, she cannot speak as they ought. Upon the whole however I am quite vain enough & well satisfied enough. – The work is rather too light & bright & sparkling; – it wants shade; – it wants to be stretched out here & there with a long Chapter – of sense if it could be had, if not of solemn specious nonsense – about something unconnected with the story; an Essay on Writing, a critique on Walter Scott, or the history of Buonaparte – or anything that would form a contrast & bring the reader with increased delight to the playfulness & Epigrammatism of the general style – I doubt your quite agreeing with me here – I know your starched Notions. – The caution observed at Steventon with regard to the possession of the Book is an agreeable surprise to me, & I heartily wish it may be the means of saving you from everything unpleasant; – but you must be prepared for the Neighbourhood being perhaps already informed of there being such a Work in the World, & in the Chawton World! Dummer will do that you know. – It was spoken of here one morng. when Mrs D. called with Miss Benn.[3]

It would seem that although Jane and her mother had endeavoured to preserve the anonymity of the work when reading it to Miss Benn, the latter had been aware of some unusual excitement in their manner and, together with Mrs Digweed, had suspected or guessed the reason.

Cassandra did not return to Chawton till late February or early March, so there was time for Jane to receive Fanny's thanks and praise from God-mersham and to write again:

I am exceedingly pleased that you can say what you do, after having gone thro' the whole work – & Fanny's praise is very gratifying; – My hopes were tolerably strong of her, but nothing like a certainty. Her liking Darcy & Elizth. is enough, She might hate all the others, if she would. I have her opinion under her own hand this morning, but your Transcript of it which I read first, was not & is not the less acceptable. – To me, it is of course all praise – but the more exact truth which she sends you is good enough.[4]

The first review appeared in *The British Critic* for February 1813:

It is very far superior to almost all the publications of the kind which have lately come before us. It has a very unexceptionable tendency, the story is well told, the characters remarkably well drawn and supported, and written with great spirit as well as vigour . . . we have perused these volumes with much satisfaction and amusement, and entertain very little doubt that their successful circulation will induce the author to similar exertions.

The Critical Review for March 1813 gave a synopsis of the plot, with quotations, and particularly praised Elizabeth's 'archness and sweetness of manner', adding that the work

rises very superior to any novel we have lately met with in the delineation of domestic scenes. Nor is there one character which appears flat, or obtrudes itself upon the notice of the reader with troublesome impertinence. There is not one person in the drama with whom we could readily dispense; – they have all their proper places; and fill their several stations, with great credit to themselves, and much satisfaction to the reader.

The New Review for the following month also gave an approving synopsis with quotations.[5]

Perhaps in some part thanks to these reviews, *Pride and Prejudice* became the fashionable novel for the spring of 1813, and the literate public were soon busily engaged in exchanging opinions and guesses as to its authorship. Sheridan the playwright asked his dinner-partner Miss Shirreff if she had seen it, 'and advised her to buy it immediately for it was one of the cleverest things he ever read'.[6] Henry Austen recorded that: 'When "Pride and Prejudice" made its appearance, a gentleman, celebrated for his literary attainments, advised a friend of the authoress [probably Henry himself] to read it, adding, with more point than gallantry, "I should like to know who is the author, for it is much too clever to have been written by a woman."'[7] The intellectual Miss Milbanke – the future Lady Byron – thought at first that it had been 'written by a sister of Charlotte Smith's', but then later in the year told her mother:

I have finished the Novel called Pride and Prejudice, which I think a very superior work. It depends not on any of the common resources of novel writers, no drownings, no conflagrations, nor runaway horses, nor lap-dogs and parrots, nor chambermaids and milliners, nor rencontres and disguises. I really think it is the <u>most probable</u> fiction I have ever read . . . I wish much to know who is the author or <u>-ess</u> as I am told –

but Lady Davy declared: '"Pride and Prejudice" I do not very much like. Want of interest is the fault I can least excuse in works of mere amusement, and however natural the picture of vulgar minds and manners is there given, it is unrelieved by the agreeable contrast of more dignified and refined characters occasionally captivating attention.' In Edinburgh Susan Ferrier was working on her own first novel, *Marriage*, and said: 'I should like amazingly to see that same "Pride and Prejudice" which everybody dins my ears with.' The first Earl of Dudley thought Mr Collins was 'quite admirable'; while Margaret Mackenzie told her brother that she had been 'much pleased' with the book and 'it is said to be by Mrs Dorset, the renowned authoress of *The Peacock at Home*.[8] The first edition sold well enough for Egerton to put out a second in the autumn of 1813, though as Jane had sold him the copyright she had no chance to correct in the second edition any of the errors which she had noticed in the printing of the first.[9]

As well as rejoicing in the publication of *Pride and Prejudice*, Jane's letters in the New Year of 1813 contain references which show that she was already halfway through *Mansfield Park*. According to Cassandra's memorandum, *Mansfield Park* was 'begun somewhere about Feby. 1811 – Finished soon after June 1813';[10] but it seems unlikely that the actual writing of this work could have started at so early a date. In the spring of 1811 Jane was not only correcting the proofs of *Sense and Sensibility* but also planning how to remodel *First Impressions* into *Pride and Prejudice*. It must be considered very doubtful that she would choose to give herself simultaneously the third task of composing a totally new novel of so different a character from its immediate predecessor; a more likely explanation would be that in February 1811 Jane made the first mention to Cassandra of her ideas for a story whose heroine would be the diametric opposite of Elizabeth Bennet, and that the actual composition of *Mansfield Park* did not commence until *Pride and Prejudice* had been finished, probably in the spring of 1812.

To keep the chronology of the plot correct in her own mind, it seems Jane used the calendars of 1808–10, though the timespan overall is from about 1801 to 1811, starting with the arrival of Lady Bertram's unhappy little ten-year-old niece Fanny Price at Mansfield Park, and ending with her marriage to Edmund Bertram at some unspecified time after the main action of the story has ended. In her letter of 24 January 1813 Jane told Cassandra that she had been reading Sir John Carr's *Travels in Spain*, and from it learned 'that there is no Government House at Gibraltar. – I must alter it to the Commissioner's'. Further on in the same letter, referring to an evening spent at Mr Papillon's rectory, she said: 'As soon as a Whist party was formed & a round Table threatened, I made my Mother an excuse, & came away; leaving just as many for <u>their</u> round Table, as there were at Mrs Grants. – I wish they might be as agreeable a set', indicating that she was then up to chapter 7 of volume II, the twenty-fifth chapter out of the total of forty-eight.[11] She was also still researching for the remaining half of the narrative, and in her letter of 29 January, after telling Cassandra about the receipt of the pre-publication copy of *Pride and Prejudice*, continued: 'Now I will try to write of something else; – it shall be a complete change of subject – Ordination. I am glad to find your enquiries have ended so well. If you cd. discover whether Northamptonshire is a Country of Hedgerows, I shd. be glad again.'[12] As Cassandra was then staying with James, the cleric of the family, Jane had evidently asked her to find out from him how long the process of ordination took, and therefore how long Edmund Bertram could reasonably be kept away from Mansfield Park for this purpose – a pertinent point for the story, as it is during his absence that Mary Crawford finds herself missing him and Henry Crawford proposes to Fanny Price. It seems that Jane was also considering the idea of someone, perhaps Fanny, overhearing others talking when hidden from sight by a hedgerow – a device which she eventually used in *Persuasion*; alternatively, she might have been wanting to check that what she had already written about hedgerows in chapter 22 was in fact correct.

Martha too had been asked to find out about hedgerows, for when she wrote to Jane from Kintbury in February 1813 she apparently apologised for her lack of success in this respect, and Jane replied: 'I am obliged to you for your enquiries about Northamptonshire, but do not wish you to renew them, as I am sure of getting the intelligence I want from Henry, to whom I can apply at some convenient moment . . .'[13] Henry was acquainted with Sir James Langham, whose estate at Cottesbrooke was not far from Northampton – facts which Jane had presumably just remembered, and so realised that she need look no further for a source of this particular information.[14] Her own knowledge of the Portsmouth scene, gained while living in Frank's company in nearby Southampton, enabled her to sketch in the Prices' home life; the Revd Thomas Leigh's improvements at Adlestrop under Repton's advice gave the correct background for the discussions about improvements to Sotherton and Thornton Lacey; Charles's gift of topaz crosses to herself and Cassandra is obviously reflected in William Price's gift of an amber cross to Fanny; and it seems possible that some of Mary Lloyd's less attractive characteristics reappear in Mrs Norris.[15] After Cassandra's return from Steventon the sisters were not separated again for any length of time until late May, so there are no letters extant from the spring of 1813 to give further details as to the progress of *Mansfield Park*.

In March 1813 the occupant of the Great House, Mr Middleton, left Chawton after a five-year tenancy of the property; although he himself does not seem to have paid much neighbourly attention towards Mrs Austen, his sister-in-law, Miss Beckford, frequently called at the Cottage and usually brought her teenage niece, Charlotte Maria Middleton, with her. Miss Beckford had some 'old complaint' that required medical treatment, and in February 1811 Jane had accompanied her to Alton for a consultation with Mr Newnham the apothecary. Jane's quick ear caught their 'conversation, as it actually took place, in prose', and rapidly converted it into verse:

> I've a pain in my head,
> Said the suffering Beckford,
> To her Doctor so dread.
> Oh! What shall I take for't?
>
> Said her Doctor so dread
> Whose name it was Newnham
> For this pain in your head
> Ah! what can you do Ma'am?
>
> Said Miss Beckford, suppose
> If you think there's no risk,
> I take a good Dose
> Of calomel brisk.
>
> What a praiseworthy notion,
> Replied Mr Newnham,
> You shall have such a potion
> And so will I too Ma'am.[16]

Young Charlotte Maria Middleton never forgot her happy adolescence at Chawton, and years later wrote:

I remember her [Jane] as a tall thin spare person, with very high cheek bones great colour – sparkling Eyes not large but joyous & intelligent . . . her keen sense of humour I quite remember, it oozed out very much in Mr Bennett's [*sic*] Style . . . We saw her often She was a most kind & enjoyable person to Children but somewhat stiff & cold to strangers She used to sit at Table at Dinner parties without uttering much probably collecting matter for her charming novels which in those days we knew nothing about – her Sister Cassandra was very lady-like but very prim, but my remembrance of Jane is that of her entering into all Childrens Games & liking her extremely. – We were often asked to meet her young nephews & nieces [and] were at Chawton with them.[17]

Now that the Great House was vacant Edward took the opportunity to move his family there while Godmersham was thoroughly redecorated and the Knights, accompanied by Edward's sister-in-law, Miss Louisa Bridges, arrived on 21 April – 'We are half frozen at the cold uninhabited appearance of the old house,' Fanny noted in her diary. The very next day, while she was still trying to get the family comfortably settled in, her brother Edward 'went to Town with Aunt Jane as we had a very bad account of poor Mrs Henry Austen'. Since Eliza's visit to Chawton Cottage in the summer of 1811, when Cassandra had told Phylly Whitaker: 'Mrs H. Austen has been spending a fortnight with us lately & I think I never saw her in such good health before –'[18] some terminal ailment had seized upon her. No description or identification of this illness is anywhere given in the Austen correspondence or in Fanny's diaries, but it seems that the family soon realised there was no hope of her recovery. Jane, in her letter to Martha of 16 February 1813, said briefly: 'We have no late account from Sloane St & therefore conclude that everything is going on in one regular progress, without any striking change.'[19] It was twenty years since Eliza had written to cousin Phylly: 'my heart gives the preference to Jane, whose kind partiality to me indeed requires a return of the same nature –'[20] and Henry knew that Jane was the person who was needed now to give help and comfort in these last few days of Eliza's life. She died on 25 April and was buried in Hampstead parish churchyard in the same grave with her mother and son – 'a woman of brilliant generous and cultivated mind' was Henry's wording for her epitaph.[21]

Jane returned to Hampshire on 1 May, but Henry soon found he could not do without her assistance in settling Eliza's affairs and so came to Chawton later in the month to collect her for another trip to London. Jane's next surviving letter is that of 20 May, describing to Cassandra their pleasant journey along the Guildford road the previous day.[22] Henry was already planning to leave the Sloane Street house and live over his banking premises at No. 10 Henrietta Street, Covent Garden, where Eliza's faithful French servants Mme. Bigeon and her daughter Mme. Perigord would continue to look after him. While these arrangements were being made during the latter part of May, Henry took his sister to three art exhibitions, starting with one in Spring Gardens. Jane's mind was still full of *Pride and Prejudice*, and after her visit there told Cassandra:

It is not thought a good collection, but I was very well pleased – particularly (pray tell Fanny) with a small portrait of Mrs Bingley, excessively like her. I went in hopes of seeing one of her Sister, but there was no Mrs Darcy; – perhaps however, I may find her in the Great Exhibition which we shall go to, if we have time; – I have no chance of her in the collection of Sir Joshua Reynolds's Paintings which is now shewing in Pall Mall, & which we are also to visit. – Mrs Bingley's is exactly herself, size, shaped face, features & sweetness; there never was a greater likeness. She is dressed in a white gown, with green ornaments, which convinces me of what I had always supposed, that green was a favourite colour with her. I dare say Mrs D. will be in Yellow . . . We have been both to the Exhibition & Sir J. Reynolds', – and I am disappointed, for there was nothing like Mrs D. at either. – I can only imagine that Mr D. prizes any Picture of her too much to like it should be exposed to the public eye. – I can imagine he wd. have that sort of feeling – that mixture of Love, Pride & Delicacy.[23]

Although Jane still wished to preserve her anonymity, whenever Henry heard *Pride and Prejudice* praised he could not resist telling the company that she had written it, and so the secret was gradually getting out. Mr and Mrs Tilson already knew it and had told their friend Miss Burdett; in her letter of 24 May, Jane said: 'I should like to see Miss Burdett very well, but that I am rather frightened by hearing that she wishes to be introduced to me. – If I am a Wild Beast, I cannot help it. It is not my own fault.'[24] There is no further information as to whether Jane did meet Miss Burdett at the end of May before returning home with Henry, but alternatively they could have been introduced at the end of the year when Jane was back in London again.

In the meantime, during the summer of 1813, both Charles and James with their respective families came to stay at Chawton. The former now had a third daughter, also named Fanny, born in December 1812, and when he and his wife returned to London they left their two elder children with Mrs Austen at the Cottage. Later in the year Jane wrote to Frank:

Charles's little girls were with us about a month, & had so endeared themselves that we were quite sorry to have them go. We have the pleasure however of hearing that they are thought very much improved at home – Harriet in health, Cassy in manners. – The latter ought to be a very nice Child – Nature has done enough for her – but Method has been wanting; – we thought her very much improved ourselves, but to have Papa & Mama think her so too, was very essential to our contentment. – She will really be a very pleasing Child, if they will only exert themselves a little. – Harriet is a truely sweet-tempered little Darling.[25]

It was probably during this visit to Chawton that James's children were finally let into the secret of their aunt's authorship of the novels which they had already read and enjoyed. James Edward, not yet fifteen, had the family talent for versifying, and dashed off the following lines,

> To Miss J. Austen:
> No words can express, my dear Aunt, my surprise
> Or make you conceive how I opened my eyes,
> Like a pig Butcher Pile has just struck with his knife,
> When I heard for the very first time in my life
> That I had the honour to have a relation
> Whose works were dispersed through the whole of the nation.
> I assure you, however I'm terribly glad;
> Oh dear! just to think (and the thought drives me mad)
> That dear Mrs Jennings's good-natured strain
> Was really the produce of your witty brain,
> That you made the Middletons, Dashwoods, and all,

And that you (not young Ferrars) found out that a ball
May be given in cottages, never so small.
And though Mr Collins, so grateful for all,
Will Lady de Bourgh his dear Patroness call,
'Tis to your ingenuity really he owed
His living, his wife, and his humble abode.
Now if you will take your poor nephew's advice,
Your works to Sir William pray send in a trice,
If he'll undertake to some grandees to show it,
By whose means at last the Prince Regent might know it,
For I'm sure if he did, in reward for your tale,
He'd make you a countess at least, without fail,
And indeed if the Princess should lose her dear life
You might have a good chance of becoming his wife.[26]

James Edward's reference to the Prince Regent's possible admiration of Jane and her works was doubtless uttered quite teasingly, as it must have been well known even to the younger generation of her family that she, in common with many others at the time, thoroughly disapproved of the heir to the throne and his dissolute life; nevertheless, within a remarkably short space of time this cheerful dig-in-the-ribs turned out to be unexpectedly prophetic.

Fanny's diary shows that throughout the summer the inhabitants of the Great House and the Cottage were in close daily contact with each other, and she notes in particular the time spent exclusively in Jane's company: 'Aunt Jane spent the morning with me . . . Aunt Jane and I had a delicious morning together . . .' and it seems that during these private morning meetings Fanny told Jane something of her romantic hopes regarding the quiet, serious-minded Mr John Pemberton Plumptre, confidences that Jane received with sympathetic approval.[27] On 5 June there is the interesting comment: 'Aunt Jane spent the morning with me and read Pride and Prejudice to me as Papa and Aunt Louisa rode out.' Henry knew that his sister could read aloud 'with very great taste and effect' and that 'Her own works, probably, were never heard to so much advantage as from her own mouth; for she partook largely in all the best gifts of the comic muse.'[28] It may be that this reading of *Pride and Prejudice* was the occasion that Fanny's sister, Marianne, then aged eleven, remembered disconsolately to the end of her very long life – how Aunt Jane had shut herself up with Fanny in one of the bedrooms to read something aloud and Marianne and the younger ones had heard 'peals of laughter through the door, and thought it very hard that we should be shut out from what was so delightful'.[29] One of these 'younger ones' was Edward's fourth daughter, Louisa (1804–89), who was

Jane's god-daughter. It was Louisa's first visit to Chawton and she listened to her aunts' conversation with great interest, for many years later she was able to tell an admirer of Jane's works that 'Miss Austen's sister Cassandra tried to persuade her to alter the end of Mansfield Park and let Mr Crawford marry Fanny Price. She [Louisa] remembers their arguing the matter but Miss Austen stood firmly and would not allow the change.'[30]

Frank was the only one of the Austen brothers who was unable to visit Chawton during this summer of 1813, for since July 1811 he had been commanding the 74-gun HMS *Elephant* as part of Admiral Young's North Sea fleet, mostly engaged in blockading Napoleon's great dockyard at Flushing. Mary Gibson had moved to Deal in order to be near him whenever he was in port – as Jane said, 'I think they must soon have lodged in every house in the Town'[31] – and their fourth child, George, was born there in 1812. In May 1813 the *Elephant* was ordered to the Baltic, as a result of the commencement of yet another phase in the war against Napoleon. Marshal Bernadotte, who had fought for his Emperor at Grezlaw and Wagram, had lately been selected to be Crown Prince of Sweden and had hoped that Napoleon would assist him in conquering Norway to add to his new kingdom. As such assistance was not forthcoming, Bernadotte first cooled into neutrality towards his old master and then in 1813 changed sides entirely, declaring himself an ally of the Russians and Austrians. He brought a contingent of 12,000 Swedish soldiers across the Baltic to fight the French, and HMS *Elephant* was now engaged in convoying the troop-transports to the Pomeranian coast.

Jane's next letter is that of 3 July 1813 addressed to Frank:

It must be real enjoyment to you, since you are obliged to leave England, to be where you are, seeing something of a new Country, & one that has been so distinguished as Sweden. – You must have great pleasure in it. – I hope you may have gone to Carlscroon . . . I have a great respect for former Sweden. So zealous as it was for Protestantism! – And I have always fancied it more like England than many Countries; – & according to the Map, many of the names have a strong resemblance to the English.

She was happy to be able to tell Frank that Henry was quite well and getting over his bereavement:

Upon the whole his Spirits are very much recovered. – If I may so express myself, his Mind is not a Mind for affliction. He is too Busy, too active, too sanguine. – Sincerely as he was attached to poor Eliza moreover, & excellently as he behaved to her, he was always so used to be away from her at times, that her Loss is not felt as that of many a beloved wife might be, especially when all the circumstances of her long and dreadful Illness are taken into the account. – He very long knew that she must die, & it was indeed a release at last.

There was other family news to be given, including the joking reminder about Dr Blackall's visit to Ashe sixteen years ago, and then Jane spoke of her own interests:

You will be glad to hear that every Copy of S. & S. is sold & that it has brought me £140 – besides the Copyright, if that shd. ever be of any value. – I have now therefore written myself into £250 – which only makes me long for more. – I have something in hand – which I hope on the credit of P. & P. will sell well, tho' not half so entertaining. And by the bye – shall you object to my mentioning the Elephant in it, & two or three other of your old Ships? – I have done it, but it shall not stay, to make you angry. – They are only just mentioned.[32]

It is evident from this that Jane had by now certainly finished chapter 7 of volume III of *Mansfield Park* (chapter 38 of modern editions), and was possibly even nearer completion of the last volume.

A few weeks after this budget of home news to Frank, Anna surprised the family by announcing that she wished to marry Ben Lefroy of Ashe. He was the youngest son of Jane's childhood friend Madam Lefroy, and although his father had died in 1806 the eldest son, J. H. George Lefroy, had succeeded him in the living, so that Ashe Rectory was still Ben's home. 'He was tall and handsome and had very good abilities, and had in addition the charms of a very gentle voice and manner'[33] – but as yet had no profession or occupation and was undecided as to his plans for the future. Not even the fact that he was Madam Lefroy's son could make Jane feel happy about the affair, and when she wrote again to Frank at the end of September she said worriedly:

I take it for granted that Mary has told you of Anna's engagement to Ben Lefroy. It came upon us without much preparation; – at the same time, there was that about her which kept us in a constant preparation for something. – We are anxious to have it go on well, there being quite as much in his favour as the Chances are likely to give her in any Matrimonial connection. I beleive he is sensible, certainly very religious, well connected & with some Independance. – There is an unfortunate dissimilarity of Taste between them in one respect which gives us some apprehensions, he hates company & she is very fond of it; – This, with some queerness of Temper on his side & much unsteadiness on hers, is untoward.[34]

The engagement was formally announced on 17 August, but the atmosphere at Steventon Rectory may well have been strained, for a few days later Anna went to Chawton Cottage and remained there for three weeks.

On 14 September the Chawton house-party finally broke up, as Mr Scudamore, Edward's Kentish physician, had advised that the family could safely return to Godmersham without fear of developing painter's colic. Edward despatched most of his vast household of children and servants across country to Kent, but himself took Jane and his three eldest daughters up to London to stay with Henry, who was now in residence at No. 10 Henrietta Street. Jane's letters of 15 and 16 September to Cassandra detail the events crammed into their three-day visit – two evenings at the theatre, painful dental appointments for poor little Lizzy and Marianne, calls upon dressmaker and milliner and much general shopping for family commissions – she was very pleased to be able to spend some of her literary earnings upon a dress-length of poplin as a present for her sister. Henry had just returned from a trip to Scotland, where he had once again spread the word that Jane was the authoress of *Pride and Prejudice*, and had also sent a copy of the book to Warren Hastings at Daylesford. Hastings had now voiced his praise of it, a letter which Jane greatly appreciated: 'I am quite delighted with what such a Man writes about it . . . I long to have you hear Mr H's opinion of P & P. His admiring my Elizabeth so much is particularly welcome to me.'[35]

Edward and his party reached Godmersham on the evening of 17 September and Jane stayed on there until the middle of November; it was her first visit since the summer of 1809 and, as events proved, was to be her last. She wrote again to Frank on 25 September with the next instalment of family news and also to acknowledge his recent letter, in which he had evidently pointed out that if she used the genuine names of his ships in *Mansfield Park* the tightly knit naval world would soon realise that some member of the Austen family was the author of the book.

I thank you very warmly for your kind consent to my application & the kind hint which followed it. – I was previously aware of what I shd. be laying myself open to – but the truth is that the Secret has spread so far as to be scarcely the Shadow of a secret now – & that I beleive whenever the 3d appears, I shall not even attempt to tell Lies about it. – I shall rather try to make all the Money than all the Mystery I can of it. – People shall pay for their Knowledge if I can make them. – Henry heard P. & P. warmly praised in Scotland, by Lady Robt. Kerr & another Lady; – & what does he do in the warmth of his Brotherly vanity & Love, but immediately tell them who wrote it! A Thing once set going in that way – one knows how it spreads! – and he, dear Creature, has set it going so much more than once. I know it is all done from affection & partiality – but at the same time, let me here again express to you & Mary my sense of the <u>superior</u> kindness which you have shewn on the occasion, in doing what I wished. – I am trying to harden myself. – After all, what a trifle it is in all its Bearings, to the really important points of one's existence even in this World!³⁶

It seems probable that during this autumn visit to Godmersham Jane was either starting to make notes for *Emma* or else writing the final fair copy of *Mansfield Park* and adding some last-minute finishing touches as she did so, for both Marianne and Louisa Knight, now aged twelve and eight respectively, later on recorded their similar memories of her at this period. Marianne remembered

how Aunt Jane would sit quietly working [sewing] beside the fire in the library, saying nothing for a good while, and then would suddenly burst out laughing, jump up and run across the room to a table where pens and paper were lying, write something down, and then come back to the fire and go on quietly working as before.³⁷

Louisa recalled that: 'She was very absent indeed. She would sit silent awhile, then rub her hands, laugh to herself and run up to her room.' It seems too that little Louisa went into her aunt's bedroom one evening as Jane was dressing for dinner, and retained imprinted on her memory a bright candle-lit image of her: 'She had large dark eyes and a brilliant complexion, and long, long black hair down to her knees.'³⁸

Jane's letters from Godmersham during this visit are filled with details of the social life amongst the Kentish neighbours whom Cassandra knew well, and also pass on other family news. Since Charles's visit to Chawton earlier in the year, he and his family had lived in a rented house at Southend for the summer but were now back on HMS *Namur* at Sheerness for the winter months. From there he proposed to make a flying visit to Godmersham during October, and Jane wrote rather ruefully: 'I shall be most happy to see dear Charles, & he will be as happy as he can with a cross Child or some such care pressing on him at the time. – I should be very happy in the idea of seeing little Cassy again too, did not I fear she wd. disappoint me by some immediate disagreableness.' The next day they came in the evening:

They were late because they did not set out earlier & did not allow time enough. – Charles did not <u>aim</u> at more than reaching Sittingbourn by 3, which cd. not have brought them here by dinner time. – They had a very rough passage, he wd. not have ventured if he had known how bad it wd. be. – However here they are safe & well, just like their own nice selves, Fanny looking as neat & white this morng. as possible, & dear Charles all affectionate, placid, quiet, chearful good humour. They are both looking very well, but poor little Cassy is grown extremely thin & looks poorly. – I hope a week's Country air & exercise may do her good . . . Cassy was too tired & bewildered just at first to seem to know anybody – We met them in the Hall, the Women & Girl part of us – but before we reached the Library she kissed me very affectionately – & has since seemed to recollect me in the same way.

Jane evidently found Charles's children very unlike her other nephews and nieces, both in looks and disposition; referring again to Cassy, she said: 'Poor little Love – I wish she were not so very Palmery – but it seems stronger than ever. – I never knew a Wife's family-features have such undue influence.'[39] A silhouette of Fanny Palmer, painted perhaps in 1812, shows her as having a snub nose and short thick neck, and already something of a double chin.[40]

Charles and his family rushed away again a week later, and Jane then had time to worry about Anna and her unsatisfactory engagement:

I have had a late account from Steventon, & a baddish one, as far as Ben is concerned. He has declined a Curacy (apparently highly eligible), which he might have secured against his taking orders; – & upon its' being made rather a serious question, says he has not made up his mind as to taking orders so early, – & that if her Father makes a point of it, he must give Anna up rather than do what he does not approve. – He must be maddish. They are going on again, at present as before – but it cannot last. – Mary says that Anna is very unwilling to go to Chawton & will get home again as soon as she can.[41]

Anna was once again banished to her grandmother's care at the Cottage, and Jane hoped that Ben would visit her there.

At the end of September Jane told Frank: 'There is to be a 2d. Edition of S. & S. Egerton advises it'[42] – and, after she had made some slight changes to the text, this was brought out at the end of October, accompanied by a second edition of *Pride and Prejudice*. Jane had heard that she was 'read and admired in Ireland too. – There is a Mrs Fletcher, the wife of a Judge, an old Lady & very good & very clever, who is all curiosity to know about me – what I am like & so forth –. I am not known to her by <u>name</u> however –' and now with brisk practicality she added: 'I hope Mrs Fletcher will indulge herself with S & S.'[43] Mary Russell Mitford, granddaughter of the Austens' one-time neighbour Dr Russell of Ashe, and herself to become famous in the 1820s for her essays on rural life in Berkshire, collected and published under the title *Our Village*, had not yet read either of Jane's books but knew of the 'two novels in high repute' and that they were ascribed now to Lady Boringdon of Saltram, near Plymouth.[44] Lady Boringdon, who had much enjoyed *Pride and Prejudice*, was in no hurry to refute this rumour, and even a year later some people still believed that she was the authoress.[45] In

Cheltenham, however, *Sense and Sensibility* was ascribed to the intellectual Elizabeth Hamilton, which made Jane feel flattered: 'It is pleasant to have such a respectable Writer named.'[46]

Jane's last engagements at Godmersham during November were a dinner party with the Wildman family at Chilham Castle, followed by a concert and a ball at Canterbury. She was now within a month of her thirty-eighth birthday and in her letter of 6 November, the last of this series from Kent, faced the prospect of advancing years with her usual wry humour. 'By the bye, as I must leave off being young, I find many Douceurs in being a sort of Chaperon for I am put on the Sofa near the Fire & can drink as much wine as I like.' After the concert she found herself 'so tired that I began to wonder how I should get through the Ball next Thursday, but there will be so much more variety then in walking about, & probably so much less heat that perhaps I may not feel it more. My China Crape is still kept for the Ball.'[47] Unfortunately Jane's letter describing this ball has not survived; Fanny noted in her diary that she herself wore 'White sarsnet, & silver, silver in my hair –' and that there was 'good company but no dancing – officers idle & a scarcity of County Beaux'.

Edward took Jane to London on 13 November and she stayed with Henry for a fortnight before returning with him to Chawton: 'it will be a great pleasure to be with him, as it always is'.[48] It was probably during this visit to London that

a nobleman, personally unknown to her . . . was desirous of her joining a literary circle at his house. He communicated his wish in the politest manner, through a mutual friend [i.e., Henry], adding, what his Lordship doubtless thought would be an irresistible inducement, that the celebrated Madame de Stael would be of the party. Miss Austen immediately declined the invitation. To her truly delicate mind such a display would have given pain instead of pleasure.[49]

It was probably also during this visit that Henry negotiated for her the acceptance of *Mansfield Park* by Egerton; the latter, although he 'praised it for it's Morality, & for being so equal a Composition – No weak parts',[50] evidently did not think it would prove so popular as *Pride and Prejudice*, and so only agreed to publish it on commission, without on this occasion offering to purchase the copyright.

CHAPTER 15

Mansfield Park *and* Emma, *1814–15*

It was lucky for Jane that she had returned home before the end of the year, for on 27 December 1813 a great frost began, accompanied in London by a thick fog which lasted for eight days. The fog was only dispersed by strong east winds bringing with them heavy snowfalls that made travelling difficult, if not impossible, for several weeks, and in February a frost fair was held on the frozen Thames. To be forced to stay indoors would have been no hardship to Jane at this time, however, for she was now ready to begin work on her next book. 'I am going to take a heroine whom no one but myself will much like' she told her family; and Cassandra recorded that *Emma* was started on 21 January 1814.[1]

Jane never made any boast or parade of her literary work, and even James's three children, who were the most frequent visitors to the Cottage, did not realise that there were occasions when their aunt was composing as distinct from merely writing letters. James Edward remembered:

She was careful that her occupation should not be suspected by servants, or visitors, or any persons beyond her own family party. She wrote upon small sheets of paper which could easily be put away, or covered with a piece of blotting paper. There was, between the front door and the offices, a swing door which creaked when it was opened; but she objected to having this little inconvenience remedied, because it gave her notice when anyone was coming . . . In that well-occupied female party there must have been many precious hours of silence during which the pen was busy at the little mahogany writing-desk, while Fanny Price, or Emma Woodhouse, or Anne Elliot was growing into beauty and interest. I have no doubt that I, and my sisters and cousins, in our visits to Chawton, frequently disturbed this mystic process, without having any idea of the mischief that we were doing; certainly we never should have guessed it by any signs of impatience or irritability in the writer.[2]

Caroline also confirmed this discretion on Jane's part: 'My Aunt must have spent much time in writing – her desk lived in the drawing room. I often saw her writing letters on it, and I beleive she wrote much of her Novels in the same way – sitting with her family, when they were quite alone; but I never saw any manuscript of that sort, in progress –'[3]

Simultaneously with the commencement of *Emma*, Jane was still occupied in seeing *Mansfield Park* through the press, the publication of which was originally intended for April 1814; when Henry took her to London again on 1 March, it seems they had with them in their carriage either a spare copy of the manuscript or else perhaps an advance copy of the printed text, for as they travelled slowly on the muddy, snowy roads he started to read it for the first time.

We did not begin reading till Bentley Green. Henry's approbation hitherto is even equal to my wishes; he says it is very different from the other two, but does not appear to think it at all inferior. He has only married Mrs R. I am afraid he has gone through the most entertaining part. – He took to Lady B. & Mrs N. most kindly, & gives great praise to the drawing of the characters. He understands them all, likes Fanny & I think foresees how it will all be.

While Henry was reading her work, Jane was occupied with E. S. Barrett's *The Heroine, or, Adventures of a Fair Romance Reader*, which diverted her exceedingly: 'It is a delightful burlesque, particularly on the Radcliffe style.'[4]

During the next few days Henry continued to read the new book, and Jane passed his comments back to Cassandra in the three letters written from London during the first half of March:

Henry is going on with Mansfield Park; he admires H. Crawford – I mean properly – as a clever, pleasant Man. – I tell you all the Good I can, as I know how much you will enjoy it. . . . Henry has this moment said that he likes my M.P. better & better – he is in the 3d vol. I beleive now he has changed his mind as to foreseeing the end; – he said yesterday at least, that he defied anybody to say whether H.C. would be reformed, or would forget Fanny in a fortnight . . . Henry has finished Mansfield Park, & his approbation has not lessened. He found the last half of the last volume extremely interesting.[5]

A fragment of a fourth letter survives, dated 21 March, in which Jane told another member of the family, probably Frank: 'Perhaps before the end of April, Mansfield Park by the author of S. & S. – P. & P. may be in the World. – Keep the name to yourself. I shd. not like to have it known beforehand.'[6]

Edward and Fanny, who had been paying a short visit to Bath, broke their journey back to Godmersham by staying at Henrietta Street from 5–9 March and, as usual, spent their time in shopping and play-going. Jane was very impressed by Kean's performance as Shylock: 'it appeared to me as if there were no fault in him anywhere; & in his scene with Tubal there was exquisite acting'. Mr John Plumptre, who was also in London, joined

himself to their party for two consecutive evenings, and Henry thought
he could see a 'decided attachment' between Fanny and the young man –
Fanny's own diary entries show that she was indeed much fluttered by his
attentions. Cassandra came to London later in March, and she and Jane
probably returned together to Chawton early in April via a call on the Hills
at Streatham.[7]

On 20 April the Godmersham family came to Chawton Great House for
a two months' visit, this time bringing with them a party of Bridges relations
headed by the Dowager Lady Bridges, Fanny's 'dearest Grand Mama' – a
description which, perhaps significantly, is never applied to Mrs Austen.
Fanny's diary again shows almost daily contact with the occupants of the
Cottage, and yet, surprisingly, contains no reference at all to the publication
of *Mansfield Park*. Although Jane had hoped that her new work would
appear during April, it was not advertised until 9 May 1814, when *The Star*
mentioned it as 'By the Author of "Sense and Sensibility", and "Pride and
Prejudice"', and priced at 18s. the three volumes. Despite the fact that it
was never reviewed, the book sold steadily and by November 1814 the first
edition (possibly no more than 1,250 copies) was exhausted, bringing Jane
a profit of £350.[8] It was perhaps because of this lack of public comment
that during the year Jane collected and listed 'Opinions of Mansfield Park'
from her family and friends. Frank, as might be expected, gave the most
balanced view:

We certainly do not think it as a <u>whole</u>, equal to P. & P. – but it has many &
great beauties. Fanny is a delightful Character! and Aunt Norris is a great favourite
of mine. The Characters are natural & well supported, & many of the Dialogues
excellent. – You need not fear the publication being considered as discreditable to
the talents of its Author.

Other opinions ranged from the total incomprehension of Miss Augusta
Bramston of Oakley Hall, who 'owned that she thought S. & S. – and
P. & P. downright nonsense, but expected to like MP. better, & having
finished the 1st vol. – flattered herself she had got through the worst' via
the technical appreciation of Frank's friend Admiral Foote: '– surprised that
I had the power of drawing the Portsmouth-Scenes so well' and the slight
regrets of those, including Cassandra, who 'thought it quite as clever, tho'
not so brilliant as P. & P.' – to the serious conclusion from Mrs Carrick:
'All who think deeply & feel much will give the Preference to Mansfield
Park.'

The appearance of a third novel by this anonymous writer set the literary
gossip going again: 'Mrs Pole also said that no Books had ever occasioned
so much canvassing & doubt, & that everybody was desirous to attribute

them to some of their own friends, or to some person of whom they thought highly.'⁹ Mrs Grant of Laggan, herself an authoress, agreed with a correspondent: 'I am glad you approve so much of Mansfield Park, it being a great favourite with me, on account of its just delineation of manners and excellent moral, which is rather insinuated than obtruded throughout – the safest and best way, I think.'¹⁰ The Dowager Lady Vernon gave a mild recommendation: 'It is not much of a novel, more the history of a family party in the country, very natural, and the characters well drawn.' Lady Anne Romilly asked Maria Edgeworth:

Have you read Mansfield Park? It has been pretty generally admired here [London], and I think all novels must be that are true to life which this is, with a good strong vein of principle running thro' the whole. It has not however that elevation of virtue, something beyond nature, that gives the greatest charm to a novel, but still it is real natural every day life, and will amuse an idle hour in spite of its faults.

It was as well that Maria Edgeworth could not know the first Earl of Dudley's opinions:

Have you read Mansfield Park? I have only just begun it . . . I am a great admirer of the two other works by the same author. She has not so much fine humour as your friend Miss Edgeworth, but she is more skilful in contriving a story, she has a great deal more feeling, and she never plagues you with any chemistry, mechanics, or political economy, which are all excellent things in their way, but vile, cold-hearted trash in a novel

– a comment which lends point to Jane's own joke with Cassandra that some 'solemn specious nonsense' should have been written into *Pride and Prejudice.*¹¹

The spring and summer of 1814 was a time of national happiness, for it was now clear that at last the twenty-year struggle against Napoleon was drawing to a close. In January the Austrians, Russians and Prussians had invaded France from across the Rhine while Wellington marched northwards from the Pyrenees, and although Napoleon himself still refused to admit defeat the French Government entered into peace negotiations during February. The invasion of Paris in March brought matters to a rapid conclusion and on 5 April Napoleon was forced to abdicate and submit to being exiled to the Mediterranean island of Elba. The cessation of hostilities of course made a great difference to the lives of Jane's sailor brothers; Frank signed off from HMS *Elephant* at Spithead in May 1814 and was thereafter free to live on shore with his ever-increasing family while retaining his naval rank and half-pay; Charles was still for the time being in command of HMS *Namur* at the Nore, but his wife, Fanny Palmer, hoped that they too would soon be 'settled on shore in some way or other'.[12] Early in June the Emperor of Russia and the King of Prussia arrived in England and stayed in London for a fortnight of celebrations, during which their every appearance was greeted with wild enthusiasm by crowds of Londoners of all ranks and ages. Henry came to collect Cassandra for a visit to Henrietta Street and Jane warned her: 'Take care of yourself, & do not be trampled to death running after the Emperor. The report in Alton yesterday was that they wd. certainly travel this road either to, or from Portsmouth',[13] where a naval review had been arranged for 24 June. At home in Hampshire, Alton celebrated on 17 and 18 June with illuminations and a civic supper for its poorer inhabitants, as Fanny noted in her diary. Edward and Fanny then also went to London to join Henry and Cassandra, and saw 'the procession going to proclaim Peace'. Henry, with his usual luck, was invited to attend the magnificent ball organised by White's Club and held at Burlington House on 21 June, at which over 2,000 people were present including the Prince Regent, the Emperor and the King, and which cost nearly £10,000. Jane was quite speechless at Cassandra's news: 'Henry at White's! Oh, what a Henry!'[14]

Once Edward and his family had left Chawton, Jane went to stay with the Cookes at Great Bookham for a midsummer fortnight. She was very pleased to hear that they admired *Mansfield Park* exceedingly – indeed, Mr Cooke called it 'the most sensible Novel he had ever read'.[15] Great Bookham was only a few miles from Leatherhead and Jane had used her knowledge of the latter small town, gained during previous visits to the Cookes, as a basis for the creation of Emma's Highbury.[16] As she was now deep in the composition of *Emma*, a further visit to the neighbourhood of Leatherhead and Box Hill would be most useful to provide more local colour for her new work. It is unfortunate that in none of her letters surviving from 1814 does Jane mention anything to do with the progress of *Emma*, as she did for that of *Mansfield Park*. However, one lucky circumstance ensured that some of her views on the art of literary composition have been preserved – this year Anna started to write a novel herself, and offered the text chapter by chapter as she completed it for her aunt's criticism. There are five letters to Anna in the second half of 1814 in which Jane discusses the developing story and in so doing demonstrates her own self-imposed standards of meticulous accuracy of detail and insistence upon natural and consistent character-drawing in order to produce the illusion of truth in fiction.

I am very much obliged to you for sending your MS. It has entertained me extremely, all of us indeed . . . Sir Tho: – Lady Helena, & St Julian are very well done – & Cecilia continues to be interesting inspite of her being so amiable. – It was very fit that you should advance her age . . . As Lady H. is Cecilia's superior, it wd. not be correct to talk of <u>her</u> being introduced; Cecilia must be the person introduced – And I do not like a Lover's speaking in the 3d person; – it is too much like the formal part of Lord Orville, & I think is not natural. If <u>you</u> think differently however, you need not mind me . . .[17]

I like the name 'Which is the Heroine?' very well, & I dare say shall grow to like it very much in time – but 'Enthusiasm' was something so very superior that every common Title must appear to disadvantage. – I am not sensible of any Blunders about Dawlish. The Library was particularly pitiful & wretched 12 years ago, & not likely to have anybody's publication . . . Lyme will not do. Lyme is towards 40 miles distance from Dawlish & would not be talked of there . . . They must be <u>two</u> days going from Dawlish to Bath; They are nearly 100 miles apart . . . And we think you had better not leave England. Let the Portmans go to Ireland, but as you know nothing of the Manners there, you had better not go with them. You will be in danger of giving false representations. Stick to Bath & the Foresters. There you will be quite at home.[18]

We are not satisfied with Mrs F's settling herself as Tenant & near Neighbour to such a Man as Sir T.H. . . . A woman, going with two girls just growing up, into a Neighbourhood where she knows nobody but one Man, of not very good character, is an awkwardness which so prudent a woman as Mrs F. would not be likely to fall into. Remember, she is very prudent; – you must not let her act inconsistently . . . You describe a sweet place, but your descriptions are often more minute than will be liked. You give too many particulars of right hand & left . . . You are now collecting your People delightfully, getting them exactly into such a spot as is the delight of my life; – 3 or 4 Families in a Country Village is the very thing to work on . . . You are but <u>now</u> coming to the heart & beauty of your book; till the heroine grows up, the fun must be imperfect . . . The scene with Mrs Mellish, I should condemn; it is prosy & nothing to the purpose – & indeed, the more you can find in your heart to curtail between Dawlish & Newton Priors, the better I think it will be. One does not care for girls till they are grown up. – Your Aunt C. quite enters into the exquisiteness of that name. Newton Priors is really a Nonpareil . . .[19]

Henry Mellish I am afraid will be too much in the common Novel style – a handsome, amiable, unexceptionable Young Man (such as do not much abound in real Life) desperately in Love, & all in vain . . . Devereux Forester's being ruined by his Vanity is extremely good; but I wish you would not let him plunge into a 'vortex of Dissipation'. I do not object to the Thing, but I cannot bear the expression; – it is such thorough novel slang – and so old, that I dare say Adam met with it in the first novel he opened . . . What can you do with Egerton to increase the interest for him? I wish you cd. contrive something, some family occurrence to draw out his good qualities more . . . I would not seriously recommend anything Improbable, but if you cd. invent something spirited for him, it wd. have a good effect.[20]

I think you are going on very well. The description of Dr Griffin & Lady Helena's unhappiness is very good, just what was likely to be. – I am curious to know what the end of them will be . . . Had not you better give some hint of St Julian's early history in the beginning of your story?[21]

This is the last letter dealing with Anna's novel, which soon afterwards had to be laid aside for some years owing to the pressure of family cares and then, in the late 1820s, was thrown into the fire one day when she was feeling despondent. Her third daughter, Fanny Caroline Lefroy (1820–85), remembered 'sitting on the rug and watching its destruction, amused with the flames and the sparks which kept breaking out in the blackened paper. In later years when I expressed my sorrow that she had destroyed it, she said she could never have borne to finish it, but incomplete as it was Jane Austen's criticisms would have made it valuable.'[22]

After returning from Bookham in July, Jane was at home for a month before once more going to Henry in London; he had recently left Henrietta Street and returned to his old Chelsea neighbourhood, taking No. 23 in Hans Place, a small square just round the corner from No. 64 Sloane Street: 'the houses bright, fresh, newly painted, looking into a garden full of shrubs and flowers . . .'[23] His partner, Mr Tilson, lived three doors away at No. 26, and it was possible to converse across the intermediate back-gardens.[24] On this occasion Jane travelled up by Yalden's coach, which was very full; as she wrote to Cassandra on the day after arrival: 'everybody either did come up by Yalden yesterday, or wanted to come up. It put me in mind of my own Coach between Edinburgh & Sterling' – a joke which shows that the sisters must recently have been rereading 'Love and Freindship'.[25] Jane stayed with Henry for nearly a fortnight, passing the days 'very pleasantly, but with not much to tell of them; two or three very little Dinner-parties at home, some delightful Drives in the Curricle, and quiet Tea-drinkings with the Tilsons',[26] as well as visiting No. 125 Pall Mall, where Benjamin West's latest enormous picture, *Christ Rejected by the Elders*, was on exhibition. She much preferred it to West's earlier work, *Christ Healing the Sick*, which she had seen in 1811, and told Martha that it was indeed 'the first representation of our Saviour whichever at all contented me'.[27]

Henry, now a wealthy widower, as tall, handsome and witty as ever and still only in his early forties, was once again a highly eligible subject for matrimony; and just as years before he had wanted Jane to get to know Miss Pearson better, so now, she told Cassandra: 'Henry wants me to see more of his Hanwell favourite, & has written to invite her to spend a day or two here with me. His scheme is to fetch her on Saturday. I am more

& more convinced that he will marry again soon, & like the idea of <u>her</u> better than of anybody else at hand.'[28] The 'Hanwell favourite' was Miss Harriet Moore, and the others 'at hand' seem to have been the Tilsons' friend Miss Burdett and a widowed Mrs Crutchley in Berkshire. It was probably Miss Burdett who had invited Henry to the White's Club ball, for Jane commented in that context: 'I do not know what to wish as to Miss B., so I will hold my tongue and my wishes'[29] and when Henry took Jane home on 3 September the plan was to 'lengthen the Journey by going round by Sunning Hill; his favourite Mrs Crutchley lives there, and he wants to introduce me to her'.[30]

Just before Jane's return from London, Charles's wife, Fanny Palmer, gave birth to her fourth daughter on 31 August, and Jane was able to tell Martha: 'We have just learned that Mrs C. Austen is safe in bed with a Girl. – It happened on board, a fortnight before it was expected.'[31] But although the birth may have been normal, post-natal complications set in – Fanny died on 6 September and the baby, Elizabeth, two weeks later.[32] Old Miss Elizabeth Leigh of Adlestrop had the news from Cassandra, and wrote in her journal: 'The Austin [*sic*] family have a great loss in the attach'd & beloved wife of Captn. C: Austin; who died (by a mistake) on board a Ship from whence she ought sooner to have removed.'[33] Edward, with the sad experience of an identical bereavement, set off at once to Sheerness to comfort his brother,[34] and during the autumn of 1814 Charles stifled his grief in the business of rearranging his domestic and professional lives. He resigned his command of HMS *Namur* at the end of September and sought instead service abroad, moving to the 36-gun HMS *Phoenix* bound for the Mediterranean station. His three little girls went to live with their Palmer grandparents at 22 Keppel Street, Bloomsbury, where their aunt Harriet, the spinster of the family, could look after them, and whence they could quite conveniently be sent to visit their Austen grandmother and aunts; and as Frank and his family were also now at Chawton, borrowing the Great House from Edward, there would be no lack of playmates for them in Hampshire.

In addition to this unexpected bereavement, the latter part of 1814 was saddened for the Austens by an attack upon the very roots of their Chawton life – an attack which caused not only financial worries but also social embarrassment, as it came from their neighbours across the road, Mr and Miss Hinton of Chawton Lodge who, together with their nephew, James Baverstock, 'a clever and rather scampish brewer of Alton',[35] brought a lawsuit against Edward for the possession of his Hampshire estates. Under the terms of the Will of the old Mrs Knight who had entailed these lands to

Mr Thomas Brodnax-May-Knight of Godmersham early in the eighteenth century, the Hinton family were to become her next heirs should his line fail. When he succeeded to her properties Mr Knight and his son, Thomas Knight II, cut off the entail, and the present claim of the Baverstocks and Hintons rested on their being able to prove some error or inexactitude in this disentailing deed, though they were not disputing the intention of the Knights to make Edward Austen their heir. They were not laying any claim to the Godmersham estate, which had never formed part of Mrs Elizabeth Knight's holdings; but if they were to win their lawsuit, Edward would lose two-thirds of his property and Mrs Austen her home at Chawton Cottage. It seems that the claimants had first made informal approaches to Edward earlier in the year, for in her letter of 5 March 1814 Jane told Cassandra: 'Perhaps you have not heard that Edward has a good chance of escaping his Lawsuit. His opponent "knocks under". The terms of Agreement are not quite settled –'[36] but this was an over-optimistic belief, and a formal writ of ejectment was served upon him in mid-October. The lawsuit dragged on for several years, a source of constant unease to the family, and was not settled until April 1818, when Edward was obliged to cut a great swathe through Chawton Park Wood in order to raise £15,000 by the sale of the timber to buy off his opponents – 'that all claims on the estate should be for ever relinquished'.[37]

A happier event in the autumn of 1814 was Anna's marriage. After his 'maddish' behaviour of the previous autumn, Ben Lefroy had presumably changed his mind over the winter and agreed with James Austen that he would take Holy Orders in the not-too-distant future, so the uncertainty surrounding the engagement was removed and the summer of 1814 passed in peaceful courtship.

Ashe and Steventon were not far apart even by road, and to one who knew the short cut across the meadows and down the avenue and through the little coppice which hung on the side of the hill, and so into the lane almost close to the Rectory gate, the distance between the two was scarcely a mile, and the young people . . . met almost daily, passing nearly every afternoon in the shrubbery walk at Steventon much to the grievance of [Mary Lloyd], who complained that she in consequence had been shut out of it all the summer, and that she had never before seen any couple so foolishly devoted.[38]

The date chosen was Tuesday 8 November, and Caroline remembered: 'Weddings were then usually very quiet. The old fashion of festivity and publicity had quite gone by, and was universally condemned as showing the great bad taste of all former generations . . . My sister's wedding was certainly in the <u>extreme</u> of quietness; yet not so as to be in any way censured or remarked upon.'[39] Apart from the bride and groom, the only other people present were their immediate families – on Ben's side his two brothers, sister-in-law and eldest niece, and on Anna's her father, stepmother, brother and sister. Anna wore 'a dress of fine white muslin, and over it a soft silk shawl, white shot with primrose with embossed white satin flowers and very handsome fringe, and on her head a small cap to match trimmed with lace', the delicate yellow tints of which 'must have been most becoming to her bright brown hair, and hazel eyes and sunny clear complexion'.[40] Little Anne Lefroy and Caroline Austen, aged six and nine respectively, were the bridesmaids, in white frocks and new straw bonnets decked with white ribbons.

The season of the year, the unfrequented road of half a mile to the lonely old church [Steventon], the grey light within of a November morning making its way through the narrow windows, no stove to give warmth, no flowers to give colour and brightness, no friends, high or low, to offer their good wishes . . . all these circumstances and deficiencies must, I think, have given a gloomy air to our wedding . . . I do not think this idea of sadness struck me at the time; the bustle in the house, and all the preparations had excited me, and it seemed to me as a festivity from beginning to end. The breakfast was such as best breakfasts then were: some variety of bread, hot rolls, buttered toast, tongue or ham and eggs. The addition of chocolate at one end of the table, and the wedding cake in the middle, marked the speciality of the day.[41]

The married couple departed soon after breakfast, as they had a long drive ahead of them to Hendon – then a straggling, pretty little village in the wooded hills of Middlesex about eight miles north-west of London – where they were going to share a house with Ben's second brother Edward;[42] and the next day Mrs Austen sent Anna her versified congratulations, adding:

The above lines were composed last May, one Sunday evening when I was on the Sopha with the head-ache and you and your Aunts were sitting round the Table; You had just told me you should depend on my writing you a congratulatory Letter on your Marriage; what I then said in Verse I now repeat in plain prose – May you both be very, very happy in this world, and perfectly so in the next.[43]

Since the spring of 1814 Fanny Knight had been growing more and more uncertain as to her feelings towards Mr Plumptre, and the event of Anna's wedding focussed her attention upon her own matrimonial prospects. On 14 November she wrote a formal letter of congratulation upon the wedding to Mrs Austen and a long private one to Jane, asking for her advice in the

matter, in response to which Jane sent her charming and sympathetic letter
of 18 November, setting out very clearly each side of the case:

I had no suspicion of any change in your feelings, and I have no scruple in saying
that you cannot be in Love . . . And with all my heart I wish I had cautioned you
on that point when first you spoke to me; – but tho' I did not think you then so
much in love as you thought yourself, I did consider you as being attached in a
degree – quite sufficiently for happiness, as I had no doubt it would increase with
opportunity. – And from the time of our being in London together, I thought you
really very much in love – But you certainly are not at all – there is no concealing
it . . . Poor dear Mr J. P.! – Oh! dear Fanny, Your mistake has been one that
thousands of women fall into. He was the first young Man who attached himself
to you. That was the charm, & most powerful it is . . . And now, my dear Fanny,
having written so much on one side of the question, I shall turn round & entreat
you not to commit yourself farther, & not to think of accepting him unless you
really do like him. Anything is to be preferred or endured rather than marrying
without Affection . . . I have no doubt of his suffering a good deal for a time, a
great deal, when he feels that he must give you up; – but it is no creed of mine, as
you must be well aware, that such sort of Disappointments kill anybody.[44]

Fanny noted in her diary on 22 November: 'A letter from Aunt Jane
Austen full of advice &c &c', and replied a few days later, evidently saying
she would be guided by her aunt's decision, for on 30 November Jane wrote
again:

Your affection gives me the highest pleasure, but indeed you must not let anything
depend on my opinion. Your own feelings & none but your own, should determine
such an important point . . . I should not be afraid of your marrying him; – with
all his Worth, you would soon love him enough for the happiness of both; but
I should dread the continuance of this sort of tacit engagement, with such an
uncertainty as there is, of when it may be completed. – Years may pass, before he is
Independant. – You like him well enough to marry, but not well enough to wait. –
The unpleasantness of appearing fickle is certainly great – but if you think you
want Punishment for past Illusions, there it is – and nothing can be compared
to the misery of being bound without Love, bound to one, & preferring another.
That is a Punishment which you do not deserve.[45]

Fanny's decision was to discourage Mr Plumptre's attentions from now
on – though this decision was not taken without long-lingering qualms.

This second letter to Fanny was written from Hans Place, for Jane had
come to London again on 25 November at Henry's insistence to discuss
with Egerton the question of a second edition of *Mansfield Park*. James
Edward, on hearing of this, sent his aunt an anonymous note:

An admirer of Miss Austen's Novels, entreats her, in the next edition of Mansfield Park to add another volume, in which the example of useful, and amiable maried [*sic*] life may be exhibited in the characters of Edmund & Fanny. – The Novel has but one fault; – it is too quickly read; and one laments that his acquaintance with persons so amiable and elegant in mind and manners is of so short duration.[46]

Now that Frank was living at the Great House, Jane had been able to discuss the book with him personally, and the changes which appear in the second edition relating to the technical nautical details in the Portsmouth scenes were undoubtedly made upon his advice.[47]

Jane spent a busy ten days in town, calling on Anna at Hendon and at Keppel Street to see Charles and his little girls, and once again being Henry's hostess to receive his 'Hanwell favourite', Harriet Moore, and her sister Eliza. Jane was rather bored now with these girls: 'for though I like Miss H. M. as much as one can at my time of Life after a day's acquaintance, it is uphill work to be talking to those whom one knows so little –' and as for Miss Eliza: 'We shall not have two Ideas in common. She is young, pretty, chattering, & thinking cheifly (I presume) of Dress, Company, & Admiration.'[48] Despite the fact that the first edition of *Mansfield Park* had already sold out, when Jane and Henry saw Egerton on 30 November he did not agree to bring out a second, and his refusal may have been the reason why her later works were published by John Murray instead.

Henry took Jane back to Chawton on 5 December, where a few days later she received the news of the wedding of her distant cousin and goddaughter, Elizabeth Matilda Butler-Harrison of Southampton, to another mutual cousin of theirs, the Revd William Austen of Horsted Keynes.[49] At Christmas Mrs Austen wrote a long letter to Anna passing on the description of the wedding, adding: 'the above particulars were written by Miss Harrison to Miss Hinton, and she communicated them to us; for we visit as heretofore and are apparently as good Neighbours as we were before the tremendous Law-suit threatened us'.[50] Mrs Austen was more honest a friend and neighbour to the Hintons than they to her, for Miss Hinton also knew Mary Russell Mitford, now living at Shinfield, Berkshire, some twenty miles to the north of Chawton, and hastened to transmit to the latter malicious comments on Jane and her works.

Miss Mitford at first was inclined to accept Miss Hinton's opinions, and in turn wrote to Sir William Elford in December 1814:

The want of elegance is almost the only want in Miss Austen. I have not read her *Mansfield Park*, but it is impossible not to feel in every line of *Pride and Prejudice*, in every word of "Elizabeth", the entire want of taste which could produce so pert, so worldly a heroine as the beloved of such a man as Darcy . . . I quite agree with you in preferring Miss Austen to Miss Edgeworth. If the former had a little more taste, a little more perception of the graceful, as well as of the humorous, I know not indeed any one to whom I should not prefer her.[51]

However, her admiration increased with time – perhaps after reading *Mansfield Park* – and three months later she wrote to him again:

I have discovered that our great favourite Miss Austen is my country-woman [i.e., both Hampshire-born]; that Mama knew all her family very intimately; and that she herself is an old maid (I beg her pardon – I mean a young lady) with whom Mama before her marriage was acquainted. Mama says she was then the prettiest, silliest, most affected husband-hunting butterfly she ever remembers and a friend of mine who visits her now says that she has stiffened into the most perpendicular, precise, taciturn piece of 'single blessedness' that ever existed, and that till 'Pride and Prejudice' showed what a precious gem was hidden in that unbending case, she was no more regarded in society than a poker or a fire screen or any other thin, upright piece of wood or iron that fills its corner in peace and quiet. The case is very different now; she is still a poker but a poker of whom every one is afraid. It must be confessed that this silent observation from such an observer is rather formidable . . . a wit, a delineator of character, who does not talk, is terrific indeed!

Miss Mitford's natural kindness then led her to qualify the above:

After all, I do not know that I can quite vouch for this account, though the friend from whom I received it is truth itself; but her family connexions must render her disagreeable to Miss Austen, since she is the sister-in-law [*sic*] of a gentleman who is at law with Miss A's brother for the greater part of his fortune.[52]

On 26 December Cassandra and Jane went to Winchester to stay with Mrs Heathcote and Miss Bigg, now living at No. 12 in the Cathedral Close,[53] and on 2 January 1815 moved to Steventon, where they stayed until 16 January. During this fortnight they called on the Bramstons at Oakley Hall and the Portals at Laverstoke, and also spent three days at Ashe Rectory with Madam Lefroy's eldest son, George, his wife, Sophia, and the first six of their eventual family of eleven children.[54] Later in 1815 their second son, Charles (1810–61), was sent to Hendon to stay with Ben and Anna, and Jane then wrote to her: 'If you & his Uncles are good friends to little Charles Lefroy, he will be a great deal the better for his visit; – we thought him a very fine boy, but terribly in want of Discipline. – I hope he gets a wholesome thump or two, whenever it is necessary.'[55]

Following the sisters' return to Chawton in mid-January, there is little further news of Jane's movements until her letters begin again in late September 1815. The Godmersham family did not come to Hampshire this year since they were busy at home arranging celebrations for young Edward's coming-of-age, and although Fanny exchanged frequent letters with Cassandra she noted receiving only five from Jane during these nine months. This probably indicates that Jane was too busy finishing *Emma* on 29 March and starting *Persuasion* on 8 August to spare time for correspondence.[56] Early in March Napoleon escaped from Elba and resumed power in Paris, so that hostilities with France and her allies were renewed until his defeat at the battle of Waterloo in June 1815 led to his final exile on St Helena. At the end of July Lord Byron published anonymously a poem beginning: 'Farewell to the Land, where the gloom of my glory / Arose, & o'ershadowed the Earth with my name . . .' – lines which, for whatever reason, Jane liked well enough to copy out and keep, giving it her own title of 'Lines of Lord Byron, in the Character of Buonaparté'.[57]

While Charles was chasing after French and Neapolitan squadrons in the Mediterranean, he wrote to Jane from Palermo on 6 May:

Books became the subject of conversation, and I praised 'Waverley' highly, when a young man present observed that nothing had come out for years to be compared with 'Pride and Prejudice', 'Sense and Sensibility', &c. As I am sure you must be anxious to know the name of a person of so much taste, I should tell you it is Fox, a nephew of the late Charles James Fox. That you may not be too much elated at this morsel of praise, I shall add that he did not appear to like 'Mansfield Park' so well as the two first, in which, however, I believe he is singular.[58]

Mrs Austen too had much enjoyed *Waverley*, as she told Anna: '[it] has afforded me more entertainment than any Modern production (Aunt Janes excepted) of the novel kind that I have read for a great while'.[59] In another letter to Anna Mrs Austen mentions Jane and Cassandra as shopping in Alton on 4 July,[60] and when Mary Lloyd came to stay at the Cottage later in the month she and her sisters-in-law called on Mrs Digweed on 24 July to drink tea.[61]

Mary had brought Caroline, now aged ten, with her, and some of Caroline's memories can be related specifically to these last two years of Jane's life:

As I grew older, I met with young companions at my Grandmother's – Of Capt. Charles Austen's motherless girls, one, the eldest, Cassy – lived there chiefly, for a time – under the especial tutorage of Aunt Cassandra; and then Chawton House was for a while inhabited by Capt. Frank Austen; and he had many children – I beleive we were all of us, according to our different ages and natures, very fond of our Aunt Jane . . . Of the two, Aunt Jane was by far my favourite – I did not dislike Aunt Cassandra – but if my visit had at any time chanced to fall out during her absence, I don't think I should have missed her – whereas, not to have found

Aunt Jane at Chawton, <u>would</u> have been a blank indeed . . . if my two cousins, Mary Jane and Cassy were there, we often had amusements in which my Aunt was very helpful – <u>She</u> was the one to whom we always looked for help – She would furnish us with what we wanted from her wardrobe, and <u>she</u> would often be the entertaining visitor in our make beleive house – She amused us in various ways – <u>once</u> I remember in giving a conversation as between myself and my two cousins, supposed to be grown up, the day after a Ball . . . she would frequently say to me, if opportunity offered, that Aunt Cassandra could teach everything much better than <u>she</u> could – Aunt Cassa. <u>knew</u> more – Aunt Cassa. could tell me better whatever I wanted to know – all which, I ever received in respectful silence – Perhaps she thought <u>my</u> mind wanted a turn in <u>that</u> direction, but I truly beleive she did always <u>really</u> think of her sister, as the superior to herself. The most perfect affection and confidence ever subsisted between them – and great and lasting was the sorrow of the survivor when the final separation was made.[62]

Mary Lloyd returned to Steventon on 4 August, and four days later Jane started work on *Persuasion*.[63] She was probably not able to make much progress at first, because later in the month Anna and Ben left Hendon and came to stay at the Cottage prior to entering a home of their own, as Anna recalled:

a House called Wyards, near the town of Alton . . . It was a large farm house belonging to a Shopkeeper in Alton – one end of the house was occupied by a sort of Bailiff or Foreman who managed the Farm, with his family, and we rented the remainder. We were within a walk of the Village of Chawton where resided my Grand Mother & Aunts.[64]

Mrs Austen was delighted to have her favourite granddaughter so close at hand, and Jane's letters from now on make frequent mention of contact with the young couple.

It was probably also during August that Jane went to London to start negotiations for the publication of *Emma*, for on Sunday 3 September Mary Lloyd noted in her diary that Henry and Jane 'came unexpectedly in the evening' to Steventon – which suggests they had been delayed on their return journey to Hampshire. It is not known whether *Emma* was first offered to Egerton or whether, after his refusal to reprint *Mansfield Park* the previous year, Jane had decided to have nothing more to do with him; but at some time in August or September the manuscript was certainly with John Murray of Albemarle Street, since by 29 September his reader, William Gifford (who was also editor of the *Quarterly Review*), was able to tell him: 'Of *Emma* I have nothing but good to say. I was sure of the writer before you mentioned her. The MS though plainly written has yet some, indeed many little omissions, and an expression may now and then be amended in passing through the press. I will readily undertake the revision.'[65]

Henry came to the Cottage again to collect Jane, and on 4 October they travelled to Hans Place together, her intention being to stay in London no more than a week or two.[66] However, Murray was in no hurry to let her think he would accept *Emma*, and it was not till 17 October that she could write to Cassandra: 'Mr Murray's Letter is come, he is a Rogue of course, but a civil one. He offers £450 but wants to have the Copyright of M. P. & S. & S. included. It will end in my publishing for myself I dare say. – He sends more praise however than I expected. It is an amusing Letter.' But she continued: 'Henry is not quite well – a bilious attack with fever – he came back early from H. St yesterday & went to bed – the comical consequence of which was that Mr Seymour & I dined together tète a tète.'[67] Presumably at some time since 1811 or 1812 Mr Seymour had formally asked Henry's permission to propose to his sister, which request Henry of course would have discussed with Jane; and yet, as time went by and Mr Seymour still said nothing, there would indeed have been a sense of embarrassment in the air on any occasion thereafter when the couple found themselves alone together.[68]

Despite being unwell, Henry did his best to attend to Jane's business, and a few days later dictated a polite message to Murray on her behalf, of which Jane kept a rough copy:

Severe Illness has confined me to my Bed ever since I received Yours of ye 15th. I cannot yet hold a pen, & employ an Amuensis [*sic*] – The Politeness & Perspicuity of your Letter equally claim my earliest Exertion. – Your official opinion of the Merits of <u>Emma</u>, is very valuable & satisfactory. – Though I venture to differ occasionally from your Critique, yet I assure you the Quantum of your commendation rather exceeds than falls short of the Author's expectation & my own. – The Terms you offer are so very inferior to what we had expected, that I am apprehensive of having made some great Error in my Arithmetical Calculation. – On the subject of the expence & profit of publishing, you must be much better informed than I am; – but Documents in my possession appear to prove that the Sum offered by you for the Copyright of Sense & Sensibility, Mansfield Park & Emma, is not equal to the Money which my Sister has actually cleared by one very moderate Edition of Mansfield Park; – (You Yourself expressed astonishment that so small an Edit: of such a work should have been sent into the World) – & a still smaller one of Sense & Sensibility. –[69]

However, a day or so after sending this, Henry had a sudden relapse and became so alarmingly ill that on 22 October Jane despatched express letters to her brothers and sister, summoning them to London.[70] Frank could not come because Mary Gibson was very near the birth of her sixth child, but Edward arrived the following evening and James, having collected Cassandra from Chawton, reached London with her on the 25th. For a time Henry's life was in danger, but after a week's anxiety he was so far on the road to recovery that his brothers were able to return home, leaving Jane and Cassandra in charge. The matter of *Emma*'s publication of course had to be put aside during this worrying period, but on 3 November Jane was at last able to acknowledge Murray's letter and ask him to call at Hans Place for a discussion.[71] Murray was not prepared to increase his offer for the three copyrights but did agree to publish 2,000 copies of *Emma* on commission, and once this agreement had been reached production of the work went ahead rapidly. He also undertook the second edition of *Mansfield Park* that Egerton had refused, printing another 750 copies of it, again on commission.[72]

A totally unexpected consequence of Henry's illness was that 'a little gleam of Court favour'[73] shone upon Jane during this visit to London, almost as James Edward had prophesied in his verse to her in 1813. Henry's first medical attention had been from young Mr Charles Haden, who lived nearby at No. 62 Sloane Street; but it seems that during the crisis of the illness a second doctor had been called in – probably Dr Matthew Baillie of Lower Grosvenor Street, who had successfully treated Henry for a chest complaint in 1801.[74] Dr Baillie was also one of the Prince Regent's physicians[75] and, as Jane's authorship was now an open secret,[76] he told her one day

that the Prince was a great admirer of her Novels; that he often read them, and had a set in each of his residences – That <u>he</u>, the physician, had told his Royal Highness that Miss Austen was now in London, and that by the Prince's desire, Mr Clarke, the Librarian of Carlton House, would speedily wait upon her – Mr Clarke came, and endorsed all previous compliments, and invited my aunt to see Carlton House, saying the Prince had charged him to show her the Library there, adding many civilities as to the pleasure his R. H. had received from her Novels.[77]

The result was that on 13 November Jane was shown over the Regent's small but luxurious palace:

A hall with walls of green and verd-antique, and Ionic columns of brown Siena marble led into ante-rooms and drawing-rooms of crimson, gold, blue and rose with flowered carpets and hangings of velvet and satin elaborately draped; the sombre richness of the blue-velvet closet, in bronze and blue and gold, contrasted with the magnificent opulence of the crimson drawing-room, in green and crimson, rose and gilded plaster, with buhl and ormolu in every corner[78] and on the south side, overlooking the garden and the Mall, were a cathedral-like conservatory, an Ionic dining-room, a Gothic dining-room and a Gothic library. Mr Clarke no doubt pointed out that 'the books in the latter are handsomely bound and arranged in classes . . . the appearance of the Library not only displays considerable taste, but convenience has also been consulted'.[79] Furthermore, in the course of this visit, 'Mr Clarke, speaking again of the Regent's admiration of her writing, declared himself charged to say, that if Miss Austen had any other Novel forthcoming, she was quite at liberty to dedicate it to the Prince.' To see for herself the Regent's extravagances if anything probably increased Jane's disapproval of him; she 'made all proper acknowledgements at the moment, but had no intention of accepting the honor offered – until she was avised [*sic*] by some of her friends [i.e., Henry and Cassandra] that she must consider the permission as a command'.[80] Having confirmed with Mr Clarke two days later that such a dedication was indeed expected, there then ensued a flurry of notes and proof-sheets between Albemarle Street and Hans Place, culminating in a set of *Emma*, bound in red morocco gilt and with a dedication page included in the preliminaries to the first volume, being sent to Carlton House in mid-December, a few days prior to general publication.[81]

This meeting with Mr Clarke led in turn to an exchange of correspondence between him and Jane during the next few months, amusing in its own right and significant inasmuch as it caused her to record her own assessment of herself as a writer. Mr Clarke, as well as being the Regent's librarian, was also his domestic chaplain, a position he had held since 1799, and prior to which he had been a naval chaplain for four years.[82] He was full of innocent self-admiration for his success in life and anxious that the rest of the world should appreciate it too, with the result that following Jane's visit to Carlton House he wrote:

Accept my sincere thanks for the pleasure your Volumes have given me: in the perusal of them I felt a great inclination to write & say so. And I also dear Madam wished to be allowed to ask you, to delineate in some future Work the Habits of Life and Character and enthusiasm of a Clergyman – who should pass his time between the metropolis & the Country – who should be something like Beatties Minstrel / Silent when glad, affectionate tho' shy / And now his look was most demurely sad / & now he laughd aloud yet none knew why – / Neither Goldsmith – nor La Fontaine in his Tableau de Famille – have in my mind quite delineated an English Clergyman, at least of the present day – Fond of, & entirely engaged in Literature – no man's Enemy but his own. Pray dear Madam think of these things.[83]

To this idea Jane gave a discreetly modest rejection:

I am quite honoured by your thinking me capable of drawing such a Clergyman as you gave the sketch of in your note of Nov. 16th. But I assure you I am not. The comic part of the Character I might be equal to, but not the Good, the Enthusiastic, the Literary. Such a Man's Conversation must at times be on subjects of Science & Philosophy, of which I know nothing – or at least be occasionally abundant in quotations & allusions which a Woman, who like me, knows only her own Mother-tongue & has read very little in that, would be totally without the power of giving. – A Classical Education, or at any rate, a very extensive acquaintance with English Literature, Ancient & Modern, appears to me quite Indispensable for the person who wd. do any justice to your Clergyman – And I think I may boast myself to be, with all possible Vanity, the most unlearned, & uninformed Female who ever dared to be an Authoress.[84]

Mr Clarke was not in the least discouraged and replied promptly:

Pray continue to write, & make all your friends send Sketches to help you – and Memoires pour servir – as the French term it. Do let us have an English Clergyman after your fancy – much novelty may be introduced – shew dear Madam what good would be done if Tythes were taken away entirely, and describe him burying his own mother – as I did, – because the High Priest of the Parish in which she died – did not pay her remains the respect he ought to do. I have never recovered the Shock. Carry your Clergyman to Sea as the Friend of some distinguished Naval Character about a Court – you can then bring forward like Le Sage many interesting Scenes of Character & Interest.[85]

Although the presentation copy of *Emma* was delivered in December 1815, Jane did not receive thanks for it until the following March. By then the Regent's daughter, Princess Charlotte, had become engaged to Prince Leopold of Saxe-Cobourg, so that Mr Clarke, writing from the Brighton Pavilion, was able to offer another helpful suggestion:

The Prince Regent has just left us for London; and having been pleased to appoint me Chaplain and Private English Secretary to the Prince of Cobourg, I remain here with His Serene Highness & a select Party until the Marriage. Perhaps when you again appear in print you may chuse to dedicate your Volumes to Prince Leopold: any Historical Romance, illustrative of the History of the august house of Cobourg, would just now be very interesting.[86]

Jane's carefully considered reply to this example of Collins-like pertinacity put a polite end to any further correspondence:

You are very, very kind in your hints as to the sort of Composition which might recommend me at present, & I am fully sensible that an Historical Romance, founded on the House of Saxe Cobourg, might be much more to the purpose of Profit or Popularity, than such pictures of domestic Life in Country Villages as I deal in – but I could no more write a Romance than an Epic Poem. – I could not sit seriously down to write a serious Romance under any other motive than to save my Life, & if it were indispensable for me to keep it up & never relax into laughing at myself or other people, I am sure I should be hung before I had finished the first Chapter. – No – I must keep to my own style & go on in my own Way; And though I may never succeed again in that, I am convinced that I should totally fail in any other.[87]

The hilarity that must have arisen in Hans Place when Jane described to Cassandra and Henry the opulence of Carlton House and Mr Clarke's overwhelming graciousness during her visit, was no doubt an excellent tonic for Henry; as he continued to improve, Edward returned to London on 15 November, bringing Fanny with him, and left again on the 20th to take Cassandra back to Chawton. Jane's letters to her therefore recommence, and the three surviving from this period, in conjunction with Fanny's diary entries, give details of Henry's convalescence and the resumption of normal cheerful life in Hans Place. Fanny as usual had many shopping commissions for the Godmersham family and drove out with Jane in the mornings to execute them, staying at home during the cold evenings: 'Aunt Jane & I very snug –'; she also hired a harp from Chappells in New Bond Street and arranged for a music-master, Mr Meyer, to call and instruct her. In the evenings some of Henry's neighbours dined or drank tea, the most frequent callers in this respect being Mr Tilson and Mr Haden. The latter, whom Jane at first had dismissed rather casually as 'the apothecary from the corner of Sloane St . . . a young man, said to be clever . . . certainly very attentive . . .'[88] in fact had a medical degree from Edinburgh and also possessed a great love of music, taking the Shakespearean view that 'a person not musical is fit for every sort of Wickedness'.[89] He was full of admiration for Fanny and her harp, and in her diary on 20 November she recorded: 'Mr Haden, a delightful clever musical "Haden" comes every evening & is agreeable.' Fanny had quite sufficiently recovered from her inconclusive romance with Mr Plumptre to appreciate Mr Haden's admiration; Jane was pleased by his 'good Manners & clever conversation' as she got to know him better, and amused at the rapidity of the decorous flirtation between the young people. 'Tomorrow Mr Haden is to dine with us. – There's Happiness! – We really grow so fond of Mr Haden that I do not know what to expect . . . Fanny played, & he sat & listened & suggested improvements,'[90] 'on the opposite side Fanny & Mr Haden in two chairs (I beleive at least they had two chairs) talking together uninterruptedly. – Fancy the scene! And what is to be fancied next? – Why that Mr H. dines here again tomorrow.'[91]

Jane was amused, but the prudent Cassandra was evidently shocked to think that their niece, Miss Knight of Godmersham, might be in danger of falling in love with a mere apothecary – a profession then at the bottom of the medical social scale[92] – and wrote back at once querying the situation; to which Jane teasingly replied:

But you seem to be under a mistake as to Mr H. – You call him an Apothecary; he is no Apothecary, he has never been an Apothecary, there is not an Apothecary in this Neighbourhood – the only inconvenience of the situation perhaps, but so it is – we have not a medical Man within reach – he is a Haden, nothing but a Haden, a sort of wonderful nondescript Creature on two Legs, something between a Man & an Angel – but without the least spice of an Apothecary. – He is perhaps the only Person not an Apothecary hereabouts.[93]

This light-hearted nonsense presumably satisfied Cassandra that no *mésalliance* was likely to occur, and Fanny had another 'delightful musical evening with Mr Haden' on 4 December before Edward took her back to Kent on the 8th. After her departure Jane and Henry, who was now almost entirely recovered, were busy with Murray regarding the Prince Regent's copy of *Emma*, and it was not until 14 December that Jane sent a note to Mr Haden asking him to call again that evening: 'I leave Town early on Saturday, & must say "Good bye" to you –'[94] and on that Saturday, 16 December, her fortieth birthday, she left London for the last time and returned to Chawton.

CHAPTER 16

Emma *and* Persuasion, *1816–17*

Although *Emma* had been first advertised in the *Morning Post* of 2 December 1815 as forthcoming soon, delays in printing meant that the book was not on sale until the last week of December and the title-page was in fact dated 1816; it was priced at one guinea the three volumes and described as 'By the Author of "Pride and Prejudice," &c. &c.'[1] Murray allowed Jane twelve presentation copies in addition to that given to the Prince Regent,[2] and as her family and friends read this latest work she collected their opinions of it, as she had done for *Mansfield Park*.[3] As before, Frank's comments headed the list: 'Captn. Austen. – liked it extremely, observing that though there might be more Wit in P & P – & an higher Morality in MP – yet altogether, on account of it's peculiar air of Nature throughout, he preferred it to either.' Cassandra liked it 'better than P. & P. – but not so well as M. P. –' while Mrs Austen took the reverse view: '– thought it more entertaining than MP. – but not so interesting as P. & P. – No characters in it equal to Ly. Catherine & Mr Collins.' Charles, out in the Mediterranean, wrote home: 'Emma arrived in time to a moment. I am delighted with her, more so I think than even with my favourite Pride & Prejudice, & have read it three times in the Passage.' Edward, as befitted the owner of a country estate, noticed a little slip in Jane's description of the Abbey Mill Farm, with its 'orchard in bloom' on the day that the strawberry party was held at Donwell Abbey, and teased her: 'Jane, I wish you would tell me where you get those apple-trees of yours that come into bloom in July.'[4]

Anna had had her first baby, Anna Jemima, on 20 October 1815 when Jane had been away in London nursing Henry, and due to the winter weather Jane had not so far been able to visit Wyards to make the acquaintance of her first great-niece. She now sent a note to Anna: 'As I wish very much to see <u>your</u> Jemima, I am sure you will like to see <u>my</u> Emma, & have therefore great pleasure in sending it for your perusal. Keep it as long as you chuse, it has been read by all here –'[5] and presently Anna returned it with the comments that she rank'd <u>Emma</u> as a composition with S. & S. – not so <u>Brilliant</u> as P. & P. – nor so <u>equal</u> as MP. – Preferred Emma herself to all the heroines. – the Characters like all the others admirably well drawn & supported – perhaps rather less strongly marked than some, but only the more natural for that reason. – Mr Knightley Mrs Elton & Miss Bates her favourites. – Thought one or two of the conversations too long. –[6]

It is interesting that Anna liked Emma the best of all her aunt's heroines, for in later years Fanny Caroline Lefroy recorded that 'when "Emma" came out many of the neighbours found in the description of her person no less than in her character a strong likeness to Anna Austen. Certainly such a likeness existed though I am sure it was unintentional on Aunt Jane's part.'[7]

Again, as for *Mansfield Park*, other opinions varied widely – the amiable simpleton, Mrs Digweed, declared that she 'did not like it so well as the others, in fact if she had not known the Author, could hardly have got through it –' while Edward's sister-in-law, Mrs John Bridges, 'preferred it to all the others'.[8] Jane sent copies to the Countess of Morley (the former Lady Boringdon, whose husband had recently been elevated to an earldom) and to Maria Edgeworth, whose novels Jane herself admired; Lady Morley wrote back politely on 27 December 1815 saying she expected to like *Emma* just as much as the previous books,[9] but in the following month told her sister-in-law, Theresa Villiers, that she ranked it below *Mansfield Park* and *Pride and Prejudice*.[10] There is no record of Miss Edgeworth expressing any thanks for the gift, and her own correspondence shows that she was totally bewildered by the placid domesticity of the setting:

There was no story in it, except that Miss Emma found that the man whom she designed for Harriet's lover was an admirer of her own – & he was affronted at being refused by Emma & Harriet wore the willow – and <u>smooth, thin water gruel</u> is according to Emma's father's opinion a very good thing & it is very difficult to make a cook understand what you mean by <u>smooth thin water gruel!!</u>[11]

Susan Ferrier, still working on her own *Marriage*, wrote: 'I have been reading "Emma", which is excellent; there is no story whatever, and the heroine is not better than other people; but the characters are all so true to life, and the style so piquant, that it does not require the adventitious aids of mystery and adventure.'[12] Miss Mitford, now quite converted to admiration of Jane, thought that it was 'delightful . . . the best . . . of all her charming works'.[13]

Apart from these private comments, between March and September 1816 no less than eight unsigned reviews or notices were published, though several were only short and generalised:

Whoever is fond of an amusing, inoffensive and well principled novel, will be well pleased with the perusal of *Emma*.[14]

The unities of time and place are well-preserved; the language is chaste and correct; and if *Emma* be not allowed to rank in the very highest class of modern Novels, it certainly may claim at least a distinguished degree of eminence in that species of composition. It is amusing, if not instructive; and has no tendency to deteriorate the heart.[15]

The fair reader may also glean by the way some useful hints against forming romantic schemes, or indulging a spirit of patronage in defiance of sober reason; and the work will probably become a favourite with all those who seek for harmless amusement, rather than deep pathos or appalling horrors, in works of fiction.[16]

Of the longer notices, the *Augustan Review* thought there was 'a remarkable sameness in the productions of this author' and that here in particular there was too little action and too much of Miss Bates's gossip;[17] the *British Lady's Magazine* considered it definitely inferior to *Pride and Prejudice* and *Mansfield Park*, and was also bored by Miss Bates.[18] *The Champion*, on the other hand, gave a very favourable review, enjoying the 'easy, unaffected, and fluent style' and the 'lively sketches of comfortable home-scenes', and complimented the author as 'a woman of good sense, knowledge of the world, discriminating perception and acute observation'.[19]

John Murray himself, however much he may tactfully have praised *Emma* in his initial letter to Jane, thought privately that it wanted 'incident and Romance';[20] but nevertheless, as founder-proprietor of the influential *Quarterly Review*, asked Walter Scott to write an article on it and Jane's preceding novels for publication in this literary journal. 'Scott accepted the invitation, and produced the first major account of Jane Austen as a novelist',[21] (though rather surprisingly he seemed to be unaware of the existence of *Mansfield Park*), praising the art involved in 'copying from nature as she really exists in the common walks of life, and presenting to the reader, instead of the splendid scenes of an imaginary world, a correct and striking representation of that which is daily taking place around him'.[22] Murray lent Jane a copy of the *Review* when it appeared in March 1816, and in returning it she wrote: 'The Authoress of <u>Emma</u> has no reason I think to complain of her treatment in it – except in the total omission of Mansfield Park. – I cannot but be sorry that so clever a Man as the Reveiwer of <u>Emma</u> should consider it as unworthy of being noticed.'[23] However, Scott quoted in his review, as an example of the 'quiet yet comic dialogue', part of the discussion in chapter 12 between Mr Woodhouse and Isabella; and Jane is reported as saying: 'Well! that *is* pleasant! Those are the very characters I took most pains with, and the writer has found me out.'[24]

From about 1813–16 a young Mrs Ann Barrett lived in Alton – although her name does not appear in Jane's surviving correspondence she and her lawyer husband had family connections with Robert Trimmer, Edward Knight's local lawyer and steward for the Chawton estate[25] – and during this period became sufficiently friendly with the Austens to discuss Jane's novels openly with her. In addition, when Mrs Barrett left Alton and returned to her own home in Manchester, she received from Jane 'a series of letters . . . of great interest'. Long afterwards (by which time, unfortunately, these letters had been lost) Mrs Barrett spoke of her contact with Jane during these years, including this comment of hers upon Scott's favourable review; and remembered also that,

on one occasion, soon after the inimitable Mr Collins had made his appearance in literature, an old friend attacked her [Jane] on the score of having pourtrayed an individual; in recurring to the subject afterwards she expressed a very great dread of what she called 'such an invasion of social proprieties'. She said she thought it fair to note peculiarities, weaknesses, and even special phrases, but it was her desire to create not to reproduce, and at the same time said 'I am much too proud of my own gentlemen ever to admit that they are merely Mr A. or Major C.' . . . To a question 'which of your characters do you like best?' she once answered 'Edmund Bertram and Mr Knightley; but they are very far from being what I know English gentlemen often are' . . . [She] was once attacked by an Irish dignitary, who preferred a residence at Bath to his own proper sphere, 'for being over particular about Clergymen residing on their cures.' This was, of course, in allusion to the conversation of Bertram & Crawford in Mansfield Park . . . [She] had on all the subjects of enduring religious feeling the deepest and strongest convictions, but a contact with loud and noisy exponents of the then popular religious phase made her reticent almost to a fault. She had to suffer something in the way of reproach from those who believed she might have used her genius to greater effect; but [Mrs Barrett] used to say, 'I think I see her now defending what she thought was the real province of a delineator of life and manners, and declaring her belief that example and not "direct preaching" was all that a novelist could afford properly to exhibit' . . . Mrs Barrett used to add, 'Anne Elliot was herself; her enthusiasm for the navy, and her perfect unselfishness, reflect her completely.'[26]

It was probably early in 1816, 'when four novels of steadily increasing success had given the writer some confidence in herself',[27] that Jane decided to recover the manuscript of *Susan* from Crosby & Co. Henry undertook the negotiation, and 'found the purchaser very willing to receive back his money, and to resign all claim to the copyright. When the bargain was concluded and the money paid, but not till then, the negotiator had the satisfaction of informing him that the work which had been so lightly esteemed was by the author of "Pride and Prejudice".'[28] Jane planned to offer again her youthful work for publication, so changed the heroine's name to 'Catherine' and wrote an 'Advertisement' as preface to the text:

This little work was finished in the year 1803, and intended for immediate publication. It was disposed of to a bookseller, it was even advertised, and why the business proceeded no farther, the author has never been able to learn . . . The public are entreated to bear in mind that thirteen years have passed since it was finished, many more since it was begun, and that during that period, places, manners, books, and opinions have undergone considerable changes.[29]

But Catherine, alias Susan, was doomed to still further delay in making her début, for in the spring of 1816 the Austens suffered two serious misfortunes in quick succession. Charles, after the final end of the Napoleonic War, had been set to the task of suppressing piracy in the Greek Archipelago and, during a hurricane in February, his ship the *Phoenix* was wrecked off the coast of Asia Minor, near Smyrna. The crew were saved and as the disaster was solely attributable to the ignorance of the local pilots then on board, Charles was fully acquitted of all blame;[30] 'yet such a misfortune is always a disparagement; and the war being over, he knew he was likely to wait long for another ship'.[31]

The news of this calamity abroad probably reached Chawton at much the same time as that of the second, more immediately distressing, event close at hand – the collapse of Henry's banking business and army agency on 15 March.[32] Many small country banks failed in the difficult economic conditions of the post-war period and the Alton partnership of Austen Gray & Vincent was declared bankrupt at the end of 1815,[33] which in turn led to the failure of Austen Maunde & Tilson in London.

My uncle [Henry] had been living for some years past at considerable expense, but not more than might become the head of a flourishing bank, and no blame of personal extravagance was ever imputed to him. He had not long before been appointed Receiver General for Oxfordshire,[34] for which a suretyship of £30,000 had been required. This sum the two sureties had to pay – Mr Leigh-Perrot £10,000, Mr Knight £20,000 – My father [James] and Captain Austen [Frank] some hundreds, on account of an Army Agency, for which <u>they</u> had bound themselves, besides what small sums were standing in the bank; so that altogether this blow fell heavily on the family.[35]

Luckily for Jane, the £600 she had already received as profits on her novels had been safely invested in Navy 5 per cent Stock, so all she lost in her account at Henrietta Street was £13.7s.0d. of the profits on *Mansfield Park*, and £12.15s.0d. just received from Egerton for the second edition of *Sense and Sensibility*.[36]

It is noticeable that these financial losses seem to have caused no division or bitterness within the family – a tribute to their 'spirit of forbearance and generosity'[37] and the strong affection which united them. 'To my uncle himself it was ruin, and he saw the world before him, to begin again. In about a fortnight [i.e., at the end of March 1816] he came to Steventon, apparently, for truly it could not have been, in unbroken spirits.'[38] As on the occasion of Eliza's death three years before, Henry's 'sanguine elastic nature' made a rebound from depression easy – indeed, almost inevitable. Giving up his Hans Place house, he divided his time between Steventon, Chawton and Godmersham, and later in the year went to France to set in motion a lawsuit against the de Feuillide family in an effort to obtain something of Eliza's long-lost property there.[39] In the meantime he returned at once to his boyhood intention of taking Holy Orders, as if the intervening military and banking careers had been nothing more than a slight interruption of his normal course, and wrote a persuasive letter to the Bishop of Winchester to this effect.[40] Nor did he intend to undertake clerical duties in a casual or perfunctory way; he was in earnest, and began by making use of his former classical knowledge to take up a serious study of the New Testament in the original language. He seems to have been in advance of current thinking in this respect; for family tradition recorded that when he went to Winchester in December 1816 to be examined by the Bishop, that dignitary, after asking him such questions as he thought desirable, put his hand on a book which lay near him on the table, and which happened to be a Greek Testament, and said: 'As for *this* book, Mr Austen, I dare say it is some years since either you or I looked into it –' and Henry, who 'had been rather proud of being able to get up his knowledge of Greek once more, felt a good deal disappointed at the bishop's conclusion'.[41] The following day he went to Salisbury for ordination to the diaconate, and was appointed to the curacy of Chawton at a stipend of fifty-two guineas a year.[42]

On 2 May 1816 Edward and Fanny came to stay at the Cottage for three weeks, and it may have been at this time that Jane composed her burlesque *Plan of a Novel, according to hints from various quarters*, as no less than four of these 'hints' were provided by Fanny. Mr Clarke's ludicrous letters of the previous winter had been cherished by Jane, and his autobiographical details now earned themselves a prominent place, word for word, in her *Plan*.[43] Fanny and her father returned to Kent on 21 May, and this short visit was the last time aunt and niece saw each other, for the insidious decline in Jane's health had already started, and she had now only fourteen months left to live.

So far as is known, up to the end of 1815 Jane had been remarkably free from ailments – there are occasional references in her letters to a headache or a cold,[44] but apart from the typhus fever of her childhood her only other recorded illnesses are the whooping cough caught from the Cooper children in 1806 and an attack of sinusitis or neuralgia in the summer of 1813.[45] But her visit to London, which marked the highest point in her modest fame, marked also a downward stage in her career as regards both prosperity and health. Perhaps the excitement of the publication of *Emma* and the close attendance at Henry's sick-bed which coincided with it, combined to diminish her strength and render her liable to infection; the worry of his sudden bankruptcy following so soon thereafter might well have precipitated the onset of any disease susceptible to being influenced by mental shock. 'I beleive that Aunt Jane's health began to fail some time before we knew she was really ill'[46] – and in recent years medical opinion has put forward the theory, based on Jane's own description of her symptoms, that early in 1816 she fell victim to the then unrecognised Addison's Disease.[47] This is a loss of function, sometimes caused by a tubercular infection, of the adrenal glands; it gives rise to an insidiously developing weakness and weight loss and to severe gastro-intestinal disturbances, possibly accompanied by some degree of pain in the back; there are intermissions during which the patient feels much better and is hopeful of recovery. One of the significant symptoms is that the skin develops patches of brownish or blackish pigmentation alternating with the whiteness of vitiligo, and crises occur during periods of mental stress. Nowadays the condition is controlled by medication, but otherwise it eventually proves fatal.

Certainly by the spring of 1816 Jane already knew there was something wrong with her and had arranged to visit Cheltenham to drink the spa water, which was advertised as being 'singularly efficacious in all bilious complaints, obstructions of the liver and spleen',[48] for on 22 May, the day after Fanny and Edward had left Chawton, Cassandra and Jane arrived at Steventon on the first stage of their journey into Gloucestershire.[49] They stayed at Cheltenham for a fortnight and on the return trip called on the Fowles at Kintbury; Fulwar Fowle's eldest daughter, Mary Jane, told Caroline Austen afterwards 'that Aunt Jane went over the old places, and recalled old recollections associated with them, in a very particular manner – looked at them, my cousin thought, as if she never expected to see them again – The Kintbury family, during that visit, received an impression that her health was failing – altho' they did not know of any particular malady.'[50]

On 11 June Jane and Cassandra were back at Steventon and on the 15th they returned to Chawton,[51] where Jane resumed work on *Persuasion*. On 8 July she noted starting work on the first draft of chapter 10 of the second volume, and wrote 'Finis. July 16. 1816' at the end of what was then planned

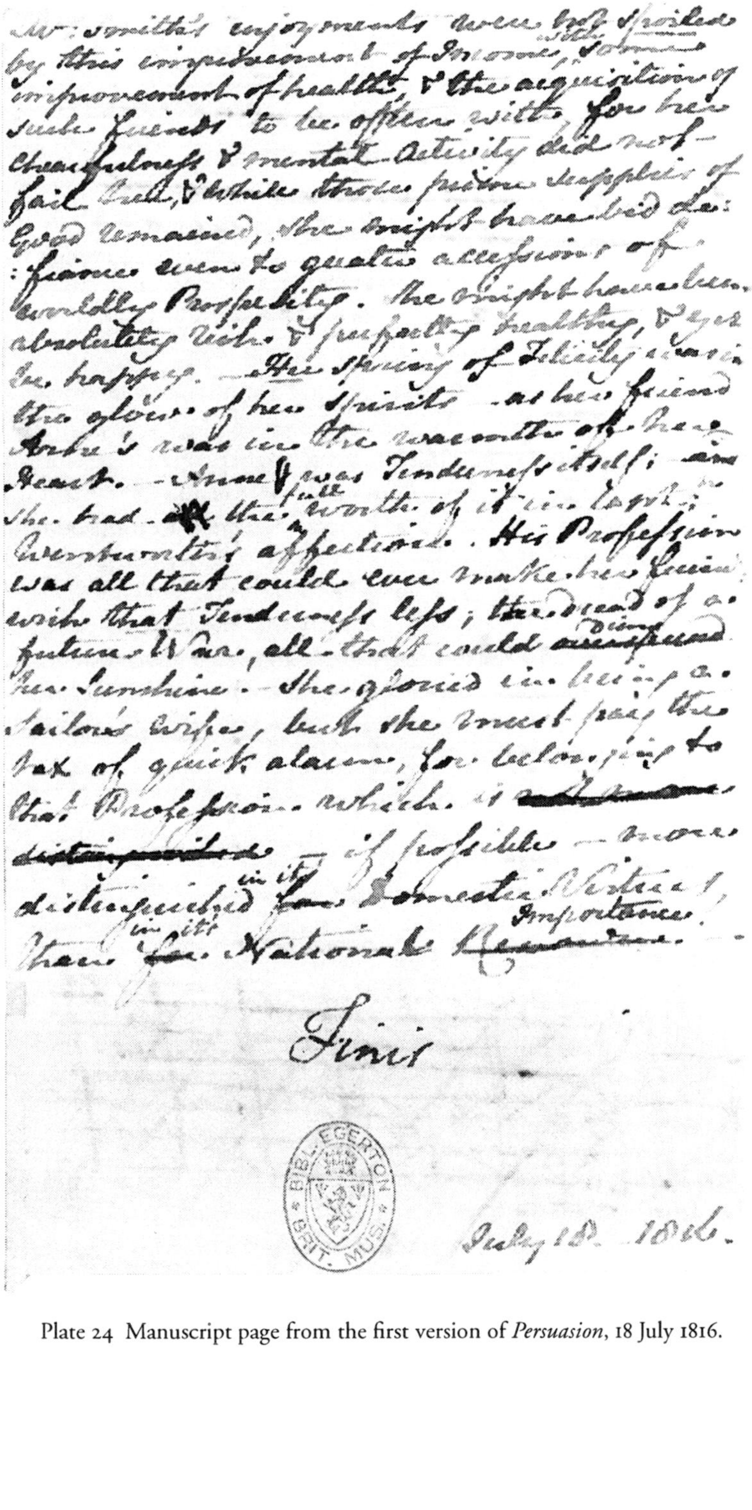

Mrs Smith's enjoyments were not spoiled by this improvement of Income, with some improvement of health, & the acquisition of such friends to be often with, for her chearfulness & mental Activity did not fail her, & while these prime supplies of Good remained, she might have bid defiance even to greater accessions of worldly Prosperity. She might have been absolutely rich & perfectly healthy, & yet be happy. Her spring of Felicity was in the glow of her Spirits — as her friend Anne's was in the warmth of her Heart. — Anne was Tenderness itself; and she had the full worth of it in Capt. Wentworth's affection. His Profession was all that could ever make her friends wish that Tenderness less; the dread of a future War, all that could dim her Sunshine. — She gloried in being a Sailor's wife, but she must pay the tax of quick alarm, for belonging to that Profession which is — if possible — more distinguished in its Domestic Virtues, than in its National Importance. —

Finis

July 18. 1816.

Plate 24 Manuscript page from the first version of *Persuasion*, 18 July 1816.

to be chapter 11; to this, however, she added a further paragraph and marked the foot of the page 'Finis. July 18, 1816'. In this first draft Anne and Captain Wentworth became re-engaged in a totally different manner in a scene laid at Admiral Croft's lodgings. But as Cassandra and James Edward knew, this version did not satisfy her.

She thought it tame and flat, and was desirous of producing something better. This weighed upon her mind, the more so probably on account of the weak state of her health; so that one night she retired to rest in very low spirits. But such depression was little in accordance with her nature, and was soon shaken off. The next morning she awoke to more cheerful views and brighter inspirations; the sense of power revived; and imagination resumed its course.[52]

The greater part of chapter 10 was cancelled and the present chapters 10 and 11 substituted, changing the way in which the lovers were re-united, while the draft chapter 11 became the present chapter 12.[53] According to Cassandra's memorandum, this second and final version of the end of the story was finished on 6 August 1816;[54] there is nothing to indicate why, of all the published novels, this first draft fragment was alone preserved. It seems that it was Jane's custom to write her novels first and choose titles for them afterwards, for in later years Cassandra told the younger generations of the family that a name for this last work 'had been a good deal discussed between Jane and herself, and that among several possible titles, the one that seemed most likely to be chosen was "The Elliots".'[55]

Of this younger generation, it was now Caroline's turn to receive a share of her aunt's attention: 'Aunt Jane was so good as frequently to write to me; and in addressing a child, she was perfect –'[56] and several letters to her survive, dating from the last three years of Jane's life. Caroline was a quiet, rather shy little girl, but intelligent and imaginative, and following her sister Anna's example she too wrote stories which were submitted for Jane's criticism. To the earliest of these Jane responded:

I wish I could finish Stories as fast as you can. – I am much obliged to you for the sight of Olivia, & think you have done for her very well; but the good for nothing Father, who was the real author of all her Faults & Sufferings, should not escape unpunished. I hope <u>he</u> hung himself, or took the sur-name of <u>Bone</u> or underwent some direful penance or other –[57]

and even during the worrying time of Henry's illness Jane did not forget to write from London: 'I have not yet felt quite equal to taking up your Manuscript, but think I shall soon, & I hope my detaining it so long will be no inconvenience.'[58] Later on there are mentions of 'your story of Carolina & her aged Father, it made me laugh heartily –' and of another called 'the

Gentleman Quack'.[59] All these little tales seem to have been comedies, for family tradition recalled that an attempt to write a tragedy was less successful – Caroline believed it to be a necessary part of a tragedy that all the dramatis personae should somehow meet their end, by violence or otherwise, in the last act; and this belief produced such a scene of carnage and woe as to cause fits of laughter among unsympathetic elders, and tears to the author, who threw the unfortunate tragedy into the fire on the spot.[60] The 'unsympathetic elders' here evidently did not include Jane, for Caroline remembered:

As I grew older, she would talk to me more seriously of my reading, and of my amusements – I had taken early to writing verses and stories, and I am sorry to think how I troubled her with reading them. She was very kind about it, and always had some praise to bestow but at last she warned me against spending too much time upon them – She said – how well I recollect it! that she knew writing stories was a great amusement, and she thought a harmless one – tho' many people, she was aware, thought otherwise – but that at my age it would be bad for me to be much taken up with my own compositions – Later still – it was after she got to Winchester, she sent me a message to this effect – That if I would take her advice, I should cease writing till I was 16, and that she had herself often wished she had read more, and written less, in the corresponding years of her own life.[61]

It seems that Jane soon realised the trip to Cheltenham had not benefited her at all, and from the summer of 1816 onwards references to her mysterious decline in strength appear with increasing frequency in her letters. It was Caroline who recorded a pen-picture of her aunt at this time:

In my later visits to Chawton Cottage, I remember Aunt Jane used often to lie down after dinner – My Grandmother herself was frequently on the sofa – sometimes in the afternoon, sometimes in the evening, at no fixed period of the day – She had not bad health for her age, and she worked often for hours in the garden, and naturally wanted rest afterwards – There was only one sofa in the room – and Aunt Jane laid upon 3 chairs which she arranged for herself – I think she had a pillow, but it never looked comfortable – She called it her sofa, and even when the other was unoccupied, she never took it – It seemed understood that she preferred the chairs – I wondered and wondered – for the real sofa was frequently vacant, and still she laid in this comfortless manner – I often asked her how she could like the chairs best – and I suppose I worried her into telling me the reason of her choice – which was, that if she ever used the sofa, Grandmama would be leaving it for her, and would not lie down, as she did now, whenever she felt inclined –[62]

During the summer of 1816 Mary Lloyd was also unwell from time to time and in August she too was advised to go to Cheltenham.[63] Cassandra went with her and they stayed at Mrs Potter's house in the High Street, where the lodgings were cold, noisy and expensive, costing three guineas a week.[64] Jane had an attack of her illness at the end of August, just as Cassandra was setting off from the Cottage to join Mary Lloyd, and her letter of 8 September, addressed to Cassandra at Cheltenham, contains the first recorded mention of her own view of her case: 'Thank you, my Back has given me scarcely any pain for many days. – I have an idea that agitation does it as much harm as fatigue, & that I was ill at the time of your going, from the very circumstance of your going.'[65]

While Cassandra was away, James Edward stayed at the Cottage for several days, and Jane much enjoyed his company. He was now nearly eighteen, in his last year at Winchester College and looking forward to going up to Oxford within the next few months, where a contemporary later recalled him as being 'Of graceful figure and complexion fair, / With pleasing features and with light brown hair, / Of cheerful converse and of sparkling wit . . .'[66] Jane and Cassandra thought him very good-looking, and a few months later Jane wrote of him to their old friend Alethea Bigg: 'He grows still, and still improves in appearance, at least in the estimation of his Aunts, who love him better & better, as they see the sweet temper & warm affections of the Boy confirmed in the young Man –'[67] He too had now started to write a book, which he read aloud at the Cottage in the evenings, as Jane told Cassandra:

Edward is writing a Novel – we have all heard what he has written – it is extremely clever; written with great ease & spirit; – if he can carry it on in the same way, it will be a firstrate work, & in a style, I think, to be popular. – Pray tell Mary how much I admire it. – And tell Caroline that I think it is hardly fair upon her & myself, to have him take up the Novel Line . . .[68]

It was probably during this visit, when discussing literary composition, that Jane showed James Edward *Volume the Third* of her juvenilia, and allowed him to make additions to her incomplete stories of 'Evelyn', and 'Catharine', written when she too was about seventeen.[69]

It was during these last two years of Jane's life, probably on this and other similar occasions when James Edward and Anna visited the Cottage, that she would, if asked, tell them

many little particulars about the subsequent career of some of her people. In this traditional way we learned that Miss Steele never succeeded in catching the Doctor; that Kitty Bennet was satisfactorily married to a clergyman near Pemberley, while Mary obtained nothing higher than one of her uncle Phillips' clerks, and was content to be considered a star in the society of Meryton; that the 'considerable sum' given by Mrs Norris to William Price was one pound; that Mr Woodhouse survived his daughter's marriage, and kept her and Mr Knightley from settling at

Donwell, about two years; and that the letters placed by Frank Churchill before Jane Fairfax, which she swept away unread, contained the word 'pardon'.

According to a less well-known tradition, the delicate Jane Fairfax lived only another nine or ten years after her marriage to Frank Churchill. It seems that Jane was not prepared to discuss her characters' lives until after they had finally appeared in print, as James Edward continued: 'Of the good people in "Northanger Abbey" and "Persuasion" we know nothing more than what is written; for before those works were published their author had been taken away from us, and all such amusing communications had ceased for ever.'[70]

Cassandra, as usual, was an exception to Jane's rule, and in later years she was able to pass on an outline of *The Watsons*.

When the author's sister, Cassandra, showed the manuscript of this work to some of her nieces [Frank's daughters], she also told them something of the intended story; for with this dear sister – though, I believe, with no one else – Jane seems to have talked freely of any work that she might have in hand. Mr Watson was soon to die; and Emma to become dependent for a home on her narrow-minded sister-in-law and brother. She was to decline an offer of marriage from Lord Osborne, and much of the interest of the tale was to arise from Lady Osborne's love for Mr Howard, and his counter affection for Emma, whom he was finally to marry.[71]

Frank and his Mary, with their six exuberant children ranging in age from Mary Jane, nearly ten, down to Herbert Grey, fifteen months, were now living again in Alton, this time in a large house in the High Street,[72] as Edward planned to let the Great House once more; during the first week of September 1816 Jane was well enough to spend the day in Alton with them and to walk home by moonlight in company with Martha and James Edward.[73] Cassandra returned from Cheltenham on 21 September,[74] and no more letters to her survive, as the sisters were not separated again for any length of time from now until Jane's death. For the remainder of the year it seems that life at Chawton was too busy for Jane to think of starting any new novel; as she said to Cassandra: 'I wanted a few days quiet, & exemption from the Thought & contrivances which any sort of company gives. – I often wonder how you can find time for what you do, in addition to the care of the House . . . Composition seems to me Impossible, with a head full of Joints of Mutton & doses of Rhubarb.'[75] Anna's second baby, Julia Cassandra, was born at Wyards on 27 September, only eleven months after Jemima's birth; Henry was constantly coming and going at the Cottage, and Edward also spent three weeks in Hampshire during November. Charles, who had returned to England at the end of June, strained and depressed following his shipwreck,[76] stayed for most of the time with the Palmer family in London, so as to keep in close touch with the Admiralty and obtain another command as soon as possible; but he too now came to Chawton in November, probably bringing his children and their aunt, Harriet Palmer, with him.[77] Luckily the Great House was not after all leased out again, so this was available to provide overflow accommodation for the family, and Charles's visit greatly improved his 'Health, Spirits & Appearance' as Jane was pleased to tell James Edward in her letter to him of 16 December.

This letter, Jane's last for 1816, was sent to James Edward to congratulate him upon being a schoolboy no longer, as he had finally left Winchester the previous week. It was brought to him at Steventon by Henry, now on the verge of ordination, and Jane continued:

Uncle Henry writes very superior Sermons. – You & I must try to get hold of one or two, & put them into our Novels; – it would be a fine help to a volume; & we could make our Heroine read it aloud of a Sunday Evening . . . By the bye, my dear Edward, I am quite concerned for the loss your Mother mentions in her Letter; two Chapters & a half to be missing is monstrous! It is well that I have not been at Steventon lately, & therefore cannot be suspected of purloining them; – two strong twigs & a half towards a Nest of my own, would have been something. – I do not think however that any theft of that sort would be really very useful to me. What should I do with your strong, manly, spirited Sketches, full of Variety & Glow? – How could I possibly join them on to the little bit (two Inches wide) of Ivory on which I work with so fine a Brush, as produces little effect after much labour?[78]

Although Jane wrote in a humourous tone, the content – as in her earlier letters to Anna and to Mr Clarke of Carlton House – shows clearly how well she understood her own literary scope and style. Since September her health had failed a little further, for in her next paragraph she said that Ben Lefroy had just recently invited her to dine at Wyards – 'but I was forced to decline it, the walk is beyond my strength (though I am otherwise very well) & this is not a Season for Donkey Carriages . . .'

However, by the New Year of 1817 an intermission in the disease had occurred, and Jane was able to write cheerfully to Alethea Bigg:

I have certainly gained strength through the Winter & am not far from being well; & I think I understand my own case now so much better than I did, as to be able by care to keep off any serious return of illness. I am more & more convinced that Bile is at the bottom of all I have suffered, which makes it easy to know how to treat myself;[79]

and to Steventon: 'I feel myself getting stronger than I was half a year ago, & can so perfectly well walk to Alton, or back again, without the slightest fatigue that I hope to be able to do both when Summer comes.'[80] Frank's children all visited the Cottage on 7 January,[81] and a week or so later Jane went to stay with the family in Alton for two or three days, as she told Caroline: '& though the Children are sometimes very noisy & not under such Order as they ought & easily might, I cannot help liking them & even loving them, which I hope may be not wholly inexcusable in their & your affectionate Aunt . . .'[82] It may well have been this last visit to his household that Frank had in mind years later, when he told an American enquirer that: 'She was fond of children and a favorite with them. Her Nephews and Nieces of whom there were many could not have a greater treat than crouding round and listening to Aunt Jane's stories.'[83]

On 27 January 1817, in this mood of hopefulness and renewed strength, Jane set to work on a fresh novel, that now known as *Sanditon*. Anna was sufficiently recovered from the birth of Julia Cassandra to be 'quite equal to walking to Chawton'[84] and during her visits in February and March Jane not only confided to her that this new work was in hand, but also to some extent discussed the characters, as Anna recalled: 'The other members of the Parker family [i.e., apart from Mr Parker] (except of course Sidney) were certainly suggested by conversations which passed between Aunt Jane & me during the time that she was writing this story – Their vagaries do by no means exceed the facts from which they were taken –'[85] Jane did not go so far as to tell Anna the plot or ending of the story, perhaps keeping this as a topic for amusing discussions between themselves. Her improvement in health was only temporary and symptoms of the illness soon reappeared, so that during February and March 'she kept a good deal in her own room, but when equal to anything she could always find pleasure in composition. The greater part of the M.S. is in her own peculiarly neat hand writing, but a few passages are in a larger & weaker hand; evidently having been first written with a pencil –'[86] Twelve chapters were completed by 18 March, when a more severe attack of fever obliged her to put the manuscript aside for the last time.[87] As with *The Watsons*, Cassandra talked about this unfinished fragment to Frank's children in later years, and their family tradition recorded that Jane had intended to call the story 'The Brothers'.[88]

Even while she was busy creating the village and inhabitants of Sanditon, Jane was simultaneously dispensing more advice to Fanny Knight on the important subjects of love and marriage. Following their correspondence at the end of 1814, Fanny had discouraged Mr Plumptre's attentions so thoroughly that he was now engaged to somebody else,[89] and the news of this engagement evidently made her think that perhaps at the age of twenty-four she was in danger of being left on the shelf, for her cousin, Anna, and her Kentish débutante friends were all now married and mothers. Young Mr Wildman of Chilham Castle was certainly very attentive, but Fanny suspected that his courtship, unlike that of the quiet Mr Plumptre, was more demonstrative than serious, and wondered if she had made a mistake in dismissing Mr Plumptre instead of marrying him when she had had the chance. These doubts she put to her aunt during the spring of 1817,[90] and on 20 February Jane wrote a kind response, sympathetic and yet gently teasing, assuring her that she need have no regrets as they would never have been truly compatible.

My dearest Fanny, You are inimitable, irresistable. You are the delight of my Life. Such Letters, such entertaining Letters as you have lately sent! – Such a description of your queer little heart! – Such a lovely display of what Imagination does . . . I cannot express to you what I have felt in reading your history of yourself, how full of Pity & Concern & Admiration & Amusement I have been . . . Why should you be living in dread of his marrying somebody else? – (Yet, how natural!) – You did not chuse to have him yourself; why not allow him to take comfort where he can? . . . You are not in love with him. You never have been really in love with him.[91]

Fanny then sent another screed concerning Mr Wildman's attentions, but these Jane discounted:

By your description he cannot be in love with you, however he may try at it, & I could not wish the match unless there were a great deal of Love on his side . . . Single Women have a dreadful propensity for being poor – which is one very strong argument in favour of Matrimony, but I need not dwell on such arguments with you, pretty Dear, you do not want inclination. – Well, I shall say, as I have often said before, Do not be in a hurry; depend upon it, the right Man will come at last; you will in the course of the next two or three years, meet with somebody more generally unexceptionable than anyone you have yet known, who will love you as warmly as ever He did, and who will so completely attach you, that you will feel you never really loved before.[92]

In these, her last three letters to Fanny, there also appear some references to *Northanger Abbey* and *Persuasion*:

I will answer your kind questions more than you expect. – Miss Catherine is put upon the Shelve for the present, and I do not know that she will ever come out; – but I have a something ready for Publication, which may perhaps appear about a twelvemonth hence. It is short, about the length of Catherine. – This is for yourself alone. Neither Mr Salusbury nor Mr Wildman are to know of it.[93]

It seems that Fanny, perhaps by way of testing Mr Wildman for compatibility, had lent him Jane's novels and sought his opinion on them without letting him into the secret of their authorship; Edward thought this was taking an unfair advantage of the young man, and so did Jane, though she was nevertheless amused and interested to have these unbiased comments relayed to her by Fanny:

Have mercy on him, tell him the truth & make him an apology. He & I should not in the least agree of course, in our ideas of Novels & Heroines; – pictures of perfection as you know make me sick & wicked – but there is some very good sense in what he says, & I particularly respect him for wishing to think well of all young Ladies; it shews an amiable & a delicate Mind. – And he deserves better treatment than to be obliged to read any more of my Works. – Do not be surprised at finding Uncle Henry acquainted with my having another ready for publication. I could not say No when he asked me, but he knows nothing more of it. – You will not like it, so you need not be impatient. You may <u>perhaps</u> like the Heroine, as she is almost too good for me.[94]

Jane's statement that her latest completed work would not be published for a year or so is not surprising, as Henry knew that 'though in composition she was equally rapid and correct, yet an invincible distrust of her own judgement induced her to withhold her works from the public, till time and many perusals had satisfied her that the charm of recent composition was dissolved'[95] – but it is not clear why 'Catherine' had once again been put aside. Perhaps Jane feared that, despite her explanatory 'Advertisement', readers would still consider it too outdated to be interesting, and her doubts as to its success may have been reinforced by the fact that the second edition of *Mansfield Park* had been selling very slowly and had resulted in an initial loss of £182.8s.3d. Admittedly, *Emma* had sold very well and the profits here amounted to £221.6s.4d.; however, Egerton offset the *Mansfield Park* loss against this sum, so that all he actually paid Jane, in February 1817, was £38.18s.0d. The second edition of *Sense and Sensibility* had yielded a profit of £12.15s.0d. in March 1816 (but this had been lost in Henry's bankruptcy) and another £19.13s.0d. now in March 1817; so Jane may well have felt unwilling to risk her small savings upon the publication of 'Catherine'.[96]

During March Jane's health fluctuated almost daily, but the overall trend was always downwards. On the 13th she was able to tell Fanny: 'I am got tolerably well again, quite equal to walking about & enjoying the Air; & by sitting down & resting a good while between my Walks, I get exercise enough'[97] – but ten days later had to admit to her:

I certainly have not been well for many weeks, & about a week ago I was very poorly, I have had a good deal of fever at times & indifferent nights, but am considerably better now, & recovering my Looks a little, which have been bad enough, black & white & every wrong colour. I must not depend upon being ever very blooming again. Sickness is a dangerous Indulgence at my time of Life.[98]

On 24 March she was strong enough to sit on one of the Cottage's donkeys and be led out by James Edward and Cassandra for a short ride up Mounters Lane – this she enjoyed very much and wrote to the Steventon family to tell them so.[99] In turn, James passed on this encouraging news to Anna, in a letter dated 3 April: 'I was happy to hear a good account of herself written by her own hand in a letter from your Aunt Jane – All who love – ie – all who know her must be anxious on her account.'[100]

Apart from anxiety over Jane's illness, the inhabitants of the Cottage were also worried by the knowledge that Mr Leigh-Perrot, at Scarlets, was very near death; he was now eighty-two and had not visited Chawton since the autumn of 1812, though contact had of course been maintained since then by correspondence.[101] The unpleasant circumstances of Mrs Leigh-Perrot's trial had not made the couple change their routine of dividing their time between Scarlets and Bath, and in fact they had given up renting No. 1 Paragon in favour of purchasing their own large house, No. 49 Great Pulteney Street, in the winter of 1810–11.[102] As Mrs Leigh-Perrot reminisced to James Edward many years later:

When the Stoneleigh settlement increased our Income, Horses & a new Chariot were purchased – but Alas! ill-health was then making the considerable addition of Fortune of less & less use to us – we could not keep the Company we had always been used to – though upon my admiring a very Elegant Barouche & 4 beautifull Horses which a Mr Parish used to parade up & down Pulteney Street, your kind Uncle told me he would keep such a one for me whenever I pleased as he could now amply afford it, & I ought to be made some Amends for late deprivations, but whilst I had him, He was the whole World to me –[103]

He died peacefully on 28 March, and Cassandra arrived at Scarlets the next day to comfort her aunt, followed by James, who was his uncle's sole trustee.

As Mr Leigh-Perrot was childless and had always shown particular favour to the Austens, it was reasonably expected that they would reap some immediate benefit under his Will; however, his devotion to his wife overruled other considerations, and all his property was left to her for her lifetime, with Scarlets and a considerable sum of money being at her free disposal. After her death some of his money was to revert to James Austen and his heirs, plus £1,000 apiece to each of Mrs Austen's children who should survive Mrs Leigh-Perrot;[104] but none of these advantages fell to them immediately and the uncertainty of these prospects was particularly distressing to the inhabitants of the Cottage. The Hinton–Baverstock lawsuit against Edward was still in progress, so that the future of two-thirds of his estate remained in doubt; since the bankruptcy of 1816 both Henry and Frank had been obliged to cease the payments of £50 apiece to Mrs Austen which they had been making since 1805, and Charles had never been able to contribute anything to his mother's upkeep. Mr Leigh-Perrot's Will had been their last hope of some improvement in their diminished income, and when the terms of it were known the disappointment was so great that Jane suffered a serious relapse. It was not until 6 April that she was able to reply to a letter from Charles, and the weakness of her handwriting confirms the content of her letter:

I am ashamed to say that the shock of my Uncle's Will brought on a relapse, & I was so ill on friday & thought myself so likely to be worse that I could not but press for Cassandra's returning with Frank after the Funeral last night, which she of course did, & either her return, or my having seen Mr Curtis, or my Disorder's chusing to go away, have made me better this morning. I live upstairs however for the present & am coddled. I am the only one of the Legatees who has been so silly, but a weak Body must excuse weak Nerves. My Mother has borne the forgetfulness of her extremely well; – her expectations for herself were never beyond the extreme of moderation, & she thinks with you that my Uncle always looked forward to surviving her.

A few months later Charles endorsed this: 'My last letter from dearest Jane.'[105]

This further stage of Jane's decline was specifically remembered by Caroline:

It had been settled that about the end of [March], or the beginning of April, I should spend a few days at Chawton, in the absence of my Father and Mother, who were just then engaged with Mrs Leigh-Perrot in arranging her late husband's affairs – it was shortly after Mr Leigh-Perrot's death – but Aunt Jane became too ill to have me in the house, and so I went instead to my sister, Mrs Lefroy, at Wyards – The next day we walked over to Chawton to make enquiries after our Aunt – She was keeping her room but said she would see us, and we went up to her – She was in her dressing gown and was sitting quite like an invalid in an arm chair – but she got up, and kindly greeted us – and then pointing to seats which had been arranged for us by the fire, she said, 'There's a chair for the married lady, and a little stool for you, Caroline.' – It is strange, but those trifling words are the last of her's that I can remember – for I retain no recollection at all of what was said by any one in the conversation that of course ensued – I was struck by the alteration in herself – She was very pale – her voice was weak and low and there was about her, a general appearance of debility and suffering; but I have been told that she never had much actual pain – She was not equal to the exertion of talking to us, and our visit to the sick room was a very short one – Aunt Cassandra soon taking us away – I do not suppose we stayed a quarter of an hour; and I never saw Aunt Jane again –[106]

During April there was once more a slight remission and Cassandra wrote in a hopeful strain to James and to Charles;[107] but Jane herself must have guessed that she would never recover, for on 27 April she quietly made her brief Will, leaving it unwitnessed in order to spare her family the additional distress of knowing she had now taken this step towards winding up the affairs of life:

I Jane Austen of the Parish of Chawton do by this my last Will & Testament give and bequeath to my dearest Sister Cassandra Elizth. every thing of which I may die possessed, or which may be hereafter due to me, subject to the payment of my Funeral Expences, & to a Legacy of £50 to my Brother Henry, & £50 to Mde. Bigeon – which I request may be paid as soon as convenient. And I appoint my said dear Sister Executrix . . .[108]

When May came, she consented to the proposal of those around her that she should move to Winchester in order to be attended by Mr Giles King Lyford, the much-respected Surgeon-in-Ordinary at the County Hospital there; during her last bout of illness, when Mr Curtis of Alton had admitted his inability to help her further, Mr Lyford had been called in and his medication had produced an improvement. In one of her last letters, that of 22 May to her governess friend, Miss Sharp, Jane spoke of this plan and also of the loving care that surrounded her:

How to do justice to the kindness of all my family during this illness, is quite beyond me! – Every dear Brother so affectionate & so anxious! – and as for my Sister! – Words must fail me in any attempt to describe what a Nurse she has been to me . . . I have not mentioned my dear Mother; she suffered much for me when I was at the worst, but is tolerably well. – Miss Lloyd too has been all kindness. In short, if I live to be an old Woman I must expect to wish I had died now; blessed in the tenderness of such a Family, & before I had survived either them or their affection.[109]

On Saturday 24 May Jane and Cassandra set off on the sixteen-mile journey to Winchester in James's carriage, sent over from Steventon for the purpose, and attended by Henry and their nephew, William Knight; it distressed Jane to see them 'riding in rain almost all the way'. Mrs Heathcote had arranged accommodation for them near the Close, at Mrs David's small house, No. 8 College Street, where they occupied rooms on the first floor. 'Our Lodgings are very comfortable. We have a neat little Drawg. room with a Bow-window overlooking Dr Gabell's Garden –' Jane told James Edward in her letter to him of 27 May. She wrote in a resolutely optimistic tone and with her usual note of wry humour:

Plate 25 No. 8 College Street, Winchester.

I will not boast of my handwriting; neither that, nor my face have yet recovered their proper beauty, but in other respects I am gaining strength very fast . . . Mr Lyford says he will cure me, & if he fails I shall draw up a Memorial & lay it before the Dean & Chapter, & have no doubt of redress from that Pious, Learned, & Disinterested Body.[110]

Her last known letter, probably addressed to her London friend, Mrs Tilson, must have been written a day or two later, before she became too weak to leave her bed:

My attendant is encouraging, and talks of making me quite well. I live chiefly on the sofa, but am allowed to walk from one room to the other. I have been out once in a sedan-chair, and am to repeat it, and be promoted to a wheel-chair as the weather serves. On this subject I will only say further that my dearest sister, my tender, watchful, indefatigable nurse, has not been made ill by her exertions. As to what I owe to her, and to the anxious affection of all my beloved family on this occasion, I can only cry over it, and pray to God to bless them more and more . . .

This letter was not posted but conveyed by hand, probably by the Chawton neighbours Captain Clement with his wife and sister-in-law, Miss Prowting, for Jane concluded with another touch of her irrepressible humour: 'You will find Captain – [the name was deleted when this letter was first published] a very respectable, well-meaning man, without much manner, his wife and sister all good humour and obligingness, and I hope (since the fashion allows it) with rather longer petticoats than last year.'[111]

Details of the last few weeks of Jane's life have now to be pieced together from diaries, reminiscences and the hasty letters exchanged almost daily amongst her anxious family. Some of these are undated, so the order in which they were written cannot be precisely determined; and it seems too that Cassandra tried to sound encouraging when writing to Mrs Austen rather than dwelling too frankly on the signs of Jane's increasing weakness. Mary Lloyd rode to Winchester on Friday 6 June to join her sisters-in-law, 'to make it more cheerful for them, and also to take a share in the necessary attendance –'[112] and Mr Lyford told her privately then that Jane's case was hopeless. There was a crisis between 9 and 13 June:

Suddenly she became much worse – Mr Lyford thought the end was near at hand, and she beleived <u>herself</u> to be dying – and under this conviction she said all that she <u>wished</u> to say to those around her – In taking then, as she thought, a last leave of my Mother, she thanked her for being there, and said, 'You have always been a kind sister to me, Mary.'[113]

James Edward was now at Oxford, in his first term at Exeter College, and on Thursday [12 June] his father wrote to him:

I grieve to write what you will grieve to read; but I must tell you that we can no longer flatter ourselves with the least hope of having your dear valuable Aunt Jane restored to us. The symptoms which returned after the first four or five days at Winchester, have never subsided, and Mr Lyford has candidly told us that her case is desperate. I need not say what a melancholy gloom this has cast over us all. Your Grandmamma has suffered much, but her affliction can be nothing to Cassandra's. She will indeed be to be pitied. It is some consolation to know that our poor invalid has hitherto felt no very severe pain – which is rather an extraordinary circumstance in her complaint. I saw her on Tuesday [10 June] and found her much altered, but composed and cheerful. She is well aware of her situation. Your Mother has been there ever since Friday and returns not till all is over – how soon that may be we cannot say – Lyford said he saw no signs of immediate dissolution, but added that with such a pulse it was impossible for any person to last long, and indeed no one can wish it – an easy departure from this to a better world is all that we can pray for. I am going to Winchester again to-morrow; you may depend upon early information, when any change takes place, and should then prepare yourself for what the next letter <u>may</u> announce . . .

To this letter Caroline added a few unhappy lines about her aunt, saying: 'I now feel as if I had never loved and valued her enough.'[114]

'Contrary to every expectation, the immediate danger passed away; she became comfortable again, and seemed really better'[115] – and Mrs Austen told Anna:

You will be happy to know that our accounts from Winchester are very good – Our Letter this Morning [probably Thursday 19 June], which was written late yesterday Evening says 'Jane has had a better Night than she has had for many weeks, and has been comfortable all day, Mr Lyford says he thinks better of her than he has ever done, tho' must still consider her in a precarious state.'[116]

James and Henry were constantly in attendance at College Street, and Jane made a point of receiving Holy Communion from them while she was still strong enough to follow the service with full attention. It seems Frank did not come to Winchester, either because his Mary had recently added a seventh baby to their family, or perhaps because the brothers had agreed that he should stay at home to support their mother.

Charles, in London, had had his particular share of worries during 1817, starting with his own illness in January and then continuing with miserable anxiety on behalf of his second daughter, Harriet Jane, now aged seven, who was believed to be developing water on the brain and had to endure painful medical treatment all through the spring months.[117] The rest of the family had evidently decided to spare him the further grief of receiving frequent accounts of Jane's decline, but her crisis in June meant they could no longer keep him in ignorance of her danger, and his diary entries at this period are self-explanatory:

Thursday 12th June: Received a letter from Henry acquainting me with Dear Jane's illness took a place in the mail for Winchester. *Friday 13th June*: Arrived at Winchester at 5 in the morning found my Sister very ill. *Saturday 14th June*: Henry went to Chawton. Jane continuing very ill. *Sunday 15th June*: Went to morning service at the Cathedral. Jane a shade better. Henry returned from Chawton. *Monday 16th June*: Rode to Chawton on Henrys Horse arrived at dinner time & found my Mother very poorly. *Wednesday 18th June*: I returned to Winchester on top of the Coach, found Dear Jane rather better. *Thursday 19th June*: Jane a little better. Saw her twice & in the evening for the last time in this world as I greatly fear, the Doctor having no hope of her final recovery. *Friday 20th June*: Left Winchester at $^1/_2$ past nine by the Telegraph Coach & arrived in Keppel Street at $^1/_2$ past five . . .[118]

During these same days Fanny at Godmersham was recording: '*12th June*: A bad account of Aunt Jane Austen from Uncle Henry from Winchester. *14th June*: A letter to me from Uncle Henry Austen – a sad account of my poor dear Aunt Jane. *15th June*: Another hopeless account from Winchester. *17th June*: A better account of dear Aunt Jane –' and in return did her best to write 'kind, amusing letters' to Jane.[119] Edward went to Chawton in mid-July to be with his mother.

The temporary improvement in Jane's condition meant that Mary Lloyd returned to Steventon on 27 June, and Caroline learned from her that

my Aunt's resignation and composure of spirit were such, as those who knew her well, would have hoped for and expected – She was a humble and beleiving Christian; her life had passed in the cheerful performance of all home duties, and with <u>no</u> aiming at applause, she had sought, as if by instinct to promote the happiness of all those who came within her influence – doubtless she had her reward, in the peace of mind which was granted to her in her last days – She was quite aware of her own danger – it was no delusive hope that kept up her spirits – and there was everything to attach her to life – Tho' she had passed by the hopes and enjoyments of youth, yet its sorrows also were left behind – and Autumn is sometimes so calm and fair that it consoles us for the departure of Spring and Summer – and <u>thus</u> it might have been with <u>her</u> – She was happy in her family and in her home; and no doubt the exercise of her great talent, was a happiness also in itself – and she was just learning to feel confidence in her own success – In no human mind was there less of vanity than in her's – yet she could not <u>but</u> be pleased and gratified as her works, by slow degrees made their way in the world, with constantly increasing favour – She had <u>no</u> cause to be weary of life, and there was much to make it very pleasant to her – <u>We</u> may be sure she would fain have lived on – yet she was enabled, without complaint, and without dismay, to prepare for death – She had for some time known that it <u>might</u> be approaching her; and <u>now</u> she saw it with certainty, to be very near at hand.[120]

A few days later Cassandra asked Mary Lloyd to return to Winchester: 'This was from no increase of my Aunt's illness, but because the Nurse could not be trusted for <u>her</u> share of the night attendance, having been more than once found asleep – so to relieve her from that part of her charge, Aunt Cassandra and my Mother and my Aunt's maid took the nights between them.'[121] Cassandra still tried to sound hopeful when writing home to Chawton, and Mrs Austen in turn wrote to Anna:

I had a very comfortable account of your Aunt Jane this morning [Monday 14 July], she now sits up a little. Charles Knight came this morning: he saw her yesterday, and says she looks better and seemd very cheerful. She hoped to be well enough to see Mrs Portal today; your Mamma is there (went yesterday by the coach), which I am very glad of. Cassandra did not quite like the nurse they had got, so wishd Mrs J. A. to come in her stead, as she promised she would whenever she was wanted . . . Your Uncle Henry goes to Winchester tomorrow & stays till Fryday Morning, Your Uncle Knight comes that evening.[122]

Aunt Jane continued very cheerful and comfortable, and there began to be a hope of, at least, a respite from death . . . Her sweetness of temper never failed her; she was considerate and grateful to those who attended on her, and at times, when feeling rather better, her playfulness of spirit prevailed, and she amused them even in their sadness.[123]

It was on the morning of Tuesday, 15 July, St Swithin's Day – and a rainy one – that this playfulness of spirit flickered up once more; and as the inhabitants of Winchester went off to watch the horse-races being held on the 'neighbouring plain' of Worthy Down, Jane dictated her very last composition – some verses pointing out teasingly the incongruity of 'races & revels & dissolute measures' taking place on a saint's day, and the aggrieved old St Swithin's punishment upon the city for this: 'Henceforward I'll triumph in shewing my powers, / Shift your race as you will it shall never be dry / The curse upon Venta is July in showers.'[124]

After this bright moment on Tuesday morning, the record of the last few hours of Jane's life and of her death in the dawn of Friday, 18 July cannot be better described than by using Cassandra's own words, as she wrote with Christian stoicism to Fanny Knight on 20 July:

Since Tuesday evening, when her complaint returnd, there was a visible change, she slept more & much more comfortably, indeed during the last eight & forty hours she was more asleep than awake. Her looks altered & she fell away, but I perceived no material diminution of strength & tho' I was then hopeless of a recovery I had no suspicion how rapidly my loss was approaching . . . Immediately after dinner on Thursday [17 July] I went into the Town to do an errand which your dear Aunt was anxious about. I returnd about a quarter before six & found her recovering from faintness & oppression, she got so well as to be able to give me a minute account of her seisure & when the clock struck 6 she was talking quietly to me. I cannot say how soon afterwards she was seized again with the same faintness . . . She felt herself to be dying about half an hour before she became tranquil and apparently unconscious. During that half hour was her struggle, poor Soul! she said she could not tell us what she sufferd, tho' she complaind of little fixed pain. When I asked her if there was any thing she wanted, her answer was she wanted nothing but death & some of her words were 'God grant me patience,

Pray for me Oh Pray for me'. Her voice was affected but as long as she spoke she was intelligible . . . Mr Lyford had been sent for, had applied something to give her ease & she was in a state of quiet insensibility by seven oclock at the latest. From that time till half past four, when she ceased to breathe, she scarcely moved a limb, so that we have every reason to think, with gratitude to the Almighty, that her sufferings were over. A slight motion of the head with every breath remaind till almost the last. I sat close to her with a pillow in my lap to assist in supporting her head, which was almost off the bed, for six hours, – fatigue made me then resign my place to Mrs J. A. [Mary Lloyd] for two hours & a half when I took it again & in about one hour more she breathed her last. I was able to close her eyes myself & it was a great gratification to me to render her these last services. There was nothing convulsed or which gave the idea of pain in her look, on the contrary, but for the continual motion of the head, she gave me the idea of a beautiful statue, & even now in her coffin, there is such a sweet serene air over her countenance as is quite pleasant to contemplate. This day my dearest Fanny you have had the melancholly intelligence & I know you suffer severely, but I likewise know that you will apply to the fountain-head for consolation & that our merciful God is never deaf to such prayers as you will offer.

The last sad ceremony is to take place on Thursday morning, her dear remains are to be deposited in the Cathedral – it is a satisfaction to me to think that they are to lie in a Building she admird so much – her precious soul I presume to hope reposes in a far superior Mansion. May mine one day be reunited to it.[125]

CHAPTER 17

Biography, 1817 and after

There were still some more sad words to be written in the ensuing days and weeks, as the family adjusted to their loss and the last few threads of Jane's earthly life were one by one knotted off. At Chawton, Frank was the first to receive the news, at noon on Friday, 18 July, and passed it on at once to Ben Lefroy: 'I do not know if you have heard how very unfavorable the accounts which were yesterday brought from Wintr. by my Brother were, if not you and Anna will be the more shocked to learn that <u>all</u> is over.'[1] Anna recorded in her diary: 'Died in College St Winchester my very dear Aunt Jane Austen',[2] and wrote to her grandmother offering to come to her, to which Mrs Austen replied:

I thank you sincerely for all your kind expressions, and offer – I am certainly in a good deal of affliction, but trust God will support me – I was not prepared for the Blow, for tho it in a manner hung over us I had reason to think it at a distance, & was not quite without hope that she might in part recover – after a 4 months illness she may be said to have died suddenly – Mr Lyford supposed some large Blood vessel had given way – I hope her sufferings were not severe, certainly not long – I had a Letter from Cassandra this morning, she is in great affliction, but bears it like a Christian – Dear Jane is to be Buried in the Cathedral, I believe on Thursday, in which case Cassandra will come home as soon as it is over –[3]

At Godmersham, Fanny had the news from her father: '*Sunday 20th July:* Evening Church. Lizzy Marianne and I did not go, in consequence of a letter from Papa announcing my poor dear Aunt Jane Austens death at 4 on Friday morning.' Two days later Cassandra's letter arrived: 'A long letter from dear Aunt Cassandra with many affecting particulars –' to which Fanny replied the next day: 'I wrote great part of a letter to Aunt Cassandra and was miserable.' Charles was now in Eastbourne with his children and Palmer in-laws, and he too received the news on 20 July: 'a letter from Henry announced my Dear Sister Janes death on the morng. of the 18th a sad day – wrote to my Mother & Henry'.[4] With stoic practicality, on 22 July Mrs Austen made her own Will, taking into account the change of family circumstances: 'I give and bequeath all my Property of every kind to my sole surviving Daughter Cassandra Elizabeth and I make her my said Daughter my sole Executrix . . .' to which Henry and Frank and Martha Lloyd were the witnesses.[5]

Before the coffin was finally closed, Cassandra cut off several locks of Jane's hair for mementoes, as was then the usual practice; and Henry arranged for the funeral to take place early on the morning of Thursday, 24 July – 'The ceremony must be over before ten oclock as the Cathedral service begins at that hour'[6] – with Jane's grave being made in the north aisle of the nave. At that period it was not the custom for women to attend funerals, on the assumption that they would be unable sufficiently to control their feelings on such distressful occasions,[7] so Cassandra and Mary Lloyd stayed in the College Street house while the men of the family accompanied the coffin into the Cathedral. Only three of the brothers – Edward, Henry and Frank – were present; Charles at Eastbourne was too far away to be able to attend, and James stayed at home, 'feeling that in the sad state of his own health and nerves, the trial would be too much for him'[8] – so that James Edward went instead to represent his father.

Afterwards, when Cassandra was home again at Chawton, she wrote to Fanny:

Thursday was not so dreadful a day to me as you imagined. There was so much necessary to be done that there was no time for additional misery. Everything was conducted with the greatest tranquillity, & but that I was determined I would see the last & therefore was upon the listen, I should not have known when they left the House. I watched the little mournful procession the length of the Street & when it turned from my sight & I had lost her for ever – even then I was not overpowered, nor so much agitated as I am now in writing of it. – Never was human being more sincerely mourned by those who attended her remains than was this dear creature. May the sorrow with which she is parted from on earth be a prognostic of the joy with which she is hailed in Heaven! . . . In looking at a few of the precious papers which are now my property I have found some Memorandums, amongst which she desires that one of her gold chains may be given to her God-daughter Louisa & a lock of her hair be set for you. You can need no assurance, my dearest Fanny, that every request of your beloved Aunt will be sacred with me. Be so good as to say whether you prefer a brooch or ring.[9]

Fanny's choice was for the hair to be set in an oval brooch, bearing simply Jane's name and the date of her death;[10] Cassandra had another lock set in pearls and made into a ring which she herself wore ever afterwards;[11] and a third went to their friend, Miss Sharp: 'I have great pleasure in sending you the lock of hair you wish for, & I add a pair of clasps which she sometimes wore & a small bodkin which she had had in constant use for more than twenty years. I know how these articles, trifling as they are, will be valued by you . . .'[12] A fourth lock went probably to James, and a fifth to Harriet Palmer;[13] Henry, Frank and Charles no doubt each had one as well, but these, or the memories of them, have not survived. To Martha, Cassandra passed on Jane's topaz cross, which she in turn kept to the end of her life.[14]

James, as always, turned to poetry in moments of emotion, and wrote an elegy for Jane, pondering on her burial in Winchester Cathedral:

> Ne'er did this venerable Fane
> More beauty, sense & worth contain
> Than when upon a Sister's bier
> Her Brothers dropt the bitter tear . . .

on her place in the family circle, both as sister and writer:

> In her (rare union) were combined
> A fair form & a fairer mind;
> Hers, Fancy quick & clear good sense
> And wit which never gave offence;
> A Heart as warm as ever beat,
> A Temper, even, calm & sweet:
> Though quick & keen her mental eye
> Poor Nature's foibles to espy
> And seemed for ever on the watch,
> Some traits of ridicule to catch,
> Yet not a word she ever penn'd
> Which hurt the feelings of a friend,
> And not one line she ever wrote
> Which dying she would wish to blot;
> But to her family alone
> Her real, genuine worth was known.
> Yes, they whose lot it was to prove
> Her Sisterly, her filial love,
> They saw her ready still to share
> The labours of domestic care,
> As if their prejudice to shame
> Who, jealous of fair female fame,
> Maintain that literary taste
> In woman's mind is much misplaced,
> Inflames their vanity & pride,
> And draws from useful works aside.
> Such wert thou Sister! while below
> In this mixt Scene of joy & woe
> To have thee with us it was given,
> A special kind behest of Heaven . . .

and on his hopes for her immortality:

> When by the Body unconfined
> All Sense, Intelligence & Mind
> By Seraphs borne through realms of light
> (While Angels gladden at the sight)
> The Aetherial Spirit wings its way
> To regions of Eternal day.[15]

James Edward, too, wrote a long elegy some weeks later, before returning to Oxford.[16]

As well as making the funeral arrangements, Henry provided obituaries for the local papers, the fullest version of which appeared in the *Hampshire Chronicle and Courier* on 22 July and in the *Salisbury and Winchester Journal* on 28 July:

On Friday the 18th inst. died, in this city, Miss Jane Austen, youngest [*sic*] daughter of the late Rev. George Austen, Rector of Steventon, in this county, and the Authoress of Emma, Mansfield Park, Pride and Prejudice and Sense and Sensibility. Her manners were most gentle, her affections ardent, her candour was not to be surpassed, and she lived and died as became a humble Christian.[17]

For Charles, either now or soon afterwards, Cassandra copied out Jane's verses on St Swithin and the Winchester races, adding on the same sheet of paper the wording of this newspaper obituary and that for the gravestone in the Cathedral.[18] Obituaries also appeared in the *Kentish Gazette* and the *Gentleman's Magazine* during August, so that on 18 August Fanny could write to Miss Chapman: 'The papers will have informed you of the sad loss we have lately sustained & you will I am sure have felt for us; & will be glad to hear that my Grandmama & Aunt Cassandra bear their loss with great fortitude & that their health is not affected by the anxiety they have undergone.'[19]

As summer turned into autumn, life at Godmersham at least returned to normality and Fanny resumed her regular exchange of correspondence with Cassandra; it was not until 15 November, when Edward brought his elder children with him to stay at the Cottage, that Fanny really saw the effect of Jane's death: 'Papa, Edward Lizzy & I came to Chawton. A melancholy meeting! & everything looking so sad!', a grief summarised in her final diary entry for 1817: 'I had the misery of losing my dear Aunt Jane Austen after a lingering illness . . .' Many years later Anna recalled: 'It comes back to me now how strangely I missed her; it had become so much a habit with me to put by things in my mind with a reference to her and to say to myself, "I shall keep this for Aunt Jane".'[20]

Jane's Will was proved on 10 September, and as it was unwitnessed Harriet Palmer and her father, Mr John Grove Palmer of Keppel Street, were called in to swear to the signature. After the payment of the legacies to Henry and to Mme. Bigeon, the funeral expenses (£92), probate costs and small debts, Cassandra received the residue of £561.2s.0d., upon which she had to pay 3 per cent legacy duty of £16.16s.8d.[21] She also of course became the owner of Jane's few possessions, chief amongst which were the manuscripts of the two completed but as yet untitled novels. Family tradition believed that Jane had asked Henry to be her literary executor, and he soon set about publishing these works, giving them the titles by which they are now known – *Northanger Abbey* and *Persuasion*. Murray brought them out on commission at the end of December 1817 (though the title-pages were actually dated 1818), printing 1,750 copies at £1.4s.0d. for the set of four volumes – I and II *Northanger Abbey*, III and IV *Persuasion*.[22]

Henry provided a brief 'Biographical Notice of The Author' as a preface to volume I, and just before publication was able to borrow from their respective recipients two of Jane's letters – that of 16 December 1816 to James Edward, and the last one from Winchester, that probably taken to Mrs Tilson by Captain Clement at the end of May 1817 – extracts from both of which he added as a 'Postscript' to his biographical sketch.[23] It was possibly for Henry's use at about this time that Cassandra made her memorandum of the dates of composition of Jane's novels:

First Impressions begun in Oct 1796 Finished in Augt. 1797 – Publishd afterwards, with alterations & contractions under the Title of Pride & Prejudice. Sense & Sensibility begun Nov. 1797 I am sure that something of the same story & characters had been written earlier & called Elinor & Marianne. Mansfield Park, begun somewhere about Feby. 1811 – Finished soon after June 1813. Emma begun Jany. 21st 1814, finishd March 29th 1815. Persuasion begun Augt. 8th 1815 finished Augt. 6th 1816. North-hanger Abby was written about the years 98 & 99.[24]

This simple note has become the basis for all subsequent literary criticism concerning the chronology of Jane Austen's literary compositions.

Surprisingly, after the numerous reviews which *Emma* had received, there were only two for this new publication – one in the *British Critic* of March 1818 and the other in *The Edinburgh Magazine and Literary Miscellany* of May 1818.[25] The anonymous reviewer in the former journal, after grumbling about the surfeit of Gothic romances and epistolary novels he had to endure in the course of his work, proceeded to pay some very backhanded compliments:

Northanger Abbey and *Persuasion*, are the productions of a pen, from which our readers have already received several admired productions; and it is with most unfeigned regret, that we are forced to add, they will be the last . . . With respect to the talents of Jane Austen, they need no other voucher, than the works which she has left behind her; which in some of the best qualities of the best sort of novels, display a degree of excellence that has not been often surpassed. In imagination, of all kinds, she appears to have been extremely deficient; not only her stories are utterly and entirely devoid of invention, but her characters, her incidents, her sentiments, are obviously all drawn exclusively from experience . . . Her merit consists altogether in her remarkable talent for observation; no ridiculous phrase, no affected sentiment, no foolish pretension seems to escape her notice . . . This is the result of that good sense which seems ever to keep complete possession over all the other qualities of the mind of our authoress; she sees every thing just as it is; even her want of imagination (which is the principal defect of her writings) is useful to her in this respect, that it enables her to keep clear of all exaggeration . . . so little narrative is there in either of the two novels of which the publication before us consists, that it is difficult to give any thing like an abstract of their contents.

The reviewer in *The Edinburgh Magazine* was far more sympathetic and even prophetic in his comments:

The singular merit of her writings is, that we could conceive, without the slightest strain of imagination, any one of her fictions to be realized in any town or village in England . . . that we think we are reading the history of people whom we have seen thousands of times, and that with all this perfect commonness, both of incident and character, perhaps not one of her characters is to be found in any other book, portrayed at least in so lively and interesting a manner. She has much observation, – much fine sense, – much delicate humour, – many pathetic touches, – and throughout all her works, a most charitable view of human nature, and a tone of gentleness and purity that are almost unequalled . . . We have always regarded her works as possessing a higher claim to public estimation than perhaps they have yet attained. They have fallen, indeed, upon an age whose taste can only be gratified with the highest seasoned food . . . In the poetry of Mr Scott and Lord Byron, in the novels of Miss Edgeworth, Mr Godwin, and the author of *Waverley*, we see exemplified in different forms this influence of the spirit of the times, – the prevailing love of historical, and at the same time romantic incident, – dark and high-wrought passions . . . yet the time, probably, will return, when we shall take a more permanent delight in those familiar cabinet pictures, than even in the great historical pieces of our more eminent modern masters . . . When this period arrives, we have no hesitation in saying, that the delightful writer of the works now before us, will be one of the most popular of English novelists . . .

But it seems that even such public estimation as Jane had gained was already on the wane – very little contemporary comment is known concerning these last two works, and although most of the edition sold out within the year following publication, thereafter sales dropped off sharply and the last 282 copies were remaindered during 1820, providing Cassandra with a total profit of £515.17s.7d.[26]

After these last tasks in settling Jane's estate, her mourners picked up the threads of their own lives again; and just as Jane had been fascinated by the interaction of three or four families in a country village, so now, had she lived, would she have watched with deep and affectionate interest the changes in her brothers' careers and families, each in his respective home, as the years went by. In 1818, apart from the mixed blessing of the costly settlement of Edward's lawsuit with the Hintons and Baverstocks,[27] a more cheerful event was the marriage in October of his second daughter, Lizzy, to a Kentish neighbour, Edward Rice of Dane Court, near Dover. Edward Rice was the younger brother of the Revd Henry Rice who had married Lucy Lefroy in 1801; however, it was not through this connection that Lizzy Knight met him, but in the course of the trip to Paris that she had made in the spring of 1817 in company with her father and Fanny. Edward Rice had been introduced to the girls by their brother, George, and for him it was love at first sight: 'How remarkably pretty your sister is!', he is reported to have told George at the conclusion of his visit.[28] They became engaged in the spring of 1818; before their marriage, Edward Rice had a riding accident one dark evening which left his face cut and bruised, and he wrote to his future father-in-law asking if he might borrow *Sense and Sensibility* until such time as his scars were sufficiently healed to enable him to reappear in society[29] – a remedy that, bearing in mind Mrs Jennings's recommendation of Constantia wine for a broken heart, Jane would undoubtedly have appreciated. In this year, too, Frank added another daughter to his family – Catherine Anne (1818–77), born at Chawton Great House. Although Catherine had never known her Aunt Jane, she and her descendants became one of the channels along which biographical information was transmitted and brought to light early in the twentieth century.

At Steventon James was in correspondence with Mrs Leigh-Perrot regarding his trusteeship of her property, and in April 1819 not unnaturally did his best to recommend his children to their rich old great-aunt: '[They] are quite well & a real comfort to their Mother & myself; Edward is well informed & studious without conceit or pedantry, & a gentlemanlike figure without being (in modern language) a <u>Dandy</u>. Caroline has that playfulness of mind united with an affectionate heart, which so peculiarly marked our lamented Jane.'[30] A month later, when Edward Knight paid his spring visit to Hampshire and brought Fanny and Marianne with him, Caroline gave James Edward her opinion of these cousins whom she had not seen for years: 'Fanny everybody says it is impossible to help loving and I beleive every body is right. I cannot admire Marianne so much as you do. She is certainly I think pretty, but I never saw her look any thing like beautiful. Her greatest personal recommendation to me, is being very like poor Aunt Jane.'[31] James did not long survive Jane; for years he had suffered from some form of digestive trouble which had caused him to restrict his diet to bread, meat and water,[32] and on 9 September 1817 Mary Lloyd recorded tersely in her diary: 'Austen seized with pain in his Bowels & took to his Bed.' He recovered sufficiently to be able to visit Worthing for a short convalescence the following month, but thereafter his decline was steady. He never lost his wish to be out of doors in the open air – sitting in a carriage when he could no longer ride, and in a bath-chair in a sheltered corner of the Steventon garden when he could no longer bear the jolting of a carriage. It was only in November 1819 that he finally became bed-ridden, though his mind remained active and for a few weeks more he was able to dictate letters and his last poetry – paraphrasing some psalms into verse. Anna and Ben Lefroy visited him frequently, and James Edward came home from Oxford in time for his father's death on 13 December and burial in the Steventon churchyard five days later.[33]

As the Steventon living was owned by Edward as part of the Knight inheritance, he was able to give it straightaway to Henry, to hold in trust for three years until Edward's fourth son, William, should be old enough to take it over. Since his ordination in 1816 Henry, with his usual chameleon-like versatility, had become 'a zealous Preacher of the Gospel, according to the religious views of the Calvinistic portion of the Evangelical Clergy, and so consistently remained to his life's end'[34] – and indeed his new-found religious enthusiasm is already visible in the wording of his 'Biographical Notice' of Jane. Apart from his curacy of Chawton, he officiated in Alton over the winter of 1817–18, and then spent some months in Berlin as Chaplain to the British Embassy.[35] Now, upon James's death, Mary Lloyd and Caroline had to vacate the rectory as soon as possible in order to make way for the new incumbent and, despite the fact that she liked him so very much,[36] Caroline could not help feeling sad as Henry moved in:

We left Uncle Henry in possession. He seemed to have renewed his youth, if indeed he could be said ever to have lost it, in the prospect before him. A fresh life was in view – he was eager for work – eager for pupils – was sure very good ones would offer – and to hear him discourse you would have supposed he knew of no employment so pleasant and honourable, as the care and tuition of troublesome young men . . . He was always very affectionate in manner to us, and paid my mother every due attention, but his own spirits he could not repress, and it is not pleasant to <u>witness</u> the elation of your successor in gaining what <u>you</u> have lost; and altogether tho' we left our home with sad hearts, we did not desire to linger in it any longer.[37]

Mary and Caroline now moved to Berkshire, where they lived together for some years in a variety of rented houses in the Newbury district, while James Edward finished his Oxford studies, took Holy Orders, and entered upon his first curacy at Newtown on the outskirts of Newbury.[38] One summer they went on holiday to the West Country, passing through Lyme Regis on the way, and from Sidmouth Mary wrote grumpily to Anna: 'I was disappointed in Lime [*sic*], as from your Aunt Janes Novel I had expected it a clean pretty place, whereas it was dirty & ugly.'[39]

On 11 April 1820 Henry married again – not one of the 'favourites' of bygone London days, but a Miss Eleanor Jackson, niece of the Revd John Papillon of Chawton. Little is known about her except that Edward Rice thought she had 'a very good pair of Eyes',[40] and she may be the same 'Eleanor' who is mentioned as a Papillon niece in Jane's letter of 24 January 1813.[41] There were no children of this marriage, which in view of Henry's extremely limited income was perhaps just as well; his claim to part of Eliza's estate was finally dismissed by the French courts in 1825,[42] so thereafter he had basically only his clerical stipends to sustain himself and his wife. When young William Knight became rector of Steventon in 1822, Henry moved to Farnham in Surrey, just over the county border from Hampshire, and combined the curacy of the town with the Mastership of the Grammar School from 1822–7. He was also appointed perpetual curate of Bentley, near Alton, in 1824, and lived there until his retirement in 1839. In 1836 there is a reference to Eleanor needing to visit Bath for her health, and after leaving Bentley in 1839 the couple lived alternately at Colchester and Tunbridge Wells, again apparently for the sake of Eleanor's well-being. It was at the latter place that Henry died and was buried in March 1850, Eleanor surviving him until 1864.[43]

Charles managed to obtain employment again in February 1820 – not, unfortunately, the command of another ship, but a post in the coastguard service at Padstow, Cornwall, as Mrs Austen told Anna: 'he will spend great part of his time on Horseback, fortunately he is very fond of that exercise, he is to ride along the Coast to a certain distance, 12 miles on one side the Town and 15 on the other, if any smuggling Vessels appear, he sends out his Boats & Men, but does not go himself.'[44] On 7 August 1820 he too remarried – his sister-in-law, Harriet Palmer. Such an alliance cannot have given much pleasure to his family, for as early as 1814 Mrs Austen had written: 'Miss Palmer to be sure is not agreable, but she is very good and very useful, and suffers so much from ill health that one must pity her, tho' one cant much like her.'[45] The younger generation were more intolerant – James Edward thought she was 'plain & sour countenanced',[46] and in 1818 James had also reproached his son: 'I think you are rather too severe upon Miss Palmer in saying she is intollerably vulgar – To Elegance indeed she has no pretensions – but as a Gentlewoman may pass muster fairly enough.'[47] Anna quite simply said: 'I cannot like Miss Palmer do what I will, which I should not care about, if I could but find out <u>why</u> I dont like her.'[48]

At that date marriage with a deceased wife's sister was not illegal but certainly subject to disapproval, as it fell within the prohibitions of the Prayerbook's Table of Kindred & Affinity, hence Mrs Austen's rueful comments to Anna at the end of August 1820:

I am <u>now</u> very glad his residence is at such a distance, by and bye wonder and censure will subside and in a year or two he may be willing to change his station for one nearer his family and friends. I hope they will be happy. She has good principles and good sense, and now that her heart is at ease (for she has suffered very much for some months past) and that she has quitted London, which always disagreed with her, she will I trust have better health and in consequence better spirits and better temper. – Charles has certainly secured a careful and attentive mother to his children for such she has proved herself during the almost six years she has had the charge of them.[49]

Four children were born of this marriage – Charles John the younger (1821–67), George (1822–4), Jane (1824–5) and Henry (1826–51) – and it was Charles's descendants from his eldest son who preserved some of Jane's letters and other memorabilia which came to light in the early years of the twentieth century.[50]

In 1826 Charles returned to sea when he was appointed to command the frigate *Aurora* on the Jamaica station, engaged in the suppression of the slave trade. From the *Aurora* he moved to become flag-captain on the *Winchester* on the North America and West India station, but late in 1830 'received considerable hurt in his Chest by a Fall from the Mast of his Ship in a Gale' and was obliged to return to England for medical advice; 'poor Charles seems to have been born under some unlucky Planet –' Mrs Leigh-Perrot commented.[51] He did, however, make a full recovery, and from 1838 to 1841 was on the *Bellerophon* in the Mediterranean, where he campaigned against the Viceroy of Egypt, Mehemet Ali, and also participated in the bombardment of St Jean d'Acre; for his services in this respect he was made a Companion of the Bath. He became a Rear-Admiral in 1846, in February

1850 was appointed Commander-in-Chief of the East India and China station, and died of cholera on 8 October 1852 while on active service up the Irrawaddy River in Burma, having 'won the hearts of all by his gentleness and kindness while he was struggling with disease'.[52] Anna's last memories of him were:

To a very remarkable sweetness of temper, & benevolence of character he joined great personal advantages, and that even to the last. When the Admiral left England in February (though in the 71st year of his age) his tall, erect figure, his bright eye & animated countenance would have given the impression of a much younger man; had it not been for the rather remarkable contrast with his hair, which, originally dark, had become of a snowy white.[53]

Yet another marriage took place in 1820 – on 24 October, when Fanny Knight at last gave up her position as mistress of Godmersham in favour of becoming the second wife of Sir Edward Knatchbull (1781–1849) of Mersham-le-Hatch, Kent, who had succeeded his father as ninth baronet the previous year and with whom, in fact, Fanny had already been acquainted even at the time when she was anxiously seeking her Aunt Jane's advice on love and marriage. Sir Edward's first wife, Annabella Honywood, had died in 1814 after the birth of their sixth child, since when he had remained a widower – 'lonely, morose and sentimental', in the opinion of one of his descendants. He now told Fanny: 'Allow me to say that you are the only person in whose Society I can find Happiness and to whose example and care I could entrust the welfare of my children.' Fanny informed Miss Chapman:

If you have heard that I am engaged to be married to Sir Edward Knatchbull I am now writing to confirm that intelligence and I need not add that it gives my family the greatest satisfaction and that with a man of his excellence of character my prospect of as much comfort as this world can bestow is well founded and I trust not unreasonable.[54]

Fanny had nine children by Sir Edward, and it was her eldest son, the first Lord Brabourne, who published in 1884 those of Jane Austen's letters which he had inherited from his mother.

Edward Knight never remarried, but lived on peacefully at Godmersham with his children and grandchildren around him till his death in 1852. Upon Fanny's marriage her sister Marianne took her place as her father's hostess; she was the only one of Edward's daughters who remained single, and became the 'Aunt May' of later generations, dying in 1896 at the great age of ninety-five.[55]

Frank had thirty years on shore after the end of the French wars, rising steadily in his profession during this period, and his last naval service was the command of the North America and West India station from 1844–8, at the end of which he became a full Admiral. He lived for some of the time at Chawton Great House, or in Alton or Gosport, before buying a home of his own, Portsdown Lodge, near Portsmouth. In 1823 Mary Gibson died at the birth of their eleventh child, Cholmeley, who survived her only a few months. For the next five years the eldest daughter, Mary Jane, was her father's companion and mistress of the household, but when she herself married early in 1828 Frank decided he must find a second wife – and chose Martha Lloyd, now aged sixty-three and still living quietly with Cassandra at Chawton Cottage. They were married in Winchester on 24 July 1828, the anniversary of his first marriage. For some reason this event annoyed old Mrs Leigh-Perrot very much, and although she had been contemplating bequeathing Scarlets to Frank she apparently could not bear the idea of Martha succeeding her as mistress there, and so gave Frank a lump sum of £10,000 in lieu of this half-promised inheritance. With this sum he was immediately able to purchase Portsdown Lodge, so perhaps the security of having that property, at least, outweighed the uncertainty he might have suffered in the future regarding Mrs Leigh-Perrot's eventual disposal of the Scarlets estate – an uncertainty which was passed on to the next generation of Austens. After his return from the West Indies Frank lived on at Portsdown with his daughters and grandsons, being finally promoted to Admiral of the Fleet in 1863 and dying on 10 August 1865 at the age of ninety-one, the last of Jane's generation. One of his grandsons, John Henry Hubback (1844–1939), recalled him as

quite a short man, about 5ft. 6in. or 5ft. 7in., of dignified manner, with perhaps more reserve in it than he himself realised. He walked with a slight stoop, but he must have been in as strong health as are most men of sixty, and his eyesight was still that of a sailor, keen to distinguish objects at a great distance, while his hearing was also quite good.[56]

Until 1827 Cassandra and Martha remained together at Chawton Cottage tending Mrs Austen, who endured continual pain from her rheumatic ailments not only patiently but with characteristic cheerfulness. James Edward remembered his grandmother saying to him: 'Ah, my dear, you find me just where you left me – on the sofa. I sometimes think that God Almighty must have forgotten me; but I daresay He will come for me in His own good time.'[57] She eventually died on 18 January 1827 aged eighty-seven, and was buried in Chawton churchyard; when her Will was proved Cassandra received £600.[58]

At the time of Jane's funeral Cassandra had written to Fanny:

I have lost a treasure, such a Sister, such a friend as never can have been surpassed, – she was the sun of my life, the gilder of every pleasure, the soother of every sorrow, I had not a thought concealed from her, & it is as if I had lost a part of myself[59] . . . I get out of doors a good deal and am able to employ myself. Of course those employments suit me best which leave me most at leisure to think of her I have lost, and I do think of her in every variety of circumstance. In our happy hours of confidential intercourse, in the cheerful family party which she so ornamented, in her sick room, on her death-bed, and as (I hope) an inhabitant of heaven.[60]

During the ensuing ten years, while her attendance upon Mrs Austen prevented her from leaving Chawton, Cassandra cherished her memories, copying out the 'Prayers composed by my ever dear sister Jane';[61] and in her copy of *Persuasion*, at the passage:

How eloquent could Anne Elliot have been, – how eloquent, at least, were her wishes on the side of early warm attachment, and a cheerful confidence in futurity, against that over-anxious caution which seems to insult exertion and distrust Providence! – She had been forced into prudence in her youth, she learned romance as she grew older – the natural sequel of an unnatural beginning –

she added in the margin: 'Dear dear Jane! This deserves to be written in letters of gold.'[62]

Cassandra also preserved every scrap of praise concerning the novels: '[Miss Shirreff] is a very great admirer of all of them herself and talked to me [? Mary Gibson] a great deal about the authoress – She used to wish as she passed Chawton that the carriage might break down opposite your door that she might be introduced. I know you like to hear any thing of this kind.'[63] From 1827 until her own death in March 1845 Cassandra frequently stayed with her brothers and their families and in turn entertained nephews and nieces at the Cottage; but for those who had been old enough to remember meeting their Aunt Jane there, such visits were always a disappointment – Frank's second son, Henry Edgar (1811–54), even though he had been only six years old when Jane died, told his cousin Caroline: 'that he could not help expecting to feel particularly happy at Chawton and never till he got there, could he fully realise to himself how all its peculiar pleasures were gone –'[64] When Anna and her daughter Fanny Caroline visited the Cottage in 1837, the latter was 'greatly struck and impressed by the way in which she [Cassandra] spoke of her sister, there was such an accent of *living* love in her voice.'[65]

It is thanks to Cassandra's contact with her brothers' children that traditions concerning Jane's life were preserved – for example, when the sudden
death of James Edward's charming friend, Henry Edridge, in 1828 startled
Cassandra into telling Caroline of the coincidental end to Jane's seaside
romance at the beginning of the century.[66] Another reminder of Jane's
youthful days occurred in the early 1830s, when Cassandra and Charles
went on a tour of the picturesque Wye Valley, taking with them Charles's
daughters, Cassy Esten and Harriet Jane, and Frank's daughter, Cassy Eliza.
Here they chanced to meet the Revd Dr Samuel Blackall who had so pon-
derously admired Jane at Christmas 1797, now grown stout and red-faced
from years of enjoyment of his 'exceeding good' living of Great Cadbury
in Somerset. Cassandra mentioned something of that past event to her
nieces and the information became confused by them in later years with
the other story of the seaside romance, hence that side of the family came to
believe Jane's love affair had been ended not by death but by her deliberate
dismissal of Dr Blackall.[67] Frank's daughter Catherine Anne understood
from Cassandra that 'she [Jane] always said her books were her children,
and supplied her sufficient interest for happiness; and some of her letters,
triumphing over the married women of her acquaintance, & rejoicing in
her own freedom from care, were most amusing.'[68]

As well as holiday trips, Cassandra paid long visits to Portsdown Lodge,
when she and Frank and Martha would reminisce about Jane and read
her novels aloud to Frank's three daughters then at home – Cassy Eliza,
Catherine Anne and Fanny Sophia. So familiar did the girls become with
the texts that in later years Catherine and Fanny could utter 'some question
or answer, expressed quite naturally in terms of the novels; sometimes even a
conversation would be carried on entirely appropriate to the matter under
discussion, but the actual phrases were "Aunt Jane's".'[69] Cassandra also
took with her the manuscripts (still untitled) of *The Watsons* and *Sanditon*;
these too were read aloud and discussed, and Catherine made for herself
a copy of the latter and possibly one of the former as well.[70] In 1842 she
married a barrister, John Hubback, but in 1847 he collapsed with a complete
mental breakdown and after three years of dwindling hopes of his recovery
Catherine was obliged to commit him to an asylum and find shelter for
herself and her three little boys under her father's roof once more. In order
to help support herself and her children, she either remembered or else
reread *The Watsons*, and provided her own completion of the story along
the lines of the plot that had been outlined by Cassandra, publishing this
version in 1850 under the title of *The Younger Sister*.[71] Between 1850 and
1863 Catherine published a further nine novels, these all being of her own

composition throughout; they were quite enjoyed by readers at the time, but none is remembered today.

As for Jane's works, in 1832 Bentley decided to reprint them in his cheap one-volume series of 'Standard Novels', and purchased the copyrights from Cassandra and Henry and from Egerton's executors (*Pride and Prejudice* only) at a total cost of £250. For this edition Henry provided a revised version of his original 'Biographical Notice', with some omissions, alterations and additions, calling it now 'Memoir of Miss Austen'. In sending this, he wrote apologetically to Bentley:

I heartily wish that I could have made it richer in detail but the fact is that My dear Sister's life was not a life of event. Nothing like a journal of her actions or her conversations was kept by herself or others. Indeed the farthest thing from her expectations or wishes was to be exhibited as a public character under any circumstances.[72]

The novels appeared in this new format in 1833 and were reprinted from time to time by Bentley and others over the next thirty years, but during the nineteenth century Scott, Dickens, Thackeray, Trollope and the Brontës were the popular authors, and Jane's works were enjoyed only by some isolated enthusiasts. In 1843 the *Foreign and Colonial Quarterly Review* published a literary article which included some praise of Jane, and Anna copied out the extract and sent it to Cassandra: 'the greatest of all female novelists, Miss Austen; great in her absence of affectation, in her wonderful knowledge of the secrets of the heart, in her power of investing common-place with interest, and of constructing works which should have the completeness demanded by art, and the unexpected turns which surprise and disappoint in daily life.'[73] For this belated praise Cassandra was almost pathetically grateful:

The Article was quite new to me & could not fail of being highly gratifying to my feelings. It was evidently written by a person of taste & discrimination. Is it not remarkable that those Books should have risen so much in celebrity after so many years? I think it may be considered as a proof that they possess intrinsic merit.[74]

Mary Lloyd and Martha both died within a few months of each other in 1843, and on 9 May that year Cassandra executed her Will[75] and wrote an accompanying testamentary letter to Charles, whom she now made her residuary legatee in Martha's stead: 'As I have leisure, I am looking over & destroying some of my Papers – others I have marked "to be burned", whilst some will still remain. These are chiefly a few letters & a few Manuscripts of our dear Jane, which I have set apart for those parties to whom I think they will be mostly valuable.'[76] Caroline remembered Cassandra's clearance at this time:

Her [Jane's] letters to Aunt Cassandra (for they were <u>sometimes</u> separated), were, I dare say, open and confidential – My Aunt looked them over and burnt the greater part (as she told me), 2 or 3 years before her own death – She left, or <u>gave</u> some as legacies to the Nieces – but of those that <u>I</u> have seen, several had portions cut out –[77]

It is usually assumed that Cassandra destroyed Jane's letters because she feared they would be published; but if that had been the case she would obviously have destroyed the whole lot at once, without bothering to sort out and preserve a particular few. Nor is it likely that Cassandra could have foreseen there would ever come a time when the public would want a biography of an authoress who was, by the mid-1840s, almost forgotten. A careful study of the letters that do survive shows that her censorship was carried out in the cause of diplomacy, destroying those which contained something that she did not wish the younger generation to read. As Caroline guessed, Jane had written her thoughts very openly to Cassandra; and while Cassandra was anxious that her nieces should have some example of Jane's amusing correspondence by which to remember her, she did not wish them to read any intimate details of illnesses, criticism of their parents and grandparents, or any jokes that might seem improper now that the robust Georgian era had given way to the primmer Victorian society.[78] She therefore kept a selection that were witty, interesting and non-controversial, and earmarked most of these for Fanny, wrapping each in a separate packet endorsed 'For Lady Knatchbull'.[79] Charles's eldest daughter, Cassy Esten, received at least a dozen letters in which she or her father were mentioned, Caroline had perhaps half a dozen and Frank's daughters probably also had some.[80] Apart from the letters, Cassandra itemised the disposal of other souvenirs: 'My gold Watch & Chain, which was dear Jane's . . . for my Brother Henry, – These articles all came from him –' and Cassy Esten and her youngest sister, Fanny Palmer, received respectively the ring containing Jane's hair set in pearls and Cassandra's own topaz cross and gold chain that Charles had given her in 1801. Each of the other nieces had some token left to her, and Cassandra concluded: 'I have marked the contents of one of the small Drawers of one of my Bureaux for Anna.'[81]

It was probably also in 1843 that James Edward's younger daughter, Mary Augusta (1838–1922) saw Cassandra at a family christening party and remembered her as 'a pale, dark-eyed old lady, with a high arched nose and a kind smile, dressed in a long cloak and a large drawn bonnet, both made of black satin. She looked to me quite different from anyone I had ever seen.'[82] In March 1845 Cassandra went to Portsdown to take leave of Frank as he set off for his West India command, and while there died suddenly of a stroke, her body being brought back to Chawton for burial next to her mother. By her Will she divided her monies equally between each branch of the family – about £1,000 apiece – with Charles being her residuary legatee and executor.[83] As well as the items of memorabilia mentioned in her testamentary letter, she also distributed Jane's surviving manuscripts in addition to the selection of her letters. *Volume the First* of the *Juvenilia* went to Charles: 'I think I recollect that a few of the trifles in this Vol: were written expressly for his amusement', *Volume the Second* to Frank and *Volume the Third* to James Edward – this latter choice probably being because Cassandra saw his handwriting in the continuation of 'Evelyn'.[84] Of the adult works, *Lady Susan* went to Fanny, Lady Knatchbull, *The Watsons* to Caroline (who also received Jane's writing desk),[85] and for Anna 'the contents of one of the small Drawers' proved to be the cancelled chapters of *Persuasion* and the *Sanditon* fragment. It is not clear whether the smaller items, *Plan of a Novel*, *Opinions of Mansfield Park*, *Opinions of Emma* and *Evening Prayers*, had been specifically allocated, but as Cassy Esten was Cassandra's executrix for her personal effects, all these too went to Charles's family along with other miscellaneous articles and papers that had belonged either to Jane or to Cassandra, most of which were subsequently sold by his descendants in the 1920s.[86] Edward disposed of the furniture in the Cottage and took it back to use as tenements for his estate workers.[87]

By the time of Cassandra's death James's three children were themselves middle-aged and busy with family cares. Anna's husband Ben Lefroy had eventually become ordained in 1817 and had succeeded his brother George as rector of Ashe in 1823, and before his early death in 1829 he and Anna had had seven children, six of whom were girls; as Cassandra wrote at the time of his death: 'She is left, poor thing! with a large family, a narrow income & indifferent health.'[88] Although *Which is the Heroine?* had been destroyed unfinished, Anna had earned herself a little money by publishing a novella, *Mary Hamilton*, in *The Literary Souvenir* for 1833, and followed this up by two small books for children – *The Winter's Tale* (1841) and *Springtide* (1842); at some time after the manuscript of *Sanditon* came into her possession she attempted to continue the story, but gave up after writing about 20,000 words.[89] During her widowhood she lived for some years at West Ham, near Basingstoke, in a house owned by her brother-in-law, Edward Lefroy, and also stayed for various periods in rented houses at Oakley, Winchester and Monk Sherborne before passing the last decade of her life in Reading.[90]

Caroline never married, but lived with her mother until 1843 and thereafter moved to be near her brother, devoting the rest of her life to being a good aunt to his nine children.[91]

As for James Edward, he had

determined to be a clergyman, as his father and grandfather had been before him . . . [even though] he offended by this decision the one person on whose good will many of his future prospects depended. Mrs Leigh-Perrot did not approve of his taking Orders. She would have preferred his being a smart young layman, and she threatened to do nothing for him in the future if he persisted in his choice. A moderate fortune was secured to him on her death, by her husband's will, but she had the power to do a great deal more if she would. This, however, did not affect his resolution.[92]

After his ordination in 1823 he became curate of Newtown, near Newbury, living with his mother and Caroline; he maintained his boyhood friendship with the Chutes at The Vyne – which dated back to the days when James, as vicar of Sherborne St John, had taken his little son there for Sunday service and dinner afterwards – and it was in that house he met his future wife, Emma Smith. It was Mrs Chute's great sorrow that she had no children, and in consequence she bestowed much affection upon the family of her widowed sister, Mrs Augusta Smith, often inviting them to visit The Vyne. Emma (1801–76) was the second of the Smith daughters, pretty and gentle, and after being acquainted for some years she and James Edward were married in 1828. Luckily for him, Mrs Leigh-Perrot had by now more or less forgiven him for taking Orders – 'so far at least as to say at times that she would still leave Scarlets to him, at other times that she would not, but would buy him a living instead';[93] but now she was delighted with his bride and could happily envisage Emma as the future mistress of her beloved Scarlets; and upon his great-aunt's death in 1836 James Edward found himself the owner of the estate, with the proviso that he should take the name of 'Leigh' in addition to his own. The Austen-Leighs lived at Scarlets for fifteen years but then found the property too expensive to maintain, so when James Edward was appointed to the vicarage of Bray, near Maidenhead, in 1852, he first leased and then sold the house to its tenant and himself continued to live in Bray until his death in 1874.

During the middle years of the nineteenth century those readers who still enjoyed Jane's works despite the changes in literary fashion began to seek information about her beyond that given by Henry in his 'Biographical Notice' and 'Memoir of Miss Austen'. One of these admirers was Mrs Mozley, wife of the Rector of Cholderton; when she and her husband passed through Amesbury on the evening of 1 November 1838 they called on their friend the Revd Fulwar William Fowle, and then it was, as Mrs Mozley wrote to her sister the next day:

I discovered that Mr Fowle is related to Miss Austin [*sic*] and his mother almost brought up with her – she discovered & persisted in Jane's being the Author of the novels from the very first – Mr F. was quite surprised & pleased at the way I spoke of them – being his cousins he said he never considered much about them & had never heard any one speak highly of them – I asked him many questions about her & he gave a very nice & satisfactory acct. of her – he said she was pretty – certainly pretty – bright & a good deal of color in her face – like a doll – no that wd. not give at all the idea for she had so much expression – she was like a child – quite a child very lively & full of humor – most amiable – most beloved –[94]

Another admirer was the aged Miss Catherine Hutton of Birmingham (1756–1846), herself an authoress and also a keen collector of autographs, who applied in 1841 to Frank, through intermediaries, asking for one of Jane's letters. To this request Frank replied:

The individual whose Autograph your friend is desirous to obtain was my Sister. I have several letters of hers in my possession, but not one that I could feel justified in parting with. I send you however her Signature such as she usually wrote it when she used (which she rarely did) more than her initials. The year is not affixed to the date, but I know it to have been 1813. She scarcely ever wrote her Christian name at full length except when writing to some of her most intimate friends, when she did not use her Sirname.

The scrap he enclosed was from the end of a letter: 'Yours very affec: ly / J. Austen / Chawton Wednesday / Feb. 17', and one of the intermediaries commented: 'perhaps no other collector can even boast of so much in their possession'. Upon receipt of this autograph Miss Hutton stuck it in her album, above some biographical notes on Jane taken from Henry's text, and added modestly below: 'I am inferior to Jane Austen in person, manners, and talents; but when she makes one of her characters speak her own mind, as she frequently does, I am delighted to think that I bear some resemblance to her.'[95]

Miss Hutton was not so lucky in her request, in fact, as were some early American enthusiasts, the Quincy family of Boston. Miss Eliza Susan Quincy wrote to Frank in January 1852 asking for a Jane autograph, and on this occasion he despatched not a mere signature but a complete letter, that addressed to Martha Lloyd on 12 November 1800.[96] In his covering letter he gave a character sketch of his sister:

Of the liveliness of her imagination and playfulness of her fancy, as also of the truthfulness of her description of character and deep knowledge of the human mind, there are sufficient evidence in her works; and it has been a matter of surprise to those who knew her best, how she could at a very early age and with apparently limited means of observation, have been capable of nicely discriminating and pourtraying such varieties of the human character as are introduced in her works. – In her temper, she was chearful and not easily irritated, and tho' rather reserved to strangers so as to have been by some accused of haughtiness of manner, yet in the company of those she loved the native benevolence of her heart and kindness of her disposition were forcibly displayed. On such occasions she was a most agreeable companion and by the lively sallies of her wit and good-humoured drollery seldom failed of exciting the mirth and hilarity of the party. She was fond of children and a favorite with them. Her Nephews and Nieces of whom there were many could not have a greater treat than crouding round and listening to Aunt Jane's stories.[97]

In a second letter to the Quincys Frank added: 'I do not know whether in the character of Capt. Wentworth the authoress meant in any degree to delineate that of her Brother: perhaps she might – but I rather think parts of Capt. Harville's were drawn from myself. At least some of his domestic habits, tastes and occupations bear a strong resemblance to mine.'[98]

A fourth enthusiast was Lady Campbell, who had been acquainted with Louisa Knight (since her marriage in 1847, Lady George Hill) without knowing that she was Jane's niece; in the spring of 1856 some chance reference brought this fact to light, as Louisa told Fanny:

Lady Campbell is . . . a most ardent admirer and enthusiastic lover of Aunt Jane's works. Aunt Cassandra herself would be satisfied at her appreciation of them – nothing ever like them before or since. When she heard I was her niece she was in extasies. 'My dear, is it possible, are you Jane Austen's niece? that I should never have known that before! – come and tell me about her – do you remember her? was she pretty? wasn't she pretty? Oh, if I could but have seen her – Macaulay says she is second to Shakespeare. I was at Bowood when Lord Lansdowne heard of her death – you cannot think how grieved and affected he was –' I told her you were her great friend and used to correspond with her. 'Oh! write and ask her if she can only send me one of her own real letters, and tell me any and every particular she may know about her life, self, everything, I should be so delighted! Pray do write and ask her. The Archbishop of Dublin is another of her staunch admirers, and we have such long conversations about her.' Then off she went, talking over and repeating parts of every one of the books, &c. –[99]

Lady Campbell wrote to Lord Carlyle on 26 March 1856 with her version of this meeting:

Only fancy the discovery we have made, dear Lord Carlyle! Lady George Hill is own niece to Jane Austen the authoress and she can tell us so much about her! She had large dark eyes and a brilliant complexion, and long, long black hair down to her knees. She was very absent indeed. She would sit silent awhile, then rub her hands, laugh to herself and run up to her room. The impression her books give one, is that she herself must have been so perfectly charming. I always fancied her Anne in Persuasion was autobiography of herself, except that the real Captain Wentworth had not been fortunate enough to marry her. Lady George says Miss Austen's sister Cassandra tried to persuade her to alter the end of Mansfield Park and let Mr Crawford marry Fanny Price. She remembers their arguing the matter but Miss Austen stood firmly and would not allow the change.[100]

Fanny, for her part, was in London when she received Louisa's letter and it was not until 2 August, at home again in Kent, that she looked out the box containing Jane's letters and endorsed it: 'Letters from Aunt Jane to Aunt Cassandra at different periods of her life – a few to me – and some from Aunt Cass. to me after At. Jane's death',[101] noting also in her diary that she had been 'Very busy looking over & arranging letters & papers'. Unfortunately, there is nothing to indicate whether she did at this date send one of Jane's letters to Lady Campbell in response to her request.

By the 1850s enthusiasts had started to visit Winchester specifically to find Jane's grave; two of these were Lady Richardson and her elderly mother Mrs Elizabeth Fletcher, and the former wrote:

we took a day at Winchester and visited the shrine of Jane Austen, with even more interest than that of William of Wickham. We talked over the happy days of reading aloud the delightful novels of Jane Austen, when the author was as little known as that of Waverley, and when some of our party gave our mother the name of Miss Bates, from the favourable view she took of all the human race and the events of the world.[102]

Such pilgrims puzzled the Cathedral verger, who asked one visitor: 'Pray, sir, can you tell me whether there was anything particular about that lady; so many people want to know where she was buried?'[103]

It was this gradually rising tide of interest in Jane and her works, not only on the part of elderly contemporary readers but also enquiries from those who had been born since she died – including James Edward's own family – which led him and his sisters to think that they owed it to posterity to provide a biography of their aunt based upon their own personal memories; as James Edward put it: 'I am the more inclined to undertake the task from a conviction that, however little I may have to tell, no one else is left who could tell so much of her.'[104] In December 1864 Anna wrote to him:

You have asked me to put on paper my recollections of Aunt Jane, & to do so would be both on your account & her's a labour of love if I had but a sufficiency of material. I am sorry to say that my reminiscences are few; surprisingly so, considering how much I saw of her in childhood, & how much intercourse we had in later years. I look back to the first period but find little that I can grasp of any substance, or certainty: it seems now all so shadowy!

However, memories returned as she wrote, and her letter eventually ran to fourteen pages, ending up modestly enough:

I have come to the end of my traditional lore, as well as of my personal recollections, & I am sorry that both should be so meagre & unsatisfactory; but if this attempt should incline others to do the same, even if no more, the contributions when put together may furnish a memorial of some value. You must have it in your own power to write something; & Caroline, though her recollections cannot go so far back even as your's, is, I know acquainted with some particulars of interest in the life of our Aunt; they relate to circumstances of which I never had any knowledge, but were communicated to her by the best of then living Authorities, Aunt Cassandra – There may be other sources of information, if we could get at them – Letters may have been preserved, & this is the more probable as Aunt Jane's talent for letter writing was so much valued & thought so delightful amongst her own family circle.[105]

At about the same time Caroline also started writing out her memories and by 1867 was able to provide James Edward with a complete essay upon which he relied quite heavily for use in his *Memoir of Jane Austen*, especially in relation to the last years at Chawton Cottage.[106]

I am very glad dear Edward that you have applied yourself to the settlement of this vexed question between the Austens and the Public. I am sure you will do justice to what there is – but I feel it must be a difficult task to dig up the materials, so carefully have they been buried out of our sight by the past generation.[107]

Unlike Anna, Caroline did not think that Jane's surviving letters would provide much useful information:

There is nothing in those letters which I have seen that would be acceptable to the public – They were very well expressed, and they must have been very interesting to those who received them – but they detailed chiefly home and family events: and she seldom committed herself even to an opinion – so that to strangers they could be no transcript of her mind – they would not feel that they knew her any the better for having read them –[108]

She considered instead that for the 'stuffing' of the projected volume

some of her light nonsensical verses might take – such as 'In measured verse I now rehearse, The charms of lovely Anna', & perhaps some few bouts rimés or charades – & I have thought that the story, I beleive in your possession, all nonsense, might be used. I don't mean Kitty's Bower, but the other – of the gentleman who wanders forth and is put in possession of a stranger's house, and married to his daughter Maria [i.e., 'Evelyn' in *Volume the Third*]. I have always thought it remarkable that the early workings of her mind should have been in burlesque, and comic exaggeration, setting at nought all rules of probable or possible – when of all her finished and later writings, the exact contrary is the characteristic. The story I mean is clever nonsense but one knows not how it might be taken by the public, tho' something must ever be risked. What I should deprecate is publishing any of the 'betweenities' when the nonsense was passing away, and before her wonderful talent had found it's proper channel. Lady Knatchbull has a whole short story [i.e., *Lady Susan*] they were wishing years ago to make public – but were discouraged by others – & I hope the desire has passed away.[109]

Caroline was embarrassed at the idea of publicising the brief romantic episodes in Jane's life:

My own wish would be, that not any allusion should be made to the Manydown story – or at least that the reference should be so vague, as to give no clue to the place or the person. Mr Wither's children are still living & in the neighbourhood – probably they never yet heard the tale – but some of them are readers, & they would be sure to fall in with the Memoir. A few people remain thereabouts who know the tradition – The Knights certainly, and perhaps the Portals; it lies very harmless now, as good as dead, but the enquiry of who the gentleman might have been would probably bring it to life again, & so the story would go the round of the neighbourhood. Now I should not like the Withers to think that the Austens had been so proud of her suitor, as to have handed down his name to all succeeding generations – I should not mind telling any body, at this distance of time – but printing and publishing seem to me very different from talking about the past . . . Mr Wither's offer was made after the family had left Steventon – tho' I suppose his love had grown in previous years of intimacy. My Aunts were on a visit to Steventon at the time. Aunt Jane I suppose was then about seven & twenty – If the circumstance is alluded to could you not make the matter less traceable by intimating that they had then left the neighbourhood?[110]

The first mention of Jane's seaside romance also occurred in this letter from Caroline to James Edward:

During the few years my Grandfather lived at Bath, he went in the summer with his wife and daughters to some sea-side. They were in Devonshire, & in Wales – & in Devonshire an acquaintance was made with some very charming man – I never heard Aunt Cassa. speak of anyone else with such admiration – she had no doubt that a mutual attachment was in progress between him and her sister. They parted – but he made it plain that he should seek them out again – & shortly afterwards he died! – My Aunt told me this in the late years of her own life – & it was quite new to me then – but all this, being nameless and dateless, cannot I know serve any purpose of your's – and it brings no contradiction to your theory that she (Aunt Jane) never had any attachment that overclouded her happiness, for long. This had not gone far enough, to leave misery behind.

As for the Tom Lefroy flirtation in 1795–6, Caroline was even more anxious:

I think I need not warn you against raking up that old story of the still-living 'Chief Justice' – That there was something in it, is true – but nothing out of the common way – (as I beleive). Nothing to call ill usage, & no very serious sorrow endured. The York Lefroys got up a very strong version of it all, & spread their own notions in the family – but they were for years very angry with their Kinsman, & rather delighted in a proof as they thought, of his early heartlessness. I have my story from my Mother, who was near at the time – It was a disappointment, but Mrs Lefroy sent the gentleman off at the end of a very few weeks, that no more mischief might be done. If his love had continued a few more years, he might have sought her out again – as he was then making enough to marry on – but who can wonder that he did not? He was settled in Ireland, and he married an Irish lady – who certainly had the convenience of money – there was no engagement, & never had been.[111]

However, only a few weeks after Caroline's letter, Tom died, aged ninety-two, and almost immediately Anna wrote to James Edward's wife, Emma, passing on just the kind of rumour that Caroline wished so much to stifle:

I am the only person who has any faith in the tradition – nor should I probably be an exception if I had not married into the family of Lefroy – but when I came to hear again & again, from those who were old enough to remember, how the Mother had disliked Tom Lefroy because he had behaved so ill to Jane Austen, with sometimes the additional weight of the Father's condemnation, what could I think then? Or what now except to give a verdict . . . [of] 'under mitigating circumstances' – As – First, the youth of the Parties – secondly, that Mrs Lefroy, charming woman as she was, & warm in her feelings, was also partial in her judgments – Thirdly – that for other causes, too long to enter upon, she not improbably set out with a prejudice against the Gentleman, & would have distrusted had there been no Jane Austen in the case. The one thing certain is, that to the last year of his life she was remembered as the object of his youthful admiration –[112]

Anna's opinions had evidently been formed from information given by her elder brothers-in-law, George and Edward Lefroy, who had been thirteen and ten years old respectively when their Irish cousin Tom had visited Ashe in 1795–6. She would also have heard more from her son-in-law, Thomas Edward Preston Lefroy (1815–87), husband of her eldest daughter, Jemima; this younger Tom Lefroy was not only a nephew of Jane's one-time admirer but also a member of that York branch of the family which, as Caroline said, had been at odds with the Lord Chief Justice in past years. James Edward later wrote direct to T. E. P. Lefroy, who cautiously confirmed that 'my late venerable uncle . . . said in so many words that he was in love with her, although he qualified his confession by saying it was a boyish love. As this occurred in a friendly & private conversation, I feel some doubt whether I ought to make it public.'[113] When it came to writing the *Memoir*, therefore,

James Edward made only the briefest of references to these three episodes in Jane's early life.[114]

Rather surprisingly, it seems that even at this late date Anna still did not know that Cassandra had kept Jane's letters and distributed some of them to the younger nieces, for she wrote to her brother:

The occasional correspondence between the Sisters when apart from each other would as a matter of course be destroyed by the Survivor – I can fancy what the indignation of Aunt Cassa. would have been at the mere idea of its being read and commented upon by any of us, nephews and nieces, little or great – and indeed I think myself she was right, in that as in most other things . . .[115]

As far as letters held by other branches of the family were concerned, James Edward's approaches met with only limited success. Herbert Austen (Frank's fourth son) knew that no letters to Henry had been kept;[116] and although Frank had carefully preserved the letters that Jane had written to his first wife, Mary Gibson, his youngest daughter, Fanny Sophia, had destroyed them all, following his death in 1865, without consulting anyone else beforehand.[117] Some of Jane's letters to Martha had come into Frank's hands, and it was one of these that he sent to the Quincy family in 1852 [118] – but how many more of them may have been in his possession at that date is unknown. Fanny Sophia went to live with her widower brother, Edward, at Barfreston in Kent, and took with her those few letters to Frank himself which still survive; in the 1860s she was prepared to let James Edward look at them but only on condition that he did not publish any, an offer which he did not feel was worthwhile accepting.[119]

As for the elder Fanny, Lady Knatchbull, she was now drifting into querulous senility and could not – perhaps would not – remember where she had put her letters from Jane. An approach to her on the subject by her sister, Marianne, brought forth a sudden pettish outburst, scribbled on the evening of 23 August 1869:

Yes my love it is very true that Aunt Jane from various circumstances was not so refined as she ought to have been from her talent, & if she had lived 50 years later she would have been in many respects more suitable to our more refined tastes. They were not rich & the people around with whom they chiefly mixed, were not at all high bred, or in short anything more than mediocre & they of course tho' superior in mental powers & cultivation were on the same level as far as refinement goes – but I think in later life their intercourse with Mrs Knight (who was very fond of & kind to them) improved them both & Aunt Jane was too clever not to put aside all possible signs of 'common-ness' (if such an expression is allowable) & teach herself to be more refined, at least in intercourse with people in general. Both the Aunts (Cassandra & Jane) were brought up in the most complete ignorance of the World & its ways (I mean as to fashion &c) & if it had not been for Papa's marriage which brought them into Kent, & the kindness of Mrs Knight, who used often to have one or the other of the sisters staying with her, they would have been, tho' not less clever & agreeable in themselves, very much below par as to good Society & its ways. If you hate all this I beg yr. pardon, but I felt it at my <u>pen's end</u>, & it chose to come along & speak the truth.[120]

After these disappointments, the help which James Edward received from Cassy Esten, Charles's eldest daughter, must have been particularly welcome. She allowed him to use those of Jane's letters which she had inherited in 1845, and it was she who proffered the two simple watercolour sketches by Cassandra – the small portrait now in the National Portrait Gallery, London, and the back view, sitting down out of doors on a summer day, which is still privately owned. Anna thought there was 'a good deal of resemblance' in the figure of the latter, but that the former was 'so hideously unlike'.[121] The family knew that no professional artist had ever painted Jane's portrait at any time in her life – as Henry had had to admit in 1832 when Bentley wanted a likeness for his new edition of the novels[122] – so James Edward commissioned a local artist, James Andrews of Maidenhead, to redraw the Cassandra-portrait, working under the superintendence of himself and his sisters. They considered his version good enough to appear in the *Memoir*, and a stipple vignette was steel-engraved from this watercolour to use as the frontispiece.[123] Steventon rectory itself had been demolished by Edward Knight in the early 1820s, when he built a new rectory on the other side of the lane for use by his son William; so for an illustration of Jane's birthplace Anna provided 'a little drawing of Julia's [her second daughter] made from my description of the Parsonage: more pretty than true: yet, some thing perhaps might be made of it . . .'[124] This joint composition formed the basis for the engraving of Steventon rectory used in the *Memoir*, and Anna added a note to the drawing in her possession: 'The Door should have more Glass, & less wood work – The Windows were Casements.'[125]

James Edward started his *Memoir* on 30 March 1869 and finished it on 7 September, and it was published on 16 December that year, though the title-page bore the date of 1870.[126] Those members of the family who had known Jane best were on the whole rather disappointed by the frontispiece; Cassy Esten wrote: 'I think the portrait is very much superior to any thing that could have been expected from the sketch it was taken from. – It is a very pleasing, sweet face, – tho', I confess, to not thinking it <u>much</u> like the original; – but <u>that</u>, the public will not be able to detect . . .'[127] Caroline was equally lukewarm:

Plate 26 Jane Austen, watercolour back view by Cassandra Austen, 1804.

The portrait is better than I expected – as considering its early date, and that it has lately passed through the hands of painter and engraver – I did not reckon upon finding any likeness – but there is a look which I recognise as hers – and though the general resemblance is not strong, yet as it represents a pleasant countenance it is so far a truth – & I am not dissatisfied with it.[128]

Lizzy Rice, now a stately matriarch, wrote from Kent to James Edward: 'I remember her so well & loved her so much & her books always were and always will be my delight . . . how well the portrait has been lithographed! I think it very like only the eyes are too large, not for beauty but for likeness, I suppose making them so was Aunt Cassandra's tribute of affection . . .'[129] Caroline agreed with this last comment: '[Mrs Rice] is right about the eyes – they are larger than the truth: that is, rounder, & more open – I am very glad she sees a general likeness tho' –'[130] but their one-time Chawton neighbour Charlotte Maria Middleton, now Mrs Beckford, considered that:

Jane's likeness is hardly what I remember there is a look, & that is all – I remember her as a tall thin spare person, with very high cheek bones great colour – sparkling Eyes not large but joyous & intelligent The face by no means so broad & plump as represented; perhaps it was taken when very young, but the Cap looks womanly –[131]

On the other side of the family, the Revd Fulwar William Fowle made no comment on the portrait, but told Caroline: 'Your dear Aunt Jane I can testify to as being the attractive, animated, delightful person her Biographer has represented her . . .' and added a few more slight memories of his own about her.[132]

The book was very well received and reviewed: 'perhaps never before has so small a volume attracted so much attention!' was Caroline's startled comment;[133] and James Edward received requests not only for more information about Jane herself but also for the publication of her other writings to which he had alluded. In the summer of 1871 he therefore brought out a second and enlarged edition, containing more of her letters and printing for the first time the cancelled chapter of *Persuasion* and *The Watsons* – a name which he himself chose for this fragment 'for the sake of having a title by which to designate it'.[134] The original manuscript of *Lady Susan* was mislaid somewhere amongst Lady Knatchbull's possessions but another copy was in the hands of either Anna or Caroline, and with his cousin's permission James Edward published the novella from this text as an appendix to the *Memoir*, though it is not known whether the title was original or also of his devising. As an example of Jane's earliest writings he included the little play 'The Mystery' from *Volume the First* of the *Juvenilia*, and ended up with a précis of *Sanditon* – this was still known to his family merely as 'The last work', though Anna herself referred to it as 'Sanditon'.[135] This fragmentary manuscript was not published in its entirety until Dr Chapman edited it in 1925, under the title *Fragment of a Novel*, but since then it has become generally known as *Sanditon*.

The historian and biographer Lord Stanhope, a great admirer of Jane's works, had hoped that James Edward would publish the 'stanzas replete with fancy & vigour' that she had composed on 15 July 1817 [i.e., the verses about St Swithin's disapproval of the Winchester races]; but Caroline thought that the insertion of 'such light words [would be] a sad incongruity' in the middle of the description of a death-bed scene, and they were consequently not included in the second or any later editions of the *Memoir*.[136] The second edition of the *Memoir* has been reprinted at intervals ever since 1871 and forms the basis of all subsequent biographies of Jane Austen.[137]

In the century and a half following the publication of the *Memoir* further information regarding Jane's life and family background has gradually come to light from a variety of sources – some of which, indeed, are still largely unpublished. When Lady Knatchbull died in 1882 her eldest son, the first Lord Brabourne, found at her home the missing letters from Jane which James Edward had been unable to use, and published these in 1884.[138] In this context he also referred briefly to his mother's diaries but evidently made no attempt to read through them systematically, and no further investigation of them was made until research for this present biography began in the early 1980s.[139] After the Brabourne letters, the next significant biography (though one which is surprisingly underrated) was *Jane Austen, Her Homes & Her Friends*, published by Constance Hill in 1902. Miss Hill, accompanied by her artist sister, Ellen, to provide the illustrations, visited all the places associated with Jane and sought personal contact with as many collateral descendants as she could find, and was allowed to quote from various family manuscripts.

In 1904 Fanny Sophia Austen died, and the letters from Jane to Frank which she had so jealously guarded presumably came at this time into the possession of her nephew, John Henry Hubback. With the help of his daughter, Edith Charlotte (later Mrs Francis Brown), and with the co-operation of his cousins in the Charles Austen line of descent, J. H. Hubback published these letters in *Jane Austen's Sailor Brothers* in 1906, a work which provides other unique anecdotes about the lives of Frank and Charles preserved in family tradition and manuscripts. In 1911 Mary Augusta Austen-Leigh published privately a memoir of her father, *James Edward Austen-Leigh*, the opening chapters of which naturally provide information about Steventon and Chawton life in the early part of the nineteenth century; and in 1913 Mary Augusta's youngest brother, William (1843–1921), collaborated with their nephew, Richard Arthur Austen-Leigh (1872–1961), to write *Jane Austen, Her Life and Letters, a Family Record*. Based upon the *Memoir*, they were now able to use the letters published by Lord Brabourne and the Hubbacks and to include family tradition and information from other miscellaneous papers collected in their hands, so that for a time their work became the definitive biography and was referred to simply as the *Life*.

However, only seven years later Mary Augusta published *Personal Aspects of Jane Austen*, which gave information not included in the *Life*; in the 1920s Charles's last surviving spinster granddaughters sold the letters and other memorabilia of Jane which their aunt, Cassy Esten, had passed on to them;[140] and in 1932 Dr Chapman published his collection of *Jane Austen's Letters to her Sister Cassandra and Others*, printing the full text of all Jane's letters as then known, which showed that in most cases the Austen-Leighs had used only very limited extracts. Elizabeth Jenkins therefore had this latest source to draw upon, as well as being allowed to see other unpublished family papers in the Austen-Leigh archive, so that her *Jane Austen* (1938), combining as it did biography with some straightforward literary criticism of the novels, was then the most reliable introduction to Jane's life and works.

Dr Chapman's *Letters* was reprinted in 1952 with a further five letters added, none of which had been known to the authors of the *Life*. In between these editions of the *Letters*, R. A. Austen-Leigh published privately in 1942 *Austen Papers 1704–1856*, a miscellaneous gathering of letters and documents which he had been collecting over the past thirty years; this volume included the Austens' letters to the Walters in the 1770s, extracts from Mr Hancock's letters to his wife Philadelphia when he was in India, extracts from the correspondence of Eliza de Feuillide and Phylly Walter, the account of Mrs Leigh-Perrot's trial in Bath, and various other items. It seems that R. A. Austen-Leigh was planning to incorporate these continuing researches into a revised and enlarged edition of the *Life*, but died before he could carry out the project.

In the years following his death many more specialised monographs and articles on particular aspects of Jane's life and works were written, but the interesting facts contained therein remained widely scattered and not easily available to the general readership. In the 1980s the present writer began collecting together this published information as well as carrying out original research, and at the request of R. A. Austen-Leigh's heirs wrote a completely revised and enlarged edition of the *Life*, retitled *Jane Austen, a Family Record*, which was published in 1989.

Since then, in 1995 the present writer has also published a completely new edition of the *Letters*, including texts and other information which had come to light since 1952. Ongoing research, especially by members of the Jane Austen Society, during the last fifteen years has resulted in a further accretion of new information regarding Jane and her family. It has therefore become desirable to publish an updated edition of the *Family Record*, so that her readers – now world-wide and including many for whom English is a second language – can keep abreast of the latest knowledge that will aid them in their study and enjoyment of the novels written by Jane Austen.

It seems that the words with which the Austen-Leighs ended their book in 1913 remain as true today as when they were first written:

From her death to 1870, there was only one complete edition of her works, and nothing, except a few articles and reviews, was written about her. Since 1870, editions, lives, memoirs, &c., have been almost too numerous to count. We, who are adding to this stream of writings, cannot induce ourselves to believe that the interest of the public is yet exhausted.

Notes

I AUSTENS AND LEIGHS, 1600–1764

1. *Pedigree* iii–vii and 1–2. In heraldic terms, the coat-of-arms is described as: argent on a chevron between three lions' gambs erased sable three bezants. The crest is: on a crown mural or a stag sejant argent attired or.
2. Hasted III 48.
3. *Pedigree* 1–2; Wilson, M. (2001) 10–12.
4. *AP* 1–16; 'New Exhibits' in *Reports* II 151; Wilson, M. (2001) 13–20; Spence 4–14.
5. *AP* 16–19; Wilson, M. (2001) 38–40.
6. *AP* 2–3, 18–19; Wilson, M. (2001) 24–8.
7. Hoole and Jarvis, 'William Walter'; Wilson, M. (2001) 31–4.
8. William Austen's Will, PROB.11/686; Spence 15–19; Wilson, M. (2001) 14, 17–19.
9. The Bishops' Transcripts of Tonbridge Parish Register show that the name is Kelk and not Holk as given in *Pedigree*.
10. *AP* 333–34; Wilson, M. (2001) 19.
11. Susanna Kelk Austen's Will, PROB.11/942; Wilson, M. (2001) 21.
12. Lefroy MS.
13. Hubback MS.
14. Lefroy MS.
15. Tucker 25–26; Wilson, M. (2001) 20–3; Southam, 'George Austen'.
16. *AP* 57, 61.
17. Vick, 'The Hancocks'.
18. *AP* 43–4; Le Faye, 'Leonora Austen'.
19. Lefroy MS.
20. Hubback MS.
21. Lefroy MS.
22. *Alum Oxon.*
23. Tucker 25; Southam, 'George Austen'.
24. Jarvis: 'JA's Clerical Connections'; Wilson, M. (2001) 23–4; Willis II 86.
25. Keith-Lucas 87–102.
26. Lefroy MS.
27. *JAOC* 12–13.

28. Vick, 'The Hancocks'.
29. *AP* 36.
30. *JAOC* 17.
31. Spence 15–19; no trace of William Walter's Will has so far been found.
32. Walter MS; Wilson, M. (2001) 31–2.
33. Le Faye: 'Three Austen Family Letters'.
34. Walter MS; Henthorn 61–91; Wilson, M. (2001) 33–4.
35. *JAOC* 169–70.
36. *JAOC* 86.
37. *Letters* Nos. 70, 71, 78.
38. Walter MS; *AP* 45, 54.
39. Walter MS; *AP* 20.
40. Walter MS; *AP* 20; Le Faye, 'Three Austen Family Letters'; *JAOC* 74.
41. *Gents Mag* for 1794, 1058.
42. Tucker 18–19.
43. Jarvis, 'JA's Clerical Connections'; also 'The Revd Thomas Bathurst'.
44. *AP* 17.
45. *JEAL* 15.
46. Leigh, Agnes E.
47. Johnson, *Cassandra*, 12.
48. Tucker 61.
49. *Memoir* 11–13.
50. Clerus List, Oxfordshire Records Office.
51. Beachcroft deposit, *c.* 570–574, Bodleian Library, Oxford.
52. *CMCA Rems* 58.
53. Still extant, but no longer used as a rectory.
54. Burn 267, 281; also G.C.R. Clay, personal communications. 1986–7.
55. Climenson 96–9.
56. FCL Family History.
57. *AP* 331; Spence 79–88.
58. 'Founder's Kin' was an Oxford University custom, originating in the thirteenth century, whereby young men descended either directly or collaterally from founders of colleges could have preferential treatment, when applying for scholarships at the University, over those not so descended. The custom was finally abolished in the middle of the nineteenth century.
59. Oxfordshire Records Office, PL.I/68–70.
60. Pope 74–6.
61. *Gents Mag* for 1764, 492.
62. The miniature of Mr Leigh-Perrot, by John Smart, has descended in a junior branch of the Austen-Leigh family; that of Jane Cholmeley has descended in the families of her maternal cousins.
63. Department of the Environment's *List of Buildings of Special Architectural or Historic Interest*, December 1983 – the extract relating to Scarlets kindly provided by John Finch, 1985; *CMCA Rems* 54.
64. *JEAL* 92–3.

65. *AP* 291; see also Vick, 'A Strikingly Elegant Pilgrim'.
66. Jane Leigh was married from Scarlets, on 29 December 1768 – information from Wargrave parish register kindly provided by Mr T. A. B. Corley.
67. Climenson 275 note 3.
68. Berkshire Records Office, personal communications 1986.
69. Mrs Leigh-Perrot to JEAL, 23 September 1835.
70. Beachcroft deposit, *c.* 570–574, Bodley.
71. Lefroy MS.
72. FCL Family History.
73. St Swithin's parish register, Somerset Records Office; Freeman 15; Spence 89–94.
74. Lefroy, F. C. 'Is It Just?', 273.
75. Lefroy MS.
76. *SB* plate facing 8 for Mr Austen's miniature; that of Mrs Austen is mentioned in CEA's testamentary letter of 9 May 1843 (Ray Collection, Pierpont Morgan Library, New York).
77. Tucker 29.
78. Lefroy MS.
79. Lefroy MS.
80. FCL Family History; but see also Vick, 'Deane Parsonage'.
81. Mr Austen's account at Hoare's Bank.
82. Hill 66.
83. Deane parish register, Hampshire Records Office.
84. Steventon parish register, Hampshire Records Office.
85. *AP* 333–4.
86. Lane, 'The Very Revd Thomas Powys'.
87. Hubback MS.

2 DEANE AND STEVENTON, 1764–75

1. Vancouver 15–20, 78–81, 107, 131–40, 390, 399–404, and tables for District Second, for descriptions of Deane and Steventon and district.
2. *Memoir* 23.
3. *Memoir* 37; also *CP James* throughout.
4. Bellas MS.
5. *Victoria County History* Hampshire, vol. IV(i), vii–ix and 171–4; also Austen-Leigh, E., *JA and Steventon*.
6. Revd J. G. Gibbs to the Austen-Leighs, 31 December 1913 – 23M93/97/1.
7. *CP James* throughout.
8. Kulisheck 39–40.
9. Lefroy MS.
10. Tucker 31.
11. *Memoir* 21–3.
12. Hubback MS.

13. *CMCA Rems* 27.
14. Austen-Leigh, Emma, *JA and Steventon* 14.
15. *Memoir* 14.
16. Bellas MS.
17. Feiling 39.
18. Gleig I 6–7; Feiling 3–6.
19. BL Add.MSS 29,227: Bills & Accounts, vol. I, 1749–77, ff. 27–28.
20. *Memoir* 13; no trace of the burial of the child has yet been found in any of the likely parishes.
21. The Deane parish register shows the baptisms of the first three Austen children.
22. The names of the godparents for all the Austen children are taken from the Lefroy MS.
23. *Alum Oxon.*
24. Oliver *Antigua* II, 296.
25. *Letters* No. 29.
26. *Memoir* 39.
27. Le Faye, 'The Austens and the Littleworths'.
28. *AP* 37.
29. Gleig I 157.
30. Tucker 40.
31. *AP* 61.
32. Mr Austen's account with Hoare's Bank shows drawing of cash when he visited London.
33. *AP* 42, 76 – Mrs Cockell was probably the wife of a member of the banking firm of Cockell & Pybus.
34. *AP* 333–4.
35. Mrs Jane Leigh's Will, PROB.11/943. At this date she describes herself as being 'of Deane'.
36. *Memoir* 14.
37. Le Faye, 'Mr Austen's Insurance Policy'.
38. *Memoir* 23.
39. Le Faye, 'Mr Austen's Insurance Policy'.
40. Hubback MS.
41. *Memoir* 23.
42. Lefroy MS.
43. Anna Lefroy to JEAL, 20 July [1869] – National Portrait Gallery archive.
44. Lefroy MS.
45. Steventon parish register.
46. Stoneleigh Papers, DR/18/20/18.
47. *AP* 333–4; Mr Austen's account at Hoare's Bank, and also that of Mrs Austen from 1806 onwards.
48. *JAOC* 37–8.
49. Le Faye, 'Jane Austen and her Hancock Relatives', 13; *JAOC* 24–6.
50. Wargrave parish register, Berkshire Records Office.

51. *Letters* No. 63.
52. Bellas MS; *CMCA Rems* 58; *AP* 334; Tucker 117.
53. *AP* 22.
54. *AP* 22–4.
55. *AP* 24–6.
56. *AP* 26–7.
57. The Steventon parish register shows the baptisms of the next five Austen children.
58. Le Faye, 'Three Austen Family Letters'.
59. *Letters* Nos. 14, 17, 25, 30, 31, 32, 33.
60. Bellas MS.
61. Mr Austen's account at Hoare's Bank.
62. *AP* 27–8.
63. Mr Austen's account at Hoare's Bank.
64. Tucker 31; *Gents Mag* for 1773, 204.
65. Vancouver, table for District Second; Tucker 31.
66. *AP* 28–30.
67. *AP* 30–31.
68. *A Genuine Report of the Proceedings in the Portsmouth Case.*
69. *Memoir* 54 note; *Letters* Nos. 24, 25.
70. *AP* 31–2.
71. *AP* 32–3.
72. Stratton and Brown 84.

3 INDIA AND FRANCE, 1752–85

1. Tucker 39; *JAOC* 12–15.
2. *AP* 34–5.
3. Feiling 39–40.
4. BL Add.MSS. 39,903.
5. *JAOC* 14–15.
6. Feiling 5–6, 88, 210, 232–3, 381–2.
7. BL Add.MSS. 29,132, ff. 147, 157–8, 159–61, 167–8.
8. Bence-Jones 220, 342.
9. *JAOC* 19–20.
10. Feiling 7.
11. *AP* 176–7.
12. Tysoe Saul Hancock, Letterbook, ff. 23r–24r. Hereafter TSH Letterbook.
13. Le Faye, 'JA and her Hancock Relatives', 12.
14. *AP* 39.
15. *AP* 40–1.
16. TSH Letterbook, ff. 7v–8v.
17. TSH Letterbook, ff. 9r–9v.
18. TSH Letterbook, ff. 5v–6r.
19. TSH Letterbook, f. 6v.

20. TSH Letterbook, f. 7r.
21. TSH Letterbook, ff. 16v–17r.
22. Grier, 'Friend of Warren Hastings', 502–3.
23. TSH Letterbook, ff. 22v–23r.
24. *AP* 27–8, 72.
25. *AP* 25; *JAOC* 25.
26. *AP* 54, 74–5.
27. *AP* 44; *JAOC* 23–4.
28. BL Add.MSS. 29,125, f. 13; *JAOC* 23.
29. *AP* 68; *JAOC* 33.
30. BL Add.MSS. 29,232, ff. 83–4; *AP* 78–9; *JAOC* 36.
31. Grier, 'Friend of Warren Hastings', 511; *JAOC* 37.
32. *AP* 81–2; *JAOC* 38.
33. *AP* 330; *JAOC* 38.
34. Mrs Hancock's account with Hoare's Bank.
35. *AP* 83–5; *JAOC* 40–2.
36. *JAOC* 46.
37. *JAOC* 47.
38. This miniature survives in the possession of Austen-Leigh descendants.
39. *JAOC* 55–6; this second miniature descended in the Walter family.
40. Devert 331–50.
41. *JAOC* 51.
42. *JAOC* 51–2.
43. *JAOC* 52–3.
44. *JAOC* 57–8.
45. *JAOC* 60.
46. Le Faye, 'Three Austen Family Letters' 331; *JAOC* 65–6.

4 CHILDHOOD AT STEVENTON, 1775–86

1. *Letters* No. 18; Bush 17 note.
2. *Alum Oxon* for dates of matriculation and graduation of the Austen sons and Steventon pupils.
3. *Memoir* 12.
4. Mr Austen's account with Hoare's Bank shows some payments that are associated by name with particular pupils, and others which, by their regularity and similarity of amount, seem likely to relate to pupils as well.
5. Lefroy MS; *CPVA* 25–6.
6. *Letters* No. 29.
7. Lefroy MS and FCL Family History; *CPVA* 27–8.
8. Sawtell 20–6.
9. *CP James* 1.
10. Son of the Thomas Brodnax-May-Knight (died 26 February 1781) who had presented Mr Austen to Steventon; see also *Gents Mag* for 1794, 1058.
11. Lefroy MS.

12. It has appeared in numerous articles and books about the Austens, and remains in the possession of the Knight family.
13. *Reports* III 354; now in the possession of the JAMT.
14. *JAOC* 71.
15. *JAOC* 38.
16. Lefroy MS and *AP* 16–19.
17. This portrait is now in the Graves Art Gallery, Sheffield, and bears a modern attribution to Ozias Humphrey.
18. Stoneleigh Papers, DR/18/31/859, /860, /861.
19. Revd Thomas Leigh's wife Mary was herself a Leigh by birth, as she was his first cousin, the elder daughter of his uncle, the Master of Balliol.
20. Beachcroft deposit, Bodleian; Leigh, Agnes 277–86.
21. *Letters* No. 29.
22. Information from the Wells Cathedral Archivist, 1986.
23. Clergy Institution Books.
24. Bath City Rate Books, 1770s and 1780s.
25. Le Faye, 'Anna Lefroy's Original Memories of JA'.
26. *CP James* 8–9.
27. Vick, 'The Sale at Steventon Parsonage'.
28. Watson, Vera 1–39, 119–20.
29. Thoyts 127, 168.
30. Anne Brydges was in fact a distant cousin of Mrs George Austen, through their common Brydges ancestry.
31. Thoyts 58, 127, 168; see also Lefroy, Helen, and Lefroy, J. A. P., for more detailed information on the Langlois and Lefroy families.
32. Lefroy, Mrs Anne 16.
33. Gore 9–12.
34. *JAOC* 56, 59.
35. *Letters* No. 69.
36. *Memoir* 36.
37. FWA to Anna Lefroy, 9 October 1855 – 23M93/63/2/1.
38. South 192.
39. Mr Austen's account with Hoare's Bank shows payments to Mrs Cawley of £30 in April 1783 and £10 in September 1783. See also Corley, 'JA's Schooldays', and 'The Revd GA's Bank Account'.
40. Phillipps, Thomas 274.
41. Bath City Rate Books, 1780s–90s.
42. Clergy Institution Books, 1784.
43. *Letters* No. 24; CEA's testamentary letter of 9 May 1843 (Ray Colln., Pierpont Morgan).
44. Gilson 440–2.
45. *NA* 14; *Letters* No. 57.
46. Gilson 433.
47. *CP James* 10–11.
48. Vick, 'Mr Austen's Carriage'.

49. Clarke 83.
50. Henry's art is mentioned in *Letters* No. 45; see also Le Faye, 'Fanny Knight's Diaries', 9; it is to Cassandra that we owe the only two authentic portraits of Jane; and for Henry's comment on Jane's art see *NA* 5 and *Memoir* 139. See also Gilson, 'Cassandra Austen's Pictures'.
51. Le Faye, 'Anna Lefroy's Original Memories of JA'.
52. Le Faye, 'New Marginalia in Jane Austen's Books'.
53. *E* 21–2.
54. Phillips, D., *Reading* 21–8, 91–3, for the history of Reading, its Abbey and the Abbey House School; see also Corley, 'JA's Schooldays', and 'The Revd GA's Bank Account'.
55. Darton 121–34, 142–51, for Mrs Sherwood's memories of the Abbey House School and Mrs La Tournelle in 1791–93.
56. *Gents Mag* for 1797, 983.
57. Darton, as above.
58. Cooper 72.
59. Darton, as above.
60. Corley, 'JA's Schooldays'.
61. *Letters* No. 4.
62. Stoneleigh Papers, DR/18/31/860.
63. FCL Family History.
64. Mr Austen's account at Hoare's Bank shows that his first payment to Mrs La Tournelle was £37.19s.0d. in August 1785, his second £36.2s.6d. in February 1786, and the third and last £16.10s.0d. in early January 1787, this being in arrears.
65. Le Faye, 'Three Austen Family Letters'.

5 FAMILY LIFE, 1786–92

1. Jarvis, 'JA's Clerical Connections'.
2. James's miniature has descended in the Austen-Leigh family; a photograph is at Jane Austen's House, Chawton.
3. *AP* 265.
4. *CP James* 70, 'Lines written at Steventon'.
5. *CP James* 14, 'Sonnet to Lady Catherine Powlet'.
6. *JAOC* 69.
7. *JAOC* 71.
8. *JAOC* 73.
9. *CP James* 23, 'Prologue to . . . Tom Thumb'.
10. EAK kept travel diaries, of which two odd volumes have survived: one, for August 1786 when in Switzerland, is in Hampshire RO; the other, for June/July 1790 when on his return journey to England, is in the Beinecke Library at Yale.
11. Mitford, Nancy 55 and note.
12. Austen-Leigh, William and Knight, Montague George, *Chawton Manor* 157–8.

13. This portrait remained in the possession of the Knight family until 1952, when it was purchased by Lt-Col. Satterthwaite; it now hangs in Jane Austen's House, Chawton.

14. Austen-Leigh, William and Knight, Montague George, *Chawton Manor* plate facing 160.

15. Lefroy MS.

16. Le Faye, 'Three Austen Family Letters'; *JAOC* 88–9.

17. Lefroy MS.

18. Photograph of miniature (original now lost) at Jane Austen's house.

19. Brabourne I 35–36.

20. *Letters* Nos. 6 and 69.

21. FWA's Memoir.

22. O'Byrne.

23. Lloyd, C., 'The Royal Naval Colleges', 145; Vick, 'The Royal Naval Academy at Portsmouth'.

24. *Letters* Nos. 1, 2, 15, 27, 63, 97.

25. Mr Austen's account at Hoare's Bank shows payments from the firm of Birch and Hercy stretching from 1780–90, which would seem to be the fees for four pupils.

26. Sawtell, 'Four Manly Boys'.

27. *Letters* Nos. 1 and 2.

28. Le Faye, 'Three Austen Family Letters', 333–4; *JAOC* 74–5.

29. *JAOC* 75.

30. *Letters* No. 31.

31. *NA* 7; *Memoir* 140–1.

32. Gilson 443, K15.

33. *Memoir* 71.

34. *NA* 241.

35. *Letters* No. 14.

36. *NA* and *P* 295–307; *MW* Index IV, 473–74.

37. Le Faye, 'JA and William Hayley'.

38. *Letters* No. 71; *Memoir* 183.

39. *Letters* No. 6; Pote 59.

40. Jane Austen, *Volume the Second* vii and 2.

41. Anna Lefroy to JEAL, 16 April [?1869], *Memoir* 183.

42. Piggott 139–40, 141–2 (in Mrs Austen's hand); Le Faye, 'Three Austen Family Letters'; *Letters* No. 4.

43. Lascelles 44–5.

44. Volumes in Austen-Leigh ownership; *Aspects* 26–8.

45. *MW* 145.

46. *NA* 7; *MAJA* 9; *Memoir* 141, 173.

47. Le Faye, 'New Marginalia in JA's Books'.

48. Brydges I 137 and II 38; Ralph 778–9.

49. *CP James* 17, 'Lines Addressed to Miss Charlotte Brydges', 'Sonnet to the same'.

50. Brydges I 5 and II 40–41.
51. *CMCA Rems* 7.
52. *NA* 15–16.
53. *MAJA* 7; *Memoir* 171. An undated sampler bearing the name Cassandra Elizabeth Austen is owned by descendants of Admiral Charles Austen; and a sampler bearing the name Jane Austen and dated 1787 is shown in *Reports* III 5. The provenance of this latter sampler is however not clear, and it probably emanates from some other branch of the Kentish Austens – see Le Faye, 'Which JA stitched this sampler?'
54. Le Faye, '*NA* and Mrs Allen's Maxims'.
55. *Letters* Nos. 35, 38.
56. *JAOC* 76.
57. *JAOC* 79–81.
58. *JAOC* 81–2.
59. *JAOC* 82–4.
60. *CP James* 20.
61. Fielding 3.
62. *CP James* 23.
63. *JAOC* 86.
64. Bellas MS; Jarvis, 'JA's Clerical Connections'.
65. *JAOC* 88–9.
66. *JAOC* 103.
67. *JAOC* 86–7.
68. *JAOC* 88.
69. MS copy made *c.* 1830 – FWA family archive; Vick, 'The Royal Naval Academy at Portsmouth'.
70. *SB* 16 (with some errors); MS in FWA family archive.
71. FWA's Memoir.

6 FIRST COMPOSITIONS, 1787–92

1. *MAJA* 10; *Memoir* 174.
2. *MW* 1–2.
3. *Hampshire Directory, 1784*, 62.
4. *JAOC* 96.
5. *CP James* 27.
6. *MW* 50; Gilson 699, M1600.
7. *Memoir* 16.
8. *The Loiterer* II No. 60; Gilson 552, M533.
9. Le Faye, 'JA and William Hayley'; see also Gore 9–12.
10. Vick, 'More on "Sophia Sentiment"'.
11. Litz, 'The Loiterer'.
12. Vick, 'Deane Parsonage'.
13. *CMCA Rems* 16.
14. *MW* 3.

15. *CMCA Rems* 7–9, 71–3; *Aspects* 102.
16. *CMCA Rems* 15.
17. *MW* 40, 12–29.
18. O'Byrne.
19. *JAOC* 96.
20. *NA* 15.
21. Austen-Leigh, Emma, *JA and Steventon* 10–12 and plate facing 12.
22. Williams 92–3, 246–9; Cobbe 23, 25, 58–60; Twining 142.
23. Brabourne I 18, 22; II 357–8.
24. Brabourne II 352–4.
25. *MW* 57–71.
26. James's signature first appears in the Overton registers in April 1790. (Personal communication, Revd W. A. W. Jarvis, 1987.)
27. *CMCA Rems* 17.
28. Poyntz.
29. Jarvis, 'JA's Clerical Connections'.
30. Bellas MS; *CMCA Rems* 58.
31. *CMCA Rems* 17.
32. FCL Family History.
33. *Letters* No. 27.
34. FCL Family History.
35. FCL Family History.
36. Jarvis, 'A Note on the Rev. James Austen'.
37. Laverstoke marriage register, Hampshire RO.
38. *CMCA Rems* 17.
39. James's account with John Ring of Basingstoke; Copeland (1993).
40. FCL Family History.
41. O'Byrne.
42. *JAOC* 108.
43. Francis Austen's Will, PROB.11/1206.
44. Revd George Austen's account at Hoare's Bank.
45. Possibly the Deacon Morrell mentioned in *Letters* No. 67, who matriculated at Christ Church on 23 October 1792; and possibly the Francis Newnham who matriculated at Wadham on 18 June 1798, as payments are received from 'Newnham' during 1793–5.
46. Crook 159.
47. *Letters* No. 43.
48. Mr Austen's account at Hoare's Bank.
49. *CPVA* 28.
50. *Letters* Nos. 2, 25, 39, 43, 44.
51. Mr Austen's account at Hoare's Bank.
52. Lefroy MS.
53. Mr Austen's account with John Ring of Basingstoke.
54. Austen, Jane, 'The History of England', ed. Jan Fergus, Acknowledgments & Note on Text, and i–iii; also personal communication from Dr Clive Caplan,

2001. Cassandra copied faces from two engravings by W. H. Bunbury, *Recruits* of 1780, and *The Relief* of 1781.

55. *Memoir* 79; Austen-Leigh, Joan, 'JA's Housewife'.
56. *JAOC* 97.
57. *JAOC* 104.
58. *JAOC* 98.
59. *JAOC* 102.
60. Le Faye, 'JA and her Hancock Relatives'; *JAOC* 111.
61. *JAOC* 112.
62. *JAOC* 116.
63. BL Add.MSS. 42,170, f.2.
64. *P* 92; Climenson 259, 264–9.
65. *JAOC* 117–19.
66. BL Add.MSS. 42,170, f. 35.
67. BL Add.MSS. 42,170, ff.35–6.
68. *JAOC* 117.
69. Steventon marriage register; Austen-Leigh, Emma, *JA and Steventon* 11; FCL Family History; Climenson 276.
70. Stoneleigh Papers, DR/18/31/861.
71. Climenson 264, 276.
72. *JAOC* 118.
73. BL Add.MSS. 39,883 – Warren Hastings's diary, under date 15 March 1794.
74. *AP* 321–3.
75. *JAOC* 122.
76. *Letters* No. 145.
77. *Letters* No. 86.
78. *JAOC* 116–17, 119.
79. *Letters* No. 27.
80. Vick, 'The Basingstoke Assemblies'.
81. *Letters* No. 14.
82. *P* 40.

7 THE YOUNG JANE, 1792–6

1. Anna Lefroy to JEAL, 20 July [1869] – National Portrait Gallery archive.
2. Le Faye, 'Anna Lefroy's Original Memories of JA', 418–19.
3. Lefroy MS.
4. *NA* 5; *Memoir* 139.
5. Le Faye, 'Anna Lefroy's Original Memories of JA', 420.
6. *Memoir* 19.
7. Watson, Vera, 119–20.
8. *AP* 228; Jarvis, 'JA's Clerical Connections'.
9. *CP James* 41, 'Lines Written at Kintbury May 1812'.
10. Brabourne 11 355–6.
11. *JAOC* 118.

12. Hubback MS.
13. FCL Family History.
14. James Austen to Anna Lefroy, [19 June 1818], 23M93/84/1.
15. *MW* 71–4, 171–8.
16. Le Faye, 'James Austen – Army Chaplain'.
17. HTA to the Bishop of Winchester, 5 November 1816 (Hampshire RO, 21M65 E1/4/2601); see also Willis 1 vi.
18. *JAOC* 116.
19. Climenson 276.
20. BL Add.MS. 42,160, under date 11 August 1793.
21. *Letters* Nos. 65 and 145; Davies, G. J. vii–xx; Collins, 'Too Much Zeal for the Bible Society'.
22. Jarvis, 'A Note on the Rev. James Austen'.
23. Mrs Chute's diary for 1793, under dates 20 and 25 October and 13 November (23M93/70/1/3).
24. Butler-Harrison MS family history.
25. *Letters* No. 62.
26. Butler-Harrison MS.
27. Leigh account book, Stoneleigh papers, DR18/31/861.
28. *Letters* No. 35; Vick, 'Cousins in Bath'.
29. *Letters* No. 52.
30. *Letters* Nos. 6, 25.
31. *Letters* Nos. 4, 6, 46, 47, 50.
32. *Gents Mag* for 1794, 1058.
33. Mr Thomas Knight's Will, PROB.11/1252; *Letters* No. 15.
34. Kaplan, 'Henry Austen and John Rawston Papillon'.
35. Jarvis, 'JA's Clerical Connections'.
36. *MW* 74–5.
37. BL Add.MSS. 29,173, f.281; and *AP* 226–7.
38. *JAOC* 84–5.
39. BL Add.MSS. 29,172, f.24, and *AP* 225.
40. BL Add.MS. 29,173, f.400 and *AP* 227.
41. BL Add.MSS. 29,174, f.25 and *AP* 153–4.
42. *MW* 243; Lascelles 13–14; *JALM* 45–7.
43. Mr Austen's account with John Ring of Basingstoke.
44. Jane's writing-desk went to Caroline Austen, and thereafter descended in a junior branch of the Austen-Leigh family until it was presented by them to the British Library, London, in 2000.
45. Dodds 405–7.
46. Stratton and Brown 91.
47. Bramston archive in Hants RO, 20M64/16.
48. Mr Austen's account with John Ring of Basingstoke, under date 2 April 1795.
49. FCL Family History.
50. FCL Family History.
51. Mr Austen's account with John Ring of Basingstoke.

52. FCL Family History.
53. FCL Family History.
54. Richardson, Joanna 31.
55. Broadley and Melville ii, 99.
56. *AP* 330.
57. Tucker 157; *Letters* No. 2.
58. Lefroy, J. A. P. 150.
59. Lefroy, J. A. P. 151.
60. *Letters* No. 1.
61. *Letters* No. 1.
62. *Letters* No. 2.
63. Le Faye, 'Tom Lefroy and JA'.
64. Powlett diary, under date 5 November 1798 (119A00/1).
65. *Letters* No. 11.
66. Lefroy, J. A. P.
67. Le Faye, 'Tom Lefroy and JA'.
68. T. E. P. Lefroy to JEAL, 16 August 1870; *Memoir* 221.

8 LATER YEARS AT STEVENTON, 1796–9

1. BL Add.MSS. 42, 161.
2. Climenson 278–9.
3. *Letters* No. 1.
4. BL Add.MSS. 29,173 f. 257; *JAOC* 122.
5. *JAOC* 122–3.
6. *JAOC* 123, 151.
7. *JAOC* 123–5.
8. *JAOC* 132, 169.
9. *Letters* No. 6.
10. *Letters* No. 3.
11. *Letters* Nos. 4, 6, 7.
12. *Letters* No. 4.
13. *Letters* No. 6.
14. *Letters* Nos. 4, 5, 6; Revd Alexander Dyce's annotated copy of *NA*, in Library of Victoria & Albert Museum.
15. *Letters* No. 7.
16. *JAOC* 129.
17. *Letters* No. 5.
18. Mrs Austen to Mary Lloyd, 30 November 1796; *AP* 228; 23M93/62/2.
19. *JAOC* 134.
20. *CP James* 39, 'To Mary, on her Wedding Day, Jany. 17th, 1812'.
21. *JEAL* 17–18.
22. FCL Family History.
23. *CMCA Rems* 17.
24. *MW* plate facing 242; *JALM* 53.

25. *Letters* No. 79.
26. Le Faye, 'Anna Lefroy's Original Memories of JA'; *Memoir* 158.
27. *JAOC* 138.
28. FCL Family History.
29. *Memoir* 105; MS now at St John's College, Oxford (MS.279); see also Gilson, 24.
30. *MW* plate facing 242, *JALM* 53.
31. *AP* 291.
32. MacKinnon 112; *Universal British Directory* 99, 111.
33. Walker 16, No. 3181.
34. Hickman, 'The JA Family in Silhouette'.
35. *Bath Chronicle* 23 November 1797; *Letters* No. 19; *AP* 167; Gilson 442, K14.
36. *JAOC* 142.
37. BL Add.MSS. 29,175, ff. 162, 184–5, 192–3, 204, 212, 218–19, 250–1 and 296; *JAOC* 150–1.
38. *JAOC* 152–6.
39. Caplan, 'JA's Soldier Brother', 135.
40. Lefroy MS.
41. Pryme and Bayne 162–4.
42. *Letters* No. 11.
43. *Letters* No. 86; Stubbings 77–81.
44. *JAOC* 153–6.
45. Vick, 'Steventon Prepares for War.'
46. *Letters* No. 8.
47. *Letters* No. 6; Lefroy MS; FCL Family History; Climenson 309.
48. *AP* 221, 229–30.
49. *Letters* p. 427.
50. Pevsner, *East Kent* 329–30; Fanny Knight's diaries for 1804 and 1807 mention the various walks and summer-houses in the Godmersham grounds; *CMCA Rems* 20.
51. *Letters* p. 427; Pevsner, *East Kent* 329–30; Hussey, 'Godmersham Park, Kent'; Nicolson, 'Godmersham Park'.
52. *Letters* No. 15.
53. *MW* plate facing 242; *JALM* 53.
54. *Letters* No. 9.
55. *Letters* No. 13.
56. *Letters* Nos. 9, 10, 11, 12, 13, 14, 15.
57. *Letters* No. 11.
58. *Letters* No. 11.
59. *Letters* No. 12.
60. Deane parish register; *Letters* No. 17.
61. *CP James* 33, 39, 41, 83: 'April 1805 To Mary', 'To Mary on her Wedding Day, Jany. 17th, 1812'. 'Lines written at Kintbury, May 1812', 'The Autumn Walk, to Mary, Jany. 16th, 1816'.
62. *JAOC* 169.

63. E.g., *Letters* Nos. 10, 18, 30, 31, 49, 53, 65, 89, 159.
64. FCL Family History.
65. Le Faye, 'Anna Lefroy's Original Memories of JA'; *Memoir* 157.
66. FCL Family History.
67. *Letters* No. 11; Vick, 'Mr Austen's Carriage'.
68. Mr Austen's account at Hoare's Bank; Corley, 'Revd George Austen's Bank Account'.
69. *Letters* No. 12.
70. *Letters* No. 10.
71. *The Lady's Monthly Museum*, vol. 2 (1799), 21–4.
72. *Letters* No. 16.
73. *Letters* No. 18.
74. *Letters* Nos. 17, 18.
75. Mrs Chute's diary for 1799 (23M93/70/1/7).
76. *Letters* No. 19.
77. *Letters* Nos. 20, 21, 22.
78. *Letters* Nos. 20, 21.
79. *Letters* Nos. 20, 21.
80. *Letters* Nos. 21, 22; see also Egerton 152, No. 111.
81. Bath City Rate Book for quarter ending March 1799 shows Mr Leigh-Perrot's name now at this address.
82. *Letters* No. 22; Gilson 436–45, K2, K4, K10, K18.
83. *Letters* No. 17.
84. *Letters* No. 21.
85. *Letters* Nos. 21.
86. *Letters* No. 18.
87. Climenson 330.
88. *CPVA* 29–30, 92–5; but see also Le Faye, 'The Ball at Basingstoke'.
89. Bigg-Wither 52. Mr Lovelace Bigg and his son had added Wither to their name upon inheriting that family's property in 1789, but his daughters did not do likewise. See also *Victoria Country History of Hampshire* IV, 239–40, for description of the parish of Wootton St Lawrence and Manydown House (demolished in 1960s).
90. *Letters* Nos. 23, 25.
91. Bigg-Wither 56–8.
92. Mrs Chute's diary for 1799 (23M93/70/1/7).

9 THE LEIGH-PERROTS AND BATH, 1799–1801

1. Edgeworth I 143–4.
2. Vick, 'A Strikingly Elegant Pilgrim'.
3. Mrs Leigh-Perrot to JEAL, 8 March 1835 (23M93/86/3); part-published *AP* 291–2.
4. *Letters* No. 22.
5. *AP* 184.

6. *AP* 188.
7. *AP* 193–5.
8. *AP* 197–8.
9. Austen-Leigh archive.
10. Austen-Leigh archive.
11. Austen-Leigh archive.
12. Ayres 29.
13. *AP* 205–6.
14. *Letters* No. 59.
15. JEAL to Anna Lefroy, 11 June 1830 (23M93/84/1).
16. *The Lady's Magazine* for April 1800, 176.
17. *AP* 211.
18. *AP* 213–14.
19. *AP* 219.
20. *The Lady's Magazine* for April 1800, 171.
21. See MacKinnon for a complete discussion of the trial.
22. Bramston archive (20M64/21).
23. *Letters* Nos. 24, 27, 32; O'Byrne; *SB* 61–73, 78–86.
24. *Letters* No. 24; O'Byrne; *SB* 48, 91.
25. *Letters* No. 27.
26. *Letters* No. 23.
27. *Letters* No. 27.
28. *Letters* No. 25.
29. *Letters* Nos. 23, 27.
30. *Letters* No. 24.
31. *Letters* No. 27.
32. *Letters* No. 25.
33. *Letters* No. 28.
34. FCL Family History; CMCA to JEAL, 1 April [1869], copy in National Portrait Gallery; *Memoir* 185; *FP* 46.
35. *FP* 46.
36. FCL Family History.
37. *Letters* No. 27.
38. Lefroy MS.
39. *Letters* No. 14; for Revd Charles Powlett, his wife, Anne Temple, and her family, see Bettany, Seccomb, Crawford, also Powlett archive in Hants Record Office, 72M92 and 119A00.
40. *Letters* No. 30.
41. Mrs Charles Powlett to Miss Peters, 20 June 1799 (72M92/18/10).
42. See *E*, chapter XIV.
43. Powlett diary, 119A00/1.
44. *Letters* No. 29.
45. *Letters* No. 31.
46. *Letters* No. 29.
47. *Letters* No. 32.

48. *Letters* No. 29.
49. *Letters* No. 31.
50. *Letters* No. 31.
51. *Letters* No. 29.
52. *Letters* No. 31.
53. *Letters* No. 30.
54. *Letters* No. 30.
55. Caplan, 'JA's Soldier Brother'; *Letters* No. 33.
56. *Letters* No. 34.
57. Steventon register of baptisms and burials, 1750–1812, pp. 34, 38, 39, 40, 41; Deane register of baptisms and burials, 1786–1812, entries late 1800.
58. Gilson 433.
59. Vick, 'The Sale at Steventon'.
60. *Letters* Nos. 35, 36.

10 BATH AND THE WEST COUNTRY, 1801–4

1. *Letters* Nos. 35, 36, 37, 38.
2. *Letters* No. 35.
3. *Letters* No. 38.
4. *Letters* No. 35.
5. *Letters* Nos. 36, 37, 38.
6. *Letters* No. 36.
7. Vick, 'Cousins in Bath'.
8. Stirling 288–94; *Gents Mag* for 1790, 1798, 1799, 1806.
9. *Letters* No. 36.
10. *Letters* No. 38.
11. Davis, M., 'JA in Bath – 4 Sydney Place'.
12. *Letters* No. 30.
13. *Letters* No. 25.
14. Extracts made by Austen-Leighs, early in the twentieth century, from Madam Lefroy's diary for 1801.
15. *JAOC* 160.
16. BL Add.MSS. 42,162.
17. Lefroy MS.
18. This miniature was bequeathed to Anna by CEA in the latter's testamentary letter of 9 May 1843 (MS Ray Colln., Pierpont Morgan), and has descended in a junior branch of the Austen-Leigh family; for a good reproduction see Collins (1993) plate 4.
19. Hickman, 'The JA Family in Silhouette'.
20. *Letters* No. 104.
21. F. C. Lefroy, 'Hunting for Snarkes at Lyme Regis'.
22. Anna Lefroy to JEAL, 8 August [1862] (23M93/86/3).
23. These summer journeyings were recorded in Mary Lloyd's diary for 1802, now lost. At some time early in the twentieth century the Austen-Leighs copied

out this information – see Austen-Leigh, Emma, *JA and Bath* viii, and also *FP* 177–78.

24. Austen-Leigh, Joan, 'New Light Thrown on JA's Refusal of Harris Bigg-Wither'.
25. FCL Family History.
26. Catherine Hubback to JEAL, 1 March 1870, copy in National Portrait Gallery; *Memoir* 191; *FP* 62.
27. BL Add. MSS. 42,162.
28. Bellas MS.
29. *JAOC* 159–60; Le Faye, 'JA and her Hancock Relatives', 12–15.
30. Caplan, 'JA's Banker Brother', 71.
31. PRO, FO.610/1: Passport no. 319 issued to Henry Austen on 28 June 1802, covering himself, his wife and Mrs Marriott for travel to France.
32. BL.Add.MSS. 39,885: Warren Hastings's diary for 13 April 1801–15 February 1804, shows that HTA stayed two nights at Daylesford in April 1803.
33. FCL Family History confirms that Henry and Eliza were accompanied by a lady who could speak only English.
34. *Memoir* 17.
35. Ramsgate Rate Book for 1803 and Poll Book for 1802.
36. Vick, 'Steventon Prepares for War'.
37. Fanny Knight to Miss Chapman, C.103/1; see also *Kentish Gazette* issues during June and July 1804.
38. Lefroy MS.
39. Fanny Knight to Miss Chapman, C.102/6.
40. Brydges II 39–41.
41. Austen-Leighs' notes from Madam Lefroy's diary for 1803.
42. *Letters* No. 57; Austen-Leigh, Richard Arthur, *JA and Lyme Regis* 48; Oldfield 6–7.
43. BL Add MSS. 42,162.
44. Fanny Knight to Miss Chapman, C.103/4.
45. *CPVA* 30.
46. *Letters* No. 39.
47. Birkenhead 56; personal communication, Prof. Peter Davison, 1986; Johnson, R. B. 25.
48. *Letters* p 381; Watson, Winifred, *JA in London* 1–2.
49. Anna Lefroy to JEAL, 8 August 1862 (23M93/86/3); and 20 July [1869] (National Portrait Gallery).
50. Oldfield 6–7.
51. *Letters* No. 39.
52. *Letters* No. 37; *Bath Chronicle* 25 October 1804; Meehan (1901) 202, gives the number of the Green Park Buildings house as 27, on the west side, but this was an error. The Bath City and Poor Rate Books for 1804–5 clearly show the name of Austen at No. 3 on the east side, and this is confirmed in the *Bath Directory* for 1805. See also Vick, 'Austen Variations'.

53. CMCA undated letter to JEAL (23M93/86/3); *FP* 65–6; FCL Family History (with abbreviations and alterations).
54. *Letters* No. 68(D); *NA* xi–xiii.
55. Gilson 82–3; Sadleir 168–71.
56. *Memoir* 59; F. C. Lefroy, 'Is It Just?'; *MW* 314.

11 BATH AND SOUTHAMPTON, 1804–8

1. *CMCA Rems* 6–7; Brydges I 137 and II 39–40.
2. *CPVA* 8–9.
3. Fanny Knight's diary for 1805.
4. *Letters* No. 40.
5. *Letters* No. 41.
6. Mr Austen's ledger-stone has now been placed in the churchyard outside St Swithin's Walcot, with an explanatory plaque.
7. *Letters* No. 42.
8. Mr Austen's Will at PRO – PROB/11/1420.
9. *AP* 234–5.
10. *AP* 235–6.
11. *SB* 152.
12. *CMCA Rems* 7.
13. *Letters* No. 43.
14. *Letters* No. 43.
15. *Letters* No. 44.
16. Le Faye, 'JA Verses'; *CPVA* 20–1.
17. *Letters* No. 52.
18. FCL Family History; JEAL to Anna Lefroy 20 September 1820 (23M93/84/1).
19. Southam, *Grandison* 1–29.
20. *Letters* No. 46.
21. *Letters* No. 57.
22. Martha Lloyd's affidavit *re* her mother's Will was sworn in Worthing on 4 November 1805, and witnessed by Jane Austen and Elizabeth Austen – PROB.11/1435; Austen-Leigh, Emma, *JA and Bath*, ix.
23. Marshall, John, II 278.
24. *SB* 155.
25. Austen-Leigh, Emma, *JA and Bath* ix; Gilson 433.
26. *Letters* No. 49.
27. *CMCA Rems* 16–17; FCL Family History.
28. *CMCA Rems* 18–19; FCL Family History.
29. Austen-Leigh, Emma, *JA and Bath* ix; Le Faye, '"A Persecuted Relation"'; *Letters* Nos. 35, 36, 37, 38.
30. *SB* 169–76; FWA family archive.
31. *AP* 237–8.
32. Austen-Leigh, Richard Arthur, *JA and Southampton* x, 1–3; Patterson 101–18.
33. FWA Memoir.

34. *Letters* No. 55.
35. *CPVA* 5–6; Gilson 'JA's Verses'; Greene, 'New Verses by JA'.
36. Lefroy MS; Le Faye, 'JA Verses'; *Letters* No. 48(C).
37. Repton, 36; see also Batey, 'JA at Stoneleigh Abbey' and 'In Quest of JA's "Mr Repton"'; for Adlestrop village see *Victoria County History of Gloucestershire*, VI, 8, also Cholmondeley.
38. Lefroy MS; Stoneleigh Papers, DR/18/17/32. Under the terms of Mary Leigh's Will, Mrs Austen and Mrs Leigh-Perrot each received a mourning ring, value 10 guineas, and Jane and Cassandra each one, value 5 guineas.
39. *AP* 222–4.
40. Pevsner, *Warwickshire*; Smith, S. C. Kaines, both edns.; *AP* 244–7.
41. Barrett, C., II 116–22.
42. Miss Elizabeth Leigh's journal of her trip to the Lakes in 1802 – Stoneleigh Papers, DR/18/26/6.
43. BL Add. MSS. 42,171 – Mrs Lybbe-Powys's journal of her trip to Staffordshire in 1800.
44. Collins, 'Too Much Zeal for the Bible Society'; Davies, G. J., vii–xx.
45. *Letters* No. 67.
46. *Letters* No. 49; Edward Cooper's letters of 23 August 1806 to Revd Thomas Leigh, and of 26 September 1806 to Mr Hill – Stoneleigh Papers, DR/18/17/32.
47. Austen-Leigh, Richard Arthur, *JA and Southampton* vi.
48. *Letters* No. 49.
49. Le Faye, 'The Business of Mothering'.
50. *Letters* No. 49.
51. *Memoir* 66.
52. Vick, 'A Tourist's view of Southampton'.
53. *Memoir* 66.
54. *Letters* No. 50.
55. *Letters* No. 50.
56. *Letters* No. 51.
57. Birkenhead 56–64; Johnson, R. B. 26; Caplan, 'JA's Banker Brother'.
58. Fanny Knight to Miss Chapman, 6 May 1807, C.106/4.
59. All Saints' parish register, Southampton City Record Office.
60. *CMCA Rems* 26; CJA journal, 29 May 1815, AUS/103.
61. CJA diary and journal, 19 May 1815, AUS/101 and /102.
62. Fanny Knight's diary for 1807 and her letter of 26 April 1807 to Miss Chapman, C.106/3; Climenson 365; BL Add. MSS. 42,162.
63. Fanny Knight to Miss Chapman, 30 August 1807, C.106/7.
64. *Victoria County History of Hampshire*, II, 498–501; Pevsner, *Hampshire*; Hussey, 'Chawton House, Hampshire'; *Chawton Manor*; Le Faye, 'Recollections of Chawton'.
65. *CPVA* 21–3; Gilson, 'JA's Verses'.
66. Le Faye, 'Journey, Waterparties & Plays'.
67. Piggott, 'JA's Southampton Piano'.

12 SOUTHAMPTON AND CHAWTON, 1808–9

1. Austen-Leigh, Richard Arthur, *JA and Southampton* vi.
2. Yonge 92.
3. *CP James* 41, 'Lines written at Kintbury May 1812'.
4. *CMCA Rems* 7–9, 71–3, plate facing 11.
5. Sawtell.
6. *Letters* No. 32; *SB* 210.
7. Tillotson.
8. Austen-Leigh, Richard Arthur, *JA and Southampton* vi.
9. *Letters* No. 52.
10. Le Faye, 'A JA Manuscript', and 'JA and the Kalendar of Flora'.
11. *Letters* No. 52.
12. *CMCA Rems* 19–20.
13. *Letters* Nos. 53, 54.
14. Gilson 434.
15. Simmons 10, 119.
16. *CPVA* 7.
17. *Letters* No. 56.
18. *Memoir* 66.
19. Fanny Knight to Miss Chapman, 24 September 1808, C.108/9.
20. *Letters* No. 56; Hurst 17, 21.
21. *Letters* No. 57.
22. *Letters* No. 61.
23. *Letters* Nos. 58, 59, 60.
24. Fanny Knight to Miss Chapman, 23 November 1808, C.108/13.
25. *Letters* No. 62.
26. *Letters* No. 62.
27. *CPVA* 8–9.
28. *Letters* No. 67.
29. *MW* 453–7.
30. *SB* 209–10; MS in Ray Colln., Pierpont Morgan.
31. Fanny Knight's diary, 20 April 1809, and her letter to Miss Chapman, 6 May 1809, C.107/4.
32. Fanny Knight to Miss Chapman, 17 June 1809, C.107/7.
33. *JAOC* 165–6.
34. *Letters* Nos. 68(D), 68(A).
35. Fanny Knight to Miss Chapman, 17 June 1809, C.107/7.
36. Gilson 83.
37. *MAJA* 19–20.
38. *Letters* No. 142.
39. Vick, 'JA's House at Chawton'.
40. *MAJA* 2–4; *Memoir* 167–8.
41. Lefroy MS.
42. Chawton Estate account book 1808–19 (79M78/MB211).

43. *Report* for December 1943–October 1946; *MAJA* 19.
44. *MAJA* 21.
45. Revd J. R. Papillon to his father, 3 May 1803, U.1015/C.77/25.
46. *Letters* No. 62.
47. *Letters* No. 82.
48. Hurst 12–14.
49. *Letters* No. 91.
50. Hurst 17, 21.
51. FCL Family History.
52. *MAJA* 5; *Memoir* 169.
53. Le Faye, 'Anna Lefroy's Original Memories of JA'; *Memoir* 157–8.
54. *MAJA* 5; *Memoir* 169.
55. Walker 16, No. 3630.
56. *Letters* No. 74.
57. FCL Family History.
58. Le Faye and Black, *The Jane Austen Cookbook*.
59. *MAJA* 7; *Memoir* 171.
60. FCL Family History; *Letters* No. 148.
61. *MAJA* 8–9; *Memoir* 172.
62. *Memoir* 71; *Letters* Nos. 87, 93, 96.
63. *Letters* No. 63.
64. *MAJA* 6–7; *Memoir* 170–1.
65. Le Faye, 'Three Missing JA Songs'.
66. *Memoir* 194; Piggott 151–2.
67. *MAJA* 7–8; *Memoir* 171–2.
68. *Memoir* 70.

13 FIRST PUBLICATION, 1809–12

1. *MAJA* 6; *Memoir* 170.
2. *Letters* No. 69.
3. Brabourne II 364–6.
4. FCL Family History.
5. Lefroy MS.
6. Le Faye, 'Anna Lefroy's Original Memories of JA'; *Memoir* 158.
7. *S&S* 246.
8. Fanny Knight's diaries for 1809 and 1810; Mary Lloyd's diary for 1810; FCL Family History.
9. Mary Lloyd's diary shows that Anna was at Chawton Cottage from 5 May to 14 July 1810.
10. *Letters* No. 90.
11. *CPVA* 12–13; *Memoir* 75.
12. *Memoir* 75.
13. Mary Lloyd's diary for 1810.
14. *Memoir* 194.
15. *Letters* Nos. 53, 64, 79.

16. *MAJA* 10–11; *Memoir* 174–5.
17. *CMCA Rems* 24–5.
18. *SB* 212–6.
19. Le Faye, 'News from Chawton', 366.
20. *S&S* xiv.
21. *NA* 6; *Memoir* 140.
22. *Memoir* 140.
23. *Letters* No. 70; von Erffa and Staley 142–5, 346–50.
24. *Letters* No. 71.
25. *Letters* No. 71.
26. *Letters* No. 70.
27. *Letters* No. 71.
28. Phillips, Richard 218–22; Granville II 444–5 note; Baring-Gould 1–25; Williamson, Lyttelton and Simeon 256–8; Wright 93–4, 107, 241–2; *JAOC* 168–9.
29. *Letters* No. 72.
30. Le Faye, 'JA's Laggard Suitor'.
31. *Letters* Nos. 73, 74, 75.
32. *JAOC* 169–70.
33. *CMCA Rems* 26.
34. *AP* 250–3.
35. *CPVA* 15–16.
36. Gilson 6–12.
37. Aspinall 26 and note.
38. Mary Lloyd's diary for 1811; Gilson 9; *CPVA* 50.
39. Southam, *Critical Heritage* I, 35–40.
40. *NA* 6; *Memoir* 140.
41. *MW* plate facing 242; *JALM* 53.
42. Gilson 24.
43. *P&P* 408.
44. *CMCA Rems* 26; Mary Lloyd's diary for 1812.
45. Le Faye, 'Anna Lefroy's Original Memories of JA'; *Memoir* 159.
46. *MAJA* 8; *Memoir* 172.
47. Le Faye, 'Anna Lefroy's Original Memories of JA'; *Memoir* 159.
48. FCL Family History.
49. Le Faye, 'JA and Mrs Hunter's Novel', and 'Anna Lefroy's Original Memories of JA'; *Memoir* 159–60; *Letters* No. 76(C); Mary Lloyd's diary for 1812.
50. Le Faye, 'JA's Laggard Suitor'.
51. *Letters* No. 77.

14 PRIDE AND PREJUDICE, 1813

1. Gilson 23–5.
2. *Letters* No. 79.
3. *Letters* No. 80.
4. *Letters* No. 81.

5. Southam, *Critical Heritage* I, 41–7; Joukovsky.
6. BL Add. MSS. 41,253, f.17.
7. HTA's revised version of his 'Biographical Notice', dated 5 October 1832, and re-titled 'Memoir of Miss Austen', prepared for Bentley's new edition of *S&S* in 1833, viii; *Memoir* 149; Gilson 212–14.
8. Gilson 25–7.
9. Gilson 34–6.
10. *MW* plate facing 242; *JALM* 53.
11. *Letters* No. 78.
12. *Letters* No. 79.
13. *Letters* No. 82.
14. *FP* 84, 131.
15. Le Faye, 'The Business of Mothering', 296–8.
16. Lefroy MS; *CPVA* 13–14.
17. Le Faye, 'Recollections of Chawton'.
18. *JAOC* 170.
19. *Letters* No. 82.
20. *JAOC* 116.
21. Le Faye, 'JA and her Hancock Relatives', 12; *JAOC* 171–2.
22. *Letters* No. 84.
23. *Letters* No. 85. Several researchers, including the present writer, have tried to identify this picture; the catalogue of the exhibition shows 250 works, from which it is possible to narrow the field to four candidates. Of these the likeliest seems to be 'Portrait of a Lady' by Huet-Villiers (No. 27); the other possibilities are three miniatures by C. J. Robertson of Lady Nelthorpe and her sisters-in-law Lady Anderson and Mrs Clarke of Welton [not Weston] Place (Nos. 15, 116 and 246). The present ownership and location of these four pictures is unknown. See Rainbolt; and also Le Faye, *JA, the World of Her Novels*, 202.
24. *Letters* No. 85.
25. *Letters* No. 86.
26. *Aspects* 149–51; *CPVA* 61.
27. *Letters* No. 109.
28. *NA* 7; *Memoir* 140.
29. Hill 202.
30. Jenkins, 'Some Notes on Background', 26.
31. *Letters* No. 82.
32. *Letters* No. 86.
33. FCL Family History.
34. *Letters* No. 90.
35. *Letters* No. 87.
36. *Letters* No. 90.
37. Hill 202.
38. Jenkins, 'Some Notes on Background', 26.
39. *Letters* No. 92.
40. Hickman, 'JA Family in Silhouette' and *Two Centuries of Silhouettes* 65–9.

41. *Letters* No. 94.
42. *Letters* No. 90.
43. *Letters* No. 95.
44. L'Estrange I 241.
45. Jarvis, 'JA and the Countess of Morley'.
46. *Letters* No. 96; see also Benger.
47. *Letters* No. 96.
48. *Letters* No. 95.
49. HTA's 'Memoir of Miss Austen', ix; Gilson 214; *Memoir* 149–50. The 'nobleman' may perhaps have been the 1st Earl of Dudley.
50. *MW* 433.

15 MANSFIELD PARK AND EMMA, 1814–15

1. *Memoir* 119; *MW* plate facing 242; *JALM* 53.
2. *Memoir* 81–2.
3. *MAJA* 9; *Memoir* 173.
4. *Letters* No. 97.
5. *Letters* Nos. 97, 98, 99.
6. *Letters* No. 100.
7. *Letters* Nos. 98, 99.
8. Gilson 49.
9. *MW* 431–5.
10. Grant, J. P. II 84.
11. Gilson 49–50.
12. Fanny Palmer Austen to her sister Mrs Esten, 8 March 1814.
13. *Letters* No. 101.
14. *Letters* No. 102; Colson 67–9.
15. *Letters* No. 101; *MW* 432.
16. 'The Original of "Highbury"', in *Reports* II 60.
17. *Letters* No. 103.
18. *Letters* No. 104; see also Le Faye, 'Another Book Owned by Mr Austen'.
19. *Letters* No. 107.
20. *Letters* No. 108.
21. *Letters* No. 113.
22. FCL Family History.
23. L'Estrange I 11–12.
24. *Letters* No. 105.
25. *Letters* No. 105; *MW* 105.
26. *Letters* No. 106.
27. *Letters* No. 106; von Erffa and Staley 142–5, 358–61.
28. *Letters* No. 105.
29. *Letters* No. 102.
30. *Letters* Nos. 105, 106.
31. *Letters* No. 106.

32. Memorial inscription in St John the Baptist, Kentish Town, London NW5.
33. Miss Elizabeth Leigh's journal, 20 September 1814.
34. Fanny Knight's diary, 8 September 1814.
35. *CMCA Rems* 39.
36. *Letters* No. 98.
37. Diary of Revd Edmund Yalden White; *Reports* 1 6; *CMCA Rems* 38, with a figure of £30,000.
38. FCL Family History.
39. *CMCA Rems* 39.
40. FCL Family History.
41. *CMCA Rems* 40.
42. The Hendon Poor Rate Book for 1814–28 shows C. E. Lefroy inhabiting Heriot House in Brent Street, the 'South End' of Hendon, from May 1814 to February 1819.
43. Le Faye, 'Anna Lefroy and her Austen Family Letters'; *CPVA* 34.
44. *Letters* No. 109.
45. *Letters* No. 114.
46. Chapman, *Critical Bibliography* 43; Gilson 50.
47. Gilson 59; *MP* 549.
48. *Letters* No. 114.
49. *Pedigree* 4, 9–10.
50. Le Faye, 'Anna Lefroy and her Austen Family Letters'.
51. L'Estrange 1 300.
52. L'Estrange 1 305; *Memoir* 133–4; Watson, Vera, 119–20.
53. The house belonged to Revd Dr Philip Williams, see Crook 167. Clanchy gives the address as No. 9 The Close, but this is due to confusion with another cleric, Dr *David* Williams, as Crook makes clear. No. 12 still exists, but was renumbered No. 11 later in the nineteenth century, when the original No. 11 was demolished.
54. Mary Lloyd's diary for 1815; Le Faye, 'Anna Lefroy and her Austen Family Letters'.
55. *Letters* No. 117.
56. *MW* plate facing 242; *JALM* 53.
57. Gilson, 'JA's Verses', 37; Southam, 'Was JA a Bonapartist?'
58. *SB* 270; BL Add. MSS. 41,253, f.19.
59. Le Faye, 'Anna Lefroy and her Austen Family Letters'.
60. Le Faye, 'Anna Lefroy and her Austen Family Letters'.
61. Mary Lloyd's diary for 1815.
62. *MAJA* 5–6, 10–11; *Memoir* 169–70, 174–5.
63. Mary Lloyd's diary for 1815; *MW* plate facing 242; *JALM* 53.
64. Bellas MS.
65. Gilson 66–7.
66. *Letters* No. 120.
67. *Letters* No. 121.
68. Le Faye, 'JA's Laggard Suitor'.

69. *Letters* No. 122(A)(D).
70. Fanny Knight's diary, 23 October 1815; Mary Lloyd's diary 24 and 25 October 1815; FCL Family History.
71. *Letters* No. 124.
72. Gilson 59–60, 66–9.
73. *MAJA* 11; *Memoir* 175.
74. *JAOC* 160–1.
75. Hibbert 88, 96–9.
76. *MAJA* 11–12; *Memoir* 175–6.
77. *MAJA* 12; *Memoir* 176.
78. Steegman 161–2; Watkin 98–126.
79. Egan 194–307.
80. *MAJA* 12; *Memoir* 176.
81. Gilson 66–9, 74; *MAJA* 12; *Memoir* 176; *Letters* Nos. 125(D), 125(A), 126, 127, 128, 129, 130, 131(C), 132(D).
82. *FP* 138–9.
83. *Letters* No. 125(A).
84. *Letters* No. 132(D).
85. *Letters* No. 132(A).
86. *Letters* No. 138(A).
87. *Letters* No. 138(D).
88. *Letters* No. 121.
89. *Letters* No. 127; Watson, Winifred, 'The Austens' London Doctor'.
90. *Letters* No. 127.
91. *Letters* No. 128.
92. Clark-Kennedy 9–11; Stuart 136–8.
93. *Letters* No. 129.
94. *Letters* No. 133.

16 *EMMA* AND *PERSUASION*, 1816–17

1. Gilson 66–9.
2. Gilson 67–9, 71.
3. *MW* 436–9.
4. Pollock, W. H. 90–1.
5. *Letters* No. 135.
6. *MW* 438.
7. FCL Family History.
8. *MW* 436–7.
9. *Letters* Nos. 134(A), 134(D).
10. Jarvis, 'JA and the Countess of Morley'.
11. Gilson 71.
12. Gilson 71.
13. L'Estrange 1 331.
14. Southam, *Critical Heritage* 1 71.

15. Southam, *Critical Heritage* I 72.
16. Southam, *Critical Heritage* I 70.
17. Ward 474–6.
18. Ward 476–7.
19. Ward 469–74.
20. Southam, *Critical Heritage* I 13.
21. Southam, *Critical Heritage* I 13.
22. Southam, *Critical Heritage* I 58–69.
23. *Letters* No. 139.
24. Le Faye, 'JA's Friend Mrs Barrett Identified'.
25. *Letters* No. 90.
26. Le Faye, 'JA's Friend Mrs Barrett Identified'.
27. *Memoir* 106.
28. *Memoir* 106.
29. *NA* 12.
30. O'Byrne.
31. *CMCA Rems* 47.
32. Mary Lloyd's diary for 1816.
33. Corley, 'JA and Her Brother Henry's Bank Failure'; Caplan, 'JA's Banker Brother'.
34. *Letters* No. 86.
35. *CMCA Rems* 47–8.
36. Austen, Jane, *Plan of a Novel* 35; Corley, 'JA and Her Brother Henry's Bank Failure'.
37. *MAJA* 6; *Memoir* 170.
38. *CMCA Rems* 48.
39. *Letters* No. 142; Devert 347; *JAOC* 173.
40. HTA to Bishop of Winchester, 5 November 1816 (Hants RO, 21M65 E1/4/2601); Willis I vi.
41. *JEAL* 28–9.
42. Willis I 139.
43. Austen, Jane, *Plan of a Novel*; *MW* 428–30.
44. *Letters* Nos. 52, 56, 57, 79.
45. Fanny Knight's diary, July–August 1813, and *Letters* No. 89.
46. *MAJA* 13; *Memoir* 177.
47. Cope; see also *Encyclopaedia Britannica* 15th edn., 1973–4.
48. *Guide to Watering-Places* 316–17.
49. Mary Lloyd's diary for 1816.
50. *MAJA* 14; *Memoir* 178.
51. Mary Lloyd's diary for 1816.
52. *Memoir* 125.
53. *Memoir* 125; MS Chapters of *Persuasion*.
54. *MW* plate facing 242; *JALM* 53.
55. *Aspects* 126.
56. *MAJA* 10; *Memoir* 174.

57. *Letters* No. 115.
58. *Letters* No. 123.
59. *Letters* Nos. 143, 154.
60. *Life* 363.
61. *MAJA* 10; *Memoir* 174.
62. *MAJA* 13; *Memoir* 177.
63. *CMCA Rems* 48.
64. *Letters* Nos. 144, 145.
65. *Letters* No. 145.
66. *JEAL* 349–51.
67. *Letters* No. 150(C).
68. *Letters* No. 144.
69. Sabor.
70. *Memoir* 119.
71. *Memoir* 4th edn. 364; Johnson, R. B. 83.
72. *Letters* Nos. 144, 145; Hurst 6.
73. *Letters* No. 145.
74. Mary Lloyd's diary for 1816; *CMCA Rems* 48.
75. *Letters* No. 145.
76. Fanny Knight's diary, 29 June 1816; CJA's diary, AUS/108.
77. *Letters* Nos. 145, 146; Mary Lloyd's diary 16 November 1816.
78. *Letters* No. 146. A small gathering of JEAL's MS of his novel is now in the Hampshire RO (23M93/103/4/2) – possibly even this missing text to which JA refers.
79. *Letters* No. 150(C).
80. *Letters* No. 149.
81. *Letters* No. 148.
82. *Letters* No. 149.
83. Howe 322.
84. *Letters* No. 150(C).
85. Le Faye, '"Sanditon": JA's MS', 58.
86. Marshall, M. G., 'Reminiscences of Aunt Jane', 153; *Memoir* 138.
87. *Letters* No. 155; *Memoir* 127; Southam, *JALM* 101–2.
88. *MW* 363 note 2; *TLS*, 19 February 1925, 120.
89. Brabourne II 129; Wilson, *Almost Another Sister* 55–6, 73.
90. Fanny Knight noted in her diary writing to JA on 27 January 1817.
91. *Letters* No. 151.
92. *Letters* No. 153.
93. *Letters* No. 153.
94. *Letters* No. 155.
95. *NA* 4; *Memoir* 138.
96. Gilson 16–17, 59–60, 69; *Letters* No. 154.
97. *Letters* No. 153.
98. *Letters* No. 155.
99. *Letters* No. 156.

100. Quoted inaccurately in Brabourne II 328 and *Life* 388; MS now in Hants RO (23M93/84/1).
101. Mary Lloyd's diary, 29 October 1812; *Letters* Nos. 81, 86, 123, 140.
102. The Bath Rate Book for the Christmas 1810 quarter shows the Leigh-Perrots at No. 1 Paragon; but Mr Leigh-Perrot was the owner of No. 49 Great Pulteney Street at the time he made his Will on 13 March 1811 – PROB.11/1591, and *AP* 332–3.
103. Mrs Leigh-Perrot to JEAL, 8 March 1835 (23M93/86/3); *AP* 291–2.
104. Mr Leigh-Perrot's Will, PROB.11/1591; *AP* 332–3.
105. *Letters* No. 157.
106. *MAJA* 14–15; *Memoir* 178–9.
107. CJA's diary, 18 and 22 April 1817 (AUS/109); Mary Lloyd's diary 26 April 1817.
108. *Letters* No. 158; Will, PROB 1/78; Spence plates 1–2.
109. *Letters* No. 159.
110. *Letters* Nos. 159, 160.
111. *Letters* No. 161(C).
112. Mary Lloyd's diary; *MAJA* 15–16; *Memoir* 179–80.
113. Mary Lloyd's diary; *MAJA* 16–17; *Memoir* 181–2.
114. *Life* 392–3, and *JEAL* 9–10, with some differences in the text; location of original MS unknown.
115. *MAJA* 17; *Memoir* 182.
116. Le Faye, 'Anna Lefroy and her Austen Family Letters'.
117. CJA's diary, 1817 (AUS/109); *Letters* Nos. 149, 153, 155, 156, 157.
118. CJA's diary, 1817 (AUS/109).
119. *Letters* No. CEA/1.
120. Mary Lloyd's diary; *MAJA* 16; *Memoir* 179–81.
121. Mary Lloyd's diary, 13 July 1817; *MAJA* 17; *Memoir* 182.
122. Austen-Leigh, Joan, 'Great Novel Readers'.
123. *MAJA* 16–17; *Memoir* 181–2.
124. Gilson, 'JA's Verses', 35–6; Le Faye, 'JA's Verses and Lord Stanhope's Disappointment'; *CPVA* 17–18.
125. *Letters* No. CEA/1.

17 BIOGRAPHY, 1817 AND AFTER

1. Le Faye, 'Anna Lefroy and her Austen Family Letters'; FCL Family History.
2. Bellas MS.
3. Le Faye, 'Anna Lefroy and her Austen Family Letters'; FCL Family History.
4. CJA's diary for 1817 (AUS/109).
5. Le Faye, 'Mrs George Austen's Will'.
6. *Letters* No. CEA/1.
7. *JEAL* 129–31.
8. CMCA to JEAL, n.d.?1868–9, copy in National Portrait Gallery; *Memoir* 187.
9. *Letters* No. CEA/3.
10. Brabourne II 332.

11. CEA's testamentary letter of 9 May 1843 (Ray Colln., Pierpont Morgan).
12. *Letters* No. CEA/2.
13. Ticknor 308; *Reports* I 16 and II 174.
14. Tucker, 'JA's Topaz Cross'.
15. *CPVA* 48–50: 'To the memory of his sister Jane Austen, who died at Winchester July 18th 1817, & was buried in that Cathedral'; Tucker 112–14.
16. Chapman papers, Bodley (MSS.Eng.misc.c.925, ff.185–8).
17. Gilson 470–1, M5.
18. Le Faye, 'JA's Verses and Lord Stanhope's Disappointment', 90–1; Gilson, 'JA's Verses', 35–6; *CPVA* 17–18.
19. Fanny Knight to Miss Chapman, 18 August 1817 (C.109/9).
20. Le Faye, 'Anna Lefroy's Original Memories of JA', 419.
21. JA's Will: PRO, PROB.1/78; *AP* 332; 'A JA Document from Somerset House', in *Reports* II 38–9.
22. Gilson 82–5.
23. *NA* 8–9; *Memoir* 142–3.
24. *MW* plate facing 242; *JALM* 53.
25. Southam, *Critical Heritage*, I, 79–84 and 266–8.
26. Gilson 84–6.
27. *CMCA Rems* 38–9; Austen-Leigh, William, and Knight, Montague George, *Chawton Manor* 171.
28. Corder 52.
29. Undated – MS in Rice archive.
30. James Austen to Mrs Leigh-Perrot, 7 April 1819 (23M93/51/2); *CMCA Rems* 1.
31. CMCA to JEAL, 4 May 1819 (23M93/86/3).
32. *Letters* No. 87.
33. *CMCA Rems* 50–6.
34. Lefroy MS.
35. Jarvis, 'JA's Clerical Connections'.
36. *CMCA Rems* 48.
37. *CMCA Rems* 57.
38. *CMCA Rems* 2.
39. Mary Lloyd to Anna Lefroy, 9 July 1829 (23M93/84/1).
40. Edward Rice to his wife, 5 September 1819 – MS Rice archive.
41. *Letters* No. 78.
42. Devert 347–8; *JAOC* 173.
43. Jarvis, 'JA's Clerical Connections'; Midgley, 'The Revd Henry and Mrs Eleanor Austen'; Wilson, M., 'JA's Family and Tonbridge', 48.
44. Le Faye, 'Anna Lefroy and her Austen Family Letters'; FCL Family History; *JEAL* 12.
45. Le Faye, 'Anna Lefroy and her Austen Family Letters'; FCL Family History.
46. JEAL to CMCA, 28 May 1865 (23M93/66/2).
47. James Austen to JEAL, 30 November 1818 (23M93/86/3).
48. Anna Lefroy to JEAL, 26 October 1818 (23M93/86/3).

49. FCL Family History.
50. Chapman, 'A JA Collection'.
51. Mrs Leigh-Perrot to JEAL, ? 12 February 1831 (23M93/86/3).
52. *Memoir* 17–18.
53. Lefroy MS.
54. Knatchbull-Hugessen 164–6.
55. Brabourne II 118.
56. *SB*, additional notes for unpublished 2nd edition – Jane Austen's House, Chawton.
57. *Memoir* 15.
58. Le Faye, 'Mrs George Austen's Will'.
59. *Letters* No. CEA/1.
60. *Letters* No. CEA/3.
61. *MW* 453–7.
62. Muir 203; Chapman, 'JA's Text'; *P* 30.
63. BL Add.MSS. 41,253, f.17.
64. Le Faye, 'The Nephew Who Missed JA'; 'JA's Nephew, a Re-Identification'.
65. Hill 258; Lefroy, F. C. 'Is It Just?', 282.
66. See chapter 10.
67. *FP* 63–8.
68. *FP* 67.
69. *SB* vii–viii.
70. Le Faye, '"Sanditon": JA's MS', 58–60.
71. Hopkinson, 233–5.
72. BL.Add.MSS 46,611, f.305; Gilson 211, 214; Le Faye, 'JA – New Biographical Comments'.
73. Gilson 482–3.
74. Le Faye, 'Anna Lefroy and her Austen Family Letters'.
75. PROB.11/2015; *Reports* II 103–6 and III 179–81.
76. Le Faye, '"Sanditon": JA's MS', 71; MS now Ray Colln., Pierpont Morgan.
77. *MAJA* 10; *Memoir* 174.
78. E.g., those missing during the winter of 1798–9 while Jane was nursing Mrs Austen; Jane's joke about an assignation with Mr Evelyn, missing between Nos. 37 and 38; and her criticism of Edward's sons, missing between Nos. 90 and 91.
79. Brabourne I x–xi.
80. *Letters* – see Notes, pp. 353–469, for provenance of individual MSS.
81. CEA to CJA, 9 May 1843 – MS now Ray Colln., Pierpont Morgan; see also Le Faye, '"Sanditon": JA's MS', 56.
82. *JEAL* 164.
83. CEA's Will, PROB.11/2015.
84. Sabor, 'James Edward Austen, Anna Lefroy and the Interpolations to JA's "Volume the Third"'.
85. *Memoir* 226; the desk descended in a junior branch of the Austen-Leigh family until it was presented to the British Library in 2000.

86. Chapman, 'A JA Collection'.
87. Austen-Leigh, William, and Knight, Montague George, *Chawton Manor* 171; *Memoir* 67–8, 168; *Reports* 1 ix, 22–3, 25 and 32.
88. Bellas MS; *AP* 284.
89. Gilson 454–6, 481; Le Faye, '"Sanditon": JA's MS'.
90. Bellas MS.
91. *CMCA Rems* 2–3.
92. *JEAL* 27–8.
93. *JEAL* 31.
94. Tillotson.
95. Beale 235; *Letters* No. 83.
96. *Letters* No. 26.
97. Howe 321–2; *AP* 296–320; 23M93/63/1.
98. Howe 326; *AP* 303; 23M93/63/1.
99. Brabourne 1 79–80.
100. Jenkins, 'Some Notes on Background', 26.
101. Brabourne 1 xi.
102. Richardson, Lady 299.
103. *Memoir* 91.
104. *Memoir* 10.
105. Le Faye, 'Anna Lefroy's Original Memories of JA'.
106. *MAJA*; *Memoir* 163–82.
107. CMCA to JEAL, 1 April [?1868 or 1869]; *FP* 140–4; *Memoir* 186–7.
108. *MAJA* 9–10; *Memoir* 173–4.
109. CMCA to JEAL, 1 April [?1868 or 1869], copy in National Portrait Gallery; *FP* 140–4; *Memoir* 185–6.
110. CMCA to JEAL, 'Wednesday Evg.' [?1868 or 1869], copy in National Portrait Gallery; *FP* 62, 66; *Memoir* 187–8.
111. CMCA to JEAL, 1 April [?1868 or 1869], copy in National Portrait Gallery; *FP* 57–8; *Memoir* 186, 188.
112. Le Faye, 'Tom Lefroy and JA'.
113. T. E. P. Lefroy to JEAL, 16 August 1870, copy in National Portrait Gallery; *FP* 58.
114. *Memoir* 28–9, 48.
115. Anna Lefroy to JEAL, 20 May [?1869], copy in National Portrait Gallery; *FP* 141; *Memoir* 184.
116. *Memoir* 184.
117. Johnson, R. B., vii.
118. Howe; *AP* 296–304.
119. Lizzy Rice to JEAL, 22 July [1870], copy in National Portrait Gallery; *FP* 140.
120. Le Faye, 'Fanny Knight's Diaries', 38–9; *Memoir* xxiv.
121. Anna Lefroy to JEAL, 20 July [1869] – National Portrait Gallery. Cassandra Esten subsequently gave this back view drawing to Anna, and it is tipped into the Lefroy MS.

122. HTA, 'Memoir of Miss Austen', xi note; *Memoir* 151; Le Faye, 'JA – New Biographical Comments'.
123. *JEAL* 264; Walker 16, No. 3630.
124. Anna Lefroy to JEAL, 20 July [1869] – National Portrait Gallery.
125. Lefroy MS.
126. *JEAL* 264; Gilson 493–4.
127. Cassandra Esten Austen to JEAL, 18 December 1869 – National Portrait Gallery.
128. CMCA to JEAL, undated, December 1869/January 1870, copy in National Portrait Gallery; *Memoir* 192.
129. Lizzy Rice to JEAL, 10 January 1870 – National Portrait Gallery.
130. CMCA to Mrs JEAL, 'Thursday' [20 or 27 January, 1870] (23M93/87/3).
131. Le Faye, 'Recollections of Chawton'.
132. Revd F. W. Fowle to CMCA, 9 January 1870, copy in National Portrait Gallery; *Memoir* 194.
133. CMCA to Mrs JEAL, 'Thursday' [20 or 27 January, 1870] (23M93/87/3).
134. *Memoir* (4th edn.) 364; *Memoir* 3, 59, 226.
135. Le Faye, '"Sanditon" – JA's MS'.
136. Le Faye, 'JA's Verses and Lord Stanhope's Disappointment'.
137. Gilson 495.
138. Gilson, 397–8; Le Faye, 'Lord Brabourne's Edition of JA's Letters'.
139. Le Faye, 'Fanny Knight'; 'Fanny Knight's Diaries'.
140. Chapman, 'A JA Collection'.

Bibliography

UNPUBLISHED SOURCES

MS material is in the Austen-Leigh archive unless otherwise stated; the bulk of this archive is now deposited in the Hampshire Record Office, Winchester (23M93). Some modern copies of manuscripts now lost are in the archives of the National Portrait Gallery, London (NPG).

Alton Poor Rate Books: Hampshire Record Office (PO.15).

Austen, Charles John. Diaries and journals, 1815–17: National Maritime Museum, Greenwich (AUS/101-/109).

Austen, Mrs Charles John (Fanny Palmer). Letters 1810–14: Gordon N. Ray Collection, The Pierpont Morgan Library, New York (MA 4500).

Austen, Francis William. Letterbooks, 1801–14: National Maritime Museum, Greenwich (AUS/7-/9).

   Memoir, and MS extracts therefrom: FWA family archive.

Austen, Mrs James (Mary Lloyd). Diaries for 1810–17: Hampshire Record Office.

Bath Rate Books, 1766–1812: Guildhall, Bath.

Beachcroft deposit, Bodleian Library, Oxford; modern copies of some Leigh family papers: dep. c. 570–4.

Bellas, Mrs Louisa Langlois. Octavo volume compiled 1872, containing copies of letters to and from her mother Mrs Anna Lefroy, and other miscellanea: Lefroy family archive. Cited as 'Bellas MS'.

Bishops' Transcripts of Tonbridge Parish Registers: Centre for Kentish Studies, Maidstone (DRb/RT1/371/2).

Bramston family archive: Hampshire Record Office (20M64).

Butler-Harrison family history: Southampton City Record Office (D/Z/676/1).

Chapman, R. W. Miscellaneous papers, Bodleian (MSS.Eng. lett. c. 759–61 and 924–5).

Chute, Mrs William John (née Elizabeth Smith) of The Vyne. Diaries for 1790, 1792–4, 1797–1800, 1802, 1804, 1807, 1813, 1815–17: Hampshire Record Office.

Clergy Institution Books: Public Record Office, London (E.331).

Clerus List: Oxfordshire Record Office.

Corder, Joan. 'Akin to Jane'. MS family genealogy, compiled 1953: Jane Austen's House, Chawton.

Hancock, Tysoe Saul. Letterbook, British Library Add.MSS.29,236. Part-published in *Austen Papers*; extracts in *JAOC*. Cited as 'TSH Letterbook'.

Hastings, Warren. Hastings Papers, British Library. Volumes consulted fall within the range Add.MSS. 29,125–41,608.

Heathcote family archive: Hampshire Record Office (63M84).

Hendon Poor Rate Books: London Borough of Barnet (PAH/3/16).

Hoare's Bank, London. Ledgers 1765 onwards, containing accounts of several members of the Austen family.

Hubback, Mrs John (Catherine-Anne Austen). Family history notes: Jane Austen's House, Chawton. Cited as 'Hubback MS'.

Jervoise family archive: Hampshire Record Office (44M69).

Knatchbull, Lady (Fanny Knight). Diaries, 1804–72: Centre for Kentish Studies, Maidstone, Kent (U951 F24/1-69).
   Letters to Miss Chapman: Centre for Kentish Studies (U951 C. 102–109).

Knight family archive: Hampshire Record Office (18M61, 39M89, and 79M78): Chawton Estate Account Book, 1808–19 (79M78MB211).

Lefroy, Mrs Anna. Quarto volume of notes on family history, compiled *c.* 1855–72; great-grandsons of Admiral Sir Francis Austen. Cited as 'Lefroy MS'.

Lefroy, Fanny-Caroline. Family history, written *c.* 1880–5. Cited as 'FCL Family History'. Hampshire Record Office (23M93/85/2).

Leigh, Elizabeth. Journal for 1811–15: Jane Austen's House, Chawton.

Leigh, Mary. 'History of the Leigh Family of Adlestrop, Glos.' (1788): modern copy in Beachcroft deposit, Bodleian.

Lybbe-Powys, Mrs Philip. Diaries and journals, 1757–1808: British Library Add.MSS. 42,160–73.

Papillon family archive: Centre for Kentish Studies (U.1015).

Powlett, Revd Charles, and wife. Letters and journals, 1785–1820: Hampshire Record Office (72M92 and 119A00).

Poyntz, William. Diary of Kempshot Hunt, 1791–3: Royal Library, Windsor.

Pym-Hales, Caroline. Diaries for 1788, 1789, 1791, 1792, 1799, 1800: Jane Austen's House, Chawton.

Ramsgate Rate Books and Poll Books: Ramsgate Reference Library.

Gordon N. Ray Collection, The Pierpont Morgan Library, New York. Various letters to and from members of the Austen family (MA 4500).

Rice family archive: H. J. B. Rice, Esq.

Ring, John, of Basingstoke. Account books, 1785–96: Hampshire Record Office (8M62/14 and /15).

Stoneleigh papers: Shakespeare Birthplace Trust, Stratford-on-Avon (DR/18/).

Terry, Stephen, of Dummer. Journals: Hampshire Record Office (24M49).

Walter, Mrs James (Frances-Maria Walter). Reminiscences, 1809; original MS lost; typescript copy made therefrom early twentieth century in Lincolnshire Record Office; MS copy of typescript made by Dr F. Henthorn. Cited as 'Walter MS'.

White, Revd Edmund Yalden. Diary, 1816–56: Gilbert White Museum, Selborne.

Wills, Administrations, etc. Public Record Office, London.

Winchester Ordinands' Papers, 1734–1827: Hampshire Record Office.
Yalden, Revd Richard. Diary, 1760–83: Hampshire Record Office (33M66PI7).

PUBLISHED SOURCES

'Æsop'. *Sporting Reminiscences in Hampshire, 1745–1862*. London, 1864.
Altick, R. D. *The Shows of London*. London, 1978.
The American War of Independence 1775–83. (Catalogue of exhibition at British Library). London, 1975.
A List of the Officers of the Army, 1784–93. London.
Annual Army List, 1794–1816. London.
The Monthly Army List, 1798–1817. London.
Arrowsmith, R. L., ed. *Charterhouse Register, 1789–1872*. Godalming, 1964.
Ashton, G., and Mackintosh, I. *The Georgian Playhouse*. (Catalogue of exhibition at the Hayward Gallery). London, 1975.
Aspinall, A., ed. *Letters of the Princess Charlotte 1811–1817*. London, 1949.
Austen, Brian. *English Provincial Posts, 1633–1840*. Chichester, 1978.
    Tunbridge Ware. Cippenham, Berks, 1992.
Austen, Caroline Mary Craven. *My Aunt Jane Austen*. Chawton, 1952, reprinted 1991.
    Reminiscences. Intro. and ed. Deirdre Le Faye. Chawton, 1986.
Austen, James. *The Loiterer*. Oxford, 1789–90.
    The Complete Poems of James Austen: Jane Austen's Eldest Brother. Ed. with intro. and notes David Selwyn. Chawton, 2003.
Austen, Jane. *Sense and Sensibility*. Ed. R. W. Chapman, 3rd edn, Oxford, reprinted 1967.
    Pride and Prejudice. Ed. R. W. Chapman, 3rd edn, Oxford, reprinted 1967.
    Mansfield Park. Ed. R. W. Chapman, 3rd edn, Oxford, reprinted 1966.
    Emma. Ed. R. W. Chapman, 3rd edn, Oxford, reprinted 1966.
    Northanger Abbey and *Persuasion*. Ed. R. W. Chapman, 3rd edn, Oxford, reprinted 1965.
    Minor Works. Ed. R. W. Chapman, rev. edn, Oxford, 1963.
    Volume the First. Ed. R. W. Chapman. Oxford, 1933.
    Volume the Second. Ed. B. C. Southam. Oxford, 1963.
    Volume the Third. Ed. R. W. Chapman. Oxford, 1951.
    Lady Susan. Ed. R. W. Chapman. Oxford, 1925, reprinted London, 1984.
    Fragment of a Novel [Sanditon]. Oxford, 1925.
    Plan of a Novel. Ed. R. W. Chapman. Oxford, 1926.
    The MS Chapters of Persuasion. Ed. R. W. Chapman. Oxford, 1926, reprinted London, 1985.
    The MS of Sanditon. Ed. B. C. Southam. Oxford and London, 1975.
    The Watsons. Ed. R. W. Chapman. Oxford, 1927, reprinted London, 1985.
    The History of England, ed. Jan Fergus and others. Edmonton, 1995.
Jane Austen and Her Family. *Charades, written a hundred years ago*. London, 1895.

Austen-Leigh, Emma. *Jane Austen and Steventon*. London, 1937.
　Jane Austen and Bath. London, 1939.
Austen-Leigh, James Edward. *Recollections of the Early Days of the Vine Hunt*. London, 1865.
　A Memoir of Jane Austen. London, 1870; 4th edn, London, 1879.
　A Memoir of Jane Austen, and Other Family Recollections. Ed. Kathryn Sutherland. Oxford, 2002. This new and revised edition includes Henry Austen's two biographical essays, Caroline Austen's *My Aunt Jane Austen*, and Anna Lefroy's 'Recollections of Aunt Jane', and is the edition referred to here in footnotes.
Austen-Leigh, Joan [Mrs Denis Mason Hurley]. 'Jane Austen's Housewife', in *Country Life*, 28 October 1982, 1323.
　'New Light Thrown on JA's Refusal of Harris Bigg-Wither', in *Persuasions*, No. 8 (1986), 34–6.
　'Great Novel Readers', in *Reports* IV (1986–95), 247–9.
Austen-Leigh, Mary Augusta. *James Edward Austen-Leigh*, a memoir by his daughter. Privately printed, 1911.
　Personal Aspects of Jane Austen. London, 1920.
Austen-Leigh, Richard Arthur. *Pedigree of Austen, of Horsmonden, Broadford, Grovehurst, Kippington, Capel Manor, etc.* Privately printed, London, 1940.
　Austen Papers, 1704–1856. Privately printed, London, 1942.
　Jane Austen and Lyme Regis. London, 1946.
　Jane Austen and Southampton. London, 1949.
Austen-Leigh, William, and Knight, Montague George. *Chawton Manor and its Owners*. London, 1911.
Austen-Leigh, William, and Austen-Leigh, Richard Arthur. *Jane Austen, her Life and Letters, a Family Record*. London, 1913.
Ayres, Jack, ed. *Paupers and Pig Killers – The Diary of William Holland, a Somerset Parson, 1799–1818*. Gloucester, 1984.
Baigent, F. J., and Millard, J. E. *A History of Basingstoke*. Basingstoke, 1889.
Bailey, Brian. *Churchyards of England and Wales*. London, 1987.
Balleine, G. R. *The Tragedy of Philippe d'Auvergne*. Chichester, 1973.
Balston, Thomas, ed. *The Housekeeping Book of Susanna Whatman, 1776–1800*. London, 1956.
Bamford, Francis, ed. *Dear Miss Heber*. London, 1936.
Banking Almanac. London, 1845.
Baring-Gould, S. *Historic Oddities*, first series. London, 1889.
Barrett, Charlotte, ed. *The Diary and Letters of Madame D'Arblay*. London, 1842–6.
Barrett, E. S. *The Heroine*. London, 1909.
Barrett, Philip. 'Philip Williams – the Acceptable Face of Pluralism', in *Winchester Cathedral Record*, No. 57 (1988), 13–26.
Batey, Mavis. 'Jane Austen at Stoneleigh Abbey', in *Country Life*, 30 December 1976, 1974–75.
　'In Quest of Jane Austen's "Mr Repton"', in *Garden History*, vol. 5, No. 1 (Spring 1977), 19–29.
　Jane Austen and the English Landscape. London, 1996.

Bath Chronicle, 1792–1805.

Bax, B. Anthony. *The English Parsonage*. London, 1964.

Beacham, R. *Cheltenham as it was . . .* Nelson, 1981.

Beale, Catherine Hutton, ed. *Reminiscences of a Gentlewoman of the Last Century; Letters of Catherine Hutton*. Birmingham, 1891.

Beaver, Alfred. *Memorials of Old Chelsea*. London, 1892, republished London, 1971.

Bellasis, Margaret. *Honourable Company*. London, 1953.

Bence-Jones, Mark. *Clive of India*. London, 1974.

Benger, Miss. *Memoirs of the late Mrs Elizabeth Hamilton*. London, 1818.

Berkshire Federation of Women's Institutes. *Berkshire Village Book*. Reading, n.d.,?1960s.

The New Berkshire Village Book. Newbury and Reading, 1985.

Bettany, Lewis, ed. *Diaries of William Johnston Temple, 1780–1796*. Oxford, 1929.

Bickerstaffe, Isaac. *The Sultan*. London, 1784.

Bigg-Wither, Revd R. F. *Materials for a History of the Wither Family*. Winchester, 1907.

Bignell, Alan. *The Kent Village Book*. Newbury, 1986.

Birkenhead, Countess of (Sheila Smith). *Peace in Piccadilly*. London, 1959.

Black, Jeremy. *The Grand Tour in the Eighteenth Century*. Stroud, 1992.

Bloomfield, Peter. *Kent and the Napoleonic Wars*. [Kentish Sources X]. Gloucester, 1987.

Blunt, Reginald. *An Illustrated Historical Handbook to the Parish of Chelsea*. London, 1900.

The Boarding School, or, Familiar Conversations between a Governess and Her Pupils. London, 1823.

Bolitho, H., and Peel, D. *The Drummonds of Charing Cross*. London, 1967.

Bowyer, Valerie. *Along the Canal*. Bath, 1985.

Boyle, Revd George David. *Recollections*. London, 1895.

Boyle, John. *In Quest of Hasted*. Chichester, 1984.

Brabourne, Edward, 1st Lord. *Letters of Jane Austen*. 2 vols., London, 1884.

Brade-Birks, Revd S. Graham. *Jane Austen and Godmersham*. Godmersham 1938, reprinted 1984.

Brannon, G. *Views of the Isle of Wight*. 1824, reprinted Wakefield, 1972.

Brett, R. (Viscount Esher). *Ionicus*. London, 1923.

City of Bristol Museum and Art Gallery. *Bristol Scenery 1714–1858*. Bristol, 1977.

The British Theatre. Vol. xxiii, London, 1808.

Broadley, A. M., and Melville, Lewis, eds. *The Beautiful Lady Craven*. London, 1914.

Brode, Anthony. *The Hampshire Village Book*. Newbury, 1980.

Bromhead, H. W. *The Heritage of St Leonard's Parish Church, Streatham*. London, 1932.

Brooke, Iris, and Laver, James. *English Costume of the Eighteenth Century*. London, reprinted 1964.

English Costume of the Nineteenth Century. London, 1929.

Brown, R., and Greer, W. *Fairdays and Tramdays – the Story of Cosham*. Horndean, n.d.,?1983.

Brownlow, Countess (Emma Cust). *The Eve of Victorianism*. London, 1940.

Bryant, Arthur. *The Years of Endurance, 1793–1802*. London, 1942.
   The Years of Victory 1802–1812. London, 1945.
   The Age of Elegance 1812–1822. London, 1975.

Brydges, (Sir) Egerton. *The Autobiography, Times, Opinions and Contemporaries of Sir Egerton Brydges*. London, 1834.

Buck, Anne. *Dress in Eighteenth Century England*. London, 1979.

Bullett, Gerald. *Sydney Smith*. London, 1951.

Burke, John Bernard. *Extinct and Dormant Baronetcies of England*. London, 1838.
   Landed Gentry, London, 1937 and 1952.
   Peerage and Baronetage, London, 1865, 1900, 1917, 1970.

Burn, John S. *A History of Henley-on-Thames*. London, 1861.

Burnett, John. *Plenty and Want: a Social History of Diet in England from 1815 to the Present Day*. London, 1979.

Burns, Robert. *Poems in the Scottish Dialect*. London, 1803.

Bush, Douglas. *Jane Austen*. London, 1978.

Bussby, Canon F. *Jane Austen in Winchester*. Winchester, 1969.

Busteed, H. E. *Echoes from Old Calcutta*. London, 1908.

Butler, Lewis. *Annals of the King's Royal Rifle Corps*. London, 1913–23.

Butterfield, Revd. R. P. *Monastery and Manor, the History of Crondall*. Farnham, 1948.
   Ordained in Powder – the Life and Times of Parson White of Crondall. Farnham, 1966.

Byrde, Penelope. *Jane Austen Fashion*. Ludlow, 1999.

Byrne, Paula. *Jane Austen and the Theatre*. London, 2002.

Byron, Lord. *Collected Poems*. London, 1904.

Cannon, R. *Historical Record of the 86th Regiment of Foot*. London, 1842.

Caplan, Clive. 'Jane Austen's Soldier Brother – the Military Career of Captain Henry Thomas Austen of the Oxfordshire Regiment of Militia, 1793–1801', in *Persuasions*, No. 18 (1996), 122–43.
   'Jane Austen's Banker Brother, Henry Thomas Austen of Austen & Co., 1801–1816', in *Persuasions*, No. 20 (1998), 69–90.

Caplan, Clive, and Breihan, John. 'Jane Austen and the Militia', in *Persuasions*, No. 14 (1992), 16–26.

Carlton House, the Past Glories of George IV's Palace. (Catalogue of exhibition at The Queen's Gallery, Buckingham Palace, 1991.)

Carter, G., Goode, P., and Laurie, K. *Humphrey Repton, Landscape Gardener 1752–1818*. (Catalogue of exhibition at Norwich 1982 and London 1983.)

Cary, John. *Great Roads*. London, 6th edn, 1815.

Chancellor, E. Beresford. *Life in Regency and Early Victorian Times*. London, 1926.

Chapman, R. W. 'A Jane Austen Collection', in *TLS*, 14 January 1926, 27.
   'Jane Austen's Text', in *TLS*, 13 February 1937, 116.

Jane Austen – Facts and Problems. Oxford, 1948, reprinted 1967.

Jane Austen – A Critical Bibliography. Oxford, 2nd edn, 1955.

Charmouth, a Guide Pub. J. Wellman, 1861.

Cholmondeley, Rose Evelyn. *Adlestrop, its Cottages and their Inmates, 1876–77*. Oxford, 1935.

Chorley, Henry, ed. *Letters of Mary Russell Mitford*. London, 1872.

Christian, E. B. V. *A Short History of Solicitors*. London, 1896.

Solicitors, an Outline of their History. London, 1925.

Chute, Chaloner. *A History of The Vyne in Hampshire*. Winchester, 1888.

Clabburn, Pamela. *The National Trust Book of Furnishing Textiles*. London, 1988.

Clanchy, V. A. 'Jane Austen and the Williams Family', in *Hampshire*, Vol. 17, No. 2 (December 1976), 56–8.

Clark, Arthur. *History of Yachting*. London, 1904.

Clark-Kennedy, A. E. *The London: A Study in the Voluntary Hospital System*, vol. 1, *The First Hundred Years, 1740–1840*. London, 1962.

Clarke, Michael. *The Tempting Prospect, a Social History of English Watercolours*. London, 1981.

Clerical Directory. London, 1858.

Clerical Guide. 1st edn, London 1817.

Clew, K. R. *Wessex Waterway: A Guide to the Kennet & Avon Canal*. Bradford-on-Avon, 1978.

Climenson, Mrs Emily J., ed. *Passages from the Diaries of Mrs Philip Lybbe Powys of Hardwick House, Oxon, AD 1756 to 1808*. London, 1899.

Coad, J. *Historic Architecture of HM Naval Base Portsmouth, 1700–1850*. Portsmouth, 1981.

Cobbe, Frances Power. *Life of Frances Power Cobbe, as Told by Herself*. London, 1904.

Cochrane, C. *The Lost Roads of Wessex*. Newton Abbot, 1969.

Cokayne, G. E. *The Complete Peerage*. London, 1887–98, reprinted Gloucester, 1982.

Collins, Irene. *Jane Austen and the Clergy*. London, 1993.

Jane Austen, the Parson's Daughter. London, 1998.

'Too Much Zeal for the Bible Society', in *Report* for 2001, 19–34.

Collyer, Graham. *The Surrey Village Book*. Newbury, 1990.

Colson, Percy. *White's, 1693–1950*. London, 1951.

Compton, William (Marquess of Northampton). *History of the Comptons of Compton Wynyates*. London, 1940.

Cook, Olive. *The English Country House*. London, 1974.

Cooke, Cassandra ('A Lady of Quality'). *Battleridge*. London, 1799.

Cooper, Revd Edward. *Sermons*. 2nd edn, London, 1805–6.

Cooper, J. J. *Some Worthies of Reading*. Reading, 1923.

Cope, Sir Zachary. 'Jane Austen's Last Illness', in *Reports*, 1 (1949–65) 267–72.

Copeland, Edward. '*Persuasion*: The Jane Austen Consumer's Guide', in *Persuasions* 15(1993), 111–23.

Women Writing About Money. Cambridge, 1995.

Copeland, Edward, and McMaster, Juliet, eds. *The Cambridge Companion to Jane Austen*. Cambridge, 1997.

Corley, T. A. B. 'Jane Austen's Schooldays', in *Report* for 1996, 10–20.

'The Revd George Austen's Bank Account', in *Report* for 1996, 21–23.

'Jane Austen and Her Brother Henry's Bank Failure 1815–16', in *Report* for 1998, 12–23.

Corney, A. *Fortifications in Old Portsmouth*. Portsmouth, 1980.

Cornish, F. W., ed. *Extracts from the Letters and Journals of William Johnson Cory*. Oxford, 1897.

Couling, D. *An Isle of Wight Camera, 1856–1914*. Wimborne, 1978.

Course, E. *The Itchen Navigation*. Southampton, 1983.

Cowley, Hannah. *Which Is the Man?* London, 1783.

Crawford, Thomas. 'Boswell's Temple and the Jane Austen World', in *Scottish Literary Journal*, Vol. 10, No. 2 (December 1983), 53–67.

Crawfurd, Gibbs Payne. *Registers of Parish of St Mary, Reading, 1538–1818*. Reading, 1891.

Recollections of St Mary's, Reading, 50 years ago. Reading, 1932.

Cresswell, J., Gower, G., and Holdaway, K. *Streatham – Pictures from the Past*. The Streatham Society, London, 1983.

Crockford's Clerical Directory for 1865, 1868, 1870.

Cronk, A. *A Wealden Rector*. Chichester, 1975.

Crook, John, ed. *The Wainscot Book: The Houses of Winchester Cathedral Close and their Interior Decoration, 1660–1800*. Hampshire Record Office for Hampshire County Council, Winchester, 1984.

Croker, Thomas Crofton. *A Walk from London to Fulham*; revised and enlarged by Beatrice Horne. London, 1896.

Crouch, Marcus. *Kentish Books, Kentish Writers*. Kent County Library, Maidstone, Kent, 1989.

Cunliffe, Barry. *The City of Bath*. Gloucester, 1986.

Cunningham, George. *London*. London, 1927.

Cunnington, P. *Costume of Household Servants*. London, 1974.

Cunnington, P., and Lucas, C. *Costume for Births, Marriages and Deaths*. London, 1972.

Curtis, William. *History of Alton*. Winchester, 1896.

The Town of Alton, With the Adjacent Villages. Winchester, 1906.

Curtis, W. H. *Quaker Doctor and Naturalist*. London, 1961.

Darton, F. J. Harvey. *The Life and Times of Mrs Sherwood, 1775–1851*. London, 1910.

Davies, Revd G. J., ed. *Homilies, Ancient and Modern*. Vol. III, sermons by Revd Edward Cooper, 1770–1835. London, 1883.

Davies, M. *The Story of Tenby*. Tenby, 1979.

Davis, Michael. 'Jane Austen in Bath: 4 Sydney Place', in *Report* for 1997, 28–34.

Davis, Terence. *Tunbridge Wells: the Gentle Aspect*. London, 1976.

Devert, Abbé Michel. 'Le Marais de Gabarret et de Barbotan', in *Bulletin de la Société de Borda*, No. 340 (1970), 330–50.

Devis, Ellin. *Miscellaneous Lessons*. London, 1782.

Introduction to Geography. London, ? 1790.

Dewar, G. A. B. *Life and Sport in Hampshire*. London, 1908.

Dickson, P. G. M. *The Sun Insurance Office, 1710–1960*. London, 1960.

Dodds, M. H. 'More Notes on Jane Austen's Novels', in *Notes and Queries*, No. 178 (1940), 405–7.

Doyle, Sir Francis Hastings. *Reminiscences and Opinions*. London 1886.

Drewett, J. *Surrey*. (Shire County Guide.) Aylesbury, 1985.

Duncan-Jones, C. M. *Miss Mitford and Mr Harness*. London, 1955.

Eason, Helena. *Walking in Bristol*. Weston-super-Mare, 1984.

Edgehill, J. Y. *About Barbados*. London, 1890.

Edgeworth, Richard Lovell, and Maria. *Memoirs of R. L. Edgeworth, Esq*. London, 1820.

Edwards, Z. *Illustrated Lyme Regis*. Bournemouth, 1902.

Egan, Pierce. *Life in London*. London, 1821.

Egerton, Judy. *George Stubbs, 1724–1806*. (Catalogue of exhibition at Tate Gallery) London, 1984.

Eggar, J. Alfred. *Life and Customs in Gilbert White's Country*. London, 1926.

Ellis, A. R., ed. *The Early Diary of Frances Burney, 1768–1778*. London, 1889.

Emden, C. S. 'Oriel Friends of Jane Austen', in *Oriel Record* (1950), 10–14.

von Erffa, Helmut, and Staley, Allen. *The Paintings of Benjamin West*. New Haven and London, 1986.

Ewing, Elizabeth. *History of Children's Costume*. London, 1977.

Dress and Undress – a History of Women's Underwear. London, 1981.

Fairbridge, Dorothea. *Lady Anne Barnard at the Cape of Good Hope, 1797–1802*. Oxford, 1924.

Farrington and Chawton, the Last 100 Years 1900–2000. Farrington and Chawton parishes, 2000.

Faulkner, Thomas. *An Historical and Topographical Description of Chelsea and its Environs*. London, 1829.

Feaveryear, Sir Albert. *The Pound Sterling*. Oxford, 1963.

Feiling, Keith. *Warren Hastings*. London, 1954.

Feltham, John. *The Picture of London*. London, 1818.

A Guide to all the Watering and Sea Bathing Places. London, n.d., post 1817.

Fergus, Jan. *Jane Austen, a Literary Life*. Basingstoke, 1991.

Fielding, Henry. *The Tragedy of Tragedies, or, The Life and Death of Tom Thumb the Great*, ed. J. T. Hillhouse. London, 1918.

Fielding, Sarah. *The Governess, or, the Little Female Academy*. 1768.

ed. Jill E. Grey. *The Governess*, facs. reproduction of 1st edn of 1749, London, 1968.

Fisher, Thomas. *The Kentish Traveller*. 1790.

Fitzgerald, Brian Vesey. *The Domestic Dog*. London, 1957.

Forster, E. M. *Marianne Thornton 1797–1887*. London, 1956.

Fortescue, S. E. D. *The Story of Two Villages*. Great Bookham, 1975.

People and Places, Great and Little Bookham. Great Bookham, 1978.

Foskett, Daphne. *John Smart*. London, 1964.
 Dictionary of British Miniature Painters. London, 1972.
Foster, Joseph. *Alumni Oxonienses 1715–1886*. London, 1887.
Francklin, Thomas. *The Tragedy of Matilda*. London, 1775.
Freeman, Jean. *Jane Austen in Bath*. Jane Austen Society, Chawton, 1969; revised
 edn 2002.
Gadd, David. *Georgian Summer*. Bath, 1971.
Gardiner, Robert, ed. *Fleet Battle and Blockade*. London, 1996.
 The Naval War of 1812. London, 1998.
Garlick, Kenneth. *Sir Thomas Lawrence*. London, 1954.
 Sir Thomas Lawrence. (Catalogue of Royal Academy Exhibition). London, 1961.
Garrick, David. *Dramatic Works*. London, 1909.
Garrick, David, and Fletcher, John. *The Chances*. London, 1773.
Gaunt, William. *Chelsea*. London, 1954.
Gay, John. *Fables*. (First complete edition 1750 – many editions thereafter.)
Gay, Penny. *Jane Austen and the Theatre*. Cambridge, 2002.
Geddes, A. *Portsmouth during the Great French Wars 1770–1800*. Portsmouth, 1970.
Gentleman's Magazine. London.
Gibbs, L. *Sheridan*. London, 1947.
Gibson, J. S. W. *Monumental Inscriptions in Sixty Hampshire Churches*. Basingstoke,
 1958.
Gilbert, C., and Wells-Cole, A. *The Fashionable Fire Place, 1660–1840*. Leeds City
 Art Galleries, 1985.
Gilbert, C., Lomax, J., and Wells-Cole, A. *Country House Floors, 1660–1850*. Leeds
 City Art Galleries, 1987.
Gill, Jennifer. *The Bristol Scene*. Bristol, 1978.
Gilson, David John. *A Bibliography of Jane Austen*. Oxford, 1982; reprinted with
 corrections, Winchester, 1997.
 'Jane Austen's Verses', in *The Book Collector*, Vol. 33, No. 1 (Spring 1984), 25–37.
 'Cassandra Austen's Pictures', in *Reports*, 4 (1986–95), 299–301.
 Jane Austen: Collected Articles and Introductions. Privately printed, 1998.
Girouard, Mark. *Life in the English Country House*. Harmondsworth, 1980.
Glasse, Hannah. *The Art of Cookery made plain and easy*. London, 1747; facs. reprint
 London, 1968.
Gleig, G. R. *Memoirs of the Life of Warren Hastings*. London, 1841.
Goldsmith, Oliver. *History of England*. London, 1771.
Gordon, Lady Lucie. *Letters from the Cape*. London, 1921.
Gore, John. 'Sophia Sentiment: Jane Austen?' in *Reports*, 2 (1966–75), 9–12.
Gotch, J. Alfred. *The English Home from Charles I to George IV*. London, 1919.
The Governess, or, the Boarding School dissected. London, 1785.
The Governess, or, Evening Amusements at a Boarding School. London, 1800.
Grant, Elizabeth. *Memoirs of a Highland Lady*. Ed. Andrew Tod, Edinburgh, 1988.
Grant, G. L. *The Standard Catalogue of Provincial Banks and Banknotes*. London,
 1977.
Grant, John Peter, ed. *Memoir of Mrs Anne Grant of Laggan*. London, 1844.

Granville, Countess, ed. *Private Correspondence of Lord Granville Leveson Gower, 1781 to 1821*. London, 1916.

Greene, Donald. 'New Verses by Jane Austen', in *Nineteenth Century Fiction*, No. 30 (1975–6), 257–60.

Greenwood, C. *Epitome of County History, Vol. 1, Kent*. London, 1838.

Greenwood, Charles. *Walking in Bath*. Weston-super-Mare, 1983.

Grier, Sydney C. 'A Friend of Warren Hastings', in *Blackwood's Edinburgh Magazine*, No. 175 (April 1904), 497–514.

    'A God-Daughter of Warren Hastings', in *Temple Bar*, No. 131 (1905), 562–71.

    The Letters of Warren Hastings to his Wife. London, 1905.

Guest, Montague, and Boulton, William. *Memorials of the Royal Yacht Squadron*. London, 1903.

A Guide to all the Watering and Sea Bathing Places. Ed. John Feltham. London, n.d., post 1817.

Haddon, John. *Bath*. London, 1973.

    Portrait of Bath. London, 1982.

Hagley, Official Guide. 1953.

    A Description of Hagley, Envil, etc. 1800.

Hall, M., and Frankl, E. *The Cotswolds*. Cambridge, 1986.

Haly, Ann, ed. *William Verrall's Cookery Book*. Lewes, 1988.

The London Art of Cookery. Lewes, 1988.

Hamilton, Mrs Elizabeth. *The Cottagers of Glenburnie*. London, 1859.

Hammond, Mabel C. 'A Lady's Letters from Ilchester Gaol', in *Notes & Queries for Somerset and Dorset*, Vol. 18 (1924–5), 1–8, 58–61, 79–81, 99–105, 135–8.

Hammond, Nigel. *The Oxfordshire Village Book*. Newbury, 1983.

The Hampshire Directory. Winchester, 1784.

Hannas, Linda. *The English Jigsaw Puzzle, 1760 to 1890*. London, 1972.

Hardy, Sheila M. *1804 – That Was the Year . . .* Ipswich, 1984.

Hardy, Paul, and Lowndes, William. *Bath: Profile of a City*. Bristol, 1984.

Harper, Charles G. *The Dover Road*. London, 1895.

    The Bath Road. London, 1899.

    The Oxford, Gloucester and Milford Haven Road. London, 1905.

    The Portsmouth Road. London, 1923.

Harris, Stanley. *Old Coaching Days*. London, 1882.

    The Coaching Age. London, 1885.

Harrison, W. *Some Aspects of Tenby's History*. Tenby, 1985.

Hart, Ann. *Engravings of Kent*. London, 1989.

Hart, Revd A. Tindal. *The Eighteenth Century Country Parson*. Shrewsbury, 1955.

    The Country Priest in English History. London, 1959.

    The Curate's Lot. London, 1970.

Hart, Revd A. Tindal, and Carpenter, Revd E. *The Nineteenth Century Country Parson*. Shrewsbury, 1954.

Hasted, Edward. *The History and Topographical Survey of the County of Kent, etc*. Canterbury, 1778–99.

Hawkins, C. W. *The Story of Alton*. Alton, 1973.

Hawkins, C. W., and Brice, M. H. *Alton – a Pictorial Biography*. Newbury, 1983.

Hayley, William. *Poems and Plays*. London, 1785.

Heathcote, E. D. *Account of Families of the Name of Heathcote*. Winchester, 1899.

Henley Archaeological and Historical Group. *A Walk Round Henley-on-Thames*. Henley, 1985.

Henthorn, Frank. *The History of Brigg Grammar School*. Brigg, 1959.

Herold, J. C. *Mistress to an Age*. London, 1959.

Hett, Francis P., ed. *Memoirs of Susan Sibbald, 1783–1812*. London, 1926.

Hewitt, V. H., and Keyworth, J. M. *As Good as Gold – 300 Years of British Bank Note Design*. London, 1987.

Hibbert, Christopher. *George IV, Prince of Wales*. London, 1972.

   George IV, Regent and King, 1811–1830. Newton Abbot, 1975.

   The Grand Tour. London, 1987.

   The French Revolution. Harmondsworth, 1988.

   George III, a Personal History. Harmondsworth, 1998.

Hickman, Peggy. 'The Jane Austen Family in Silhouette', in *Country Life*, 14 December 1961, 1522–23.

   Two Centuries of Silhouettes. London, 1971.

Hicks Beach, Mrs William. *A Cotswold Family: Hicks and Hicks Beach*. London, 1909.

Hill, Constance. *Jane Austen, Her Homes and Her Friends*. London, new edn, 1904.

Hoare, H. P. R. *Hoare's Bank*. London, 1932.

Hobhouse, Thomas. *Kingsweston Hill, a poem*. London, 1787.

Hodge, Jane Aiken. *The Double Life of Jane Austen*. London, 1972.

Hodgson, J. *Southampton Castle*. Horndean, n.d.,?1986.

Holden's Triennial Directory. London, 1811.

Hollingworth, Geoffrey. *The Story of Henley*. Newbury, 1983.

Holt-White, Rashleigh. *Life and Letters of Gilbert White*. London, 1901.

Holyoake, G. 'Jane in Kent', in *Bygone Kent*, Vol. 3, No. 5 (May 1982), 301–8, and Vol. 3, No. 6 (June 1982), 349–56.

Hoole, G., and Jarvis, Revd W. A. W. 'William Walter', in *Reports*, 3 (1976–85), 344–6.

Hope, J. F. R. *A History of Hunting in Hampshire*. Winchester, 1950.

Hopkinson, David. ('Jane Austen and Another'). *The Watsons*. London, 1978.

Howard, Maurice. *The Vyne, Hampshire*. National Trust guidebook, London, 1998.

Howe, M. A. DeWolfe. 'A Jane Austen Letter', in *The Yale Review*, n.s. Vol. 15 (January 1926), Oct. 1925–July 1926, 319–35.

Holme, Thea. *Chelsea*. London, 1972.

Hubback, Edith C. (Mrs Francis Brown). *The Watsons*. London, 1928.

Hubback, J. H. and Edith C. *Jane Austen's Sailor Brothers*. London, 1906.

Hubback, Sir John. *The Parents in Jane Austen's Novels*. London, 1960.

Hubback, Mrs J. *The Younger Sister*. London, 1850.

Hughes, J. *The New Law List*, London, 1798–1802; continued as *Clarke's New Law List*, London, 1809–19.

Hughes, P. *The Isle of Wight*. London, 1967.

Hull, Felix. *Kent*. (Ordnance Survey Historical Guides). London and Southampton, 1988.

Hunt, Violet. 'The Village of Chawton in the Time of Jane Austen', in *Reports*, 4 (1986–95), 101–7.

The History of the Parish of Chawton from 1894. Chawton, 1994.

Hunter, Mrs Rachel. *Letters from Mrs Palmerston*. London, 1803.

Lady Maclairn. London, 1806.

Hurst, Jane. *Jane Austen and Alton, a Walk around Jane Austen's Alton*. Privately printed, Alton, 2001.

Hussey, Christopher. 'Chawton House, Hampshire', in *Country Life*, 2 February 1945, 200–3, and 9 February 1945, 244–7.

'Godmersham Park, Kent', in *Country Life*, 16 February 1945, 288–91; 23 February 1945, 332–5; 2 March 1945, 376–9.

Hyett, W. *A Description of the Watering Places on the South East Coast of Devon*. Exeter, ?1805.

Jackson, Mrs E Nevill. *History of Silhouettes*. London, 1911.

Ancestors in Silhouette. London, 1921.

Jane Austen Society, Chawton, Hampshire. *Collected Reports*, Vol. 1, 1949–65; Vol. 2, 1966–75; Vol. 3, 1976–85; Vol. 4, 1986–95; also individual annual *Reports* for 1996 and continuing.

Jane Austen Society of North America (JASNA). *Persuasions*, 1979 and continuing annually.

Jarvis, Revd W. A. W. 'Some Information about Jane Austen's Clerical Connections', in *Reports*, 3 (1976–85), 11–17.

'Rev. Thomas Bathurst', in *Reports*, 3 (1976–85), 80–2.

'A Note on the Rev. James Austen', in *Reports*, 3 (1976–85), 179–81.

'Jane Austen and the Countess of Morley', in *Reports*, 4 (1986–95), 6–14.

'Jane Austen and the Countess of Morley, a Footnote', in *Reports*, 4 (1986–95), 79.

'These Will Last Us Some Time', in *Reports*, 4 (1986–95), 108–12.

Jenkins, Elizabeth. *Jane Austen: A Biography*. London, 1938, 3rd imp. 1948.

'Some Notes on Background', in *Reports*, 3 (1776–85), 152–68.

Johnson, Joan. *Excellent Cassandra: The Life and Times of the Duchess of Chandos*. Gloucester, 1981.

Princely Chandos: James Brydges 1674–1744. Gloucester, 1984.

Johnson, R. Brimley. *Jane Austen, Her Life, Her Work, Her Family and Her Critics*. London, 1930.

Joukovsky, Nicholas A. 'Another Unnoted Contemporary Review of Jane Austen', in *Nineteenth Century Fiction*, Vol. 29, No. 3 (December 1974), 336–8.

Kaplan, Deborah. 'Henry Austen and John Rawston Papillon', in *Reports*, 4 (1986–95), 60–4.

Jane Austen among Women. Baltimore and London, 1992.

Kaye, Sir J. W., ed. *Autobiography of Miss Cornelia Knight*. London, 1861.

Keith-Lucas, Bryan. 'Francis and Francis Motley Austen, Clerks of the Peace for Kent', in Detsicas, A., and Yates, N., eds., *Studies in Modern Kentish History*, 87–102. Maidstone, Kent, 1983.

    Parish Affairs, the Government of Kent under George III. Kent County Library, Maidstone, Kent, 1986.

Keith-Lucas, Bryan, and Ditchfield, G. M., eds. *A Kentish Parson.* Kent Arts and Libraries, Maidstone, Kent, 1986.

Kemble, Fanny. *Record of a Girlhood.* London, 1878.

    Records of Later Life. London, 1882.

    Further Records. London, 1890.

King, R. G. *Itchen Ferry Village.* Itchen, 1981.

Kitz, Norman and Beryl. *Pains Hill Park.* Cobham, 1984.

Knatchbull, Lady. 'Aunt Jane', in *The Cornhill Magazine* (ed. Peter Quennell), Vol. 163 (1947), 72–3.

Knatchbull-Hugessen, Sir Hughe. *Kentish Family.* London, 1960.

Knipe, H. R. ed. *Tunbridge Wells and Neighbourhood.* Tunbridge Wells, 1916.

Kulisheck, Patricia Jo. 'Steventon Parsonage', in *Persuasions*, No. 7 (1985), 39–40.

The Lady's Magazine, 1796–1808.

The Lady's Monthly Museum, 1798–99.

Landmann, Capt. George. *Adventures and Recollections.* London, 1852.

Lane, Maggie. *Jane Austen's Family, Through Five Generations.* London, 1984.

    Jane Austen and Food, London, 1995.

    'The Very Revd Thomas Powys', in *Reports*, 4 (1986–95), 290–4.

Lascelles, M. M. *Jane Austen and her Art.* Oxford Paperbacks, 1963.

Latter, Mr *Catalogue of the Library at Chevening.* 1865.

Laurie, Lt. Col. G. B. *History of the Royal Irish Rifles.* London, 1914.

LeFanu, W., ed. *Betsy Sheridan's Journal.* London, 1960.

Le Faye, Deirdre 'Jane Austen and her Hancock Relatives', in *RES*, NS Vol. 30, No. 117 (February 1979), 12–27.

    'The Business of Mothering: Two Austenian Dialogues', in *BC* (Autumn 1983), 296–314.

    'The Nephew Who Missed Jane Austen', in *N&Q*, Vol. 31, No. 4 (December 1984), 471–2; see also 'Jane Austen's Nephew, a Re-identification', in *N&Q* 235/4 (NS 37/4) (December 1990), 414–15.

    'Recollections of Chawton', in *TLS*, 3 May 1985, 495.

    'Tom Lefroy and Jane Austen', in *Reports*, 3 (1976–85), 336–8.

    'Fanny Knight', in *TLS*, 16 August 1985, 901.

    'Three Austen Family Letters', in *N&Q*, Vol. 32, No. 3 (September 1985), 329–35.

    'Jane Austen and Mrs Hunter's Novel', in *N&Q*, Vol. 32, No. 3 (September 1985), 335–6.

    'Journey, Waterparties and Plays', in *Reports*, 4 (1986–95), 24–30.

    '"Sanditon": Jane Austen's Manuscript and her Niece's Continuation', in *RES*, NS Vol. 38, No. 149 (February 1987), 56–61.

    'Jane Austen Verses', in *TLS*, 20 February 1987, 185.

'Jane Austen and William Hayley', in *N&Q*, continuous series Vol. 232, No. 1 (March 1987), 25–6.

'News from Chawton: A Letter from Mrs George Austen', in *RES*, NS Vol. 38, No. 151 (August 1987), 364–8.

'Jane Austen: Some Letters Re-Dated', in *N&Q*, continuous series Vol. 232, No. 4 (December 1987), 478–81.

'The Austens and the Littleworths', in *Reports*, 4 (1986–95), 64–70.

'Jane Austen's Verses and Lord Stanhope's Disappointment', in *BC*, Vol. 37, No. 1 (Spring 1988), 86–91.

'Anna Lefroy's Original Memories of Jane Austen', in *RES*, NS Vol. 39, No. 155 (August 1988), 417–21.

Jane Austen, a Family Record. London, 1989, 1993. (Revised and updated version of the Austen-Leighs' *Life and Letters*.)

'To Dwell Together in Unity', in *Reports*, 4 (1986–95), 151–63.

'A Jane Austen Manuscript', in *TLS*, 27 April 1990, 445.

'Jane Austen – More Letters Re-dated', in *N&Q* 236/3 (NS 38/3) (September 1991), 306–8.

'James Austen's Poetical Biography of John Bond', in *Reports*, 4 (1986–95), 243–7.

'Jane Austen – New Biographical Comments', in *N&Q* 237/2 (NS 39/2) (June 1992), 162–3.

'Jane Austen's Letters', in *Persuasions*, No. 14, December 1992 (1993), 76–88.

'James Austen, Army Chaplain', in *Reports*, 4 (1986–95), 338–41.

The Jane Austen Cookbook (with Maggie Black). London, 1995.

'A Literary Portrait Re-examined: Jane Austen and Mary Anne Campion', in *BC* 45/4 (Winter 1996), 508–25.

'Mrs George Austen's Will', in *Report* for 1996, 23.

'The Devonshire Roots of *Sense and Sensibility*', in *Report* for 1996, 32–3.

'The Geographical Settings of *Pride and Prejudice*', in *Report* for 1996, 43.

'Jane Austen and the Rice Portrait', in *TLS*, 20 March 1998, 17.

'"A Persecuted Relation": Mrs Lillingston's Funeral and Jane Austen's Legacy', in *Bath History*, Vol. VII, Bath, 1998.

Jane Austen (The British Library's Writers' Lives series). London, 1998.

'Zincke Miniature Purchased for the Society', in *Report* for 1998, 8–9.

'Silhouettes of the Revd William Knight and His Family', in *Report* for 1998, 10–12.

'Leonora Austen', in *Report* for 1998, 54–7.

'*Northanger Abbey* and Mrs Allen's Maxims', in *N&Q* 244/4 (December 1999), 449–50.

'Jane Austen and the "Kalendar of Flora" – Verses Identified', in *N&Q* 244/4 (December 1999), 450–1.

'Jane Austen's Friend Mrs Barrett Identified', in *N&Q* 244/4 (December 1999), 451–4.

'Three Missing Jane Austen Songs', in *N&Q* 244/4 (December 1999), 454–5.

'Jane Austen's Friends at Canterbury Cathedral', in *Report* for 1999, 9–14.

'Mr Austen's Insurance Policy', in *Report* for 1999, 26.

'Another Book Owned by Mr Austen', in *Report* for 1999, 27–8.

'Which Jane Austen Stitched This Sampler?', in *Report* for 1999, 30–2.

'New Marginalia in Jane Austen's Books', in *BC*, 49/2 (Summer 2000), 222–6.

'Jane Austen's Laggard Suitor', in *N&Q*, 245/3 (NS vol. 47) (September 2000), 301–4.

Fanny Knight's Diaries: Jane Austen through her Niece's Eyes. Chawton, 2000.

'The Lime Tree at Steventon Rectory', in *Report* for 2000, 18–20.

'The Ball at Basingstoke', in *Report* for 2000, 38–40.

'Lord Brabourne's Edition of Jane Austen's Letters', in *RES*, NS Vol. 52, no. 205 (May 2001), 91–102.

Jane Austen's 'Outlandish Cousin': the Life and Letters of Eliza de Feuillide. London, 2002.

Jane Austen, the World of her Novels. London, 2002.

'Anna Lefroy and her Austen Family Letters', in *Princeton University Library Chronicle*, vol. 62/3, Spring 2001 issue (2003).

Le Faye, Deirdre, ed. *Jane Austen's Letters*. Oxford, 1995.

Lefroy, Mrs Anne, ed. C. E. Lefroy. *Carmina Domestica*. London, 1812.

Lefroy, F. C. 'Hunting for Snarkes at Lyme Regis', in *Temple Bar*, Vol. 57 (1879), 391–7.

'Is It Just?', and 'A Bundle of Letters', in *Temple Bar*, Vol. 67 (January–April 1883), 270–84 and 285–8.

Lefroy, Helen. 'Strangers', in *Reports*, 3 (1976–85), 208–13.

'Everyone Here Talks of War', in *Report* for 1998, 23–9.

Lefroy, J. A. P. 'Jane Austen's Irish Friend: Rt. Hon. Thomas Langlois Lefroy, 1776–1869', in *Proceedings of the Huguenot Society of London*, 23(3) (1979), 148–65.

Leigh, Agnes E. 'An Old Family History', in *National Review*, No. 49 (1907), 277–86.

Leonard, A. G. K. *Stories of Southampton Streets*. Southampton, 1984.

L'Estrange, Revd A. G., ed. *A Life of Mary Russell Mitford, Related in a Selection from her Letters to her Friends*. London, 1870.

Letts, Malcolm. *The Old House*. London, 1942.

Levey, Michael. *Catalogue of the Paintings of Sir Thomas Lawrence, 1769–1830*. (National Portrait Gallery exhibition, 1979–80.) London, 1979.

Lewis, Samuel. *A Topographical Dictionary of England*. 4th edn, London, 1840.

Little, B. *Cheltenham*. London, 1952.

Litz, A. Walton. 'The Loiterer: A Reflection of Jane Austen's Early Environment', in *RES*, NS Vol. 12, No. 47 (August 1961), 251–61.

Lloyd, Christopher. *Fanny Burney*. London, 1936.

'The Royal Naval Colleges at Portsmouth and Greenwich', in *Mariners' Mirror*, Vol. 52, No. 2 (May 1966), 145–56.

Lloyd, David. *Historic Towns of Kent and Sussex*. London, 1991.

Locker-Lampson, Frederick. *The Rowfant Library*. London, 1886.

An Appendix to the Rowfant Library. London, 1900.

Lowe, J. A., ed. *Records of the Portsmouth Division of Marines 1764–1800*. Portsmouth, 1990.

Lowndes, William. *The Royal Crescent in Bath*. Bristol, 1981.

The Theatre Royal at Bath. Bristol, 1982.

Luard, C. G., ed. *Journal of Clarissa Trant*. London, 1925.

McClatchey, Diana. *Oxfordshire Clergymen 1777 to 1869*. Oxford, 1960.

Mackenzie, Faith C. *William Cory*. London, 1950.

MacKinnon, Sir Frank Douglas. *Grand Larceny, being the Trial of Jane Leigh Perrot, Aunt of Jane Austen*. Oxford, 1937.

Mackintosh, Robert James, ed. *Memoirs of the Life of Sir James Mackintosh*. London, 1835.

Major, Alan. *Who's Buried Where in Kent*. Gillingham, 1990.

Hidden Kent. Newbury, 1994.

Mangnall, Richmal. *Historical and Miscellaneous Questions*. London, 1800.

Manners, Lady Victoria. *Matthew William Peters*. London, 1913.

Markham, Sarah. 'A Gardener's Question for Mrs Leigh-Perrot', in *Reports*, 4 (1986–95), 213–14.

Marshall, John. *Royal Naval Biography*. London, 1824–35.

Marshall, Mary Gaither, ed. *Jane Austen's Sanditon: A Continuation, with 'Reminiscences of Aunt Jane' by Anna Austen Lefroy*. Chicago, 1983.

Masefield, John. *Sea Life in Nelson's Time*. London, 1920.

Mavor, W. *The British Tourist*. London, 1798–1800.

May, Leonard. *A Master of Silhouette*. London, 1938.

Meehan, J. F. *Famous Houses of Bath*. Bath, 1901.

More Famous Houses of Bath. Bath, 1906.

Midgley, Graham. *University Life in Eighteenth-Century Oxford*. New Haven and London, 1996.

Midgley, W. 'The Revd Henry and Mrs Eleanor Austen', in *Reports*, 3 (1976–85), 86–91.

Mitchell, B., and Penrose, H., eds. *Letters from Bath 1766–67 by the Rev. John Penrose*. Gloucester, 1983.

Mitford, Mary Russell. *Recollections of a Literary Life*. London, 1852.

Mitford, Nancy. *The Stanleys of Alderley*. London 1939, reissued 1968.

Montagu of Beaulieu, Lady. *To the Manor Born*. London, 1971.

de Montolieu, Mme. E. J. L. P. *Caroline of Lichtfield*. London, 1817.

Montgomery, Florence M. *Textiles in America 1650–1870*. London, 1984.

Moore, Thomas. *Poetical Works*. Paris, 1829.

Morriss, Richard K. *The Buildings of Winchester*. Stroud, 1994.

Morton, H. V. *I Saw Two Englands*. London, 1942.

Moss, Thomas. *Poems on Several Occasions*. Wolverhampton, 1769.

Muir, Percy. *Minding My Own Business*. London, 1956.

Mundy, H. G., ed. *Journal of Mary Frampton, 1779–1846*. London, 1885.

Murray, Venetia. *High Society in the Regency Period*. Harmondsworth, 1999.

Murry, Ann. *Mentoria*. 4th edn, London, 1785.

The Sequel to Mentoria. London, 1799.

Nicoll, Allardyce. *A History of English Drama, 1600–1900*. Cambridge, 1952.

Nicolson, Nigel. *Kent*. London, 1988, 1999.

    Godmersham Park, Kent. Chawton, 1996.

Norman, Philip. 'Queen Square, Bloomsbury, and its Neighbourhood', in *London Topographical Record*, vol. 10 (1916), 1–16.

Nugent, Lady. *Journal of a Voyage to Jamaica*. London, 1839.

O'Byrne, William R. *A Naval Biographical Dictionary*. London 1849, also revised enlarged edn, 1859–61.

Oldfield, John. 'Removing the Myths from Jane Austen and Lyme Regis', in *Dorset*, No. 43 (April-May 1975), 6–11.

Oliver, Vere Langford. *History of the Island of Antigua*. London, 1894–9.

    Monumental Inscriptions of Barbados. London, 1915.

    Monumental Inscriptions of the West Indies. London, 1927.

Oman, Carola. *Britain against Napoleon*. London, 1943.

    Nelson. London, 1950.

Oxley, J., ed. *Excavations at Southampton Castle*. Southampton, 1986.

Palmer, Arnold. *Movable Feasts – Changes in English Eating Habits*. Oxford, 1984.

Papworth, John. *British Armorials*. London, 1874.

Parker, Eric. *Highways and Byeways in Surrey*. London, 1925.

Parry, Dr J. D. *The Coast of Sussex*. 1833, facs. reissue London, 1970.

Pascoe, Michael. *The Clifton Guide*. Bristol, ?1980.

Patterson, A. Temple. *A History of Southampton 1700–1914*. Southampton, 1966.

Pearson, Alicia, ed. *A Journey through France and Belgium 1784–1785, the Letters and Journals of Catherine Knatchbull, Mrs Thomas Knight*. Privately printed, n.d.,?1964.

Peppitt, G. F. *Cubbington*. ?Cubbington, 1971.

Percival, Thomas. *A Father's Instructions to his Children*. London, 1777.

Perkins, Angela. *The Book of Sonning*. Chesham, 1977.

Perrott, D., ed. *The Ordnance Survey Guide to the Waterways*: 1, South. London and Southampton, 1985.

Pevsner, Nikolaus, and others, eds. *The Buildings of England*. Harmondsworth. *Berkshire*. 1966; *South Devon*. 1952; *Dorset*. 1972; *Gloucestershire, The Cotswolds*. 1979; *Hampshire and the Isle of Wight*. 1967; *North-East and East Kent*. 1983; *West Kent and the Weald*. 1976; *Northamptonshire*. 1973; *Oxfordshire*. 1974; *North Somerset and Bristol*. 1958; *Surrey*. 1971; *Warwickshire*. 1966; *Wiltshire*. 1975; *Worcestershire*. 1968.

Phillipps, Sir Thomas, ed. *Monumental Inscriptions in the County of Wilton*. Privately printed, 1821.

Phillips, C. J. *History of the Sackville Family*. 1930.

Phillips, Daphne. *The Story of Reading*. Newbury, 1980.

    The Great Road to Bath. Newbury, 1983.

Phillips, Sir Richard. *A Morning's Walk from London to Kew*. 1817.

Phillips, Robert. *Henley and its Volunteer Forces*. Peppard Common, Oxon., 1980.

Phillips-Birt, D. 'Jane Austen and Old Portsmouth', in *Country Life Annual* for 1966, 12–13.

The Picture of London, ed. John Feltham. London, 1818.

Piggott, Patrick. *The Innocent Diversion – Music in the Life and Writings of Jane Austen*. London, 1979.

'Jane Austen's Southampton Piano' in *Reports*, 3 (1976–85), 146–9.

Pike, Leslie. *Charmouth – The Official Guide*. 1957.

Pitcher, A. *Pictorial Album of Overton, Whitchurch, Laverstoke and Freefolk*. ?Laverstoke, n.d.,?1985.

Plumptre, George. *British Gardens*. London, 1985.

Pollock, J. *Wilberforce*. London, 1977.

Pollock, Walter Herries. *Jane Austen, her Contemporaries and Herself*. London, 1899.

Pope, E. B. *History of Wargrave*. Hitchin, 1929.

A Genuine Report of the Proceedings in the Portsmouth Case. London, 1823.

Post Office Annual Directory. London, 1810.

Pote, J. *Introduction to the Latin Tongue* (Eton Latin Grammar). Eton, 1769.

Pound, Christopher. *Genius of Bath*. Bath, 1986.

Pressnell, L. S. *Country Banking in the Industrial Revolution*. Oxford, 1956.

Pressnell, L. S., and Orbell, J. *A Guide to the Historical Records of British Banking*. Aldershot, 1985.

Price, Anthony. *The Eyes of the Fleet*. London, 1990.

Pryme, Jane Townley, and Bayne, Alicia. *Memorials of the Thackeray Family*. 1879.

Pyne, William H. *British Costumes*. London, 1805, reprinted Ware, 1989.

Quaritch, Bernard. *A Catalogue of the Printed Books, Manuscripts, Autograph Letters, Drawings and Pictures, collected by Frederick Locker-Lampson*. London, 1886.

Radcliffe, Susan M. *Sir Joshua's Nephew*. London, 1930.

Rainbolt, Martha M. 'The Likeness of Austen's "Jane Bennet"', in *English Language Notes* (December 1988), 35–43.

Ralph, H. V. 'Book Man and Printer Extraordinary', in *Country Life*, 23 March 1978, 778–9.

Rance, Adrian. *A Victorian Photographer in Southampton: Thomas Hibberd James*. Southampton, ?1980.

Southampton Then and Now. Horndean, 1985.

Ransom, P. J. G. *The Archaeology of the Transport Revolution 1750–1850*. Tadworth, Surrey, 1984.

Read, D. H. Moutray. *Highways and Byways in Hampshire*. London, 1923.

Repton, Humphry. *Observations on the Theory and Practice of Landscape Gardening*. London, 1803.

Ribeiro, Aileen. *The Eighteenth Century*. London, 1983.

Dress in Eighteenth Century Europe. London, 1984.

Fashion in the French Revolution. London, 1988.

The Art of Dress, Fashion in England and France 1750 to 1820. New Haven and London, 1995.

Richards, R. D. *The Early History of Banking in England*. London, 1929.

'The Lottery in the History of English Government Finance', in *Economic History* Vol. 3, No. 9 (January 1934), 57–76.

Richardson, Joanna. *The Disastrous Marriage*. London, 1960.

Richardson, John. *Covent Garden.* New Barnet, Herts., 1979.

Richardson, Lady, ed. *Autobiography of Mrs Elizabeth Fletcher, 1770–1858.* Edinburgh, 1875.

Robbins, Revd Mills. *Gleanings of the Robins or Robbins Family of England.* Devizes, 1908.

Robertson, Archibald. *Topographical Survey of the Great Road from London to Bath and Bristol.* London, 1792.

Robinson, John Martin. *The English Country Estate.* London, 1988.

Roderick, Colin. *John Knatchbull – from Quarterdeck to Gallows.* London, 1963.

Rodger, N. A. M. *The Wooden World.* London, 1986, 1988.

Roe, F. Gordon. *The Georgian Child.* London, 1961.

 Women in Profile: A Study in Silhouette. London, 1970.

Rolt, L. T. C. *The Aeronauts: A History of Ballooning 1783–1903.* Gloucester, 1985.

Romilly, Samuel, ed. *Letters to 'Ivy' from the First Earl of Dudley.* London, 1908.

Rothstein, Natalie, ed. *Barbara Johnson's Album of Fashions and Fabrics.* London, 1987.

Rowland, A. M., and Hudson, T. P. *A History of Worthing.* London, 1980, reprinted Chichester, 1983.

Ruff's Beauties of Cheltenham. 1806, rep. ?Cheltenham, 1981.

Rugby School Register, Vol. 1, 1675–1849. Rugby, 1881.

Russell-Barker, G. F. and Stenning, A. H. *Westminster School: The Record of Old Westminsters.* London, 1928.

St Aubyn, Fiona, ed. *Ackermann's Illustrated London.* Ware, Herts., 1985.

Sabor, Peter. 'James Edward Austen, Anna Lefroy, and the Interpolations to Jane Austen's "Volume the Third"'. *N&Q*, Vol. 245 (NS Vol. 47), No. 3 (September 2000), 304–6.

Sadleir, Michael. *Things Past.* London, 1944.

Savidge, Alan. *The Parsonage in England, its History and Architecture.* London, 1969.

Sawtell, George. 'Four Manly Boys', in *Reports*, 3 (1966–75), 222–8.

Scott, A. F. *Every One a Witness: the Georgian Age.* London, 1970.

Seccomb, Thomas, ed. *Letters of James Boswell to Rev. W. J. Temple.* London, 1908.

Selwyn, David. *Jane Austen and Leisure.* London, 1999.

Selwyn, David, ed. *Jane Austen: Collected Poems and Verse of the Austen Family.* Manchester, 1996.

Shaida, Margaret. *Views of Henley-on-Thames.* Barnstaple, 1984.

Shepherd, T. H., with Britton, J. *Bath and Bristol displayed in a Series of Views.* London 1829, reprinted Newcastle on Tyne, 1969.

Sheridan, R. B. *The Rivals.* First edn London 1775 and many subsequent editions.

Simmons, Jack. *Southey.* London, 1945.

Skrine, Henry. *Two Successive Tours thro'out Wales.* London, 1798.

Smith, Charlotte. *Minor Morals.* London, 1798.

Smith, E. *The Compleat Housewife.* London, 1753, facs. reprint London, 1968.

Smith, Georgia. *Bentworth: the Making of a Hampshire Village.* Alton, 1988.

Smith, Horace and James. *Rejected Addresses.* London, 1929.

Smith, S. C. Kaines. (Guidebook to) *Stoneleigh Abbey.* Derby, n.d., and rev. edn, Norwich 1984.

Smithers, Sir David Waldron. *Jane Austen in Kent*. Westerham, Kent, 1981.

'The Austen Fortune and some Austen Parsons in Kent and Sussex', in *Bygone Kent*, Vol. 7, No. 6 (June 1986), 363–74.

Smyth, Ethel. *Impressions That Remained*. London, 1919.

Smyth, Sir John. *In This Sign Conquer*. London, 1968.

Catalogue of Exhibition of Society of Painters in Oil & Watercolours, at Spring Gardens. London, 1813.

South, M. L. 'Epidemic Diseases, Soldiers and Prisoners of War in Southampton, 1550–1800', in *Proceedings of the Hants Field Club and Archaeological Society*, Vol. 43 (August 1987), 185–96.

Southam, B. C. *Jane Austen's Literary Manuscripts*. Oxford, 1966.

Jane Austen and the Navy. London, 2000.

'George Austen, Pupil, Usher & Proctor', in *Report* for 2000, 6–11.

'Was Jane Austen a Bonapartist?', in *Report* for 2000, 38–40.

Southam, B. C. ed. *Jane Austen: The Critical Heritage*, I. 1811–70. London, 1968.

Jane Austen: The Critical Heritage, II, 1870–1940. London, 1987.

Jane Austen's 'Sir Charles Grandison'. Oxford, 1980.

The Southampton Guide. Southampton, 1774.

Directory for Town of Southampton. Southampton, 1803.

Southey, Robert. ['Espriella'] *Letters from England*. London, 1807.

The Life of Horatio Lord Nelson. London, 1813.

Sparrow, John. 'Jane Austen and Sydney Smith', in *TLS*, 2 July 1954, 429.

Spence, Jon. *A Century of Wills from Jane Austen's Family 1705–1806*. The Jane Austen Society of Australia, inc.[JASA]. Paddington, NSW, Australia, 2001.

Sprange, John. *Tunbridge Wells Guide*. Tunbridge Wells, 1797.

Sprott, Duncan. *1784*. London, 1984.

Staff, Frank. *The Penny Post 1680–1918*. Cambridge, 1992.

Standen, Hugh W. *Kippington in Kent*. Sevenoaks, Kent, 1958.

Stanhope, Philip Dormer. *Genuine Memoirs of Asiaticus*. 3rd edn, Hugli, India, 1909.

Stark, J. A. *History and Guide to Barbados*. Boston, Mass., 1893.

Stead, Jennifer. *Food and Cooking in Eighteenth Century Britain*. London, 1985.

Steegman, John. *The Rule of Taste, from George I to George IV*. London, 1986.

Steuart, A. Francis. 'A Correspondent of Jane Austen', in *Chambers's Journal*, 7th Series, Vol. 10 (Dec. 1919–Nov. 1920), 731–3.

Stevens, L. R. *Byfleet, a Village of England*. Woking, 1953.

Stirling, A. M. W., ed. *The Diaries of Dummer*. London, 1934.

Stovold, J. *Bygone Southampton*. Chichester, 1984.

Stratton, J. M., with Brown, J. H., and ed. Whitlock, Ralph. *Agricultural Records AD 220–1977*. London, 1978.

Stuart, D. M. *Regency Roundabout*. London, 1943.

Stubbings, Frank. 'Samuel Blackall and Jane Austen', in *Emmanuel College Magazine*, Quatercentenary issue (1984), 77–81.

Summerson, Sir John. *Georgian London*. London, new rev. edn 1988.

Sutton, A. *A Story of Sidmouth*. Sidmouth, 1959.

Syrett, David, and DiNardo, R. L., eds. *The Commissioned Sea Officers of the Royal Navy, 1660–1815*. London, 1994.

Tames, Richard. *Earls Court and Brompton Past*. London, 2000.

Taylor, Lou. *Mourning Dress, a Costume and Social History*. London, 1983.

Teignmouth, a Guide and Complete Handbook to the Town. 1875.

Thompson, John Cargill. *An Introduction to Fifty British Plays 1660–1900*. London, 1979.

Thomson, Clara Linklater. *Jane Austen – A Survey*. London, 1929.

Thoyts, Revd F. W. *A History of Esse or Ashe*. London, 1888.

Ticknor, Caroline. *Glimpses of Authors*. London, 1922.

Tillotson, Kathleen. 'Jane Austen', in *TLS*, 17 September 1954, 591.

Tomalin, Claire. *Jane Austen, a Life*. London, 1997.

Townley, J. *High Life Below Stairs*. London, 1759.

Tristram, W. Outram. *Coaching Days and Coaching Ways*. London, 1888.

Tucker, G. H. 'Jane Austen's Topaz Cross', in *Reports*, 3 (1976–85), 4–5.

   A Goodly Heritage – a History of Jane Austen's Family. Manchester, 1983. (Reissued as *A History of Jane Austen's Family*, Stroud, 1992.)

Twining, Louisa. *Recollections of Life and Work*. London, 1893.

Tyack, G. *Warwickshire Country Houses in the Age of Classicism 1650–1800*. Warwick, 1980.

The Universal British Directory of Trade, Commerce and Manufacture. London, 1791.

Vancouver, Charles. *General View of the Agriculture of Hampshire*. London, 1813.

Venn, J. A. *Alumni Cantabrigienses*. Cambridge, 1922.

Verey, D., ed. *The Diary of a Cotswold Parson – Rev. F. E. Witts, 1783–1854*. Gloucester, 1979.

Vick, Robin. 'The Sale at Steventon Parsonage', in *Reports*, 4 (1986–95), 295–8.

   'The Basingstoke Assemblies', in *Reports*, 4 (1986–95), 304–7.

   'Deane Parsonage', in *Reports*, 4 (1986–95), 343–5.

   'The Alton Book Society', in *Reports*, 4 (1986–95), 353–5.

   'Jane Austen's House at Chawton', in *Reports*, 4 (1986–95), 388–91.

   'A Strikingly Elegant Pilgrim', in *Reports*, 4 (1986–95), 393.

   'Cousins in Bath', in *Reports*, 4 (1986–95), 394–9.

   'Austen Variations', in *Reports*, 4 (1986–95), 414.

   'The Royal Naval Academy at Portsmouth', in *Report* for 1996, 24–8.

   'A Tourist's View of Southampton and Portsmouth in 1811', in *Report* for 1996, 34–6.

   'Rural Crime', in *Report* for 1996, 37–42.

   'More on "Sophia Sentiment"', in *Report* for 1999, 15–17.

   'The Hancocks', in *Report* for 1999, 19–23.

   'Mr Austen's Carriage', in *Report* for 1999, 23–5.

   'Steventon Prepares for War', in *Report* for 1999, 28–30.

Vickers, William. *Companion to the Altar*. Dublin, 1773.

Victoria County History of Gloucestershire. London.

Victoria County History of Hampshire. London.

Vigar, John E. *Kent Curiosities*. Wimborne, Dorset, 1992.

    Kent Churches. Stroud, 1995.

Walker, Annabel, and Jackson, Peter. *Kensington and Chelsea*. London, 1987.

Walker, Richard. *Regency Portraits*. National Portrait Gallery, London, 1985.

Walter, Henry. *History of England*. London, 1828.

Walter, James Conway. *Stray Leaves on Travel, Sport and Animals*. London, 1910.

Ward, William S. 'Three Hitherto Unnoted Contemporary Reviews of Jane Austen', in *Nineteenth Century Fiction*, Vol. 26, No. 4 (March 1972), 469–77.

Wardroper, John. *The Caricatures of George Cruikshank*. London, 1977.

Warner, Oliver. *A Portrait of Lord Nelson*. Harmondsworth, 1963.

Warner, Richard. *Excursions from Bath*. Bath and London, 1801.

Warren, W. T., ed. *Winchester Illustrated*. Winchester, 1905.

Waterston, Anna. 'Jane Austen', in *Atlantic Monthly*, 11 (1863), 235–40.

Watkin, David. *The Royal Interiors of Regency England*. London, 1984.

Watson, James. *The Dog Book*. London, 1902.

Watson, Steven. *The Reign of George III*. Oxford, 1960.

Watson, Vera. *Mary Russell Mitford*. London, 1949.

Watson, Winifred. 'The Austens' London Doctor', in *Reports*, 1 (1949–65), 189, 194–7.

    Jane Austen in London. Chawton, 1960.

Webb, J., *An Early Victorian Street – The High Street, Old Portsmouth*. Portsmouth, 1977.

Webb, J., ed. *An Early Nineteenth Century Dockyard Worker*. Portsmouth, 1971.

Weiner, Margery. *The French Exiles 1789–1815*. London, 1960.

Wellman, J. *A Guide to Charmouth and its Neighbourhood*. Charmouth, 1866.

Wells-Cole, Anthony. *Historic Paper Hangings*. Leeds City Art Galleries, 1983.

Whitaker, A. *Compton & Shawford*. Compton, 1985.

White, T. H. *The Age of Scandal*. Harmondsworth, 1962.

Whitaker, John. *Mary Queen of Scots Vindicated*. London, 1787.

Whyman, John. *The Early Kentish Seaside (1736–1840)*. [Kentish Sources VIII.] Gloucester, 1985.

Wild, Antony. *The East India Company, Trade and Conquest from 1600*. London, 1999.

Wilkinson, Henry C. *Bermuda in the Old Empire*. London, 1950.

    Bermuda from Sail to Steam. London, 1973.

Williams, Clare, ed. *Sophie in London, 1786*. London, 1936.

Williamson, George. *Life and Works of Ozias Humphrey*. London, 1918.

Williamson, V. A., Lyttelton, G. W. S., and Simeon, S. L., eds. *Memorials of Brooks's, 1764–1900*. London, 1907.

Willis, Arthur J., comp. *Winchester Ordinations, 1660–1829*. Folkestone, 1964–5.

Willoughby, Rupert. *Chawton, Jane Austen's Village*. Chawton, 1998.

Wilson, C. Anne. *Food and Drink in Britain*. Harmondsworth, 1976.

Wilson, Margaret. *Almost Another Sister – the Story of Fanny Knight, Jane Austen's Favourite Niece*. Maidstone, 1998.

    Jane Austen's Family and Tonbridge. Chawton, 2001.

Winbolt, S. E. *Kent*. London, 1930.

Wood and Cunningham. *The New Bath Directory, corrected to May 1812*. Bath, 1812.

Woodforde, John. *Georgian Houses For All*. London, 1978.

Woodgate, Revd Gordon, and Woodgate, G. M. G. *A History of the Woodgates of Stonewall Park, and of Summerhill in Kent*. Wisbech, 1910.

Woodman, Richard. *The Victory of Seapower*. London, 1998.

Woodiwiss, John. *British Silhouettes*. London, 1965.

Worsley, R. *Prince of Places – a Pictorial & Social History of Tenby*. Haverfordwest, n.d.

Wright, Constance. *Louise, Queen of Prussia*. London, 1970.

Yonge, Charlotte M. *John Keble's Parishes*. London, 1898.

Young, Hilary, ed. *The Genius of Wedgwood*. London, 1995. (Catalogue of exhibition at the Victoria & Albert Museum, 1995.)

Family pedigrees

1. JOHN AUSTEN

John Austen I, of Horsmonden,
1560–1620

John II,
1585–1650

Francis I, of Grovehurst,
1600–88

John III,
1629–1705

John IV, of Broadford,
d. 1704
= Elizabeth Weller

Anne = John Holman

Jane = Stephen Stringer.
See Pedigree IX

Francis II = Anne Motley
1698–1791
See Ped. II

Thomas,
1699–1772

William,
1701–87.
See Pedigree III

Robert,
1702–28

Stephen,
1704–51

Elizabeth = George Hooper
b. 1695

son b. 1732

three children

John V = Mary Stringer
1696–1728

Elizabeth = John Fennor

Rev. Henry
1725–1807

Elizabeth-Matilda 1766–1855
Harriet-Lennard 1768–1839
Francis-Edgar 1771–1804

Francis Motley,
of Kippington,
1717–1815

John VI = Joanna Weeks
1716–1807

Mary,
d. unmarried
1803

Francis Lucius,
1773–1815,
no male issue
See Pedigrees II & VII

Col. Thomas,
1775–1859,
MP for West Kent;
no issue;
inherited Kippington

Jane,
1776–1857,
m. W. J. Campion

John VII,
1777–1851,
inherited Broadford
and Grovehurst

Henry 1779–1850
Elizabeth 1780–
Marianne 1781–96
George Lennard 1782–1811
Frances 1783–
Edward 1785–1815
William 1787–1851

John Francis,
of Capel Manor,
1817–93;
no male issue; sold Kippington.
See Pedigree II

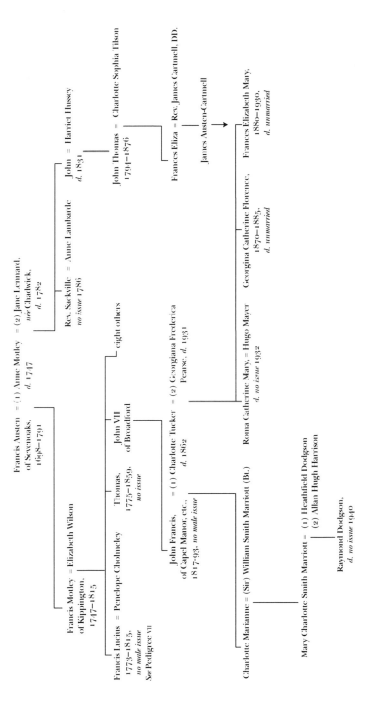

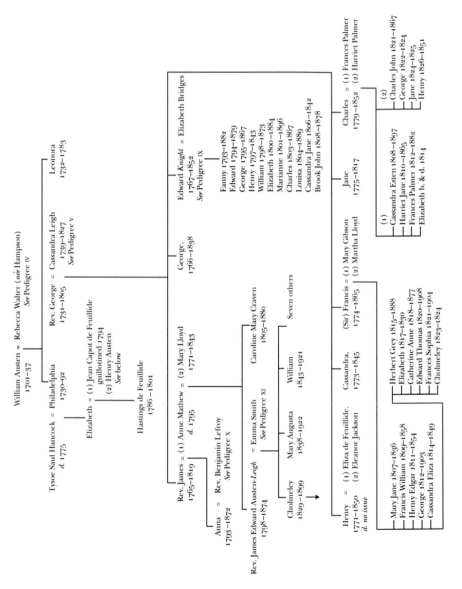

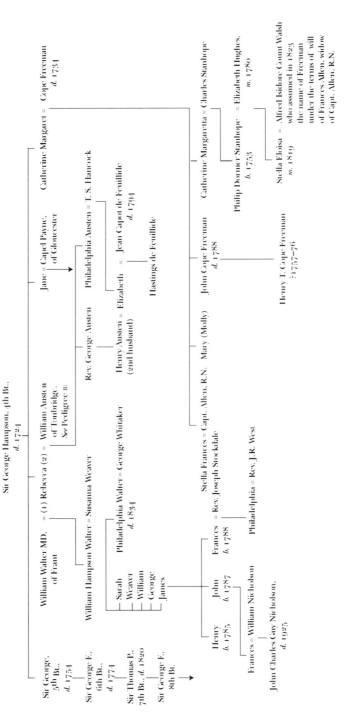

iv. Hampson

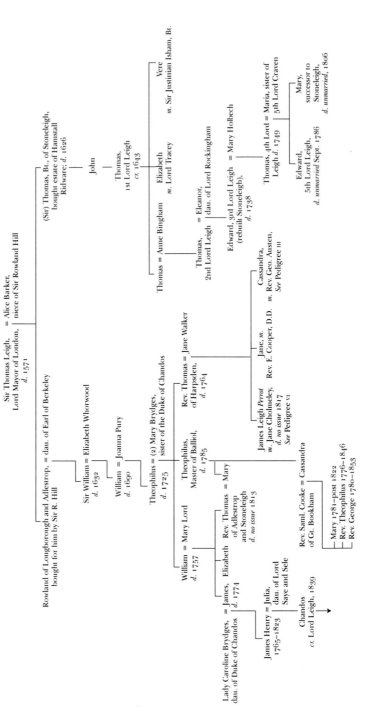

v. LEIGH

Sir Thomas Leigh, = Alice Barker,
Lord Mayor of London, | niece of Sir Rowland Hill
d. 1571

Rowland of Longborough and Adlestrop, = dau. of Earl of Berkeley
bought for him by Sir R. Hill

(Sir) Thomas, Bt., of Stoneleigh,
bought estate of Hamstall
Ridware; *d.* 1626

Sir William = Elizabeth Whorwood
d. 1632

John

Thomas.
1st Lord Leigh
cı. 1643

William = Joanna Pury
d. 1690

Thomas = Anne Bingham

Elizabeth
m. Lord Tracey

Vere
m. Sir Justinian Isham, Bt.

Theophilus, = (2) Mary Brydges,
d. 1725 | sister of the Duke of Chandos

Rev. Thomas = Jane Walker
of Harpsden,
d. 1764

Thomas, = Eleanor,
2nd Lord Leigh | dau. of Lord Rockingham

Edward, 3rd Lord Leigh = Mary Holbech
(rebuilt Stoneleigh),
d. 1738

Theophilus,
Master of Balliol,
d. 1785

Jane, *m.*
Rev. E. Cooper, D.D.

Cassandra,
m. Rev. Geo. Austen,
See Pedigree III

Thomas, 4th Lord = Maria, sister of
Leigh *d.* 1749 | 5th Lord Craven

William = Mary Lord
d. 1757

Rev. Thomas = Mary
of Adlestrop
and Stoneleigh
d. no issue 1813

James Leigh *Perrot*
m. Jane Cholmeley,
d. no issue 1817
See Pedigree VI

Edward,
5th Lord Leigh,
d. unmarried Sept. 1786

Mary,
successor to
Stoneleigh,
d. unmarried, 1806

Lady Caroline Brydges, = James, | Elizabeth
dau. of Duke of Chandos | *d.* 1774

Rev. Saml. Cooke = Cassandra
of Gt. Bookham

James Henry = Julia,
1765–1823 | dau. of Lord
Saye and Sele

Mary 1781–*post* 1822
Rev. Theophilus 1776–1846
Rev. George 1780–1853

Chandos
cı. Lord Leigh, 1839 →

VI. PERROT

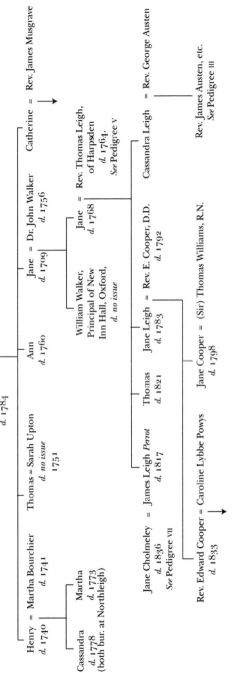

James Perrot, = Anne Dawtrey
of Northleigh, Oxon.,   d. 1729
d. 1784

Henry = Martha Bourchier
d. 1740   d. 1741

Thomas = Sarah Upton
d. no issue
1751

Ann
d. 1760

Jane = Dr. John Walker
d. 1709   d. 1756

Catherine = Rev. James Musgrave

Cassandra
d. 1778
(both bur. at Northleigh)

Martha
d. 1773

William Walker,
Principal of New
Inn Hall, Oxford,
d. no issue

Jane =
d. 1768

Rev. Thomas Leigh,
of Harpsden
d. 1764.
See Pedigree V

Jane Cholmeley = James Leigh Perrot
d. 1836   d. 1817
See Pedigree VII

Thomas
d. 1821

Jane Leigh = Rev. E. Cooper, D.D.
d. 1783   d. 1792

Cassandra Leigh = Rev. George Austen

Rev. Edward Cooper = Caroline Lybbe Powys
d. 1833

Jane Cooper = (Sir) Thomas Williams, R.N.
d. 1798

Rev. James Austen, etc.
See Pedigree III

VII. CHOLMELEY

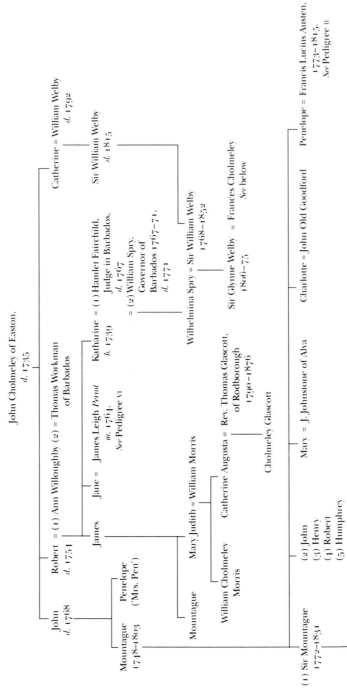

John Cholmeley of Easton.
d. 1735

Catherine = William Welby
d. 1792

Robert = (1) Ann Willoughby (2) = Thomas Workman
d. 1751   of Barbados

Sir William Welby
d. 1815

John
d. 1768

James   Jane =   James Leigh Perrot   Katharine = (1) Hamlet Fairchild,
                        m. 1764.   b. 1739   Judge in Barbados,
                        See Pedigree VI   d. 1767
                                                           = (2) William Spry,
                                                                Governor of
                                                                Barbados 1767–71,
                                                                d. 1771

Mountague   Penelope
1748–1803   ('Mrs. Pen')

Wilhelmina Spry = Sir William Welby
                  1768–1852

Mary Judith = William Morris

Catherine Augusta = Rev. Thomas Glascott,
                    of Rodborough
                    1790–1876

Sir Glynne Welby = Frances Cholmeley
1806–75   See below

Mountague

William Cholmeley
Morris

Cholmeley Glascott

Charlotte = John Old Goodford

Penelope = Francis Lucius Austen.
           1773–1815.
           See Pedigree II

(1) Sir Mountague
1772–1831

(2) John
(3) Henry
(1) Robert
(5) Humphrey

Mary = J. Johnstone of Alva

Frances = Sir Glynne Welby
          1806–75

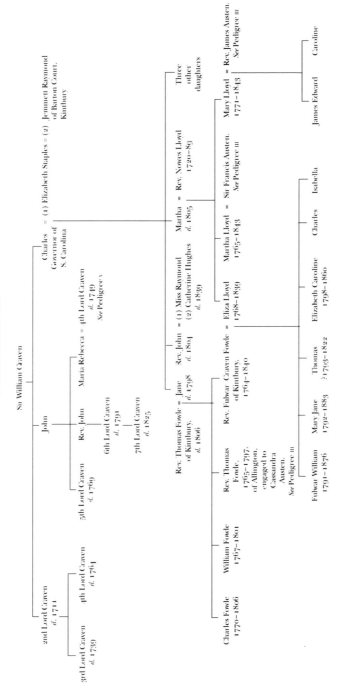

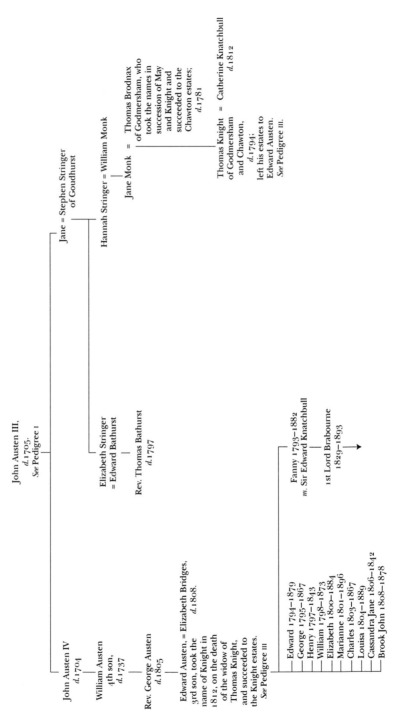

IX. AUSTEN AND KNIGHT

John Austen III,
d.1705,
See Pedigree 1

Jane = Stephen Stringer
of Goudhurst

Hannah Stringer = William Monk

Jane Monk = Thomas Brodnax
of Godmersham, who
took the names in
succession of May
and Knight and
succeeded to the
Chawton estates;
d.1781

Thomas Knight = Catherine Knatchbull
of Godmersham   d.1812
and Chawton,
d.1794;
left his estates to
Edward Austen.
See Pedigree III.

Elizabeth Stringer
= Edward Bathurst

Rev. Thomas Bathurst
d.1797

John Austen IV
d.1704

William Austen
4th son,
d.1737

Rev. George Austen
d.1805

Edward Austen, = Elizabeth Bridges,
3rd son, took the   d.1808.
name of Knight in
1812, on the death
of the widow of
Thomas Knight,
and succeeded to
the Knight estates.
See Pedigree III

Fanny 1793–1882
m. Sir Edward Knatchbull

1st Lord Brabourne
1829–1893   →

Edward 1794–1879
George 1795–1867
Henry 1797–1843
William 1798–1873
Elizabeth 1800–1884
Marianne 1801–1896
Charles 1803–1867
Louisa 1804–1889
Cassandra Jane 1806–1842
Brook John 1808–1878

X. LEFROY

Anthony Lefroy = Elizabeth Langlois
of Leghorn and Canterbury,
1703–79

Anthony Peter, Lt.-Col.
1712–1819

Rev. Isaac Peter George = Anne,
1745–1806   dau. of Edward Brydges
Rector of Ashe   of Wootton Court, Kent

Thomas Langlois
1776–1869
Chief Justice of Ireland

(Irish Branch)
of Carrigglas,
co. Longford

Jemima-Lucy
1779–1862
m. Rev. Henry Rice

Rev. John Henry George
1782–1823
Rector of Ashe 1800–23

Charles Edward
of Itchel, Crondall, Hants.
and ten others

Christopher Edward
1785–1856

Rev. Benjamin
1791–1829
Rector of Ashe
1823–29

= Anna,
dau. of Rev. James Austen
1793–1872

Anna-Jemima 1815–55 = T. E. P. Lefroy
Julia-Cassandra 1816–81
George-Benjamin 1818–1912
Fanny-Caroline 1820–85
Georgiana-Brydges 1822–82
Louisa-Langlois 1824 [–1910 = Rev. S. Bellas
Elizabeth-Lucy 1827–96

XI. SMITH

John Smith

Joshua of Erlstoke = Sarah Gilbert
1735–1819
MP for Devizes

John, = Margaret Burges
took name of
Smith-Burges,
cr. a baronet 1793;
d. no issue 1803

Sir Drummond = (1) Mary Cunliffe
1st Bt.,   (2) Elizabeth, dau of
1740–1816,   2nd Viscount
d. no issue   Galway

Maria = Charles,
d. 1843   1st Marquess
of Northampton

Elizabeth = William Chute, M.P.,
of The Vine;
d. no issue

Augusta = Charles Smith,
d. 1845   1757–1814
of Suttons,
MP for Saltash,
etc.

Emma,
d. unmarried
1860

Emma = Rev. James Edward Austen Leigh
1801–76   1798–1874
See Pedigree III

Sir Charles Joshua Smith, = (1) Belinda Colebrooke
2nd Bt., of Suttons,   (2) Mary, dau. of
1800–31   William Gosling

Sir Charles Cunliffe Smith,
3rd Bt., 1827–1905

Sir Drummond Cunliffe Smith,
4th Bt.

Augusta 1799–1836
Frances 1803–71
Spencer 1806–82
Sarah 1808–94
Charlotte 1810–40
Drummond 1812–32
Maria 1814–87

Cholmeley 1829–99
Emma-Cassandra (Amy) 1831–1902
Charles-Edward 1832–1924
Spencer 1834–1913
Arthur-Henry 1836–1917
Mary-Augusta 1838–1922
Edward-Compton 1839–1916
Augustus 1840–1905
George-Raymond 1841–42
William 1843–1921

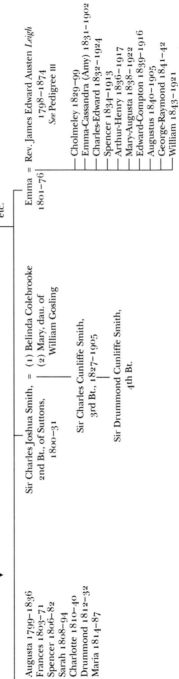

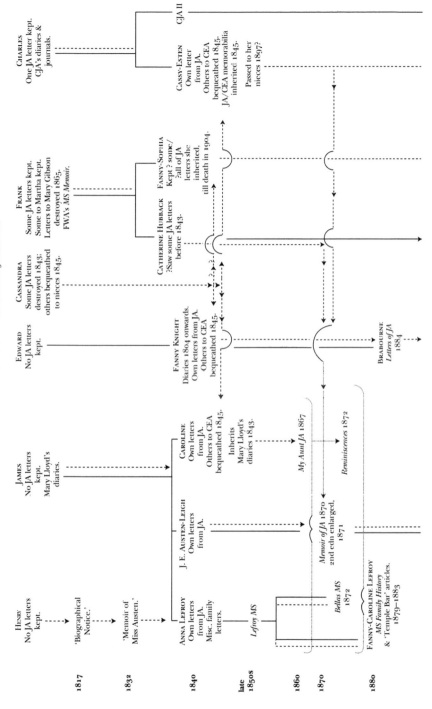

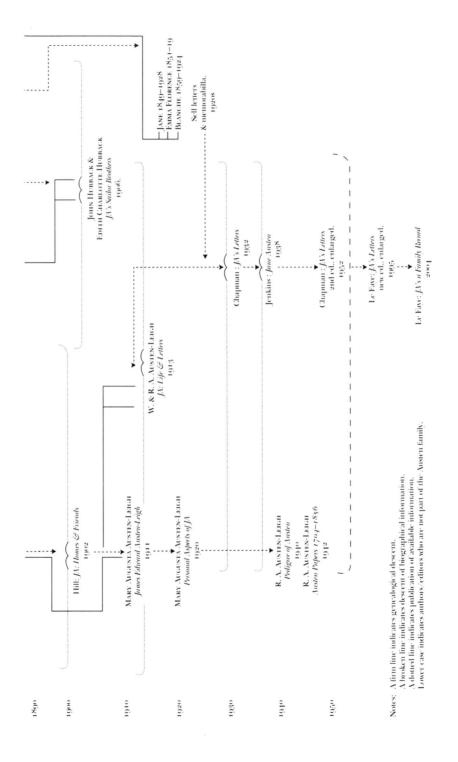

1890

1900

1910

1920

1930

1940

1950

Hill: *JA: Homes & Friends*
1902

Mary Augusta Austen-Leigh
James Edward Austen-Leigh
1911

Mary Augusta Austen-Leigh
Personal Aspects of JA
1920

R. A. Austen-Leigh
Pedigree of Austen
1940

R. A. Austen-Leigh
Austen Papers 1704–1856
1942

W. & R. A. Austen-Leigh
JA: Life & Letters
1913

John Hubback &
Edith Charlotte Hubback
JA's Sailor Brothers
1906

Jane 1849–1928
Emma Florence 1851–19
Blanche 1859–1921

Sell letters
& memorabilia,
1920s

Chapman : *JA's Letters*
1932

Jenkins : *Jane Austen*
1938

Chapman : *JA's Letters*
2nd ed., enlarged,
1952

Le Faye: *JA's Letters*
new ed., enlarged,
1995

Le Faye: *JA's a Family Record*
2004

Notes: A firm line indicates genealogical descent.
A broken line indicates descent of biographical information.
A dotted line indicates publication of available information.
Lower case indicates authors/editors who are not part of the Austen family.

Index

The conventions and abbreviations used in this index are as shown on pages xvi–xvii above.

Lightning Source UK Ltd.
Milton Keynes UK
UKOW04f2000220215

246680UK00001B/75/P